The Jo Anne Stolaroff Cotsen Prize Imprint
honors outstanding studies in archaeology
to commemorate a special person whose
appreciation for scholarship was recognized
by all whose lives she touched.

Excavations at Cerro Azul, Peru

THE ARCHITECTURE AND POTTERY

Monograph 62

Cotsen Institute of Archaeology Monographs

CONTRIBUTIONS IN FIELD RESEARCH AND CURRENT ISSUES IN ARCHAEOLOGICAL METHOD AND THEORY

EXCAVATIONS AT CERRO AZUL, PERU

THE ARCHITECTURE AND POTTERY

BY

JOYCE MARCUS

COTSEN INSTITUTE OF ARCHAEOLOGY
UNIVERSITY OF CALIFORNIA, LOS ANGELES
2008

THE COTSEN INSTITUTE OF ARCHAEOLOGY at UCLA is a research unit at the University of California, Los Angeles that promotes the comprehensive and interdisciplinary study of the human past. Established in 1973, the Cotsen Institute is a unique resource that provides an opportunity for faculty, staff, graduate students, research associates, volunteers and the general public to gather together in their explorations of ancient human societies.

Former President and CEO of Neutrogena Corporation Lloyd E. Cotsen has been associated with UCLA for more than 30 years as a volunteer and donor and maintains a special interest in archaeology. Lloyd E. Cotsen has been an advisor and supporter of the Institute since 1980. In 1999, The UCLA Institute of Archaeology changed its name to the Cotsen Institute of Archaeology at UCLA to honor the longtime support of Lloyd E. Cotsen.

Cotsen Institute Publications specializes in producing high-quality data monographs in several different series, including Monumenta Archaeologica, Monographs, and Perspectives in California Archaeology, as well as innovative ideas in the Cotsen Advanced Seminar Series and the Ideas, Debates and Perspectives Series. Through the generosity of Lloyd E. Cotsen, our publications are subsidized, producing superb volumes at an affordable price.

THE COTSEN INSTITUTE OF ARCHAEOLOGY AT UCLA
Charles Stanish, Director
Elizabeth Klarich, Assistant Director
Shauna K. Mecartea, Executive Editor & Media Relations Officer
Eric Gardner, Publications Coordinator

EDITORIAL BOARD OF THE COTSEN INSTITUTE OF ARCHAEOLOGY:
Jeanne Arnold, Christopher B. Donnan, Shauna K. Mecartea, John Papadopoulos, James Sackett, Charles Stanish, and Willeke Wendrich

EDITORIAL ADVISORY BOARD OF THE COTSEN INSTITUTE OF ARCHAEOLOGY:
Chapurukha Kusimba, Joyce Marcus, Colin Renfrew, and John Yellen

This book is set in Janson Text
Edited and produced by Leyba Associates, Santa Fe, New Mexico
Cover design by William Morosi
Index by Robert and Cynthia Swanson

Library of Congress Cataloging-in-Publication Data

Marcus, Joyce.
    Excavations at Cerro Azul, Peru : the architecture and pottery / by Joyce Marcus.
        p. cm. — (Cotsen Institute of Archaeology monographs ; 62)
    Includes bibliographical references and index.
    ISBN 978-1-931745-55-0 (pbk. : alk. paper) — ISBN 978-1-931745-56-7 (cloth : alk. paper)
1. Cerro Azul Site (Peru) 2. Indian architecture—Peru—Cañete (Province) 3. Indian pottery—Peru—Cañete (Province) 4. Excavations (Archaeology)—Peru—Cañete (Province) 5. Cañete (Peru : Province)—Antiquities. I. Title. II. Series.

F3429.1.C44M37 2008
985'.25—dc22
                                            2008001540

Copyright © 2008 Regents of the University of California
All rights reserved. Printed in the U.S.A.

CONTENTS

LIST OF ILLUSTRATIONS

DEDICATION

This book is dedicated to the memory of Craig Morris, a wonderful friend, scholar, and generous colleague. Although we had known each other before 1980, Craig and I began to see more of each other during the 1980s when I was working in the Cañete Valley and he was working in Chincha, the neighboring valley to the south.

As archaeologists are wont to do, he would come to visit Cerro Azul and I would visit La Centinela. After reviewing each other's pottery during these reciprocal visits, he and I had many discussions about the architecture and pottery of La Centinela and Cerro Azul. Most conversations ended with Craig saying, "You know, Joyce, I am going to postpone publishing my pottery until you describe your Cerro Azul pottery." Then he would pause and smile before adding: "That way I can compare my Chincha ceramics to yours." I replied, "Gee, I was thinking the same thing—how much easier it would be for me if you publish *your* pottery first."

With Craig's tragic death on June 14, 2006, I had to face the fact that I would not have his La Centinela pottery volume to compare to the pottery of Cerro Azul. Nonetheless, Craig's words continue to encourage me. He often told me how important it would be if *any* archaeologist were to illustrate a complete assemblage of pottery from a site on the south-central coast, especially if that assemblage came from meaningful contexts.

Although it is deeply satisfying to bring out one's data, this is also a sad day for me because I cannot send Craig a copy of this report and thank him for all his encouragement.

ACKNOWLEDGMENTS

I visited the site of Cerro Azul for the first time in January of 1980. The field work reported on in this volume was conducted over five field seasons. The first field season at Cerro Azul took place in 1982, when we were supported by a small University of Michigan Faculty Fund Grant to conduct the preliminary mapping. This vital pilot season supplied us with the kinds of data we needed to write a detailed grant proposal for external funding. Following that 1982 mapping season came four seasons dedicated to excavation and artifact analyses. Those four seasons (1983–1986) were generously supported by the National Science Foundation (Grant BNS–8301542). I appreciate not only the funding but also the excellent advice offered by Charles Redman, Mary Greene, John Yellen, and Craig Morris throughout the project.

Permission to excavate Cerro Azul was granted by Peru's Instituto Nacional de Cultura in Credencial No. 102–82–DCIRBM, Credencial No. 041–83–DCIRBM, Credencial No. 018–84– DPCM, and Resolución Suprema No. 357–85– ED.

I want to thank everyone who participated in the Cerro Azul Project, especially my Peruvian co-director María Rostworowski de Diez Canseco; Ramiro Matos Mendieta, a key member of the archaeological team; the late C. Earle Smith, Jr., my ethnobotanist; Charles M. Hastings, my cartographer; Kent V. Flannery, Jeffrey Sommer, and Chris Glew, my archaeozoologists; Sonia Guillén, who analyzed the human burials; John G. Jones, who analyzed coprolites; James B. Stoltman, who did ceramic petrography; and Dwight Wallace, who analyzed textiles.

Several colleagues provided unflagging enthusiasm and encouragement during the excavation and write-up, especially Charles Stanish, Christopher B. Donnan, Michael E. Moseley, Robert L. Carneiro, Guillermo Cock, Alana Cordy-Collins, Charles S. Spencer, Elsa M. Redmond, Rogger Ravines, Duccio Bonavia, Jorge Silva, Helaine Silverman, John O'Shea, Jason Yaeger, John Hyslop, Henry Wright, Christina Elson, Bruce Mannheim, Luis Jaime Castillo, Marc Bermann, Paul Goldstein, Guillermo Algaze, Susan deFrance, Steve Plog, Robert D. Drennan, Jeremy A. Sabloff, Geoffrey Braswell, E. Wyllys Andrews V, Jane Buikstra, Cynthia Beall, Bruce Smith, Geoffrey W. Conrad, Richard W. Keatinge, Allison R. Davis, Howard Tsai, Conrad Kottak, Betty Kottak, Evon Z. Vogt, Gordon R. Willey, Steve Bourget, Claude Chapdelaine, Jean-François Millaire, Véronique Bélisle, Patrick Ryan Williams, Kenny Sims, Loa Traxler, Robert J. Sharer, Don Rice, and Prudence Rice.

I want to offer very special thanks to Geoffrey Braswell, who calibrated all my ^{14}C dates, and to R. Alan Covey, who provided many insights and comments that helped me to refine my thinking on key issues. In addition, I very much appreciate all the thoughtful suggestions and sage advice offered by the anonymous reviewers.

In the modern town of Cerro Azul we found informants, friends, and good people who wanted to work for us, either in town or at the archaeological site. We thank all the residents of Cerro Azul, but especially Diomides Aguidos, Edalio Aguidos, Marcelina Aguidos, Urbano Aguidos, Zenobio Aguidos, Pedro Álvarez, Alberto Barraza, Adolfo Casella, don José Chumpitaz y su familia, Emilio Cordero, Rosa

Cordero, Ruperto Corral, Cirilo Cruz, Victor de la Cruz Álvarez, Pablo Cubillas, Victor Cubillas, Ramón Espinosa, César (Chinaco) Francia, Iván Francia, Roberto García, Luis Gómez, José Huaratapaira, Ramón Landa, Carlos Manco Flores, José Antonio Manco Flores, Rufino Manco Flores, Francisco Padilla, Camilo Quispe, Edgar Zavala, and Pedro Manuel (Pato Loco) Zavala.

I will end this acknowledgment section by thanking three special people—John Klausmeyer, Kay Clahassey, and David West Reynolds—the wonderful artists who made this archaeological report come to life.

CHAPTER 1

An Introduction to the Kingdom of Huarco

They're anglin' in Laguna and Cerro Azul,
They're kickin' out in Dohini too.
I tell you surfin's runnin' wild, it's gettin' bigger
    ev'ry day
From Hawaii to the shores of Peru.
               —Wilson and Love (1962)

It was the summer of 1975, and I was cruising down the Pacific Coast Highway in a white Ford Thunderbird with my surfboard tied to the roof. Over the radio came "Surfin' Safari," a Beach Boys standard, already 13 years old. All I knew about Cerro Azul then was that it was considered the southern limits of surfing in the Americas. I could not have imagined a reason to go there other than to "hang 10."

Fast forward five years to 1980. Archaeologist Ramiro Matos had invited Kent Flannery and me to visit important sites up and down the coast of Peru. Part of his mission, unbeknownst to me, was to introduce me to María Rostworowski de Diez Canseco, a leading Andean ethnohistorian. Matos was acting as a matchmaker. He had heard me say that I would love to excavate a Peruvian site for which there were ethnohistoric documents. He had also heard Rostworowski say that she had discovered such a site, if only she could find an archaeologist willing to work with her. Matos believed it would be a match made in anthropological heaven. The site was none other

than Cerro Azul, and sure enough, when we arrived we saw two young surfers actually catching a wave.

HUARCO AND LUNAHUANÁ

Cerro Azul lies some 130 km south of Lima, at 13° 01´ south latitude and 76° 29´ west longitude, in the lower valley of the Río Cañete (Figure 1.1). Rostworowski's ethnohistoric research had showed that during the Late Intermediate period (A.D. 1100–1470) this region had been divided between two complementary *señoríos* or polities: the Kingdom of Huarco (Quechua, *Warku*) and the Kingdom of Lunahuaná (Quechua, *Runawanak*) (Rostworowski 1978–1980). The Huarco polity controlled the *yunga* or coast proper, while the Lunahuaná polity controlled the *chaupi yunga* or piedmont.

For its part, Huarco drew canals off the Río Cañete and irrigated the coastal plain. Huarco also caught large numbers of marine fish, many of which were dried for shipment inland. Lunahuaná lay far enough upstream to grow orchard crops in the quebrada of the Río Cañete; it also was an area with enough natural forage to support domestic camelids. Roadcuts through middens in the Lunahuaná region reveal llama bones; those on the coast near Cerro Azul yield predominantly fish bone, shellfish, and plant remains. There can be little doubt that products flowed between the two kingdoms.

The documents reveal Huarco's allies and enemies. Their relations with Lunahuaná were good, as was their relationship with the Valley of Chincha to the south. It is therefore no surprise that the Late Intermediate ceramics of Huarco and Chincha show a great number of similarities, both at the level of shared pottery types and at the level of shared individual motifs and vessel attributes. Huarco shows many fewer ties with Late Intermediate centers to the north, such as Pachacamac (Uhle 1903; Strong and Corbett 1943).

The closeness of Huarco's ties with Chincha makes it instructive to look at the rich ethnohistoric data from the latter polity. According to one 1570 Spanish Colonial *aviso* (Biblioteca del Palacio Real de Madrid, Miscelánea de Ayala—Tomo XXII, fols. 261–273v; Rostworowski 1970: Ap. I), the Chincha *señorío* included 30,000 male tribute-payers—6,000 traders or *mercaderes*, 12,000 agriculturalists, and 10,000 fishermen. The fishermen occupying the Chincha coast were described as living along one long street, with each fisherman entering the sea every day in a *balsa* with his nets, proceeding to his own familiar area to fish without competing with others.

Several documents emphasize that Chincha fishermen did not farm. For example, Lizárraga ([1605] 1946:Ch. XLVII, p. 90) states that fishermen did not have to till the land; using their fish, they could get all the agricultural products they needed through exchange. He goes on to add that Chincha agriculturalists, for their part, did not have to go fishing; they could exchange their agricultural products for all the fish they wanted. This situation was similar to one described for the Jequetepeque Valley on the north coast of Peru, where one local lord stated that he and the Indians of his *parcialidad* had few lands for cultivation, so they exchanged their fish for plant foods:

> digo que yo y los indios de la dicha parcialidad tenemos pocas tierras para sembrar e sustentarnos e ansy nuestro trato es pescar y vender el pescado [Archivo General de Indias, Justicia 45, fol. 1928].

Additional ethnohistoric information can be used to show specialization even among fishermen. Several indigenous terms suggest that the Indians distinguished between two categories: "he who went out and caught the fish" (*challua hapic*) and "he who exchanged or possessed the fish" (*challua camayoc*) (Biblioteca Nacional de Madrid, MS. No. 3042, año 1571, fol. 225v; fray Domingo de Santo Tomás [1560] 1951a, 1951b; local informants at Cerro Azul, 1982). In another document, there seems to be evidence for a distinction between "those who navigated the watercraft" and "those who fished" ("*tienen el exercicio de la mar; unos navegan y otros son pescadores*") (Museo Naval de Madrid, MS. No. 468). These data on coastal Peruvian fishermen made us curious to see if similar patterns existed in Huarco.

THE INKA CONQUEST

Ethnohistoric documents indicate that Chincha and Huarco were treated very differently by the Inka when the latter expanded into the area around A.D. 1470. The señorío of Chincha made a deal with the Inka that allowed the Chincha ruler both to continue living in his palace and to be carried from place to place by litter bearers. The Inka built his own palace next to that of the Chincha ruler, and the former supplied Chincha nobles with elegant pottery from Cuzco (Morris 2004, in press). The rulers of Huarco, on the other hand, fought stubbornly for more than four years to retain their independence but were eventually conquered, with great loss of life.

When the Inka arrived in the Cañete region in A.D. 1470, they came down the quebrada of the Río Cañete and subdued Lunahuaná first. There they built a major Late Horizon center, Inkawasi (Figure 1.1; Cieza de León [1553] 1943, Ch. 73; Villar Córdova 1935:268–269; Villar Córdova 1982; Hyslop 1985). Cerro Azul valiantly refused to submit to the Inka, causing the imperial army to remain upstream for some time while it worked out a strategy for conquest. The stalemate was broken when the Inka ruler pretended that he had a desire for peace in the polity. To celebrate the "peace," the people of Huarco got into their balsas and went out to hold a ceremony at sea. While

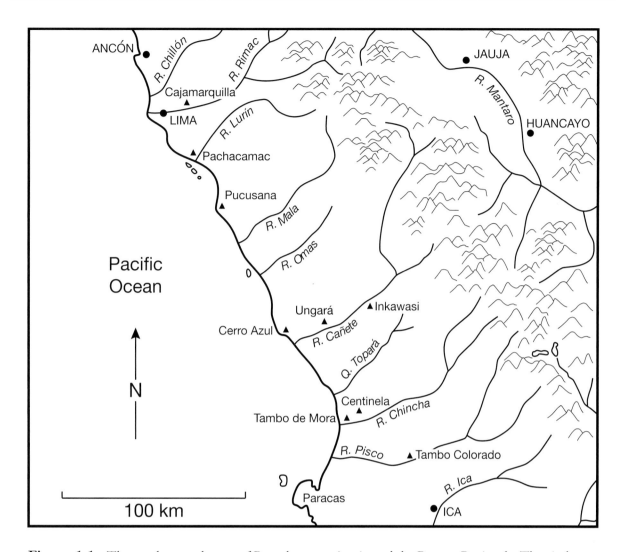

Figure 1.1. The south central coast of Peru, between Ancón and the Paracas Peninsula. The circles are cities; the triangles are archaeological sites. The valleys of the Ríos Cañete, Chincha, and Pisco and the Quebrada Topará shared stylistic similarities during the Late Intermediate period.

the celebrants were offshore, Inka troops quietly descended to the coast and conquered Huarco (Acosta [1550] 1940:Bk. 3, Ch. 15).

Bernabé Cobo ([1653] 1956) adds other details of this period, noting that Huarco at that time was actually administered by a cacica, or female ruler. When the wife of the Inka (the *coya*, or queen) heard that the cacica of Huarco would not submit to the will of her husband, she laughed and devised a plan to deceive her. Cobo says that it was the *coya* who sent a messenger to tell the cacica of Huarco that the Inka ruler had decided to leave her in office, suggesting that she hold a great celebration in honor of the sea to confirm

this peaceful end to hostilities. Believing in the word of the Inka ruler, the cacica of Huarco ordered that preparations be made, and on the day of celebration all of her people set out to sea accompanied by music and drumbeats. When they were far enough from the coast, the Cuzco armies took control of the lower Cañete Valley (Cobo [1653] 1956:Vol. II, Ch. 15):

De todos estos relatos lo único que se puede asegurar es la resistencia de los Guarco ante la pujanza inca y las crueles represalias posteriores. En las versiones de Acosta y Cobo es interesante notar la mención de grandes fiestas o de pescas ceremoniales en honor del mar, en las que todos los habitantes tomaban parte embarcándose en balsas. Esta debió ser una costumbre costeña [Rostworowski 1978–1980:157].

To celebrate their conquest of Huarco, the Inka decided to build several important buildings in Cuzco style at Cerro Azul. One of these was a multiroomed adobe structure with trapezoidal niches (Marcus 1987a, 1987b; Marcus et al. 1985). Another was a sillar stone ceremonial building atop a sea cliff, visible from far out at sea (Marcus 1987a, 1987b). Since the sillar building appeared to the Spaniards to be a fort, it was christened "la Fortaleza de Huarco." One chronicler (Cieza de León [1553] 1943:Ch. 73) describes the "Fortaleza" as

> built on a high hill of the valley the most beautiful and ornate citadel to be found in the whole kingdom of Peru, set upon great square blocks of stone, and with very fine gates and entrance ways, and large patios. From the top of this royal edifice a stone stairway descends to the sea. The waves beat against the structure with such force and fury that one wonders how it could be built so strong and handsome. … In all this mighty building, which is as large as I have said, and the stones are of great size, there is no mortar or any sign of how the stones have been fitted together, and they are so close that it is hard to see the joining.

In the late 1800s, historian Eugenio Larrabure y Unánue ([1893] 1935) visited Cerro Azul and identified it as the site of Cieza de León's "Fortaleza de Huarco." At that time one could still see traces of the high adobe walls that once protected the Cuzco-style sillar building, as well as a stone balcony projecting out over the ocean and some traces of a stone stairway winding its way 50 m down the sheer cliff to the sea (Marcus 1987a: Fig. 69B). However, it appeared to members of my project that the adobe building was the one that had the "façades and reception rooms."

As Larrabure y Unánue notes, the removal of nicely dressed stones from the sillar construction was proceeding so rapidly even then that all but the least accessible stones would one day be gone.

Today all that remains of the building are the lowest courses or foundation stones (Marcus 1987a: Fig. 69A), but these are enough to confirm the location of the "Fortaleza de Huarco."

SOME HIGHLIGHTS OF THE KINGDOM OF HUARCO

At the time the Inka arrived, the Kingdom of Huarco occupied roughly 140 km^2. It would be well worth subjecting it to an intensive settlement pattern survey, a task my project had neither the budget, time, nor staff to undertake. In preparing for my work, however, I was able to consult the publications of several earlier investigators: (1) historian Eugenio Larrabure y Unánue (1874, [1893] 1935); (2) architect Emilio Harth-Terré (1923, 1933); and (3) archaeologists Pedro Villar Córdova (1935), Alfred L. Kroeber (1937), Dwight Wallace (1963), Louis Stumer (1971), William Duncan Strong and John Corbett (1943), and Carlos Williams and Manuel Merino (1974).

Let us begin by examining the map of Huarco (Figure 1.2) drawn by Larrabure y Unánue ([1893] 1935:270), which shows details that would be difficult to recover today. Crucial to the entire kingdom were the numerous irrigation canals that took off from the "Río de Lunahuaná" (now called the Río Cañete) near the southeastern border of the kingdom. One of the most important was the canal shown coming off the river near a hill marked with the number 4, which bifurcates into a pair of canals labeled "Acequia de la Quebrada de Hualcará" and "Acequia de Chome."

Acequia de la Quebrada de Hualcará is the name assigned by Larrabure y Unánue to the northernmost branch of the canal. However, according to documents in the Archivo General de Indias in Seville, the canal's more ancient name was Chumbe (AGI Escribanía de Cámara 498B, fol. 792 and 797v [A.D. 1575]). In Colonial times, this same branch was renamed María Angola; it is said to have run for 24 km and featured 34 water takeoff points (ONERN 1970).

The more southerly Acequia de Chiome (or Chome), renamed San Miguel during Colonial times, ran for 35 km. This branch of the canal

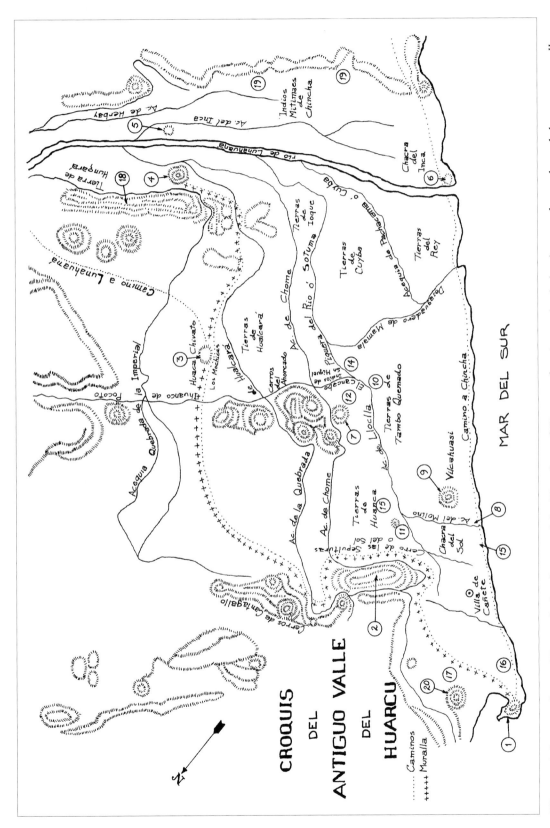

Figure 1.2. Larrabure y Unánue's sketch map of the Kingdom of Huarco, showing major irrigation canals, roads, and the great muralla or fortification wall. The author used numbered circles to indicate landmarks such as Cerro Azul (1), Canchari (7), Los Huacones (9), the Fortress of Ungará (4), the Fortress of Huaca Chivato (3), and Cerro del Oro (2); not all landmarks are discussed in this chapter (redrawn from Larrabure y Unánue [1935:270] by K. Clahassey).

provided water to irrigate the lands of farmers living inland of Cerro Azul bay, and it is said that some of its water even ponded up to form pools and *pántanos*.

Together, these two branches—the Chumbe/Quebrada de Hualcará/María Angola and the Chome/San Miguel—traversed virtually the entire length of the Kingdom of Huarco, from the Río Cañete on the southeast to the Bay of Cerro Azul on the northwest.

It is significant that this bifurcated canal system lay just inside, and was protected by, the great tapia wall called the muralla on Larrabure y Unánue's map (Figure 1.2). This wall seems to have enclosed most of the Kingdom of Huarco. It began at the "Fortaleza de Ungará," a hilltop fortress (marked "4" in Figure 1.2) that protected the takeoff point of the canal before its bifurcation, and continued all the way to Cerro del Fraile near Cerro Azul (marked "1" in Figure 1.2). An ancient road seems to have followed the inner edge of the defensive wall from Cerro Azul to Ungará, interrupted only by the fortified hill of Huaca Chivato (marked "3" in Figure 1.2). The latter hill is where the road to the Kingdom of Lunahuaná began.

Still another road, labeled "Camino a Chincha," is shown running along the coast near the sea, all the way from Cerro Azul past the southeastern edge of the map. While this was probably the main route between Cañete and Chincha, it may also have been a road along which fishermen moved up and down the coast, depending on where the fish were running. It is clear in some ethnohistoric documents from Chincha that fishermen sometimes had their own roads (Castro and Ortega Morejón [1558] 1974) and even their own patois or vernacular idiom (Brüning 2004).

Larrabure y Unánue's map shows several more irrigation canals coming off the Río Cañete. However, some of the latter may have been Late Horizon or Colonial additions. The easternmost of these canals, called the "Acequia Quebrada de La Imperial," lies outside the defensive wall of the Kingdom of Huarco and therefore may not have existed during the Late Intermediate. A Colonial document describes

this canal as watering "700 or 800 *fanegas* of land," according to reports "about half of it heavy soil and the remainder thin soil" (Angulo 1921:83, documento de 1593).

Two more westerly canals, the "Acequia de Lloclla" and the "Acequia de Pachacama o Cuyba," took off from the Cañete River west of Ungará (Figure 1.2); they clearly did water lands within the muralla or "great wall" of Huarco. In 1556 the Acequia de Lloclla was still watering the lands of the *ejidos* of the *cabildo*, passing near the hill called "Cerro de las Sepulturas" (known today as Cerro del Oro and marked "2" in Figure 1.2). At that time, the Acequia de Pachacama o Cuyba watered the lands of the community of Cuyba.

Finally, two more canals are shown to the south of the Cañete River. One, the "Acequia del Inca" (which arose from a takeoff named "Pinta" in Colonial times), seems to have watered lands known as "Chacra del Inca" near the town of Herbay. This canal may have been created in the Late Horizon, after the Inka conquest, in order to water lands belonging to the Inka state. Figure 1.2 also suggests that the Inka set aside lands dedicated to the Sun, calling them the "Chacra del Sol." These fields were located to the north of Vilcahuasi (marked "9" in Figure 1.2), and the Inka placed their Temple of the Sun there, on top of one of the archaeological mounds at the sprawling ruin known today as Los Huacones.

Still another canal south of the river, labeled "Acequia de Herbay," is shown watering lands belonging to the "Indios Mitimaes de Chincha." This must have been a Late Horizon project for which the Inka deliberately resettled *mitimaes*, or immigrants, from Chincha after they had conquered that part of the coast. The Inka placed the Chincha immigrants to the south of the Cañete River, with two *tambos* delimiting their lands: the Tambo de Locos (now called Herbay Bajo) near the coast, and the Tambo de Palo upstream on the route to Lunahuaná. A document in the Archivo General de Indias (AGI, Audiencia de Lima, 1630) says that the lands of the Chincha *mitimaes* ran from the Tambo de Locos to the sandy hills along the road to Chincha.

In addition to ordering *mitimaes* from the south to the Huarco area, the Inka also brought Mochica *mitimaes* from the north. As shown near point "3" in Figure 1.2, these Mochica *mitimaes* were placed on the lands of Hualcará, near the Huaca Chivato. During this same period, the Inka also placed Mochica *mitimaes* in the Ica Valley to the south of Huarco (Rostworowski 1978–1980:166).

Because Larrabure y Unánue's map includes Late Intermediate, Late Horizon, and Colonial landmarks, it is difficult to know how many of the canals in Figure 1.2 existed during the apogee of the Kingdom of Huarco. To be sure, it seems likely that the bifurcated "Quebrada de Hualcará" and "Chome" canal system already existed in the Late Intermediate (if not before), since those canals would have watered the lands near Cerro del Oro (marked "2" in Figure 1.2).

Cerro del Oro was a major site of the "Middle Cañete culture" (Kroeber 1937), one whose occupation largely antedated that of Cerro Azul; it would have needed these canals to flourish. However, Cerro del Oro eventually declined and seems not to have been included within the defensive *muralla* of the Kingdom of Huarco.

Before leaving Larrabure y Unánue's map (Figure 1.2), let us look at three more sites to which he assigned numbers. These are Canchari (numbered "7"), the Fortress of Ungará (numbered "4"), and the large site of Los Huacones (numbered "9"). We will look briefly at each of these.

The Palace of Canchari

According to ethnohistoric sources, the *kuraka*, or ruler, of Huarco lived in a hilltop palace near the geographic center of his realm. The hilltop, known as Canchari, is the place marked "7" on Larrabure y Unánue's map (Figure 1.2). Architect Emilio Harth-Terré (1933), who sketched the hill and the still-visible walls of the palace, opined that the ruler had chosen the summit of a centrally located hill because it afforded him an excellent vantage point from which to appreciate "the beauty of his valley" and watch his subjects busy at agricultural tasks.

Significantly, Canchari was a defensible stronghold where the ruler, his staff, and his troops could all be protected. It featured multiple thick walls with buttresses, which created concentric rings of defense to protect the site from attack. It was considered especially important to prevent an attack from the Quebrada de Pócoto, a major route entering Huarco from the Sierra de Yauyos (see Figure 1.2).

Figure 1.3 shows Harth-Terré's sketch of the palace on its defensible hilltop; Figure 1.4 gives Harth-Terré's plan and interpretation of the palace, based on walls that were visible during his visit to the site.

One of the most interesting features seen in Figure 1.3 is the extent to which the hilltop was supplied with water. On the lower slopes, the canal known as "San Miguel" looped around the entire hilltop before continuing on to the valley's irrigated fields. Nearer to the summit, an aqueduct originating from the canal known as "María Angola" carried potable water to the palace complex (Larrabure y Unánue [1893] 1935:307). This aqueduct would have provided water to the ruler and his warriors even if Canchari were under siege. Villar Córdova (1935:262) describes these canals as "true works of hydraulic engineering," and Harth-Terré says that both canals served to protect the site because they were difficult to cross, analogous to the moats that protected feudal European castles.

As for the palace plan shown in Figure 1.4, one should bear in mind that we are dealing with Harth-Terré's interpretation of an unexcavated building. His plan shows two access ramps. One leads to the trapezoidal plaza flanked by room complexes A–D, the other to a centrally located and more rectangular plaza. Beyond this plaza lies a complex of elongated rooms (E–G) and an area Harth-Terré interprets as "servants' quarters."

Harth-Terré's interpretation is that the plaza and room complex marked A–D had a religious function, while the area behind Rooms E–G was the ruler's palace; he bases the latter interpretation on the area's privacy, low accessibility, kitchen remains, and storage areas. (It should be mentioned that Harth-Terré's use of terms like "eastern" and "western" are sometimes contradicted by the north arrow on his own map.)

The palace itself was surrounded by thick tapia walls that served to protect it from attack. Harth-Terré (1933:103) says that these walls were not less than 4 m high, and some had been finished off with three or four layers of red clay that gave the walls an almost perfect gloss. Some inner walls were buttressed by thick outer walls; Villar Córdova (1935:263) reports two or three reinforcement walls in places. At the base of the hill of Canchari is a cemetery where Villar Córdova (1935:263) reports seeing tombs that appeared to be stone-walled circular cists covered over with logs, branches, or *caña brava*. These cists sound similar to those excavated by Kroeber's project (and mine) in the quebradas of Cerro Camacho at Cerro Azul (Kroeber 1937; Marcus 1987a).

All the comments made by visitors to Canchari, of course, remain to be confirmed by careful excavation in the future. To mention only one unanswered question about dating: We do

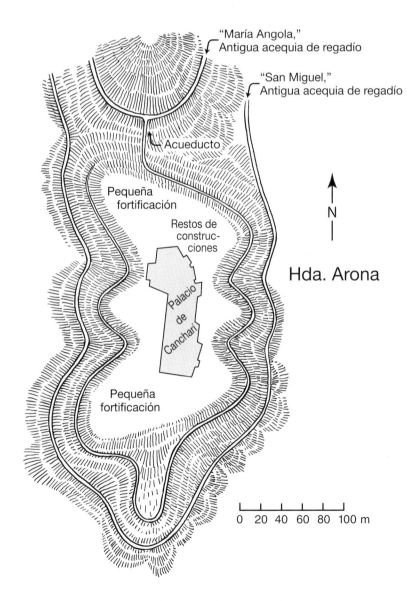

Figure 1.3. Sketch map of the ruins of Canchari, featuring the palace of the ruler of Huarco. Note the way that two irrigation canals (María Angola and San Miguel) encircle the hill (redrawn from Harth-Terré [1933] by John Klausmeyer).

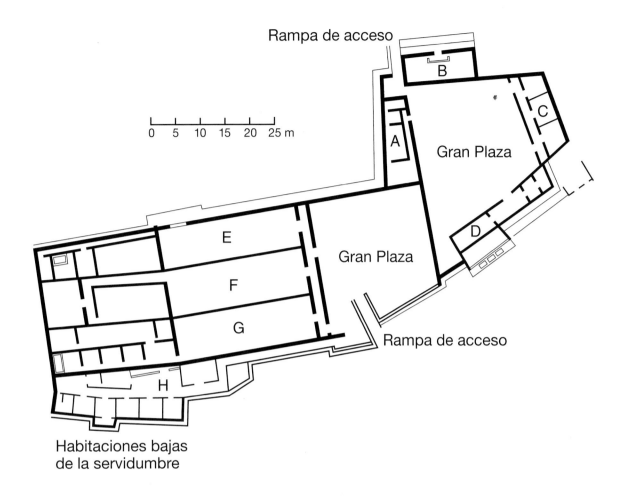

Figure 1.4. Plan of the palace of the ruler of Huarco atop the hill of Cancharí in the Cañete Valley (redrawn from Harth-Terré 1933). For orientation, see Figure 1.3.

not even know whether the Palace of Cancharí dates wholly to the Late Intermediate period, or contains additions and modifications made by the Inka. Williams and Merino (1974) report finding sherds from both periods at Cancharí, suggesting the latter.

The Fortress of Ungará

Guarding the takeoff point of the bifurcating Hualcará/Chome canal system was the Fortress of Ungará (marked "4" in Figure 1.2). This fortress occupied the summit and slopes of an irregular hill near the Río Cañete and is estimated by Williams and Merino (1974) to have covered 40 hectares.

Harth-Terré (1933) undertook a sketch map of the fortress, which I reproduce as Figure 1.5. His map shows large defensive walls at the base of the hill and a smaller wall partially surrounding the architectural complex on the summit. Williams and Merino (1974) describe the hill as defended by three walls on the southwest and northwest flanks, and a single wall on the side facing the river. Harth-Terré's sketch of the complex on the summit shows large open plazas, possible elite residences, commoner residences, and storage units. One prominent rectangular building with a stairway is interpreted by Williams and Merino as a "temple."

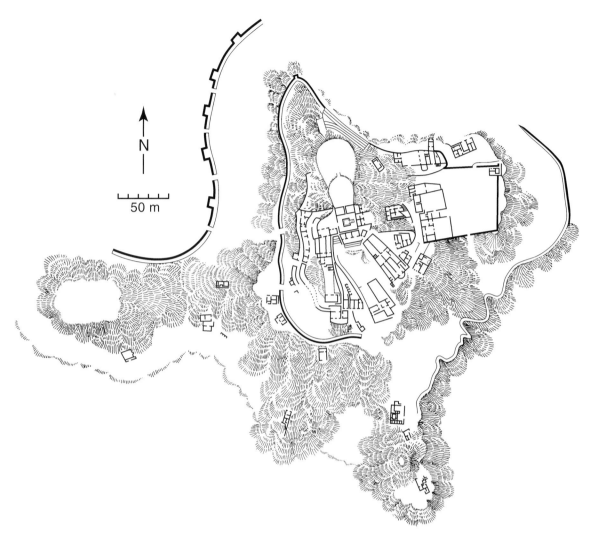

Figure 1.5. The Fortress of Ungará, which guarded the takeoff of the most important irrigation canals of the Kingdom of Huarco (redrawn from Harth-Terré 1933).

Ethnohistoric documents provide two reasons for the location of the fortress. One obvious reason is that it was positioned to protect the lower valley from invasion by highland peoples. A 1562 document, in fact, refers to Ungará as the "fortress of the highland road" (Rostworowski 1978–1980:197).

A second reason, equally obvious, is that Ungará was perfectly situated to guard the take-off for the bifurcated canal bringing water from the Cañete River to the rich agricultural lands of the lower valley (Harth-Terré 1923:44–49; Hyslop 1985:41–43; Larrabure y Unánue [1893] 1935:282, 367–374; Middendorf [1894] 1973:99–

100; Williams and Merino 1974:Site 04F01). Such elaborate defenses were necessary because one of the Inka strategies for subduing a coastal valley was to seize its irrigation canals and cut off the water upstream. Hyslop (1985:43) suggests that the principal reason the Kingdom of Huarco was initially able to fend off the Inka (at least for a few years) was that it had a fortress to protect its main canal, while most other coastal valleys did not.

Hyslop (1985:43), in fact, attributes the founding of Inkawasi (an Inka site on the Cañete River, upstream in the *chaupi yunga* zone) to Huarco's initial resistance to conquest. "Since well-protected Huarco could probably not be conquered with one brief campaign," he says, "the Inka found it necessary to construct a garrison, Inkawasi." Inkawasi then became the staging area for the Inka, the place where they stored provisions and began their campaigns against the resistant lower valley. The Inka garrison at Inkawasi had two main roads: one leading upriver to the highlands and another leading to the Quebrada de Topará and on to the Chincha Valley. So long as the lower Cañete Valley remained hostile, this latter road avoided the Kingdom of Huarco by crossing over the inland hills of Lunaguaná to connect up with Chincha (Hyslop 1985:43).

Ungará has abundant Late Intermediate pottery and the kind of impressive tapia walls typical of the Late Intermediate period in Cañete. However, it also yields Late Horizon sherds, presumably because "once Huarco was conquered, Ungará was occupied, and perhaps remodeled, by the Inkas" (Hyslop 1985:43). While the site at Ungará has been sketched and photographed, it has never received the detailed archaeological mapping it deserves. The descriptions of various authors agree on some details and disagree on others. All visitors were impressed by the defensive walls at the base of the mountain, whose lower portions are of stone (often to a height of 1.4 m), above which they usually change to tapia.

Villar Córdova (1935:263) describes Ungará as having four *ciudadelas* on the summit of the hill, each facing one of the four cardinal directions. One of the lower defensive walls protected a stretch of the María Angola canal. Owing to the irregular riverbed and the steep, irregular terrain, the walls are not continuous or well preserved everywhere, but all authors agree that they are massive.

Projecting from the west side of the fortress is a seemingly independent hill, which is actually connected at its base to the rest of the hill (Figure 1.5). This peninsular formation is surrounded by terraces on whose summit is a ciudadela with numerous rooms, a place where Villar Córdova suggests large numbers of defenders lived, ready to descend rapidly to guard the first wall from attack. Villar Córdova also describes a great rectangular plaza encircled by tapia walls with bastions and two to three retaining walls. On the southeast

were well-preserved rooms in what may have been a palace, a building with burnished walls covered with glossy yellow clay. The palace had an atrium, trapezoidal doors, corridors, narrow streets, and platforms that descended to different levels or terraces of the mountain. Another visitor to the fortress, Larrabure y Unánue ([1893] 1935), noted storage rooms of different sizes, as well as great vessels buried in the ground and capable of holding from 300 to 500 gallons of liquid; he inferred that such vessels were used for *chicha*, "the favorite beverage of the inhabitants of Peru."

The walls of the fortress have turrets, merlons, and watchtowers, places where guards could stand to see if anyone was approaching. At the very top of the eastern part of the summit is an impressive "pyramidal altar," a stepped clay platform 2 m in height. This is the building Williams and Merino (1974) consider a temple; Larrabure y Unánue speculates on whether it functioned as an observatory for the movements of approaching enemies, an *intihuatana* where the Sun could be adored, or some kind of altar or adoratory.

Villar Córdova (1935, 1982) concludes his description of the fortress by saying that he was impressed by the great military organization it showed and the engineering skills displayed by the massive fortifications; he left feeling truly awed by it all. My own impression, based on my visit, is that the Fortress of Ungará was a complex hilltop community with military barracks, residences for all strata of society, and both religious and secular public buildings. This is an important site which the University of Michigan would love to have mapped and excavated, had time and money permitted.

Los Huacones

While Canchari and Ungará are extremely important ruins, the largest archaeological site within the great muralla of Huarco was Los Huacones, the locality Larrabure y Unánue called "Vilcahuasi" (marked "9" in Figure 1.2). Williams and Merino (1974) considered Los Huacones the most important architectural complex in the Cañete Valley and estimated its size as 80 hectares (Figure 1.6).

Figure 1.6. Sketch map of the site of Los Huacones in the Cañete Valley (redrawn from Williams and Merino 1974).

According to Williams and Merino, Los Huacones can be divided into 11 sectors, featuring more than two dozen pyramids. Near the site center is a set of pyramids that delimit several patios; close to this central complex are major structures. Farther from the center of the site are more dispersed and isolated pyramidal mounds.

During our own visit to Los Huacones, we found evidence of copper slag in looters' backdirt; we therefore would not be surprised to learn that Los Huacones was involved in producing metal objects, a craft for which we saw little or no surface evidence at other sites.

The northwest part of Los Huacones's central sector includes well-preserved tapia walls. Unfortunately, the central part of the site is damaged by a road and canal, and even the lower patios are now being cultivated. The architectural and ceramic variation suggests that Los Huacones's various sectors may have been occupied during different time periods. In the central part of the site (Sector F), Williams and Merino report that they found ceramics from three periods: Early Intermediate, Late Intermediate, and Late Horizon or Inka.

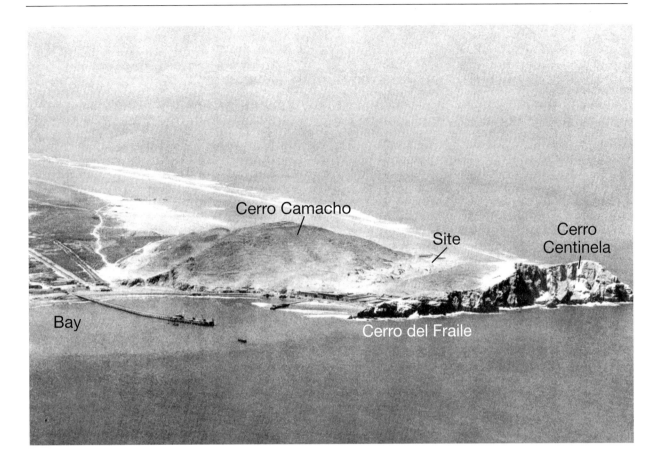

Figure 1.7. Cerro Azul seen from the north, showing the relationship of the bay, Cerro Camacho, Cerro del Fraile, Cerro Centinela, and the Late Intermediate archaeological site. Enhanced version of aerial photo from Johnson (1930:Fig. 103).

Cerro Azul

Finally we come to Cerro Azul, a Late Intermediate and Late Horizon community on the bay of the same name (marked "1" in Figure 1.2). One of Cerro Azul's main roles was evidently to supply fish to the rest of the Kingdom of Huarco.

Aerial photography, which initially developed after World War I for military purposes, eventually began to be applied to geographical and archaeological surveys in Peru. From 1928 to 1929, U.S. Navy Lieutenant George Robbins Johnson taught aerial photography in Peru and took several flights along the coastline. Cerro Azul was one of the sites he selected for aerial photography (Johnson 1930). I present labeled and computer-enhanced versions of three of his photographs in Figures 1.7–1.9.

Figure 1.7 shows how the Late Intermediate site at Cerro Azul lay in a protected saddle between Cerro Camacho (an inland mountain) and the twin sea cliffs of Cerro del Fraile and Cerro Centinela. Figure 1.8 shows the port of Cerro Azul as it looked during the 1920s, emphasizing the proximity of Late Intermediate Structure E to the bay. In the chapters that follow, I will examine Late Intermediate Cerro Azul in more detail.

Figure 1.8. Photo of Cerro Camacho from the southwest, with Cerro Azul bay indicated by the pier on the left. The coastal ranges of the Andes can be seen in the background. Enhanced version of aerial photo from Johnson (1930:Fig. 104).

Figure 1.9. The community of Cerro Azul as it looked in the 1920s. Cerro del Fraile can be seen in the foreground, just west of the bay. Kroeber's Structure E appears in the upper right corner. Enhanced version of aerial photo from Johnson (1930:Fig. 105).

CHAPTER 2

The Architecture and Layout of Late Intermediate Cerro Azul

As we saw in Chapter 1, the setting of Cerro Azul was dramatic. On the northwest it featured a 480-m stretch of sea cliffs, falling almost vertically into the Pacific Ocean. Just offshore are rocky outcrops and small islands where the sea lions can sun themselves during the day. The two highest peaks in this area are Cerro Centinela (55 m above sea level), which features a lighthouse, and Cerro del Fraile (28 m above sea level), which projects north into the bay. This half-kilometer stretch of coast is referred to as *peña*, an area where fish that arrive to pull mollusks off the submerged cliff can be caught with cast nets (Marcus 1987a:16–17).

After their conquest of Huarco, the Inka built several important buildings on both Centinela and El Fraile (Marcus 1987a:93–103). Two of these Inka buildings, designated Structures 1 and 3 by the University of Michigan Project (Marcus et al. 1985), will be described in a later volume. It seems likely that the Inka chose rocky promontories for both buildings so that they could be seen from a distance. The pottery from Structures 1 and 3, while not particularly abundant, shows us what local Late Horizon ceramics looked like.

To the north and east of Cerro del Fraile lies the crescent-shaped bay of Cerro Azul. It features the kind of sandy beach known by today's fishermen as *playa* (Marcus 1987a:20–22). In prehispanic times the bay teemed with anchovies, sardines, and larger fish, which could be caught with everything from wicker baskets to large nets called *redes de cortina* (Marcus 1987a:Fig. 8). The modern town of Cerro Azul sits on this bay, which is a very pleasant setting. The approach to the bay, however, is across a level plain that would be difficult to fortify and defend. Significantly, the Late Intermediate occupants chose a more defensible location.

Inland and to the southeast of Cerros Centinela and El Fraile is an even larger mountain, Cerro Camacho, which rises to 86 m above sea level. It is composed of extrusive igneous rock that is bluish-black in color; this is the mountain that, when seen from the sea, inspired the name "Cerro Azul."

Between the peaks of Camacho and Centinela/El Fraile lies a protected saddle of sloping land that could accommodate a 200 × 400 m complex of structures, contoured to rocky spurs and low rises in the natural terrain (Figures 2.1, 2.2). This is where the Late Intermediate nobles chose to put their settlement—a community visible only from the sea, yet within walking distance of three contrasting environments for fishing. In addition to the *peña* and *playa* zones already mentioned, the Late Intermediate site overlooks a half-kilometer stretch of cobble beach of the type local fishermen call *costa* (Marcus 1987a:16–20). This environment is one that produces some of Peru's most highly prized fish, including corvina and róbalo, two large members of the drum family (Marcus et al. 1999).

In this protected saddle, the Late Intermediate nobles directed the building of ten large multi-roomed structures, which we now suspect were

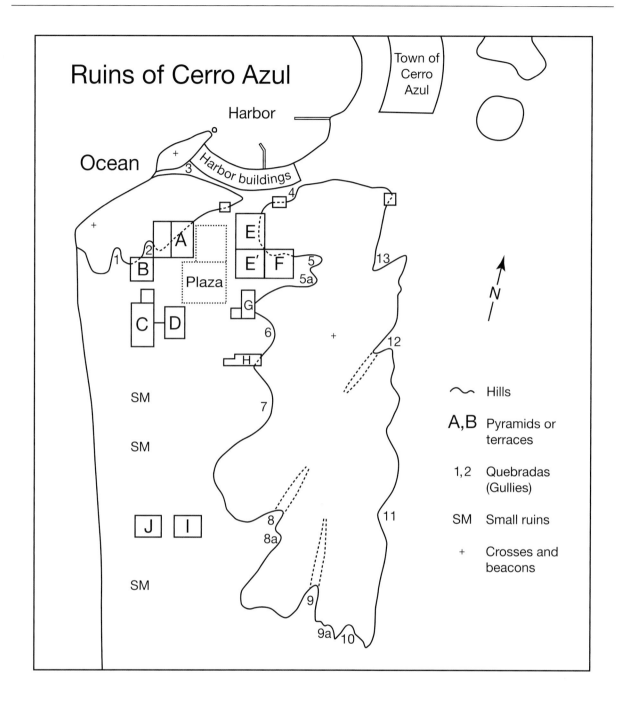

Figure 2.1. Kroeber's sketch map of Cerro Azul, showing major structures (*A–J*), "small ruins" (*SM*), and quebradas (*1–13*) (redrawn from Kroeber 1937:Pl. LXXXI).

elite residential compounds. The walls of these compounds were constructed of mud or clay, poured in place into wooden frames that were removed once the material had dried; these constructions are called *tapia* in Spanish or *allpa pirca* in Quechua. Tapia walls are very thick (often a meter or more) and are built up in stages, with bedding lines visible where an upper section rests on a lower section. In the Cañete region, tapia is particularly characteristic of the Late Intermediate kingdoms;

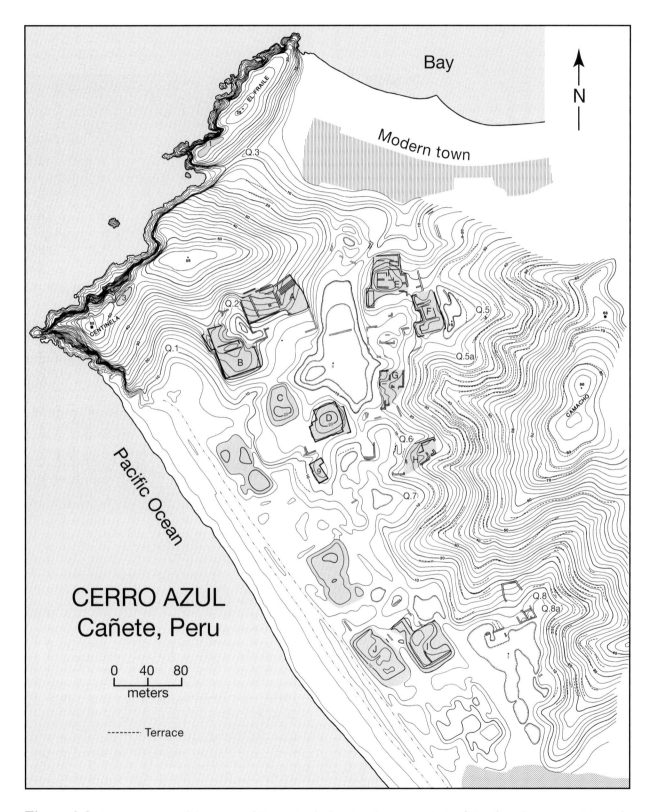

Figure 2.2. Contour map of the ruins of Cerro Azul, showing Structures A–J of Kroeber; Structures 1, 3, and 9 of the University of Michigan project; and Quebradas 5–8a of Cerro Camacho. Elevations in meters above sea level (cartography by Charles M. Hastings; drafted by Kay Clahassey).

the later Inka preferred adobe brick. The source of the clay used for the tapia at Cerro Azul is foreign to the saddle on which the site lies. It likely comes from an area of fine alluvium to the northeast called Ihuanco, also a probable source of the clay used for the site's major pottery types (see Chapter 3).

In addition to its ten major residential compounds, Cerro Azul has scores of smaller tapia buildings scattered throughout, some visible from the surface, others buried by erosion and thus accessible only after excavation. These smaller buildings vary in size from one or two rooms to more than a dozen rooms. Some buildings were clearly used for storage, but it would be impossible to assign a single function to all of them.

Test excavations away from the major compounds often produce chunks of clay with cane impressions, like those found in and around the wattle-and-daub buildings for which Andeanists use the term *kincha*. Our suspicion is that while elite families and their retainers lived in the large tapia compounds, a great many commoners (including most of the actual fishermen) lived in kincha houses outside the compounds. This would not be a pattern without precedent; Moseley and his associates (see discussion on Chan Chan later in this chapter) believe that the large elite compounds at Chan Chan on the north coast were surrounded by kincha houses occupied by commoners.

Finally, there are the terraces of Cerro Camacho. Descending from the slopes of that mountain is a series of gullies, or quebradas, growing wider as they merge with the protected saddle. These quebradas have been artificially terraced almost to the summit of Cerro Camacho. We now know that these terraces were built of midden debris, almost certainly carried from the tapia compounds and kincha houses basketload by basketload, dumped in the quebradas and regularized into horizontal terraces with the help of the loose stones available all over Cerro Camacho. Once these terraces had become deep enough, they became an ideal place in which to hide dry-laid stone masonry burial cists for people who died in the compounds. These

burials will be described in a future volume, but a preview can be found in an earlier report (Marcus 1987a:68–92).

KROEBER'S EXCAVATIONS

From April to May of 1925, legendary anthropologist Alfred L. Kroeber excavated at Cerro Azul. His first task was to produce a sketch map (Kroeber 1937:Pl. LXXXI), our redrafted version of which is given in Figure 2.1. Kroeber assigned capital letters A through J to the ten large tapia compounds. Not having time to excavate any of them, he assumed that they were giant terraces built to support pyramids, and recorded them as such. He did not number the smaller tapia structures, but he called them "small ruins" and put some of them on his map with the symbol "SM." Kroeber marked a naval beacon on Cerro Centinela and a cross atop Cerro del Fraile with plus signs (+).

Kroeber also assigned numbers to the 13 major quebradas on Centinela, El Fraile, and Cerro Camacho. Owing to the activity of looters before his arrival, Kroeber correctly identified the quebrada terraces as containing many burial cists. He had no way of knowing, of course, that the terraces had originally been created as a kind of "landfill" for midden material from the tapia buildings.

Kroeber noted that his major buildings A, B, C, and D lay on high points to the west of an open area, while his E/E´, F, G, and H lay to the east. On the assumption that these major buildings might be pyramids for temples, he considered the open area "a central level plaza" (Figure 2.1). Now that we have an actual contour map of the site (Figure 2.2), it seems more likely that the open area was simply a natural depression, unsuitable for the placement of buildings. In fact, given the amount of dust, sand, and disintegrated tapia that has partially filled the depression over time, it is even possible that during the Late Intermediate period it was a marshy depression, even a source of water. Marshy depressions or groundwater seeps can still be found to the northeast of Cerro Camacho.

Kroeber spent most of his brief time at Cerro Azul salvaging looted burials in the quebradas. The associated funerary offerings allowed him to define a "Late Cañete culture," which he correctly compared to the Late Chincha culture defined by Uhle to the south (Uhle 1924; Kroeber and Strong 1924a; Menzel 1966). Today we would assign both Late Cañete and Late Chincha to the Late Intermediate period, immediately pre-Inka on the south central coast. Kroeber (1937:244) saw the pottery of these two neighboring cultures as "no more than local variants of the same type . . . the cultural relation is not one of complete identity but of a strong and pervading similarity." I would agree, and add that two of the Cerro Azul pottery types Kroeber relied upon are those I have called Camacho Black and Pingüino Buff (Chapter 3), both of which have counterparts in Chincha.

THE UNIVERSITY OF MICHIGAN EXCAVATIONS

My project members arrived at Cerro Azul with a photocopy of Kroeber's 1937 report in hand. Since so much of what Kroeber had done was useful, we decided to build on it by retaining his letter and number scheme.

One key to our work was to have an accurate contour map of the site. The map shown in Figure 2.2 was produced by Charles M. Hastings using an alidade, two workmen with ranging poles graduated in centimeters, and stereo pairs of overhead aerial photographs. Hastings mapped all major visible walls and quebrada terraces. We retained Kroeber's number designations for Quebradas 1–8a, and numbered the terraces within each quebrada from the top down. We preserved Kroeber's capital letters for the ten major tapia compounds, and decided that any of his "small ruins" we chose to excavate would be given numbers. Eventually this numbering system was extended to the small rooms and stone masonry cists we excavated in the quebradas as well.

Figures 2.3–2.7 provide views of the ten major compounds as they looked when we arrived. Owing to centuries of erosion, all were buried under many meters of fine dust from decomposing tapia and windblown sand. Only the major walls were still visible on the surface. One detail of construction that we could see was the use of massive tapia buttresses on the exterior of each compound. Our excavations revealed that while some buttresses served to prevent outer walls from slumping under their own weight,

Figure 2.3. Structure A, arguably the most impressive of all the elite residential compounds at Cerro Azul, seen from the southeast.

Figure 2.4. Two views of Structure D at Cerro Azul. (*Top*): A telephoto shot of Structure D, looking east from the Cerro Azul lighthouse. (*Bottom*): The north flank of Structure D, showing an artificially created, flat work area outside the walls of the elite compound.

others were probably added later to brace walls weakened by earthquakes. Structure D, the compound we chose to excavate, had sustained considerable earthquake damage (see Chapter 5).

Structure A (Figure 2.3) appeared to be the largest of the tapia compounds and occupied the highest promontory. It seemed to consist not only of room complexes but of the large walled spaces

Figure 2.5. Two elite compounds at Cerro Azul, looking east from the lighthouse. (*Top*): Structure C (note traces of a recent building on the flat area at center). (*Bottom*): Structure E with its massive tapia buttresses.

Figure 2.6. Two elite compounds at Cerro Azul, looking east from the lighthouse. (*Top*): Structure F, with Quebrada 5 in the background. (*Bottom*): Structure G.

some Peruvian archaeologists refer to as *can-chones*, a hispanicized augmentative for the Quechua term *kancha*, which can refer either to a corral or an open space delimited by domestic structures. We saw no evidence that these large, unroofed enclosures were corrals of any kind; they seemed, instead, to be areas for outdoor activity that had been walled off for privacy.

Figure 2.4 presents two views of Structure D, the compound we chose to excavate. Structure D

Figure 2.7. Two elite compounds at Cerro Azul. (*Top*): A telephoto shot of Structure H, looking east from the lighthouse. This compound rests against the rocky ridge which separates Quebrada 6 (*at left*) from Quebrada 7 (*at right*). (*Bottom*): Structure I, looking west from a spur of Cerro Camacho.

was selected because of its unlooted condition, along with the fact that, in the words of my collaborator Ramiro Matos, it was "*tamaño, no más.*"

That colloquialism meant that Structure D was large enough to be important, yet small enough to be excavated extensively in the time we had.

We managed to excavate the 1640 m² elite residential compound in its entirety, but I hasten to add that it was surrounded by smaller outlying structures that may have been related. For example, the lower photo in Figure 2.4 shows an artificially created, potential activity area on the north slope below the residential compound, an area we did not have time to excavate.

Structure C, a tapia compound not far from D, was also "*tamaño, no más,*" but we declined to excavate it in part because we could see an intrusive, more recent building atop it (Figure 2.5, top). Structure E was a very large compound across the central depression from Structure A (Figure 2.5, bottom).

No two compounds had the same layout. Structure F gave the impression of having the greatest degree of bilateral symmetry (Figure 2.6, top). We knew, of course, that our impression could change once the overburden of disintegrated tapia and sand had been removed.

Structure G (Figure 2.6, bottom) was a medium-sized compound built on a rocky spur between Quebradas 5a and 6 of Cerro Camacho. Structure H (Figure 2.7, top) occupied a similar setting on a rocky spur between Quebradas 6 and 7. The locations of Structures G and H made it clear that the builders had sought exposed bedrock for the heavy tapia foundations of the compounds.

Finally we come to Structures I and J, the closest to the ocean. As can be seen in the bottom photo of Figure 2.7, these structures had been subjected to the destructive effects of *garúa* (salt fog), and few of their walls were visible.

Figure 2.8 shows two of the mounds Kroeber referred to as "small ruins." While areas of tapia wall were exposed in places on these two buildings, many of the small ruins close to the ocean showed evidence of having been built largely of rounded beach cobbles. Trying to excavate such buildings can be an archaeologist's worst nightmare, especially if they have been exposed to wave action over the centuries.

We decided to sample one of Kroeber's small ruins. We did this by excavating completely a

Figure 2.8. Two of Kroeber's "small ruins," located between Structure C and the ocean.

modest tapia-walled building just to the south of Structure D. This building, designated Structure 9 (Figure 2.2), turned out to be a fish storage facility (see Chapter 8). We suspect that the two small ruins in Figure 2.8 will turn out to look very different if and when they are excavated.

In addition to excavating one large tapia compound and one small ruin, we conducted stratigraphic excavations in Quebradas 5, 5a, and 6 (see Chapter 9). Some of these excavations were made in order to discover how the terraces were created. Others were designed to investigate small tapia structures that had been placed in the quebradas; at least some of these were evidently used to store plant foods under drier conditions than would have been available nearer to the ocean. Still other excavations in the quebradas were undertaken to salvage as much as we could from burial cists that had been partially looted. In the course of this salvage, we found undisturbed cists and mummy bundles that will be described in a later volume.

Overview

Figure 2.9 is an artist's conception of Cerro Azul as it might have looked from the sea during the Late Intermediate period. All ten of the major tapia compounds are indicated.

An unresolved question is whether or not all ten compounds were occupied simultaneously. Supporting simultaneity is the fact that, based on all currently available evidence, the sherds from the area of the ten compounds do not suggest a long temporal sequence. However, the deepest stratigraphic levels of some terraces on Cerro Camacho produced ceramics that probably date to an earlier stage of the Late Intermediate than the bulk of the occupation of Structure D (Chapter 9). And since these levels look like midden debris from one or more of the tapia compounds, it is likely that one or more of those compounds have a longer sequence than does Structure D. We saw no evidence, however, of material as old as the Middle Horizon.

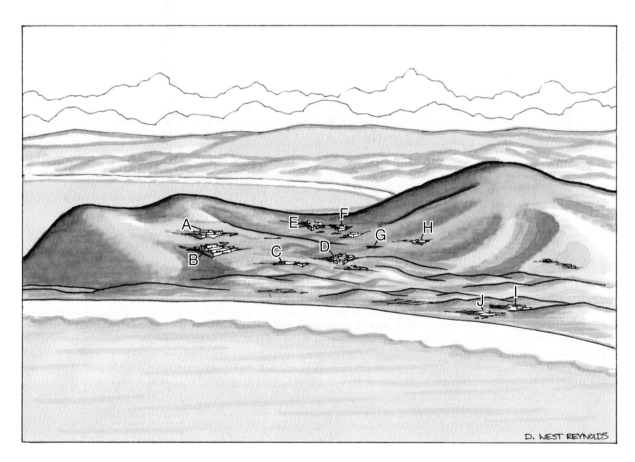

Figure 2.9. Artist's conception of Cerro Azul as it might have looked from the sea during the Late Intermediate period.

To put the problem of simultaneity in perspective, let us consider the case of another Late Intermediate center with large residential compounds, Chan Chan on the north coast of Peru. To be sure, the disparity in site size is considerable: Chan Chan covers 6 km², while Cerro Azul is less than 1 km². Both sites, however, raise questions about simultaneity.

Chan Chan had ten large compounds, or *ciudadelas*, and in their case various lines of information have been used to show that they were built in a sequence (Conrad 1974, 1982; Day 1973; Kolata 1982). For one thing, Chan Chan was built of adobe bricks, and changing brick sizes can be used to show that not all *ciudadelas* were occupied simultaneously. Conrad (1982:108) has proposed that the ten compounds at Chan Chan

> were the palaces of the kings of Chimor. Each ruler built one such structure to house himself, be the seat of his government, and serve as the center for the management of his wealth. In accordance with a law of split inheritance the palace passed to the king's corporation of secondary heirs after his death. His principal heir became the next king of Chimor and built a new palace.

The radiocarbon dates for the ten compounds complicate this picture somewhat in that they suggest a span of more than 500 years for the *ciudadela* sequence, but I have no suggestion for resolving the ambiguity.

Cerro Azul is significantly different. In the first place, its compounds are all built of tapia and appear so similar in construction that one would be hard put to arrange them in a sequence. In the second place, Cerro Azul was not the seat of the king of the Huarco polity; that ruler's palace (and there seems to be only one) is at Canchari.

It is possible, therefore, that what we have at Cerro Azul is a group of ten noble families who built their residences to either side of a natural depression in the center of a defended saddle between mountains. Each of the residences is a different size and has a different layout. Only by digging to the lowest level of each compound could we be sure that they were built in sequence rather than occupied simultaneously.

THE PROBLEMS WITH LATE INTERMEDIATE RADIOCARBON DATES

It would be nice if we could resolve all our problems of simultaneity with radiocarbon dates. Unfortunately, the Late Intermediate falls in a period of cosmic-ray flux that makes accurate dating notoriously difficult. Three periods when sunspots were apparently absent—and cosmic-ray flux increased—were the Wolf minimum (A.D. 1282–1342), the Spörer minimum (A.D. 1416–1534), and the Maunder minimum (A.D. 1654–1714) (Stuiver and Quay 1980). The first two of these minima, Wolf and Spörer, are relevant to the Late Intermediate. Recently it has been discovered that the Northern and Southern Hemispheres were differentially affected between A.D. 950 and 1850. As McCormac et al. (2002:650) put it,

> While our model study is still in the preliminary stages, it does point out that increased upwelling in the Southern Ocean, caused by either deep water formation there or in the North Atlantic, could be responsible for the increased difference in atmospheric ^{14}C around AD 1300–1400. Whatever the cause of the variation in the inter-hemispheric difference, correction of Southern Hemispheric ^{14}C ages with a constant offset could result in an error of up to 50 yr.

Our stratigraphic excavations at Cerro Azul produced 12 radiocarbon dates, which are presented where appropriate throughout the text. These dates suggest that "Late Cañete" culture probably reached its peak between A.D. 1300 and the Inka conquest of A.D. 1470. They also hint that trash was being dumped in Quebrada 5a of Cerro Camacho earlier than A.D. 1300, though still within the Late Intermediate period. However, given the broad two-sigma ranges of our calibrated dates, and the problems of cosmic-ray flux mentioned above, we must rely on changing ceramic attributes to mark the transition from Late Intermediate to Late Horizon.

CHAPTER 3
Late Intermediate Pottery Types

I arrived in Cañete by way of Mesoamerica. In that culture area there is a tradition of defining ceramic complexes in terms of binomial pottery types, some of which are further divided into varieties. I discovered that while there was widespread agreement on many of the stylistic attributes of Late Intermediate pottery (A.D. 1000–1470), neither Cañete nor any adjacent valley had a binomial typology into which I could fit the ceramics of Cerro Azul. The creation of such a typology thus became one of my principal tasks.

To be sure, for some neighboring valleys there were published seriations of whole vessels from tombs; unfortunately, many of the vessels were looted, in private collections, or from poorly documented contexts. In addition, many of the collections were strongly biased in favor of attractive funerary offerings, while coarse utilitarian pottery was underrepresented (e.g., Kroeber and Strong 1924a, 1924b; Menzel 1976; Strong and Corbett 1943; Uhle 1903, 1924). Thus, while I expected my painted and special funerary vessels to have counterparts in the literature from neighboring valleys, it became clear that I was on my own as far as the utilitarian pottery was concerned. In the end, I wound up creating four binomial types: Camacho Reddish Brown, Camacho Black, Pingüino Buff, and Trambollo Burnished Brown. Both Camacho Black and Pingüino Buff came in distinguishable varieties— some common, some relatively rare.

SOURCES OF CLAY AND TEMPER

The site of Cerro Azul does not sit on clay deposits appropriate for pottery making. According to local informants, the nearest source of alluvial clay for making pottery (or tapia walls) is a place called Ihuanco, not far to the north of the site. (As Villar Córdova [1935:32] notes, the people of Cañete call any such clay deposit *ihuanco*.) The temper added to this alluvial clay by the Cerro Azul potters was usually an extrusive igneous rock of the latite/trachyte group, not unlike that of Cerro Camacho. In order to better understand our Cerro Azul pottery types, I asked James B. Stoltman of the University of Wisconsin to undertake petrographic thin-section analyses, not only of the local bedrock but also of the seven most common pottery types/varieties found at Cerro Azul (see Appendix A). I direct the reader to Stoltman's appendix at the end of this chapter, to which I will refer repeatedly during my definition of pottery types and varieties.

Stoltman analyzed the Cerro Azul pottery using a quantitative ("point counting") approach he created in the late 1980s (Stoltman 1989). He reports that the basic clay used for all local Cerro Azul types is relatively clean, being more than 85% clay, less than 10% silt, and less than 5% sand. The coarsest of the local wares, understandably, is that used for the giant maize-beer storage vessels (*hatun maccma*) sunk into the floor of the North Central Canchón of Structure D. This walled area was a "kitchen/brewery" (see Chapter

7). Such giant storage vessels are 25% temper, and that tempering material shows less uniform use of latite/trachyte, probably because each storage vessel was made in situ in the kitchen/brewery with whatever ingredients were available, rather than in a standardized potters' workshop.

It is no surprise that our *hatun maccma* has the coarsest temper grain size of all the sherds in Stoltman's sample. Stoltman uses a scale of 1 to 5 to calculate a grain size index for the temper in each sherd. On this scale, very fine sand (grains in the 0.0625–0.1249 mm range) would have an index of 1; very coarse sand (grains in the 1.0–1.99 mm range) would have an index of 4. Our *hatun maccma* have a grain size index of 2.9, near the transition from medium to coarse sand.

In contrast, the finest of the local wares is the highly burnished or "graphite" variety of Camacho Black, which was most common in elite residential areas or as offerings with elite burials. This variety has only 11% temper, with an average grain size index of only 1.4 (closer to fine sand than to medium sand). Because this variety was never used for cooking, it needed little protection from thermal shock. Its body appears fine and standardized, which is what I would expect if it were made by the best local potters.

Another type virtually never used for cooking is Trambollo Burnished Brown, which occurs mainly in the form of hemispherical bowls. This type has only 16% temper, with an average grain size index of 1.48.

The type most often used for cooking at Cerro Azul was Camacho Reddish Brown. Typical cooking pots in this ware, which would often have been subjected to thermal shock, have 25% temper, with an average grain size index of 1.76 (closer to medium sand than to fine sand).

The Cerro Azul type with the greatest potential for shared stylistic attributes with other regions is Pingüino Buff, whose geometric and naturalistic painted motifs resemble those of the valleys of Chincha and Ica to the south. Typical Pingüino Buff is well made and has 22% temper, with an average grain size index of 1.69. However, we also found a less well-made, atypical orange variety of Pingüino Buff, with an average grain size index of 2.44. Stoltman's analysis (Appendix

A) suggests that this variety may have been non-local; its temper looks more like dacite, an extrusive igneous rock with more quartz than one expects to see in latite or trachyte.

CAMACHO REDDISH BROWN

Camacho Reddish Brown is the most common pottery found in Late Intermediate contexts. It is a coarse utilitarian ware used mainly for cooking and storage, the kind of pottery that we presume every household made for its own use. Many of the cooking vessels were blackened by soot or from direct contact with fire. Even vessels destined for storage rather than cooking have firing clouds that contribute to the range of surface colors in Camacho Reddish Brown.

Paste
The paste is generally in the light red range, 2.5 YR 6/6 to 2.5 YR 6/8 in the Munsell system (Munsell 1954). Petrographic thin sections are about 25% temper, with an average size index of 1.76.

Surface treatment
Most vessels were smoothed on the interior with a bundle of fiber or a strip of coarse textile. On the exterior, most were left wiped but not carefully smoothed or burnished, although those included as burial offerings might show some smoothing and even light burnishing. The vessel surface is on average brick red, ranging to light red or maroon (2.5 YR 6/6, "light red," grading to 2.5 YR 4/4 "reddish brown" or 5 YR 4/2 "dark reddish gray"). Firing clouds can be brownish gray or 7.5 YR 6/4 ("light brown").

Common vessel shapes
A few of the most common vessel shapes are shown in Figures 3.1–3.11, and many more examples are illustrated later in the volume. Among the most common shapes is a *cooking pot with a slightly restricted orifice and two strap handles* which would have allowed it to be lifted on and off the fire (Figure 3.1).

Also common is a *jar with a cambered rim*, meaning that the lip hangs down over the rim like a shingle on a roof (Figures 3.2, 3.3). A series of

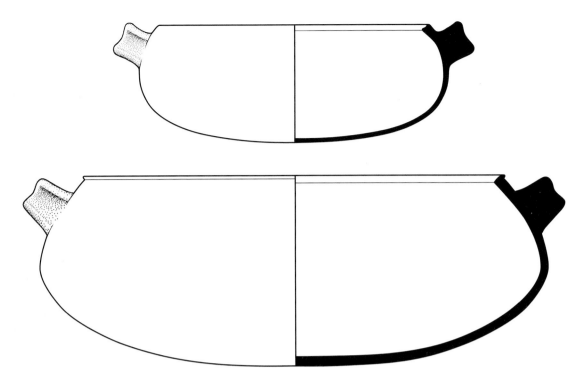

Figure 3.1. One of the most common vessel shapes in Camacho Reddish Brown was a cooking pot with a slightly restricted orifice and two horizontally set strap handles. Many of these pots were fire-blackened on the exterior.

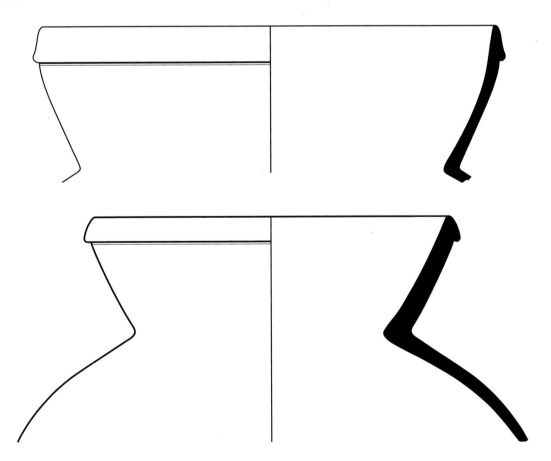

Figure 3.2. One of the most common rim forms seen on Camacho Reddish Brown jars was the cambered rim, which hung down like a shingle on a roof.

alternative rim forms are shown in Figure 3.4; these include *plain rims, rolled rims, beveled rims,* and *everted rims*.

While the vast majority of Camacho Reddish Brown vessels are undecorated, there are exceptions. Jars can be decorated with *cane-end impressions* or *punctate nipples* (Figure 3.5). Perhaps the most elaborate plastic decoration on jars of this type is an occasional *modeled human face* (Figure 3.6b). Such faces were usually reserved for burial offerings, and sometimes appear to represent dead people with puffy "coffee-bean" eyes.

Many Camacho Reddish Brown vessels have handles, usually a pair set on opposite sides. Such handles can be *loop type* or *strap type* (Figure 3.7)

and might be set vertically on the vessel (Figure 3.7b) or horizontally (Figure 3.1). Where and how the handle is set depends on how the vessel was to be lifted, and whether the lifting was to be done with one's fingers or with a rope harness. Figure 3.7a and c also show an alternative rim form, the *bolstered rim*.

While many Camacho Reddish Brown jars are globular, the *amphora* vessel shape was also used (Figure 3.8). It is particularly common in burial cists, probably serving as a water jar.

While most human faces on Camacho Reddish Brown jars are modeled (Figure 3.9a), there are occasional examples of *faces painted on jar necks in white, black, and red* (Figure 3.9b). Such

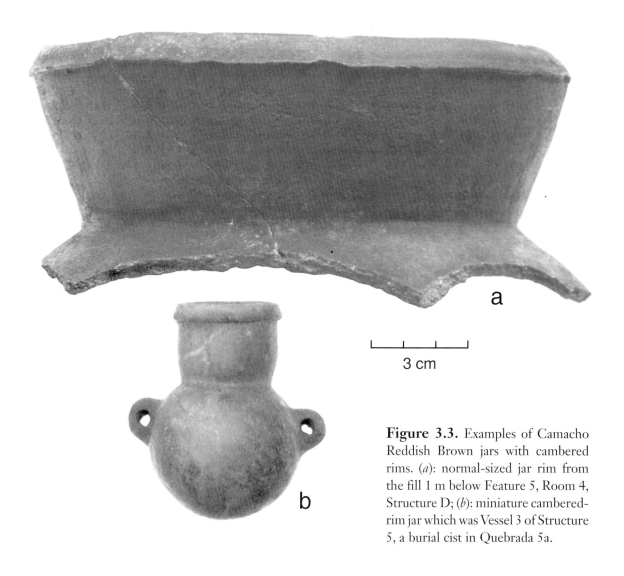

3 cm

Figure 3.3. Examples of Camacho Reddish Brown jars with cambered rims. (*a*): normal-sized jar rim from the fill 1 m below Feature 5, Room 4, Structure D; (*b*): miniature cambered-rim jar which was Vessel 3 of Structure 5, a burial cist in Quebrada 5a.

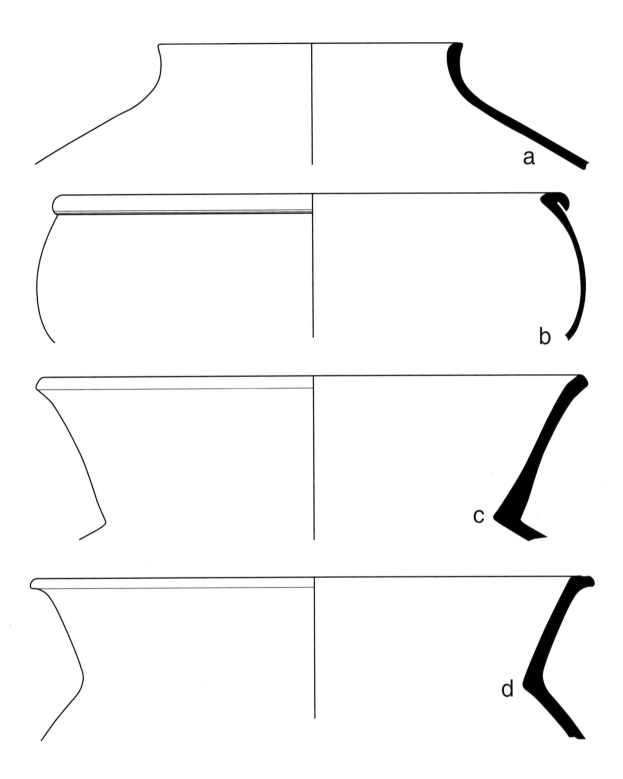

Figure 3.4. Among the rim profiles seen on Camacho Reddish Brown jars were plain (*a*), rolled (*b*), beveled (*c*), and everted (*d*).

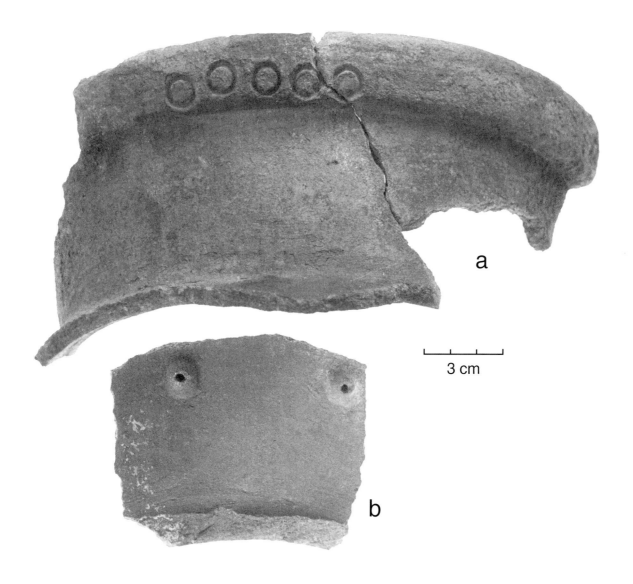

Figure 3.5. Examples of Camacho Reddish Brown jars with plastic decoration. (*a*): jar with bolstered rim, decorated with cane-end impressions; found in the North Central Canchón, Structure D; (*b*): jar neck with modeled and punctate nipples, found in Feature 4, Structure D.

painted faces are far more common in Pingüino Buff, which provide a much better surface for painting. Another point illustrated by Figure 3.9 is that while most modeled faces look dead, most painted faces seem open-eyed and alive.

Another attribute of Pingüino Buff jars which, on rare occasions, can be found on Camacho Reddish Brown vessels is a *lug modeled in the shape of a maize cob* (Figure 3.10). For reasons that will become clear during our discussion of the kitchen/brewery in Structure D (Chapter 7), we believe that these lugs are a reference to *chicha*, or maize beer, and may suggest the original contents of the jar.

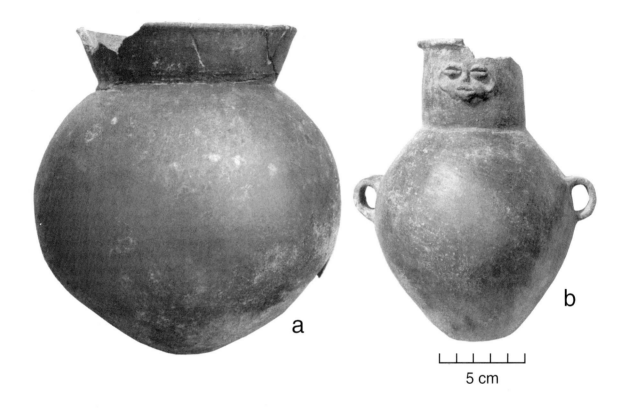

Figure 3.6. Examples of Camacho Reddish Brown jars. (*a*): globular jar with plain rim; this is Vessel 1 found with Individual 2 of Burial 7 in Quebrada 5a. (*b*): jar with strap handles and a tall neck with a modeled human face; this is Vessel 1 of Burial 1, Quebrada 5a.

Finally, we come to a distinct vessel form within Camacho Reddish Brown, one clearly related to the storage of *chicha*. These are very large vessels, known in Quechua as *hatun maccma*, which could hold 700 to 2000 liters of maize beer. A number of these were found set into the floor of Structure D's North Central Canchón (Marcus 1987a, 2008). They are so heavy that we suspect that they were formed and fired in situ out of an even coarser variety of Camacho Reddish Brown. Figure 3.11 shows two rims from such *hatun maccma*, whose paste is 25% temper. This ware has an average grain size index of 2.9, the highest index of any vessel at Cerro Azul.

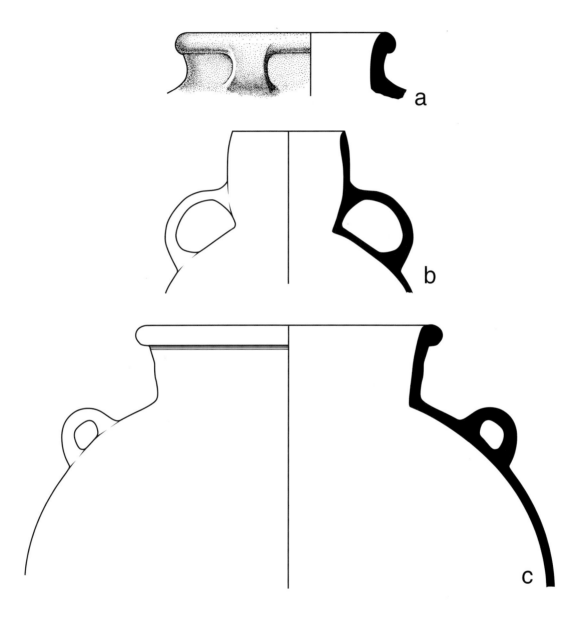

Figure 3.7. The handles on Camacho Reddish Brown jars could be attached to the rim (*a*), the shoulder (*b*), or the upper body (*c*). Handles could vary from loop type (*c*) to strap type (*a*, *b*). The rim profile shown in (*a*) and (*c*) is the bolstered type.

5 cm

Figure 3.8. Camacho Reddish Brown amphora from stratigraphic Zone A of Terrace 9, Quebrada 5a.

3 cm

Figure 3.9. Examples of Camacho Reddish Brown jar rims decorated with human faces. (*a*): neck with modeled face featuring coffee-bean eyes, found in the *kincha* layer above the floor of Room 3, Structure D; (*b*): neck with face painted in white/black/red, found while sweeping the surface of Structure 9 before excavation, in the area above the south entrance.

Figure 3.10. Lug in the shape of a maize cob, broken off a large Camacho Reddish Brown jar; found in the North Central Canchón, Structure D.

3 cm

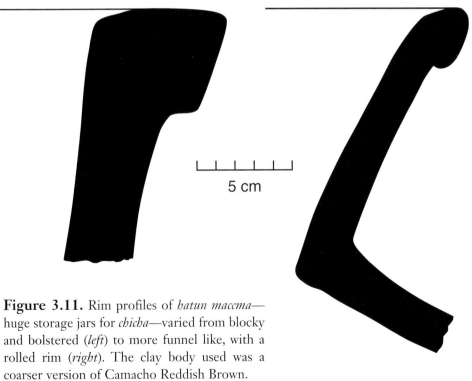

5 cm

Figure 3.11. Rim profiles of *hatun maccma*— huge storage jars for *chicha*—varied from blocky and bolstered (*left*) to more funnel like, with a rolled rim (*right*). The clay body used was a coarser version of Camacho Reddish Brown.

CAMACHO BLACK

Camacho Black is a black to grayish black ware produced under reduced-firing conditions. It has two varieties. The more common "standard" variety was used primarily for amphorae and storage jars. The less common "highly burnished" or "graphite" variety was used more often for burial offerings and effigy vessels, many of them miniatures. (Our use of the term *graphite* here refers to the appearance of the vessel surface and does not imply the presence of actual graphite.)

Paste
The paste in both varieties resembles cigarette ash, light gray (2.5 Y 7/0 in the Munsell system) to gray (2.5 Y 6/0). However, the standard variety is about 31% temper, with an average grain size index of 1.46. The highly burnished variety is much finer, only about 11% temper, with an average grain size index of 1.40 (Stoltman, Appendix A).

Surface treatment
When the surface of the vessel is well preserved, the two varieties are easily distinguished by surface treatment. Jars of the standard variety might be left rough or minimally wiped smooth, while amphorae are usually smoothed or even lightly burnished. Better-made vessels seem to have been given a float or wash of the same clay before being subjected to a light burnish.

In the case of the highly burnished variety, vessels were burnished twice—once when leather-hard, and a second time when completely dry. In addition to closing the pores on the surface, this double burnish produced a metallic sheen which gave the vessel its graphite-like surface. In our room-by-room inventories, we took note of all Camacho Black vessels with a "graphite" finish.

The more highly burnished the vessel, the darker its surface color. Large amphorae with minimal burnishing vary from dark gray to charcoal, with firing clouds ranging from light brown-

ish gray (10 YR 6/2) to light olive brown (2.5 Y 5/2). Highly burnished miniature vessels are more likely to be very dark gray (10 YR 3/1) to pure black or even metallic black.

I debated whether or not the two varieties of Camacho Black should be considered separate types. In the end I decided against it because the deterioration of many sherd surfaces, under exposure to marine salt (*salitre*), made it impossible to tell just how highly burnished they had once been.

Common vessel shapes
Among the most common vessel shapes in this ware are *jars and amphorae* (Figure 3.12). In the case of small rim sherds, it was not always possible to tell whether the vessel had had the more globular body of a jar or the more conical body of an amphora. Necks vary from *vertical* (Figure 3.12a) to *funnel shaped* (Figure 3.12b), and the vessels can have *strap handles* or *loop handles* on the shoulder or body (Figure 3.12c, d). Many standard variety amphorae included with burials have a *human face modeled on the neck* (Figure 3.13). In Figure 3.13 one can see the pitting of the vessel surface caused by the penetration of salt crystals over time.

Figure 3.14 shows additional globular jars (standard variety) with *rolled to plain rims* on *wide or restricted mouths*.

Human faces modeled on amphora necks come in many varieties, as seen in Figure 3.15. They can have *coffee-bean eyes* (Figure 3.15c), *modeled and incised eyes* (Figure 3.15d), or simple *pinched nipples* as eyes (Figure 3.15a).

In Figure 3.16 we show two examples of the highly burnished variety of Camacho Black. Both are small to miniature vessels included with burials. They do not by any means exhaust the variety of small burial offerings in Camacho Black, which will be discussed in detail in a future volume on the burials found in the quebradas of Cerro Camacho. Figure 3.16 makes clear how shiny and graphite-like the surface of these double-burnished vessels can be.

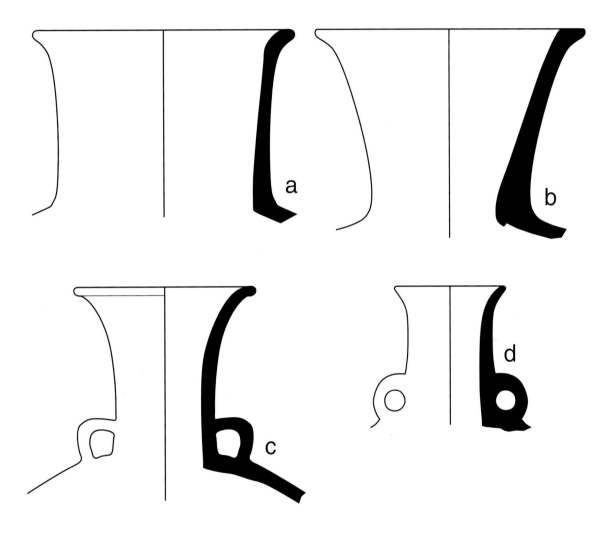

Figure 3.12. The necks of Camacho Black jars and amphorae varied from vertical (*a*) to funnel shaped (*b*) and could have strap handles (*c*) or loop handles (*d*) linking them to the shoulder.

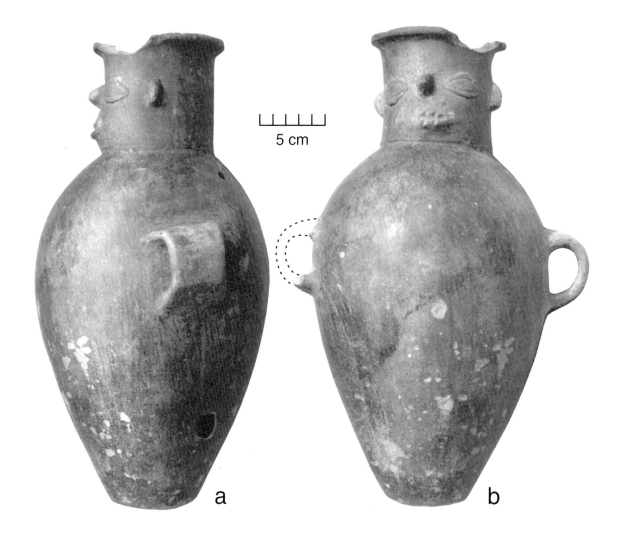

5 cm

a

b

Figure 3.13. Front and side views of a standard variety Camacho Black amphora with a human face modeled on the neck. This amphora was Vessel 2 of Burial 8.

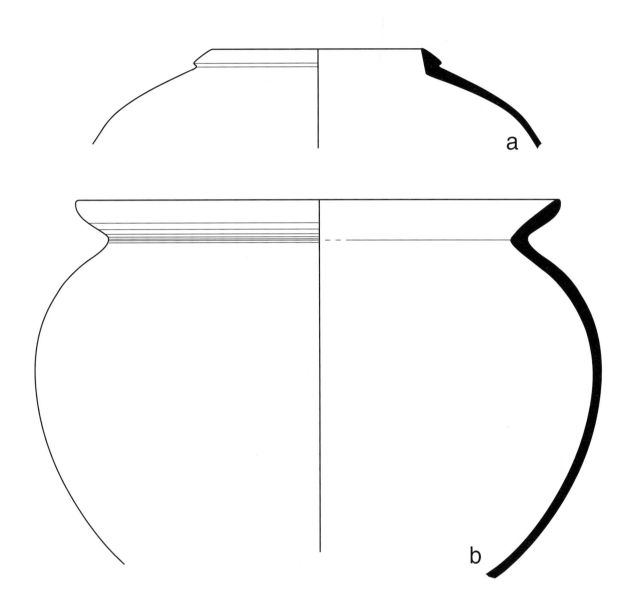

Figure 3.14. The mouths of Camacho Black globular jars varied from small and restricted (*a*) to wide (*b*). Rims could be tightly rolled (*a*), cambered, or plain (*b*).

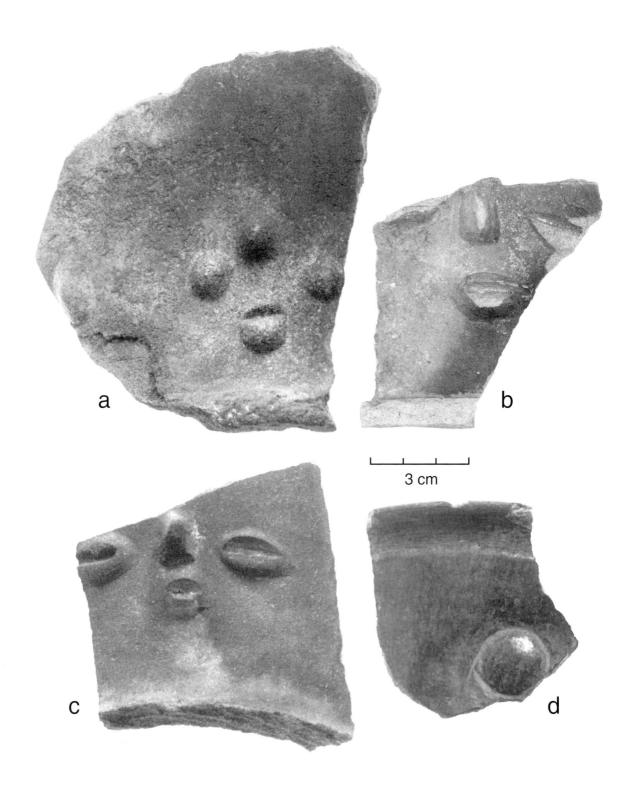

Figure 3.15. Fragments of modeled human faces from Camacho Black vessels. (*a, c*): from Feature 4, Structure D; (*b*): from Northeast Canchón, Structure D; (*d*): showing a modeled and incised "eye," from Feature 6, Structure D.

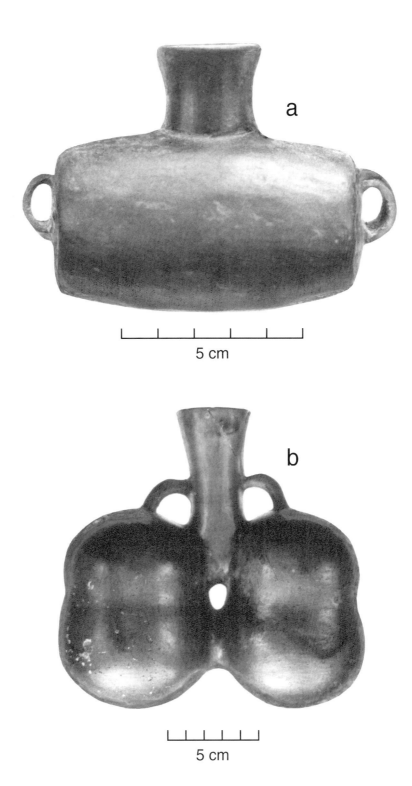

Figure 3.16. Examples of the highly burnished variety of Camacho Black. (*a*): miniature drum-shaped vessel found with Burial 1; (*b*): double vessel found with Burial 4. The highly burnished variety was more common among burial offerings than in general midden debris.

PINGÜINO BUFF

Pingüino Buff is an oxidized, pinkish buff ware whose light-colored surface provides an ideal background for elaborate painting in white, black, and red. As the most decorated Late Intermediate pottery type found at Cerro Azul, it also provides some stylistic ties to other valleys.

Pingüino Buff was rarely, if ever, used for cooking. It occurs mainly in the form of small globular jars, larger jars for the storage of liquids, individual serving bowls, and occasional exotic effigy vessels. The vast majority of Pingüino Buff specimens are pinkish to buff in color, but there is a minor, atypical orange variety that is less expertly made. As mentioned earlier, petrographic analysis suggests that this atypical orange variety may have been nonlocal.

Paste

Standard Pingüino Buff is about 22% temper, with an average grain size index of 1.69 (Stoltman, Appendix A). The atypical orange variety is also about 22%, but has a coarser grain size index of 2.44. Standard Pingüino Buff paste ranges from light red (2.5 YR 6/8) to light brown (7.5 YR 6/4) in color. The atypical variety, as its name implies, is closer to orange in color.

Surface treatment

Pingüino Buff can be smoothed, burnished, or occasionally double burnished. The interiors of jars seem to have been wiped with a handful of fiber or grass; exteriors are always smoothed and sometimes even burnished. In the case of bowls, both interior and exterior surfaces are smoothed or even burnished. Wiped surfaces tend to be browner in color (7.5 YR 5/4, "brown," to 7.5 YR 6/4, "light brown," in the Munsell system). Burnished surfaces tend to be pink, buff, or pinkish buff, ranging from 7.5 YR 5/4 to 2.5 YR 6/6 or 2.5 YR 6/4. Surfaces of the atypical variety are closer to orange in color.

Painting

Jars can be painted on the neck, the shoulder, the interior of the rim, or all three areas. Bowls are painted on the interior, exterior, or both, depending on the size of the orifice and the areas of greatest visibility. Vessels often have a layer of cream paint or wash (2.5 Y 8/2) that serves as a background for further painting. Over this, designs might be painted in black (7.5 YR 3/0) and/or red (10 R 4/6, "red," to 10 R 5/2, "weak red").

It should be stressed that the paint colors used on Pingüino Buff are highly variable, showing a greater range of Munsell colors than the few noted in the preceding paragraph. I have attempted to provide a sense of this variation in later chapters, where specific sherds from specific proveniences are illustrated. Where appropriate, I give the actual Munsell colors of these specimens.

Common vessel shapes and decoration

Some of the most common vessel shapes in Pingüino Buff are *globular jars with wide mouths* which can be either small (Figure 3.17a) or large (Figure 3.18b). There are also *globular jars with restricted mouths* (Figure 3.17d) and *large globular jars with funnel necks* (Figure 3.18a). The larger jars, which were probably used for the storage of water, *chicha*, and other liquids, can have paired strap handles, set either vertically or horizontally. The small globular jars with wide mouths more likely held porridge-style meals for one to two people. They are frequently painted on all visible surfaces (Figure 3.17a).

Bowls in Pingüino Buff can be *hemispherical* (Figure 3.17c) or have *a restricted orifice* (Figure 3.17b). These vessels were probably used for individual servings of food.

Cerro Azul did not yield a long chronological sequence. Nevertheless, thanks to a few key stratigraphic contexts, we were able to document some significant changes in decoration or vessel attributes over time. The oldest ceramics we found came from the deepest stratigraphic levels in the quebradas of Cerro Camacho (Chapter 9). The youngest or most recent ceramics we found came from the Late Horizon deposits on Cerros Centinela and El Fraile (Marcus et al. 1985). These excavations gave us parameters for the beginning and end of the occupation of Cerro Azul.

Figures 3.19 and 3.20 provide examples of what I believe to be relatively early motifs painted on Pingüino Buff. Figure 3.19 shows sherds of Pingüino Buff bowls whose interior walls are painted neatly with diamonds, narrow triangles, and parallel black lines. Most were given a red wash, after which the design was outlined in black; finally, the diamonds or triangles were filled with yellow paint (Figure 3.19a, b, d) or iridescent purple paint (Figure 3.19c). Three of the sherds came from deep stratigraphic levels in Quebrada 5a of Cerro Camacho, while the fourth was redeposited in room fill in Structure D. The bowl form, the motifs, and the neatness of the painting are reminiscent of pottery at earlier sites such as Cerro del Oro (Kroeber 1937).

Figure 3.20 shows Pingüino Buff jar body sherds bearing what I have called the "Life Saver" motif. In that figure, sherds *a* and *b* are from a Pingüino Buff jar that has a black-painted zone, over which cream-colored Life Savers have been painted. Sherd *c* is from a jar whose exterior surface has been divided into two zones, one painted red, the other painted purple. The Life Savers painted over the red zone are yellow; those painted over the purple zone are cream-colored. This is a rare motif at Cerro Azul, occurring mainly in the deep levels of the quebradas on Cerro Camacho, but occasionally found redeposited in the fill of later buildings. As in the case of the motifs in Figure 3.19, I suspect that the Life Saver motif was a survival from earlier times.

Far more common at Cerro Azul are human faces modeled and painted on Pingüino Buff jar necks (Figure 3.21). In contrast to the dead-looking faces on Camacho Black jars and amphorae, these Pingüino Buff faces look very much alive, with large, open eyes painted in black and white. These specimens also have a distinctive and standardized form of red facial paint, with the bridge of the nose painted, and L-shaped red areas extending from cheek to ear. The same type of facial painting can be found on some figurines at Cerro Azul (Marcus 1987a:Fig. 21a). We do not know whether this style of facial painting was related to sociopolitical status, ethnic identity, or something else. Some of the figurines with this kind of facial paint have female bodies.

Other Pingüino Buff jars are decorated with white paint over the natural buff surface (Figure

3.22). Motifs range from geometric (Figure 3.22a, b) to zoomorphic (Figure 3.22c). In other cases, simple geometric motifs are painted in white over a black wash, which causes the white design to stand out more prominently (Figure 3.23).

Figures 3.24–3.27 provide the reader with a sample of motifs painted on Pingüino Buff jars in black and white or black/white/red. Geometric motifs include nested black/white/red chevrons (Figure 3.24b), zones of dots set off by white lines (Figure 3.24a), checkerboards (Figure 3.27b), combinations of crosses, discs, and dots (Figure 3.27a), and the crosshatched "mountains" already shown in Figure 3.17a. Zoomorphic motifs may be naturalistic (Figure 3.25a) or stylized (Figure 3.25b, c). In the case of some motifs, it is not clear whether the painter was trying to produce stylized animals or simply abstract motifs (Figure 3.26).

Some Pingüino Buff vessels appear to be effigies. Among the most interesting of these are *globular jars that seem to depict skeletal individuals* (Figure 3.28). By combining three-dimensional modeling with incising, the potter has given these effigies spindly arms, prominent spinal columns, and carefully delineated ribs. Because these effigies combine skeletal characteristics with a large globular vessel shape, our crew dubbed them "fat skeletons."

Like Camacho Reddish Brown, Pingüino Buff features three-dimensional *jar lugs modeled to resemble maize cobs* (Figure 3.29), a possible reference to *chicha* or maize beer, which was produced in quantity in the North Central Canchón of Structure D (Chapter 7).

A few effigy bowls in Pingüino Buff seem to represent *the inverted carapace of a turtle*. These bowls feature small protuberances that resemble the tails and feet of a turtle (Figure 3.30).

Figures 3.31 and 3.32 illustrate a few of the vessels from Cerro Azul that are atypical either in paste or decoration. The vessel in Figure 3.31 is made with the atypical orange variety of Pingüino Buff. It is painted in a style common to burial wrappings of the Late Intermediate period: alternating brown and white stripes. In the case of the burial wrappings, the effect is created without dye, simply by alternating the yarn of two local types of cotton, *algodón pardo* (brown) and *algodón blanco* (white).

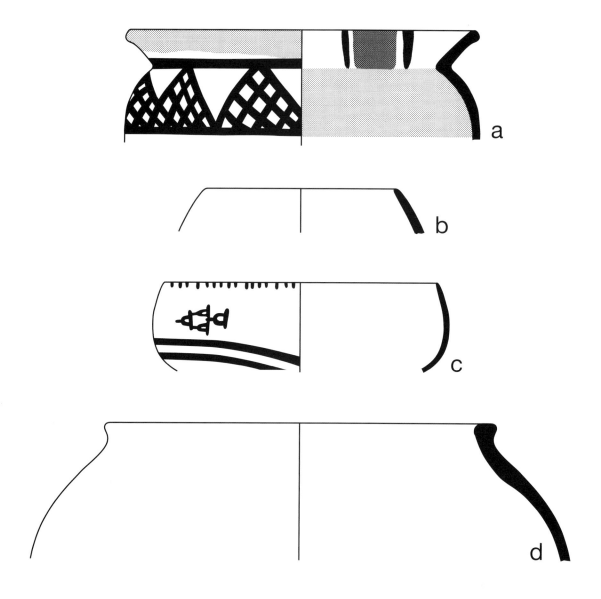

Figure 3.17. Among the vessel shapes in which Pingüino Buff occurred were globular jars with wide mouths (*a*), globular jars with restricted mouths (*d*), hemispherical bowls (*c*), and bowls with a restricted orifice or incurved rim (*b*). Painted designs were added in black and white or black/white/red.

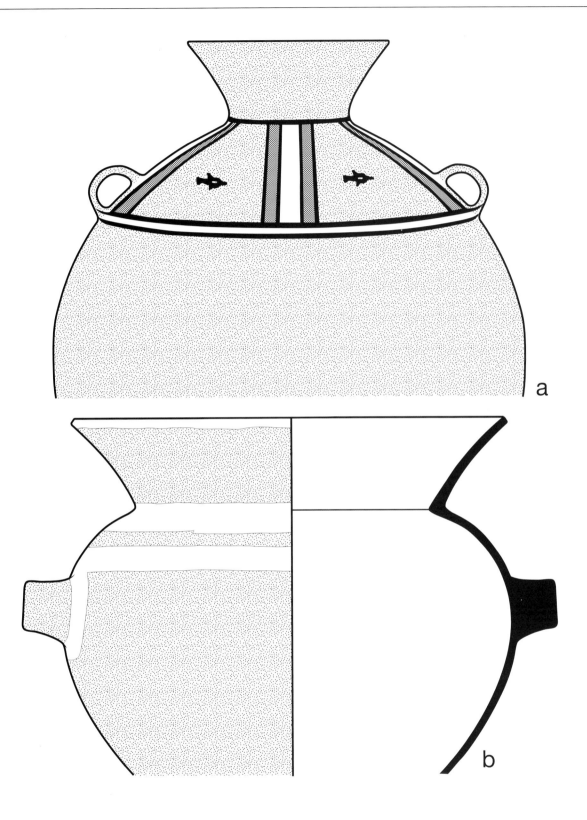

Figure 3.18. The strap handles on Pingüino Buff jars could be set vertically (*a*) or horizontally (*b*) on the vessel. The difference may reflect whether the vessel was to be lifted by ropes through the handles or directly by the hands. The vessel shown in *a* is the atypical orange variety of Pingüino Buff.

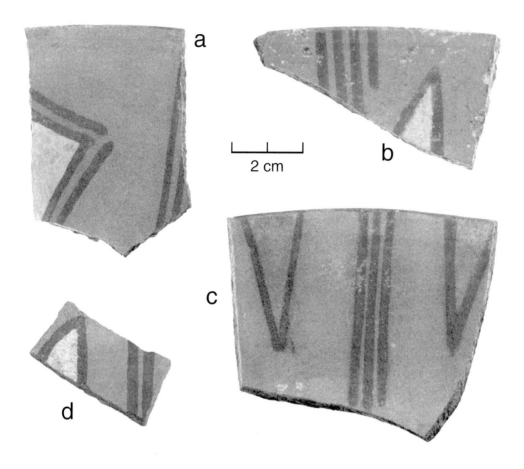

Figure 3.19. Pingüino Buff bowl sherds, painted in a style that may antedate most of the occupation of Structure D. Sherds *a–c* were redeposited in Structure 4, a burial cist found on Terrace 9 of Quebrada 5a, and probably originated in the midden into which the cist was excavated. (*a, b*): bowls given a red wash and painted in black and yellow; (*c*): bowl given a red wash and painted in black and iridescent purple; (*d*) sherd found in the fill above the floor in Room 1, Structure D.

The two jars shown in Figure 3.32 are painted in typical Pingüino Buff style but are made from pastes not typical of that type. Figure 3.32a is made on a paste similar to that of Trambollo Burnished Brown, while Figure 3.32b is made on Camacho Reddish Brown paste but is painted as if it were a Pingüino Buff vessel. Both jars in

Figure 3.32 feature the "school of fish" motif, which is often found on Pingüino Buff.

Finally, we come to a series of vessels whose shape or decoration I consider to fall relatively late in the occupation of Cerro Azul. The two specimens shown in Figure 3.33 came from Feature 4, a Late Horizon *kincha* hut built in a

3 cm

Figure 3.20. Pingüino Buff jar sherds featuring the "Life Saver" motif. It is suspected that this motif goes back further in time than the bulk of the occupation of Structure D. (*a, b*): sherds with "Life Savers" painted in cream on black, found between Floors 1 and 2 of Room 6, Structure D; (*c*): sherd with "Life Savers" painted in yellow on red (*top*) and cream on purple (*bottom*), redeposited in Structure 5, a burial cist on Terrace 9 of Quebrada 5a. This sherd probably originated in the midden into which the cist was excavated.

patio of Structure D after the Late Intermediate occupation of that building had ended (Chapter 5). Figure 3.33b is a sherd from a Pingüino Buff imitation of an Inka *aryballos*, complete with a three-dimensionally modeled lug. Figure 3.33a is a three-dimensionally modeled human head from an effigy vessel of some kind. Neither vessel in Figure 3.33 is typical of the Late Intermediate.

Globular jars with tightly rolled rims in the highly burnished variety of Camacho Black are also more typical of the Late Horizon. Another relatively late attribute of Cerro Azul pottery is the *low annular base* (or "ring base"). Such bases occur at the very end of the Late Intermediate period and continue into the Late Horizon and early Colonial period (Figure 3.34).

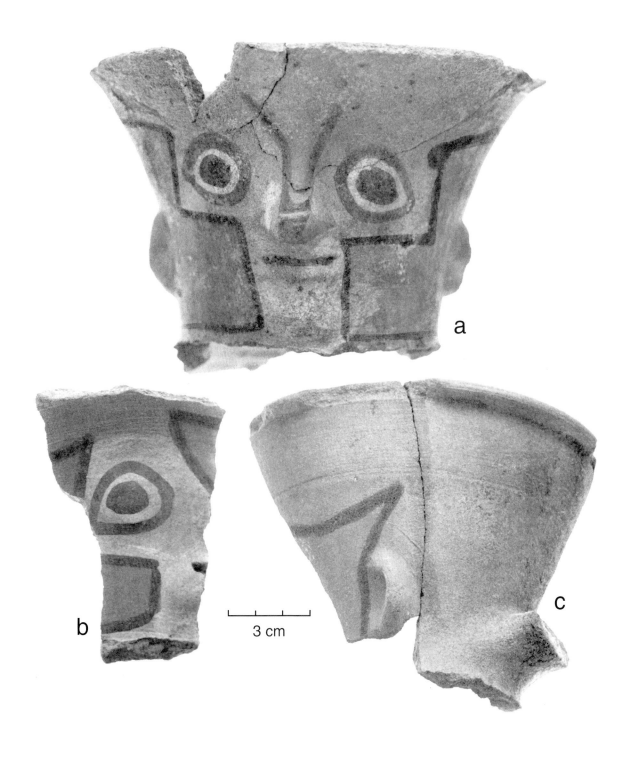

Figure 3.21. Examples of Pingüino Buff jars with painted and modeled human faces on the neck. (*a*): from the South Corridor, Structure D; (*b*): from the floor of Room 3, Structure D; (*c*): from the floor of the North Central Canchón, Structure D.

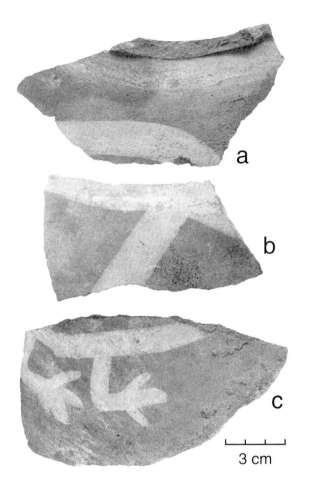

a

b

c

3 cm

(LEFT):
Figure 3.22. Sherds from Pingüino Buff jars with white-on-natural-buff painting. (*a, b*): sherds left by the looters of Structure 6, Terrace 9, Quebrada 5a; (*c*): sherd from the North Central Canchón, Structure D.

(BELOW):
Figure 3.23. Three conjoining Pingüino Buff sherds from a jar painted with white-on-black disks over natural buff. Found in the fill above the low wall dividing Rooms 9 and 10, Structure D.

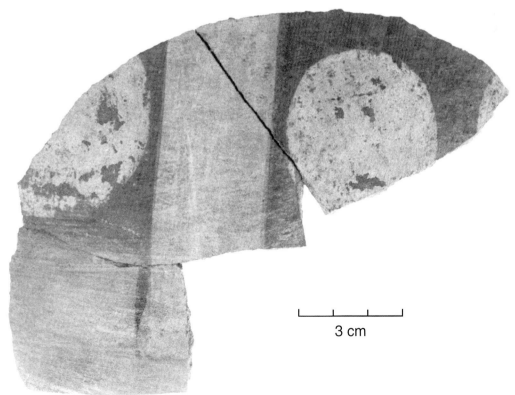

3 cm

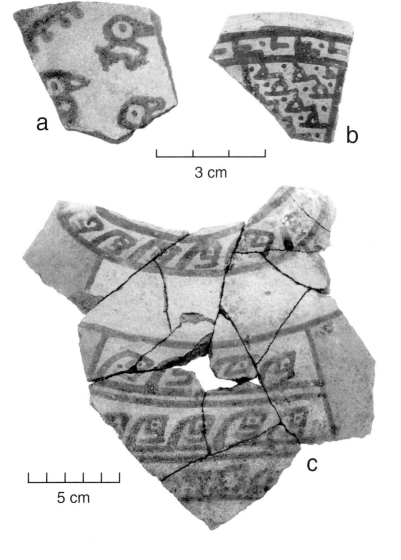

Figure 3.24. Pingüino Buff jar sherds painted in black/white/red: sherd *a* was found on the surface of the Northeast Canchón, Structure D; *b* was found in the fill of Room 11, Structure D.

Figure 3.25. Pingüino Buff sherds with bird motifs painted in black on white. (*a*): found with a pile of maize cobs in the South Corridor of Structure D, features realistic birds; (*b*): from Room 6 of Structure 9, this sherd has a horizontal row of stylized birds above a "school of fish" motif; (*c*): conjoining sherds from a jar found in the *kincha* layer above the Room 3 floor, Structure D, have horizontal rows of stylized bird heads with long necks and curving beaks.

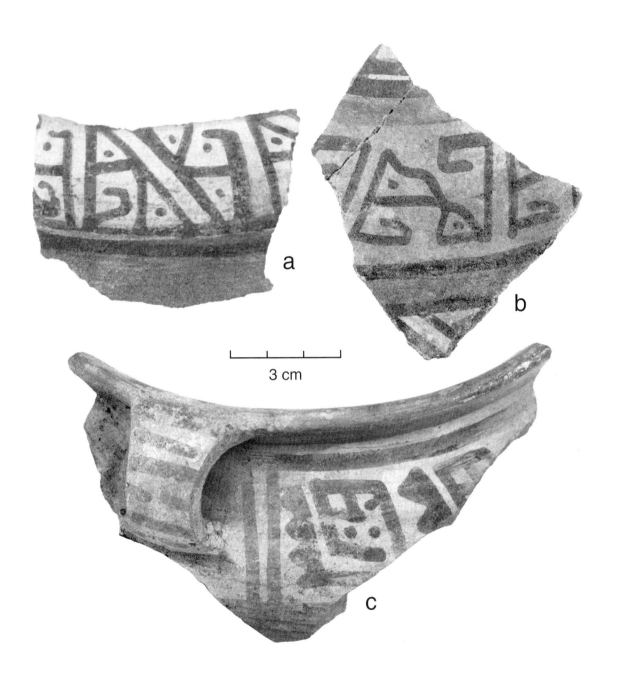

Figure 3.26. Pingüino Buff sherds with step-fret or other geometric motifs painted in black on white. Sherd *a* is from the fill above the North Platform of the Southwest Canchón, Structure D; *b* is from Room 3, Structure D; *c* is from Feature 4 of Structure D.

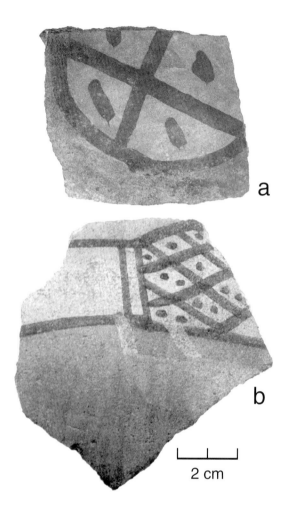

Figure 3.27. Pingüino Buff sherds with geometric motifs painted in black on white. (*a*): from the South Corridor, Structure D; (*b*): from Collca 1, Structure D.

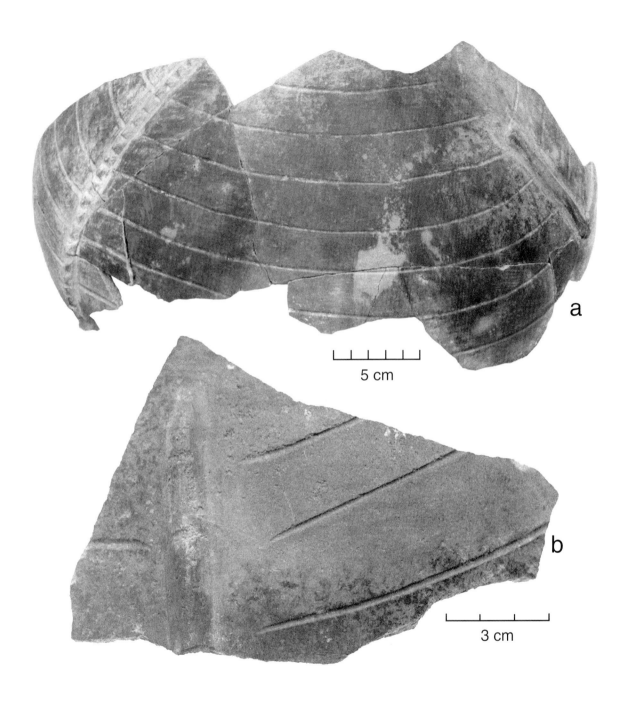

Figure 3.28. Pingüino Buff vessels depicting "fat skeletons." (*a*): partially restorable jar from inside Feature 9 of the North Central Canchón, Structure D. A modeled vertebral column appears at far left; a modeled spindly arm appears at far right. In between are horizontal incisions representing ribs. (*b*): sherd found while sweeping above Rooms 3–5, Structure 9, prior to excavation.

2 cm

Figure 3.29. Pingüino Buff jar lug in the shape of a maize cob from Room 7, Structure 9.

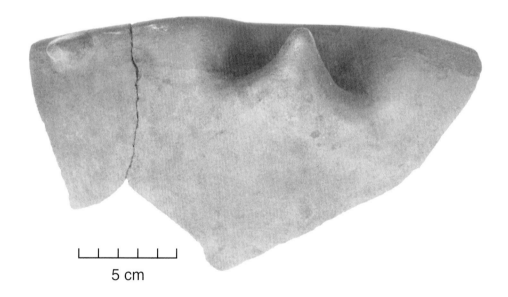

5 cm

Figure 3.30. Conjoining sherds from a Pingüino Buff bowl which features a "turtle tail" and stubby "turtle foot"; found in Room 3, Structure D.

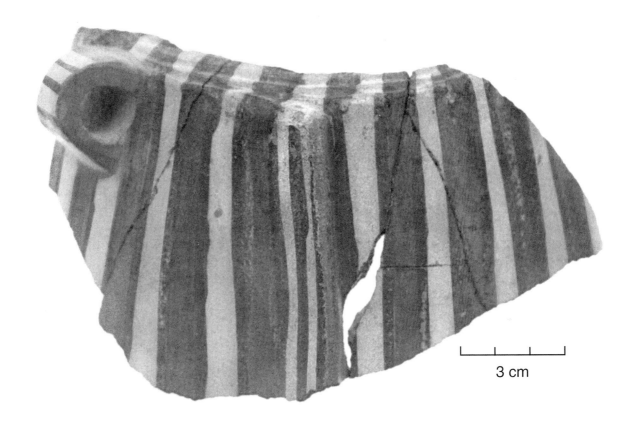

Figure 3.31. Conjoining sherds from a vessel made with the atypical orange variety of Pingüino Buff, found in Room 5 of Structure 9. This vessel appears to have been painted in imitation of the typical Late Intermediate brown-and-white-striped burial wrappings. On such wrappings, *algodón pardo* alternates with *algodón blanco*.

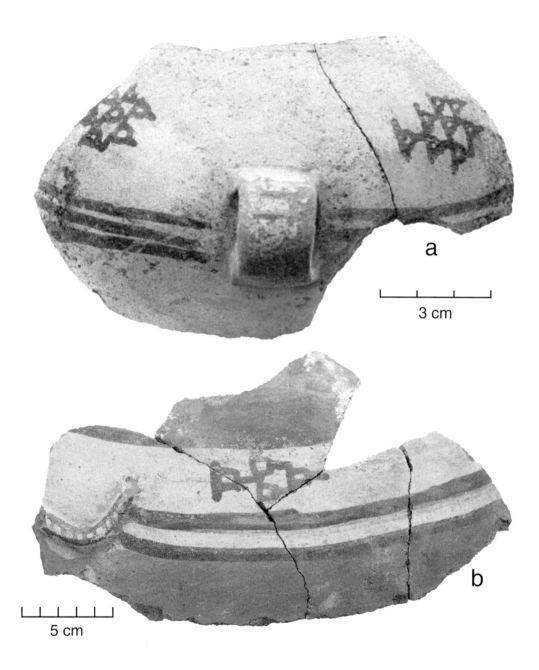

Figure 3.32. Vessels painted in Pingüino Buff style, but with atypical paste. Both feature the "school of fish" motif. (*a*): found in Room 5 of Structure 9, this is painted in black over a cream slip and has paste similar, but not identical, to that used for Trambollo Burnished Brown; (*b*): from an ash-filled hollow in the floor of the Northeast Canchón, Structure D; this is made on Camacho Reddish Brown paste, but painted in black/white/red as if it were Pingüino Buff.

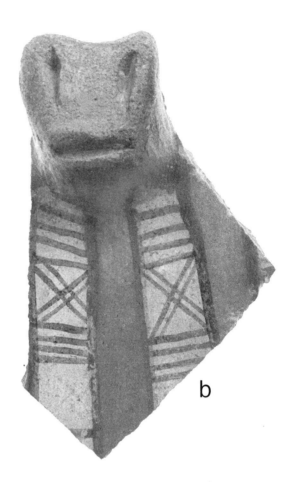

3 cm

(ABOVE):
Figure 3.33. Unusual Pingüino Buff items from Feature 4, a Late Horizon *kincha* hut built atop Structure D. (*a*): three dimensionally modeled head from an effigy vessel of some kind, painted black/white/red; (*b*): sherd from a local imitation of an Inka *aryballos*, with a modeled lug and areas painted in black/white/red.

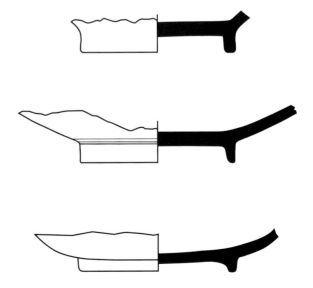

(RIGHT):
Figure 3.34. Ring bases on Pingüino Buff vessels seem to have been a relatively late attribute, only occurring toward the end of the Late Intermediate and continuing into the Late Horizon.

TRAMBOLLO BURNISHED BROWN

Trambollo Burnished Brown is a relatively fine, thin-walled ware which I suspect was a holdover from earlier time periods. It is used almost exclusively for *hemispherical bowls, slightly incurved-rim bowls,* and other vessels with gourd-like shapes. There seems to be little question about its function: most Trambollo Burnished Brown hemispherical bowls strongly resemble *mates,* the gourd vessels used for individual food servings in Cerro Azul structures and burial cists. These bowls are as thin as gourds (4–6 mm in wall thickness) and have a similar surface color range, pumpkin-colored (or orange-buff) to mahogany or reddish brown.

Paste

The paste is fine: only about 16% temper, with an average grain size index of 1.48 (Stoltman, Appendix A). In contrast to Pingüino Buff, whose sherd sections are generally of one color throughout, Trambollo Burnished Brown sherd sections can display a gray core sandwiched between buff or reddish brown layers (2.5 YR 5/6), or even a mixture of brownish to grayish colors.

Surface treatment

Trambollo Burnished Brown bowls are burnished once, on both interior and exterior surfaces. The burnishing is sometimes the streaky kind erroneously referred to as "stick polish," which in reality must have been done with something like a quartz pebble. Burnished surfaces can show a bit of crazing and usually have a slick or soapy feel. Surface colors range from 2.5 YR 5/6 ("red") to 2.5 YR 3/6 ("dark red") in the Munsell system.

Decoration

At Cerro Azul, Trambollo Burnished Brown ware is almost never painted or incised.

Common vessel shapes

Figures 3.35 and 3.36 present the most common vessel shape in which Trambollo Burnished Brown appears: a hemispherical bowl that is about the right size for an individual serving. Except for its slightly cambered rim, there is little to distinguish it from a gourd vessel of the same size.

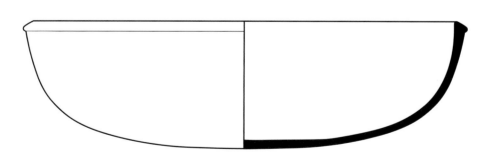

Figure 3.35. The most common vessel form in Trambollo Burnished Brown was a hemispherical bowl closely resembling a *mate,* or gourd bowl.

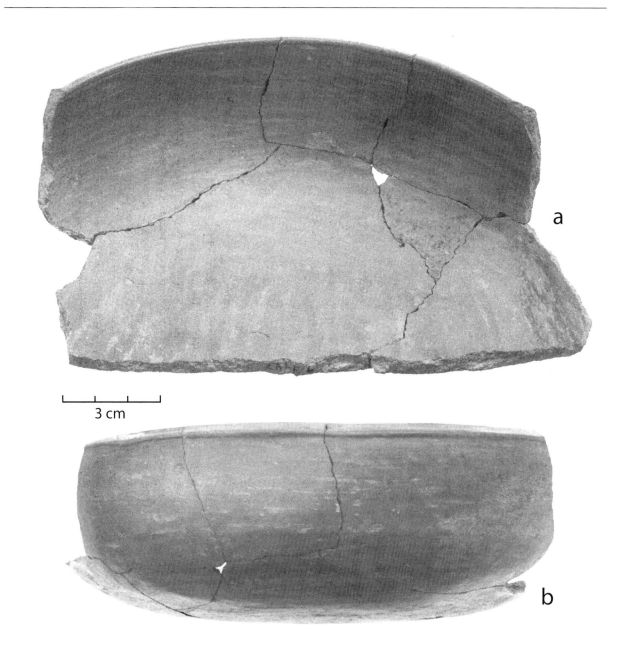

3 cm

Figure 3.36. Two views of a typical Trambollo Burnished Brown hemispherical bowl from Feature 6 of Structure D.

THE TOTAL CERAMIC SAMPLE FROM CERRO AZUL: PRIMARY, SECONDARY, AND TERTIARY CONTEXTS

This chapter does no more than scratch the surface of the Late Intermediate pottery assemblage from Cerro Azul. In the chapters that follow, we present the total sherd counts from our excavations in Structure D, Structure 9, and several terraces in the quebradas of Cerro Camacho. Sherd counts are given separately for each room and feature, and in the case of rooms with a sequence of superimposed floors, the counts for each of the floors are given separately. This detailed reporting was necessary for two reasons: (1) I wanted to see what effect the functional differences among rooms would have on their sherd assemblages, and (2) I wanted to monitor any changes in ceramics that took place over time.

Our sherd collections come from at least three contexts. *Primary contexts* are those where the vessels were in situ or virtually so. For example, Feature 5 in Room 4 of Structure D consists of vessels that had been left sitting on a floor; they eventually broke under the weight of the earth above them. *Secondary contexts* are those where the sherds appear to have been moved only once. For example, Feature 6 of Structure D is a small midden that appears to have resulted from the sweeping of the Southwest Canchón, a large unroofed court. These sherds were no longer in situ, but probably all came from nearby and dated to a short time period. *Tertiary contexts* are those in which we have reason to believe that the sherds had been moved several times, and fragments from different proveniences and different episodes of time might have been combined. For example, the midden debris in the terraces of Cerro Camacho not only appear to have been carried to the quebrada from one or more of the tapia compounds, but could even represent a mixture of sherds from several different structures.

Our counts include every diagnostic sherd from every provenience: rim sherds, decorated body sherds, handles, lugs, basal sherds, and so on. In the case of collections that seemed unusually large and important, we also counted the undecorated body sherds, even though they did not add a lot of information. (Just as I discovered earlier while working in Mesoamerica, most of the undecorated body sherds appear to have come from utilitarian cooking and storage wares.)

A note on sherd counts from primary, secondary, and tertiary contexts

Our excavations at Cerro Azul allowed us to investigate one other by-product of archaeological context. In some ceramic reports, a great deal is made of sherd counts. They provide us with quantification and the opportunity to draw conclusions from it. My subjective impression, however, was that every time groups of sherds were moved at Cerro Azul, they broke into smaller fragments. Obviously, moving sherds from place to place could affect sherd counts.

To test this possibility, I decided to weigh a sample of 100 body sherds from four different proveniences. The proveniences chosen were (1) Feature 5, an already-mentioned primary context in Structure D; (2) Feature 6, an already-mentioned secondary context in Structure D; (3) Feature 20 of Structure 9, a midden whose sherds I suspected had been moved only slightly farther than those of Feature 6; and (4) the matrix of Terrace 9 in Quebrada 5a on Cerro Camacho, a tertiary deposit whose sherds may have been moved several times. To avoid problems of differential breakage among pottery types, all the sherds counted were Camacho Reddish Brown.

The results of our experiment are as follows:

Feature 5 (primary)	100 sherds = 4700 g
Feature 6 (secondary)	100 sherds = 2400 g
Feature 20 (secondary)	100 sherds = 1903 g
Quebrada 5a, Terrace 9 (tertiary)	100 sherds = 1090 g

I conclude from these results that context does, in fact, affect sherd size. One hundred sherds from primary context weigh twice as much as 100 from secondary context; 100 from secondary context weigh twice as much as 100 from tertiary context. In other words, if you want higher sherd counts, just keep moving your sherd collections.

Petrographic Analyses of the Cerro Azul Pottery Types

James B. Stoltman

Following her excavations at Cerro Azul, Joyce Marcus asked if I would be willing to undertake a petrographic analysis of her seven Late Intermediate pottery types/varieties: (1) Camacho Black, standard variety; (2) Camacho Black, highly burnished ("graphite") variety; (3) Camacho Reddish Brown, standard variety; (4) the coarser variety of Camacho Reddish Brown used for *hatun maccma*, or immense storage jars; (5) Pingüino Buff, standard variety; (6) the atypical orange variety of Pingüino Buff; and (7) Trambollo Burnished Brown.

I subjected sherd samples of these ceramics not only to standard petrographic thin-section analysis, but to the quantitative analysis I introduced in an *American Antiquity* article (Stoltman 1989). This technique is a version of point counting that estimates with considerable precision the amounts of human additives (temper) and natural inclusions (silt and sand) in ceramic pastes.

LOCAL BEDROCK

Before looking at the ceramics, I decided to familiarize myself with the local bedrock from which at least some of the pottery tempers were likely to have been derived. I did this by thin sectioning a chunk of bedrock from Cerro Camacho, the hill overlooking the archaeological site. It turned out to be an extrusive igneous rock, originally of andesitic composition, that had been subjected to metamorphic alteration. It has little or no quartz or orthoclase; the original feldspars were probably plagioclase and mafics but have since been extensively altered. The most common mineral in the phenocrysts is sericite (fine-grained musco-

vite), which is a common alteration product of feldspar. The next most common mineral in the phenocrysts is green amphibole, with pumpellyite being the third most common. Smaller amounts of epidote, apatite, and opaques are also present.

While none of the thin sections contained the particular rock described above, it was no surprise to find that most Cerro Azul pottery types/varieties contain fragments of igneous rock temper. In five of the varieties, the preponderance of the temper inclusions derives from a volcanic (that is, extrusive), porphyritic rock that ranges in composition along a continuum from trachyte to latite to andesite. The two exceptions to this observation are (1) the coarser variety of Camacho Reddish Brown used for *hatun maccma*, vessels that may have been made in situ in the North Central Canchón of Structure D, and (2) the atypical orange variety of Pingüino Buff, which may be a nonlocal ware. I will have more to say about these ceramics later.

With the exception of these two varieties, the porphyritic rock in the Cerro Azul ceramics is composed preponderantly of cryptocrystalline to dark, nearly opaque "groundmass," comprised of various minerals that are too fine grained to be identified reliably by microscope. Embedded in the groundmass, but often loose as isolated grains within the paste, are larger mineral crystals, "phenocrysts," that *can* be reliably identified. Feldspars, both alkaline (Kspar) and sodic (plagioclase), dominate, with lesser amounts of mafic minerals such as amphibole and biotite also present. Quartz occurs only in minor amounts or may even be absent.

THE PROBLEMS OF DISTINGUISHING TRACHYTES, LATITES, AND ANDESITES

The primary distinguishing features of the porphyritic rocks used as temper at Cerro Azul depend upon the representation of feldspars, as follows. *Trachytes* have alkali feldspar dominance, with no (or minor) amounts of sodic plagioclase (< 35%) (Shelley 1993; LeMaitre 2002). *Latites* have sodic plagioclase and alkali feldspars in roughly equal amounts. *Andesites* have sodic plagioclase dominance, with no (or minor) amounts of alkali feldspars (< 35%) (Shelley 1993; LeMaitre 2002).

Distinguishing among these rock types is difficult because of the gradational differences among them, along with the cryptocrystalline character of the groundmasses that comprise the preponderance of their makeup. This problem is compounded in pottery thin sections, because the relatively small particle sizes (due to temper preparation) make it highly unlikely that the visible grains are truly representative of their parent rock. Identifying these rocks via petrography depends mainly upon identifying the coarser-grained phenocrysts, which by themselves are not fully representative of the composition of the rock. As noted above, the main phenocrysts observed in the Cerro Azul pottery are plagioclase and alkali feldspar, with lesser amounts of such mafic minerals as amphibole and biotite. Since quartz is so rare in these rocks, it is assumed that any "loose" silt- and sand-size quartz grains are natural inclusions within the clays used to make the pots.

In addition to these problems, the term *latite* itself, as defined above, is subject to considerable disagreement among geologists. For example, some prefer the term *trachyandesite* (Shelley 1993:52). In the ensuing discussion I employ the term *latite* with this proviso: that it be understood not as a definitive identification, but only a convenient shorthand for the most common volcanic rock seen in these thin sections, one that is believed to fall somewhere along the trachyte-to-latite-to-andesite continuum.

The coarse variety of Camacho Reddish Brown used for huge storage jars (*hatun maccma*) is distinct in its mineralogical diversity, possibly because these vessels were individually created in situ in a concavity in the floor of a kitchen/brewery, rather than being produced in a standardized workshop. While latite is present in my *hatun maccma* sample, even predominant, it is accompanied by several other rock types that appear to possess higher incidences of quartz. These include both fine-grained volcanics, ranging in composition from rhyolitoid to dacitoid, as well as coarser-grained granitoid plutonic rocks (see Shelley 1993; LeMaitre 2002). Also present are a few grains of a quartzless plutonic rock composed mainly of plagioclase and amphibole—that is diorite. A single grog grain, which could easily be an accidental inclusion, was also observed in my *hatun maccma* sample.

The atypical orange variety of Pingüino Buff is also distinctive, possibly possessing nonlocal temper. As with the other vessels, the prevalent temper is a fine-grained volcanic rock. However, the incidence of quartz appears to be greater than in the "latite" of the other ceramics, suggesting a dacitoid composition (plagioclase > alkali feldspar along with > 20% quartz). Accompanying this rock is a more coarsely crystalline (plutonic) rock that is granitoid in composition. I think it can be considered a granodiorite—that is, similar in composition to dacite but more coarsely crystalline.

COMPARING MATRIX, SILT, SAND, AND TEMPER: THE RESULTS OF "POINT COUNTING"

Before proceeding to the individual thin sections, let us examine Figures A.1–A.3, which present the basic data for all seven Cerro Azul pottery types/varieties in terms of their percentages of ingredients and aplastic grain sizes. Overall, it can be said that the basic clay for all seven varieties of ceramics is relatively clean—less than 10% silt and less than 5% sand (Figures A.1 and A.3). The standard variety of Camacho Black has the greatest amount of temper (about 30%), while the highly burnished ("graphite") variety of that same type has the least (about 10%). Trambollo Burnished Brown has the second smallest amount of temper (16%), while the remaining four varieties tend to have 22%–25% temper (Figure A.2).

Paste

Type	Thin Section #	% Matrix	% Silt	% Sand	Sand Size Index
Camacho Black (Standard)	P.1	96	1	3	1.20
Camacho Black ("Graphite")	P.2	94	4	2	1.50
Camacho Reddish Brown	P.3	95	4	1	1.00
Hatun Maccma Sherd	P.4	95	3	2	2.00
Pingüino Buff (Standard)	P.5	93	4	3	1.40
Atypical Orange Variety	P.6	91	8	1	1.00
Trambollo Burnished Brown	P.7	93	6	1	1.50
Mean & Std Dev	[n=7]	93.9±1.7	4.2±2.2	1.9±0.9	1.37±.35

Body

Type	Thin Section #	% Matrix	% Sand	% Temper	Temper Type	Temper Size Index
Camacho Black (Standard)	P.1	67	2	31	Latite	1.46
Camacho Black ("Graphite")	P.2	87	2	11	Latite	1.40
Camacho Reddish Brown	P.3	75	o	25	Latite	1.76
Hatun Maccma Sherd	P.4	74	1	25	Latite+	2.90
Pingüino Buff (Standard)	P.5	76	2	22	Latite	1.67
Atypical Orange Variety	P.6	77	1	22	Dacite+	2.44
Trambollo Burnished Brown	P.7	81	1	18	Latite	1.50
Mean & Std Dev	[n=7]	76.7±6.2	1.3±0.8	22.0±6.3		1.88±.57

Figure A.1. Seven types/varieties of pottery from Cerro Azul, compared with regard to the percentage of matrix, silt, and sand in the paste (*top*) and matrix, sand, and temper in the body (*bottom*). Mean grain size in sand and temper are given in millimeters.

When grain size of the temper is considered, it is perhaps no surprise that the coarsest grain size (index, 2.90) can be found in the *hatun maccma* of the North Central Canchón kitchen/brewery (Figure A.1). These huge storage vessels, buried below floor level and perhaps even fired in place, are the coarsest of all Cerro Azul vessels. The ceramics with the finest grain size are the highly burnished variety of Camacho Black (index, 1.40), the standard variety of the same type (average, 1.46), and Trambollo Burnished Brown (index, 1.50).

It is interesting to compare standard Pingüino Buff to its atypical orange variety. Standard Pingüino Buff, presumably made locally with latite-derived temper, has an average temper grain size index of only 1.67. The atypical orange variety, possibly made elsewhere with granodiorite-and-dacite-derived temper, has a much larger temper grain size (index, 2.44). Thus, several variables—Munsell color, overall appearance, temper size, and mineralogical origin—suggest that the atypical orange variety is indeed nonlocal.

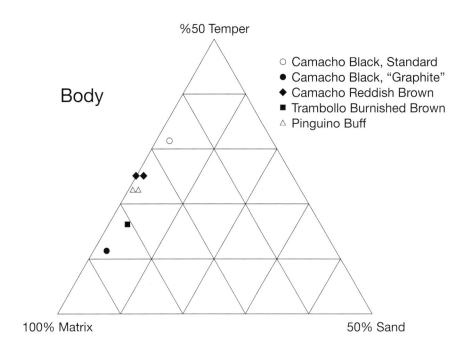

Figure A.2. Ternary graph comparing types/varieties of Cerro Azul pottery with regard to matrix (clay), sand (natural inclusions of sand size), and temper (added by humans) in the body. The main variable is temper, since the kind, amount, and size of temper particles reflect conscious decision making on the part of the potter (see text).

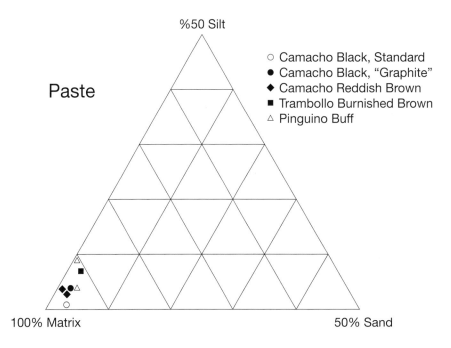

Figure A.3. Ternary graph comparing types/varieties of Cerro Azul pottery with regard to matrix, silt, and sand in the paste (the natural clayey sediment from which the vessels were made). Excluded from this graph is the temper added by humans. While all thin sections show paste values of greater than 90% matrix, less than 10% silt, and less than 5% sand, the atypical orange variety of Pingüino Buff has the siltiest paste (8%). When one combines this difference in paste with its orange color and the fact that the temper is granodiorite/dacite rather than latite, there are grounds for viewing this atypical variety as of non-local derivation (see text).

THE THIN SECTIONS

Let us now turn to the photomicrographs of the actual thin sections (Figures A.4–A.10). All were taken at the same magnification, 10X. Each variety of pottery is shown in two photographs, the first taken under plane-polarized light and the second under cross-polarized light. Some minerals show up better under the first type of light, others under the second.

In viewing the photomicrographs, here are some things to look for: (1) the dark, speckled grains or parts of grains are the fine-grained groundmass of the volcanic rock; (2) the larger, "clear" grains embedded in groundmass are the phenocrysts, most commonly plagioclase (distinctive twinning visible only under crossed polars, and unfortunately, not always even then) and alkali feldspars (either untwinned or with simple twinning, and often brownish or cloudy); (3) grains with red to blue to green coloration are mainly amphiboles, but could also be biotite; (4) isolated "clear" grains within the paste are usually quartz and, as discussed above, can be treated as natural inclusions; and (5) phenocrysts are derived from temper grains, which commonly also occur as "loose" grains within the paste and may sometimes be mistaken for natural inclusions, especially when viewed under plane polars. Twinning, when present (it is only visible under crossed polars) readily distinguishes feldspars from quartz (which has no visible twinning). Also, feldspars often show signs of metamorphic alteration (cloudiness or brownish coloration) that is sometimes visible, though not always.

Camacho Black, Standard Variety (Figure A.4)

This ware has latite temper. The largest grain, located just above the center of the photo and marked with an "x," is a rock fragment containing plagioclase phenocrysts in a fine-grained groundmass. It has a maximum dimension of 0.475 mm.

Camacho Black, Highly Burnished ("Graphite") Variety (Figure A.5)

This ware has latite temper which is the finest in grain size (index, 1.40) of all seven varieties and makes up the smallest percentage (11%) of the body among the thin-sectioned vessels. Just below the center of the photo is a plagioclase grain (a loose phenocryst) measuring 0.35 mm; it is marked with a "2." Also marked in the cross-polarized photo are grains of alkali feldspar ("1"), quartz ("3"), and amphibole ("4").

Camacho Reddish Brown, Standard Variety (Figure A.6)

This ware has latite temper, and its volume of temper (25% of the body) is the greatest of any type in my Cerro Azul sample. This high volume of temper is presumably intentional, designed to improve the vessel's resistance to thermal shock, since Camacho Reddish Brown was often used for cooking. Near the top of the photo can be seen a rock fragment measuring 0.675 mm, consisting of four plagioclase phenocrysts surrounded by dark, nearly opaque groundmass; it is marked with a "1." Other grains marked are amphibole ("2"), and a rock fragment containing both plagioclase and alkali feldspar in a dark groundmass ("3").

Coarse Variety of Camacho Reddish Brown used for hatun maccma (Figure A.7)

These large storage vessels, which Marcus believes were individually formed in situ below floor level in a kitchen/brewery, have multiple tempers, including rhyolite and diorite. This may be because each vessel was "made to order" with whatever materials were locally available.

Hatun maccma, like vessels of Standard Camacho Reddish Brown, have 25% of the body devoted to temper, and show the coarsest temper size index (2.90) in my entire Cerro Azul sample. This is probably an intentional property, designed to prevent the walls from collapsing during manufacture and firing. Shown in the photo are a 1.125-mm grain of rhyolite marked "1," composed of quartz and sanidine (an alkali feldspar in a fine-grained groundmass); and a 1.725-mm grain of diorite marked "2," composed of twinned plagioclase, brown amphibole, and an opaque mineral that may be magnetite.

Pingüino Buff, Standard Variety (Figure A.8)

Pingüino Buff, the distinctive black-and-white or polychrome painted ware at Cerro Azul, has latite

Figure A.4. Two views of a thin section of Camacho Black, standard variety. (*Top*): Under plane polarized light. (*Bottom*): Under cross-polarized light. This pottery type features latite temper. The large particle marked with an "x" (*bottom*) contains multiple plagioclase crystals in a fine-grained groundmass and measures 0.475 mm. Note that its structure appears clearer under cross-polarized light.

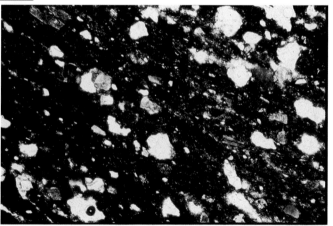

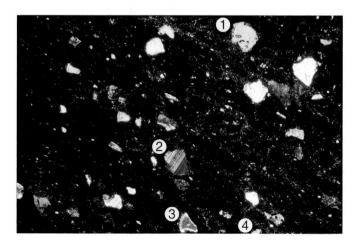

Figure A.5. Two views of a thin section of Camacho Black, highly burnished ("graphite") variety. (*Top*): Under plane polarized light. (*Bottom*): Under cross-polarized light. Like its standard counterpart, the highly burnished variety of this type features latite temper, but the particles are finer and sparser. Under cross-polarized light (*bottom*) can be seen (1) alkali feldspar with zoicite inclusions, measuring 0.325 mm; (2) plagioclase; (3) quartz (appearing red owing to the thickness of the slide); and (4) amphibole.

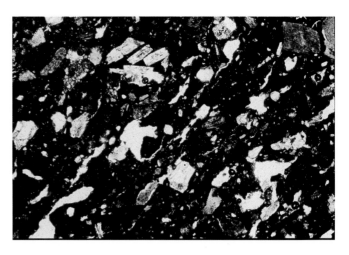

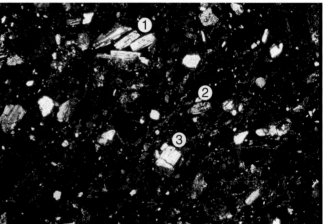

Figure A.6. Two views of a thin section of a standard Camacho Reddish Brown cooking vessel. (*Top*): Under plane polarized light. (*Bottom*): Under cross-polarized light. This pottery type features latite temper. Under cross-polarized light (*bottom*) can be seen (1) four plagioclase phenocrysts in a dark, nearly opaque groundmass measuring 0.675 mm; (2) greenish colored amphibole; and (3) a rock fragment containing both plagioclase and alkali feldspar in a dark groundmass.

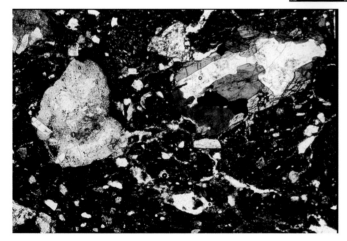

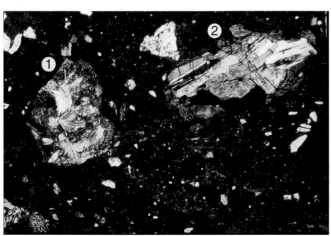

Figure A.7. Two views of a thin section of the coarser version of Camacho Reddish Brown used for *hatun maccma*, or massive storage jars. (*Top*): Under plane polarized light. (*Bottom*): Under cross-polarized light. The very large vessel analyzed here appears to have contained coarse tempers of multiple origins. The two numbered temper particles (*bottom*) are (1) a 1.125-mm piece of rhyolite, a cryptocrystalline rock with quartz and sanidine phenocrysts; and (2) a 1.725-mm piece of diorite containing twinned plagioclase and both brown amphibole and black opaques.

temper. This temper makes up 22% of the body and has a size index of 1.67. The largest grain in the photomicrographs, marked "3," measures 0.6 mm and is composed of plagioclase and alkali feldspar. Other grains marked in the photos are twinned plagioclase ("1"), sanidine ("2"), and a fragment of cryptocrystalline groundmass ("4").

Atypical Orange Variety of Pingüino Buff (Figure A.9)

This ware combines two rock tempers, granodiorite and dacite, and may be nonlocal. It is similar to standard Pingüino Buff in having 22% temper in its body, but differs in its Munsell color range and coarser temper size (index, 2.44).

The granodiorite (marked "3") is a coarsely crystalline plutonic rock with quartz-plagioclase intergrowth (myrmekite). The dacite is a porphyritic volcanic rock, in this case with plagioclase the only clearly identifiable phenocryst, although quartz is also suspected.

In the photos, the particle marked "1" is a 1.325-mm grain of what appears to be dacite, featuring two distinctive groundmasses, cryptocrystalline at the upper end and glassy (nearly opaque) at the lower end; the lower end incorporates a plagioclase phenocryst, marked "2." Other minerals, marked in the cross-polarized photo, are the aforementioned granodiorite ("3") and polycrystalline plagioclase ("4").

Trambollo Burnished Brown (Figure A.10)

This ware, used mainly for hemispherical bowls resembling gourd vessels, has latite temper. Its temper is fine (index, 1.50) and makes up only 18% of the body. In the photomicrographs, the largest grain (marked "1") is a loose phenocryst of altered plagioclase with sericite. Other grains marked include a clear grain of quartz ("3") and a piece of biotite (mica) which appears nearly opaque in the thin section ("2").

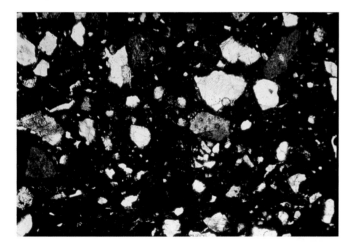

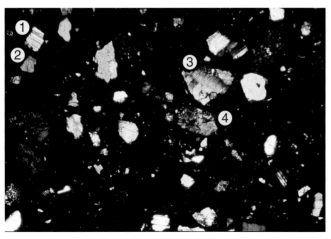

Figure A.8. Two views of a thin section of a standard Pingüino Buff painted vessel. (*Top*): Under plane polarized light. (*Bottom*): Under cross-polarized light. This pottery type features latite temper. Four particles of interest have been numbered in the cross-polarized photo (*bottom*). They are (1) twinned plagioclase; (2) sanidine, a twinned alkali feldspar, whose other half is visible under plane polarized light; (3) a grain of plagioclase and alkali feldspar measuring 0.6 mm; and (4) a fragment of cryptocrystalline groundmass.

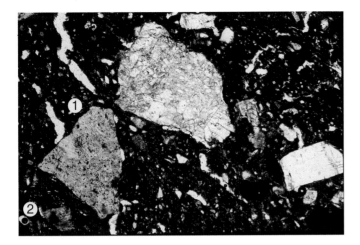

Figure A.9. Two views of a thin section of the atypical orange variety of Pingüino Buff. (*Top*): Under plane polarized light. (*Bottom*): Under cross-polarized light. This variety, which may be nonlocal, features dacitoid-granitoid temper rather than latite. The particle marked "1" (*top*) is a 1.325-mm piece of what appears to be dacite, incorporating a plagioclase phenocryst (2) in a dark groundmass which has both cryptocrystalline and glassy areas. Under cross-polarized light (*bottom*) we see (3) a 1.5-mm grain of granodiorite and (4) a piece of polycrystalline plagioclase.

Figure A.10. Two views of a thin section of Trambollo Burnished Brown. (*Top*): Under plane polarized light. (*Bottom*): Under cross-polarized light. This pottery type features latite temper. The particle numbered "1" is a grain of altered plagioclase with sericite measuring 0.675 mm. In the cross-polarized photo (*bottom*), we see (2) a piece of biotite measuring 0.70 mm, which appears nearly opaque; and (3) a large clear grain of quartz measuring 0.575 mm.

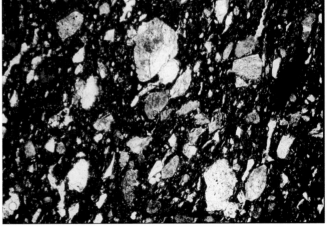

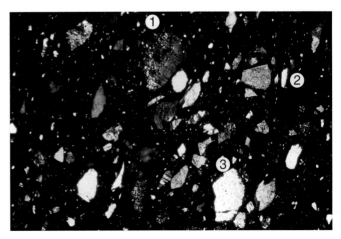

Plate I. Structure D, seen from the west during excavation

Plate II. The North Platform and *llamkana pata* in the Southwest Canchón, Structure D (Chapter 4)

Plate III. The South Corridor, leading from the Southwest Canchón into the interior of Structure D (Chapter 4)

Plate IV. The "Room 2" patio of Structure D.
At the far right can be seen the last few meters of the South Corridor (Chapter 5)

Plate V. Room 1 of Structure D, an elite residential apartment that suffered earthquake damage (Chapter 5)

Plate VI. Room 7 of Structure D, a storage room that suffered earthquake damage (Chapter 7)

Plate VII. Feature 8, a hearth trench in the kitchen/brewery of Structure D (Chapter 7)

Plate VIII. Feature 9, a 2000-liter chicha storage vessel in the kitchen/brewery of Structure D (Chapter 7)

Plate IX. Rooms 9 and 10 of Structure D, where the guinea pigs were kept (Chapter 7)

Plate X. Room 11 of Structure 9, a room used to store fish in layers of bluish-green sand (Chapter 8)

Plate XI. Rooms 2, 3, and 4 of Structure 9, showing the effects of long-term wind erosion on the tapia walls (Chapter 8)

Plate XII. Excavation of Terrace 11 in Quebrada 6, Cerro Camacho (Chapter 9)

Plate XIII. Among the oldest ceramics at Cerro Azul are bowls finely painted in black, yellow, and iridescent purple (Chapter 3)

Plate XIV. Camacho Reddish Brown amphora (Chapter 3)

Plate XV. Camacho Reddish Brown jar with human face modeled on the neck (Chapter 3)

Plate XVI. Neck of Pingüino Buff jar with human face modeled and painted in black, white, and red (Chapter 3)

79

Plate XVII. Pingüino Buff jar with maize cob lugs, painted with crabs, birds, and geometric motifs (Chapter 3)

Plate XVIII. Sherds from vessel with modeled human arm, painted in black/ white/red with "school of fish" motif (Chapter 3)

Plate XIX. Sherds from Pingüino Buff jar painted with rows of stylized bird heads (Chapter 3)

Plate XX. Jar with painted fish motif, atypical orange variety of Pingüino Buff (Chapter 3)

CHAPTER 4

Structure D:
The Southwest Quadrant

One of my first tough choices at Cerro Azul was to decide which of Kroeber's major tapia compounds to excavate. Although all the compounds were tempting, I settled on Structure D because it was centrally located, it appeared relatively unlooted, and its size was such that it could be fully excavated in the time available.

Our first step was to have a team of workmen sweep the entire surface of the structure with ordinary household brooms. Such is the nature of disintegrated tapia on the arid coast that when a building is swept in this way, the sweeping removes the uppermost 2–3 cm of powdery room fill, leaving the harder wall stubs exposed. As sweeping progresses, the plan of the underlying building begins to emerge, much like the image on a negative placed in a pan of developer. Soon we could see that we were dealing with a building approximately 38 × 42.5 m, divided into at least a dozen rooms and four major patios, covering about 1640 m². We could virtually draw the plan of the structure and name (or number) the rooms before excavation began.

At this point we decided to rule out three excavation strategies. (1) We decided against laying out a trench across the center of the building, as is sometimes done; that would simply have destroyed the walls (and integrity) of the rooms. (2) We also decided against drawing a random sample of rooms and excavating only those; since we could already see that the rooms had different sizes, shapes, and (almost certainly) functions, we

decided that we wanted to excavate them all. (3) We also decided not to place a test pit in one corner of each room, as a few colleagues had suggested to us; based on my experiences elsewhere, I was not convinced that a corner could fully represent the whole room. We decided instead that we would make every visible room or patio a unit of analysis, and dig each in its entirety.

After preparing a preliminary plan that showed every wall visible after sweeping, we established two permanent datum points. One, marked T on Figure 4.1, lay on a flat surface near the center of the building, where the tripod for our alidade could be set up. Our cartographer, Dr. Charles M. Hastings, had determined that this point could be seen from the other compounds for the purposes of triangulation and mapping. The alidade station turned out to be approximately 20.3 m above sea level.

The second datum point, marked D on Figure 4.1, was the actual high point of the building. While not sufficiently level to support a tripod, it served as the arbitrary "zero point" from which all depths of floors and features in Structure D could be taken. We drove a permanent stake made from steel reinforcing rod into point D. All depths below datum given in this volume refer to the top of this stake.

We excavated the entire tapia compound atop Structure D in the Andean winter of 1984. Three sizes of sieves were used in the excavation. The coarsest was a 6-mm mesh screen, which stopped

81

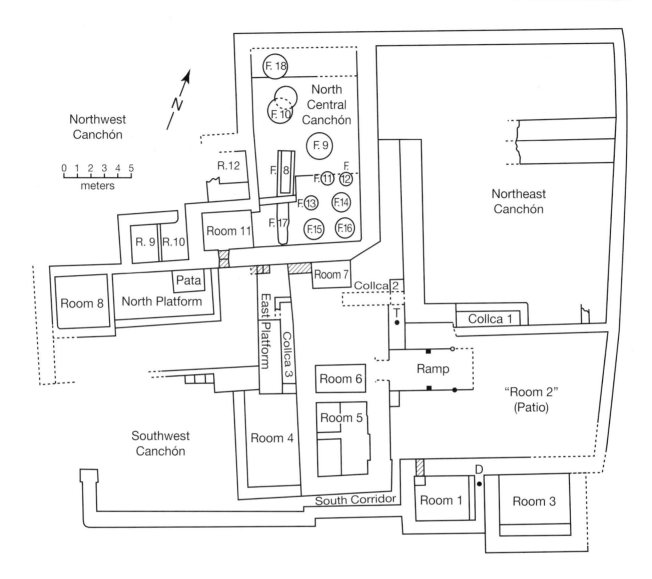

Figure 4.1. Ground plan of Structure D at Cerro Azul. R. = Room. F. = Feature. T = Alidade station. D = Datum point established on the building's highest spot. Blocked doorways and corridors are shown as hachured. The dashed-line area near Collca 2 is a looter's trench; other dashed-line areas indicate wind erosion.

all potsherds, most artifacts, and 20% of the fish bone. Our medium-sized screen was 1.5-mm mesh, which stopped tiny artifacts and 80% of the fish bone. Under special circumstances, such as the discovery of a midden with small-scale debris, we turned to our finest sieves, which had a 0.6-mm brass mesh. This brass mesh appeared to stop virtually 100% of the fish bone, including anchovy vertebrae.

Which screen to use was frequently a judgment call. Indeed, we even encountered situations where using any screen at all seemed like overkill. For example, there were (1) areas of completely sterile tapia wall decomposition products and (2)

areas of windblown sand containing eighteenth- to twentieth-century refuse. We removed such deposits with care but did not fine-screen them. This allowed us to move rapidly through recent overburden, while proceeding very slowly through genuine prehispanic deposits.

By the time the excavation was completed, we were in a position to interpret Structure D as the residence of an elite family and its support staff (Figure 4.1). We found clear living quarters with built-in sleeping benches; multiple collcas or storage cells; several canchones, or walled but unroofed work areas; a large *chicha* brewery and/or kitchen; places where weaving had been carried out; rooms for keeping guinea pigs; and units where massive numbers of fish had been stored in layers of sand.

We also found that the original layout of Structure D had been changed several times during the occupation of the building. Some of this modification appeared to have been forced on the occupants by earthquake damage. Some residential quarters, severely compromised by seismic tremors, had been converted to fish storage units. New walls had been added to create additional rooms or storage cells. A few doorways and corridors had been blocked off in order to change the flow of traffic. Multiple layers of tapia buttresses had been added to reinforce walls whose stability had been undermined by earthquakes. Finally, after the Late Intermediate compound had been largely abandoned—presumably around the time of the Inka conquest of Huarco—some low-status families had built houses of *kincha*, or wattle-and-daub, in the ruins of the building. We do not believe that these families were in any way connected to the original occupants; they were simply "squatters" who made use of the level surfaces that had fallen into disuse. These later modifications of Structure D are shown in drawings and photographs throughout this volume.

Given all the things that we learned during the course of our excavation, we were glad that we had excavated Structure D in its entirety. Consider what we would know had we only sampled a few units. For example, had we sampled only the North Central Canchón, we might have considered Structure D a brewery. Had we sampled only Room 8, we might have considered the building a fish storage facility. Had we sampled only Room 9, we might have considered Structure D a guinea pig nursery. Had we sampled only the Northeast Canchón, we might have considered the building a workshop for weaving. Had we excavated only Rooms 1 and 3, we might have considered it an elite dormitory. In fact, Structure D was all those things, and only by having our dedicated crew (Figure 4.2) excavate the compound completely did we discover that fact.

Figure 4.2. Under the watchful eye of Professor Ramiro Matos, the excavators of Structure D assemble for their group photo.

A major goal of this volume is pottery analysis, and here our experiences led to similar conclusions. Had we excavated only the kitchen/brewery, our pottery sample would have contained many Camacho Reddish Brown cooking and storage vessels and many Pingüino Buff *chicha* jars, but little Camacho Black. Had we excavated only Room 4, we would have recovered an outstanding sample of Pingüino Buff painted vessels, but would know less about utilitarian pottery. Had we missed the Feature 6 midden—a distinct possibility, since it occupied only a few square meters of the Southwest Canchón—we would know much less than we do about the range of variation in Late Intermediate pottery. There are certainly situations in which sampling is the correct choice to make, but it would have been foolish of us not to excavate all of Structure D when we could see virtually the whole plan beforehand.

One cautionary flag should be raised, however, by Figure 2.4 of Chapter 2. Structure D was built on a natural rise, and from the surface it appears that there may well have been open-air activity areas on the slopes below the tapia compound. Even excavating an entire compound, therefore, does not necessarily mean that one has learned everything there is to know about the activities associated with it.

A GUIDED TOUR OF STRUCTURE D

One of the points I hope to stress most strongly in this volume is that context matters. The Late Intermediate pottery assemblage of Cerro Azul (or any site of that period) is made up of functionally distinct vessels that occur in varying frequencies, depending on depositional context. Kitchens produce lots of coarse utilitarian wares. Elite residential quarters produce lots of elegant painted wares, not to mention trade pieces. Many of the vessels used to define the Late Intermediate in the past have come from burials, contexts that often contain unique or atypical pieces. The Cerro Azul burials, for example, produced many more highly burnished, miniature Camacho Black vessels than did household middens.

In this volume, therefore, I present the pottery collections from each room or canchón sep-

arately and, where appropriate, call attention to the extent to which context probably influenced the frequency of various types.

The order in which the rooms, canchones, and collcas are presented amounts to a counterclockwise tour of Structure D, beginning with the entrance (near the building's southwest corner) and following the traffic routes designed by the compound's architects. In Chapter 4, we enter the Southwest Canchón first and examine its associated units and features. Next, in Chapter 5, we follow the South Corridor into the more private southeast quadrant of the building. From there we travel to the Northeast Canchón and nearby units (Chapter 6). Finally, we examine the northwest quadrant, with its kitchen/brewery, storage rooms, and guinea pig nursery (Chapter 7).

THE SOUTHWEST QUADRANT

Figure 4.3 shows an artist's conception of the southwest quadrant of Structure D. Visitors to the compound would have passed through a wide entryway into the Southwest Canchón, a large walled enclosure that underwent modifications during the occupation of the building. This canchón might originally have covered an area of some 16 × 17 m but was eventually reduced in size by the creation of Room 4 and several platforms. Its floor was irregular, averaging 3.78 to 4.78 m below datum near the center and sloping down to 5.68 m below datum near the entrance.

The entryway to the Southwest Canchón was wide enough to allow a caravan of llamas to enter and spend some time in the canchón while their burdens were being loaded or unloaded. Evidence that this had happened was provided by hundreds of llama dung pellets on the floor of the canchón. Among the products that may have arrived on the backs of llamas were maize (for the *chicha* brewed in the North Central Canchón) and camelid wool (to be spun into yarn in the Northeast Canchón). The most likely products carried away from Structure D by llama caravans were dried anchovies and sardines.

While it was designed to accommodate numerous llamas and their burdens, the Southwest Canchón was as far into Structure D as the animals

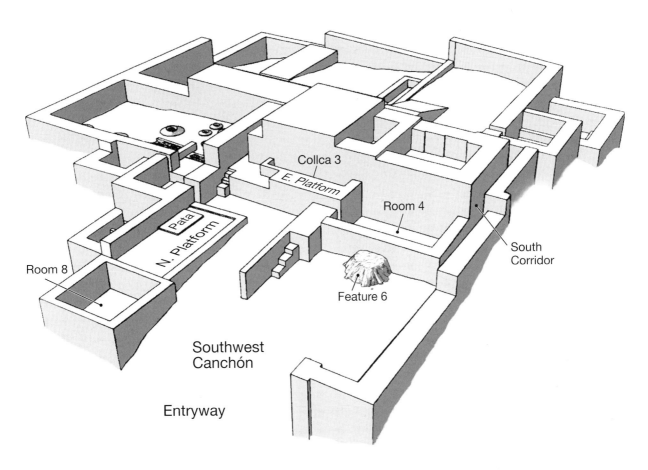

Figure 4.3. Artist's conception of the southwest quadrant of Structure D.

got. Entry into the interior of the building was deliberately restricted by the South Corridor, a passageway so narrow that it could only be traversed by humans traveling single file. Presumably for this reason, the Southwest Canchón was the only unit in the building whose floor yielded llama dung.

The Southwest Canchón was flanked by two raised tapia structures, the North Platform and the East Platform. We suspect that the North Platform, measuring 8.2 × 3.7 m, was designed for a lower-level administrator whose job it was to record the movement of products into and out of the building. This platform rose to a depth of 2.79 m below datum, and its surface had been carefully plastered with white clay (Figures 4.4, 4.5). The diagnostic sherds recovered from the surface of the North Platform (Figure 4.6) come mostly from cooking and storage vessels, although there are occasional sherds from serving bowls. The collection is Late Intermediate in date, but we do not consider it an in situ sample because the

North Platform is a location that was undoubtedly swept clean while in use.

Camacho Reddish Brown (Figure 4.6a–d)
    Jar rim, plain: 1
    Jar rim, everted: 1
    Jar rims, cambered: 3 (2 are fire-blackened)
    Jar shoulder: 1
    Cooking pot with restricted orifice: 1 (fire-blackened)

Camacho Black (Highly Burnished Variety)
    Tiny rim sherd from hemispherical (?) bowl: 1

Pingüino Buff (Figure 4.6e–h)
    Jar rims, plain, unpainted: 2
    Jar neck showing face with paint, modeled and painted in black: 1
    Painted jar, black on white: 1 sherd (showing pupil from eye on jar neck?)

Figure 4.4. The North Platform of the Southwest Canchón, Structure D, seen from the southeast. Pedro Manuel Zavala is sweeping the *llamkana pata*, or raised work platform.

Conical base of jar or amphora: 1
Hemispherical bowl rim, slipped white on
　　the interior and exterior, painted black
　　on white on the exterior: 1

Atop the North Platform was a smaller raised area that we interpret as a *llamkana pata/puñunu pata* (in Ayacucho Quechua), a working and/or sleeping platform. The *pata* measured 2.38 × 1.66 m, and its surface lay 2.68 m below datum (Figures 4.5, 4.7). Like the platform below it, the

pata was plastered white. As Figure 4.7 shows, two posts from a much later "squatters' house" had intruded through it. A single sherd was found on the *llamkana pata*, as follows:

Pingüino Buff (Figure 4.8)
　　Jar neck with plain rim: 1
　　This rim sherd is painted cream (10 YR 8/4),
　　black, and brownish red (10 R 4/4) over bur-
　　nished buff on the exterior; left unslipped and
　　unpainted on the interior.

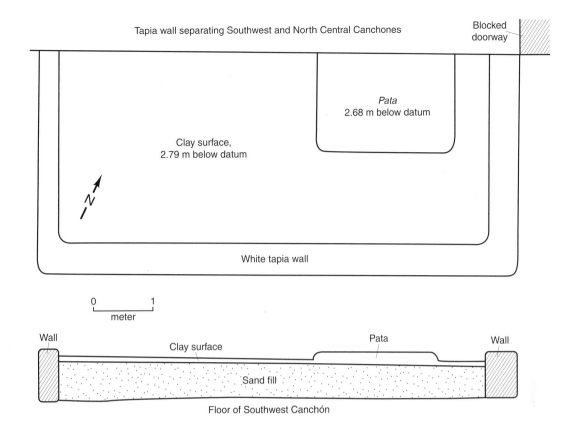

Figure 4.5. Plan and cross section of the North Platform in the Southwest Canchón, Structure D. This platform's most important feature is a *llamkana pata*, or raised work platform.

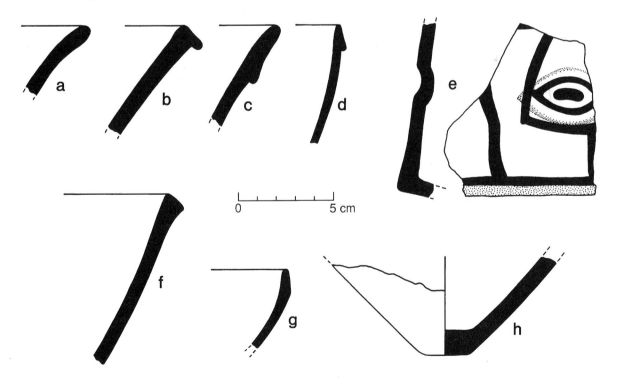

Figure 4.6. Ceramics from the surface of the North Platform in the Southwest Canchón, Structure D, near the *llamkana pata* (raised work platform). Sherds *a–d* are Camacho Reddish Brown jar rims. *(a)*: plain rim; *(b)*: everted rim; *(c, d)*: cambered rims. Sherds *e–h* are Pingüino Buff. *(e)*: jar neck with modeled face painted black on natural; the pupil of the eye has been pushed out from the interior; *(f)*: jar rim; *(g)*: rim of hemispherical bowl, slipped white on interior and exterior, painted black on white on exterior; *(h)*: conical base of jar or amphora.

Figure 4.7. The *llamkana pata* atop the North Platform of the Southwest Canchón, Structure D. Measuring 2.38 × 1.66 m, this *pata* may have been assigned to the person overseeing activities in the Southwest Canchón. The two dark circles represent damage caused by much later intrusive posts (arrow points north).

Figure 4.8. Pingüino Buff jar rim sherd, found on the *llamkana pata* (raised work platform) atop the North Platform of the Southwest Canchón, Structure D. The sherd is painted cream, black, and brownish red over its burnished buff exterior; the interior was left unslipped and unpainted. The cream is 10 YR 8/4; the brownish red is 10 R 4/4.

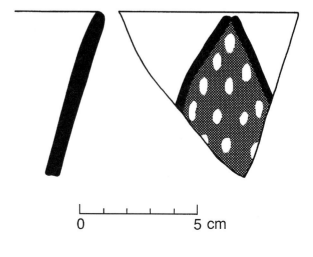

0   5 cm

In order to expose the North Platform and the *llamkana pata*, we had to dig down through an overlying layer of fill, essentially the finely granulated weathering product of tapia walls. We found sherds in this fill, stratigraphically above the platform but still typologically Late Intermediate in age. The diagnostic sherds are as follows (Figures 4.9, 4.10):

Camacho Reddish Brown (Figure 4.9)
    Jar with plain rim: 1 (fire-blackened on the
        exterior)
    Jar with bolstered rim: 1
    Jar with everted rim: 1 rim sherd
    Small jar with bolstered rim, strap handle,
        and brushed body: 1 rim (fire-blackened
        on the exterior)
    Cooking pot with restricted orifice: 1 rim
    Jar shoulder with panel of black-and-white
        decoration: 1
    Basal sherds, possibly from the vessel shown
        as Figure 4.9f, g: 2

Camacho Black (Highly Burnished Variety) (Figure 4.10a)
    Small composite silhouette bowl with rolled
        rim: 1 rim sherd

Pingüino Buff (Figures 4.10b–d, 4.11)
    Jar with flaring rim, slightly beveled rim: 1
    Jar with restricted orifice and rolled rim,
        black rim ticking, body painted in black
        and white over very weak whitewash: 1
        rim (sherd has bird motif)
    Jar body sherd, area of white paint zoned
        with black line, natural buff below: 1
    Hemispherical bowl, slipped white, painted
        black on white on the exterior: 1 rim
    Jar neck sherd with modeled human arm,
        painted black and white: 1

The East Platform of the Southwest Canchón measured 9.8 × 2.5 m and included Collca 3, a storage cell that had been created by the addition of an L-shaped wall (Figures 4.12, 4.13). The original surface of the East Platform was 1.95 m below datum.

There would originally have been two ways to reach the East Platform. One approach was from a stubby wall with an inset three-step stairway, leading east from the middle of the Southwest Canchón (Figure 4.3). We suspect that this stairway, whose middle step was 3.38 m below datum, would have been used by laborers

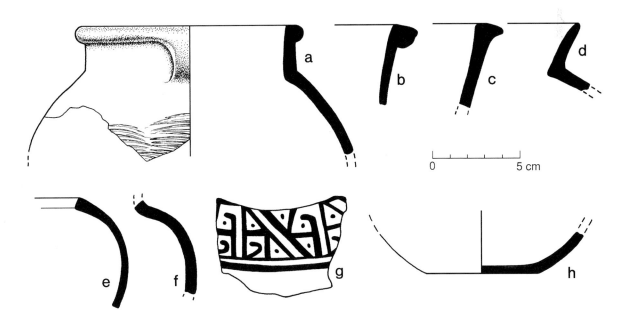

Figure 4.9. Camacho Reddish Brown vessels from the fill above the North Platform of the Southwest Canchón, Structure D. *(a):* small jar with bolstered rim and strap handle, fire-blackened; the shoulder shows brushing, while the rim is smoothed; *(b):* bolstered jar rim; *(c):* everted jar rim; *(d):* plain jar rim; *(e):* cooking pot with restricted orifice; *(f, g):* profile and plan view of atypical jar shoulder, given a band of black-and-white painting usually reserved for Pingüino Buff; *(h):* jar base which could have come from the vessel shown in *f* and *g*.

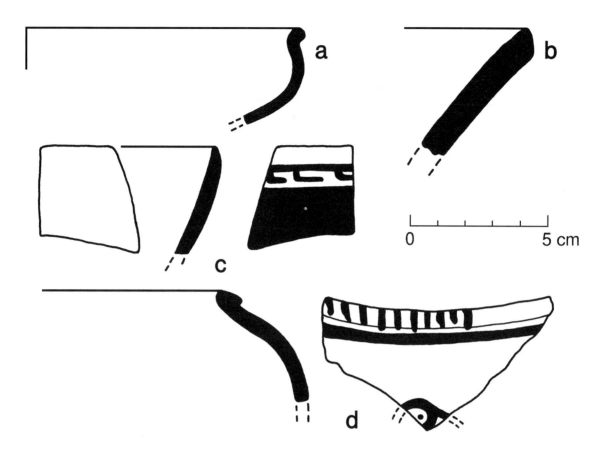

Figure 4.10. Ceramics from the fill above the North Platform of the Southwest Canchón, Structure D. *(a)*: Camacho Black (highly burnished variety) small composite silhouette bowl with rolled rim; *(b)*: Pingüino Buff jar with flaring, slightly beveled rim; *(c)*: Pingüino Buff hemispherical bowl, slipped brilliant white on interior and exterior, then painted black on white on the exterior; *(d)*: Pingüino Buff jar with restricted orifice and rolled rim, painted black and white on the exterior.

Figure 4.11. Sherd from the neck of a Pingüino Buff jar, showing a modeled human arm in an area painted black and white over natural buff. Found in the fill of the Southwest Canchón, Structure D.

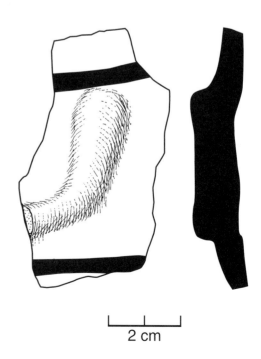

2 cm

Figure 4.12. The East Platform of the Southwest Canchón, Structure D, seen from the west. The L-shaped wall that created Collca 3 can also be seen. Edgar Zavala squats on the North Platform. (The two wooden posts are from an intrusive *kincha* house built over the ruins of Structure D.)

Figure 4.13. Collca 3 of Structure D seen from the north, with Cirilo Cruz serving as scale.

carrying products from llama caravans directly to the collca. The other approach was by way of a small stairway at the extreme north end of the East Platform (Figure 4.14). Given the location of this stairway, we suspect that it would have been used by the administrator on the North Platform whenever he wanted to enter the interior of the building. At a later stage of the building's history, this small stairway and the narrow passageway just to the east of it were blocked with tapia (Figures 4.14, 4.15). The narrow passageway had formerly led to Room 7 (Figure 4.1).

Collca 3, the storage cell on the East Platform, measured roughly 6.01 × 1.1 m, depending on how one took the measurement. The collca's floor was 1.65 m below datum. Two sherds were found in Collca 3, as follows:

Figure 4.14. Looking east from the *llamkana pata* atop the North Platform of the Southwest Canchón, Structure D. Victor de la Cruz kneels on the floor of the Southwest Canchón. To the left, one can see the broken remains of a small stairway that ascended to the East Platform of the canchón. At *a* is a blocked corridor that formerly led to Room 7. At *b* we see Collca 3, still unexcavated at this stage of the work.

Collca 3

Figure 4.15. Victor de la Cruz kneels on the surface of the East Platform of the Southwest Canchón, Structure D. Just to the left of his whisk broom is the blocked entrance to a corridor which once led toward Room 7. (This is one of many places where the traffic flow was altered during the occupation of Structure D.) In the lower right foreground, one can see the corner of Collca 3.

Camacho Reddish Brown
    Jar body sherd: 1

Trambollo Burnished Brown (Figure 4.16)
    Punctate lug from a miniature vessel: 1

One other doorway in the Southwest Canchón proved to have been blocked off. This was a door that had once led to Room 11, an apparent storage room or "pantry" just off the kitchen/brewery or

North Central Canchón. This doorway, shown in Figure 4.17, lay just beyond the east end of the North Platform. Originally, therefore, any administrator stationed on the North Platform could have supervised the transport of foodstuffs or *chicha*-making ingredients from the backs of llamas in the Southwest Canchón through the doorway into Room 11, and from there to the kitchen/brewery. At a later stage in the building's occupation, this door was blocked with tapia.

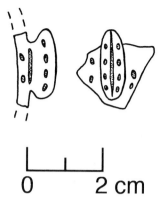

Figure 4.16. Punctate lug from a Trambollo Burnished Brown vessel, found in Collca 3, Structure D.

Figure 4.17. Pedro Manuel Zavala squats near the northeast corner of the Southwest Canchón, Structure D. Beside him is a blocked doorway that once led from the Southwest Canchón to Room 11 (see Figure 7.28 for the other side of this doorway). At the far right in the photo, we see the stairway (now broken) that led up to the East Platform of the Southwest Canchón. Extensive earthquake damage can be seen on the wall nearby.

FEATURE 6

We suspected that from time to time, the floor of the Southwest Canchón had been swept and its debris piled against a wall until such time as it could be removed from the building. (Given what we discovered in later seasons, the ultimate resting place for all trash from the compounds seems to have been the terraces in the quebradas of Cerro Camacho.) Luckily for us, the final load of debris swept from the floor of the canchón was never carried to the quebradas; it remained piled against the L-shaped wall built to create Room 4. This large heap of debris—essentially a midden 50 cm deep and 2 m in diameter—was designated Feature 6 (see Figures 4.3, 4.18).

We consider our discovery of Feature 6 a fortunate one, since it gave us considerable insight into the range of debris-producing activities carried out in the final months of occupation in the Southwest Canchón. We isolated Feature 6 on a pedestal (Figure 4.18) and assigned two of our most careful excavators to it. They were each given two sieves,

using the 1.5-mm mesh first and then the 0.6-mm mesh to screen whatever had passed through the first sieve. We even fashioned small scoops from soft-drink bottle caps, which allow the workers to lift tiny anchovy vertebrae from each sieve and amass them in aluminum foil packets.

The contents of Feature 6 revealed a remarkable range of activities that had taken place in the Southwest Canchón. All the non-ceramic items will be listed in future volumes on Cerro Azul. The fish remains alone included more than 8000 specimens of sardines (*Sardinops sagax*), 2800 specimens of anchovies (*Engraulis ringens*), and 1000 specimens of the lorna (*Sciaena deliciosa*), a medium-sized drum or croaker (Marcus et al. 1999:Table 1). There were also llama bones, mollusks, crabs, chitons, and crayfish in the midden. Beans and maize had been shelled in the canchón, and there were also squash, gourds, chili peppers, peanut hulls, and Andean fruits. Cotton and camelid wool had been spun into yarn; pieces of cotton cloth had been embroidered, with the needles used present, some still strung with colored

Figure 4.18. Southwest Canchón, Structure D. The final squares of the Feature 6 midden are being removed for fine screening.

thread. One of the most unexpected discoveries was a whole series of fingernail and toenail trimmings, cut very carefully with something like a sharp flint or obsidian flake.

So numerous are the ceramics from Feature 6 that it has taken us 12 illustrations to do them justice (Figures 4.19–4.30). Camacho Reddish Brown utilitarian vessels are common. Note, however, that Pingüino Buff and highly burnished Camacho Black are more abundant than is standard Camacho Black.

1. Diagnostic sherds

Camacho Reddish Brown (Figures 4.19–4.20)
　　Cambered rims from jars: 27 (Figure 4.19f–k)
　　　Tinajón: 1 rim (Figure 4.20a); 3 sherds from neck

Cooking pots with restricted orifice: 20 rims
Cooking pots with restricted orifice, horizontally set strap handles: 7 rims (Figure 4.19a–d)
Cooking pot with restricted orifice: 1 rim without handle
Cooking pots with restricted orifice: 15 fire-blackened body sherds
Jar shoulders: 13
Jar shoulder (?) with modeled nipple: 1
Jar rims, everted: 5
Jar shoulder, perforated for suspension: 1 (Figure 4.20d)
Vertical necks from small globular jars: 3 (Figure 4.20e, f)
Jar bases: 2
Strap handles from large jars: 5
Small bowl rims (hemispherical to incurved): 5
Reworked sherd disk: 1

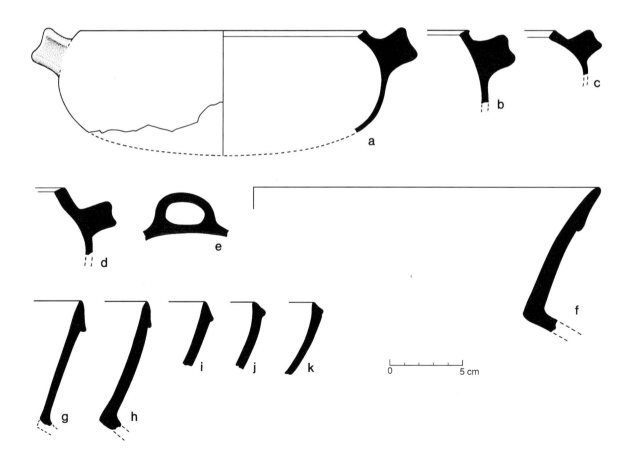

Figure 4.19. Camacho Reddish Brown vessels from Feature 6, Structure D. *(a-d)*: Cooking pots with restricted orifice and horizontally set strap handles; fire-blackened; *(e)*: top view of typical strap handle; *(f-k)*: cambered rims from jars; fire-blackened.

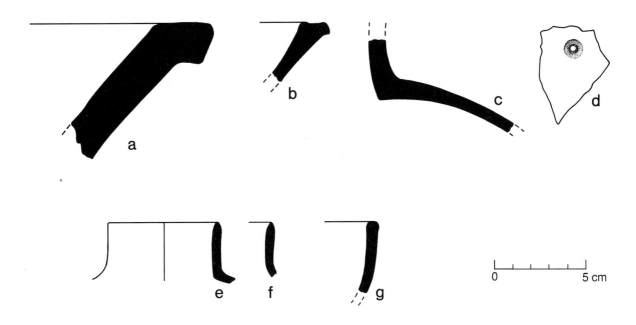

Figure 4.20. Camacho Reddish Brown vessels from Feature 6, Structure D. *(a)*: rim of giant *tinajón* or *hatun maccma* like those in the North Central Canchón; *(b)*: everted rim from jar; *(c)*: jar shoulder; *(d)*: jar sherd showing hole drilled for suspension; *(e, f)*: vertical necks from small jars; *(g)*: rim of hemispherical bowl.

Camacho Black (Standard Variety) (Figure 4.21b, l)
    Large amphora rims, slightly everted: 2

Camacho Black (Highly Burnished Variety) (Figure 4.21a, c–h)
    Large composite silhouette bowl, "graphite" finish: 1 rim (Figure 4.21a)
    Amphora (?) neck with human face modeled on it, highly burnished: 1 (Figure 4.21c)
    Flaring necks from small jars: 3 (Figure 4.21d–f)
    Strap handles from small jars: 2
    Lug from amphora: 1 (Figure 4.21g)

Miniature Camacho Black Vessels (Highly Burnished) (Figure 4.21i–k, m–r)
Many miniatures have oxidized interiors, so the paste is not uniformly gray; interiors may be buff to reddish brown.
    Globular jars with strap handles linking neck and body: 2 rims (Figure 4.21o, p)
    Fragments of above, but without handles: 3
    Rims of miniature ollas/amphorae: 10 (Figure 4.21n)
    Incurved rim bowls: 3 rims (Figure 4.21q, r)

    Ear from face on neck of miniature amphora, atypical pink paste, slipped black and burnished ("graphite" finish): 1 (Figure 4.21m)
    Vessel supports (?): 2
    Modeled effigy vessels: 8 (Figure 4.21k)
    Possible legs from modeled effigy vessels: 3 (Figure 4.21i, j)
    Miniature spout (?): 1

Pingüino Buff (Figures 4.22–4.29)
    Small globular jars with wide mouth, painted black and white or black/white/red on the exterior and the inner rim: 5 rims (Figures 4.22, 4.23)
    Globular jar with wide mouth, painted black and white on exterior of body and interior of rim, shoulder sherd: 1 (Figure 4.25f)
    Globular jars with rolled rim: 3 rims (one painted black/white/red) (Figure 4.25a, b)
    Large bowls with cambered rim: 10 rims (Figure 4.24b–f)
    Large jars with everted rim, funnel necks: 5 (one painted white) (Figure 4.25c, d)

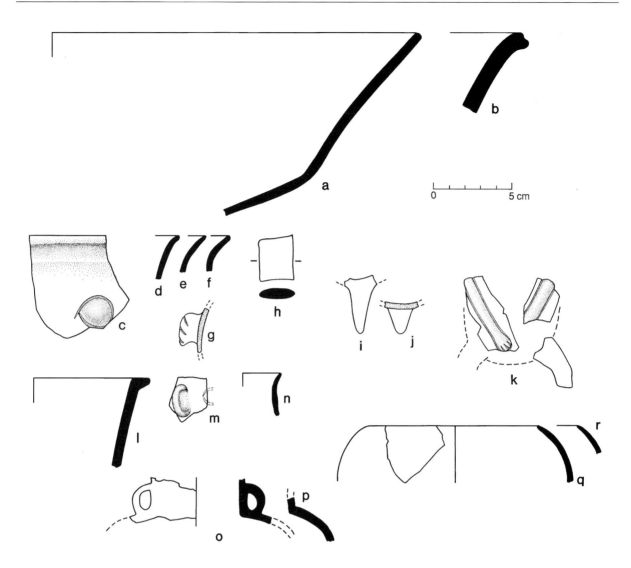

Figure 4.21. Camacho Black vessels from Feature 6, Structure D. *(a)*: large composite silhouette bowl with graphite-like double-burnished surface; *(b)*: everted rim from neck of large amphora (standard variety); *(c)*: sherd from neck of amphora with modeled and incised human eye (highly burnished variety); *(d–f)*: flaring necks from small jars; *(g)*: incised lug from shoulder of amphora; *(h)*: fragment of strap handle; *(i, j)*: possible vessel supports (solid); *(k)*: fragments of human effigy like the one found in Collca 1; *(l)*: everted rim from amphora (standard variety); *(m)*: modeled ear (and part of incised eye) from face on neck of miniature amphora (highly burnished "graphite" variety); *(n)*: neck of miniature amphora; *(o, p)*: globular jars with strap handle linking neck and body; *(q, r)*: small bowls with incurved rim.

Fragment of modeled and black-and-white painted face from jar neck: 1

Fragment of jar neck, white paint stripe on exterior: 1 (Figure 4.25e)

Vertical jar necks with modeled and/or painted human faces: 7 (Figure 4.29b)

Unusual tall-necked jar, painted black and white, with wavy parallel lines painted on it and a handle connecting neck to body; has effigy modeling (Figures 4.26, 4.27): 2 handle fragments; 12 body sherds

Strap handles from large jars: 15

Lugs from large jars: 2

Bases from large jars: 3

Jars with cambered rim: 2 rims

Large bowl (?) with rim ticking: 2 rims (Figure 4.24a)

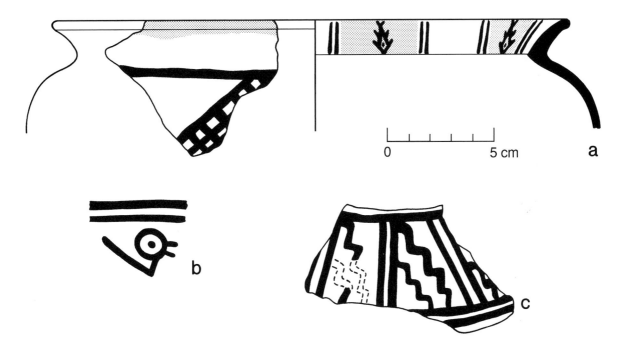

Figure 4.22. Pingüino Buff vessels from Feature 6, Structure D. *(a)*: globular jar with wide mouth, painted on the exterior of the body and the interior of the neck in black and white, with some areas left natural buff; *(b)*: reconstruction of bird motif from body sherd of globular jar; *(c)*: body sherd from globular jar, painted black and white.

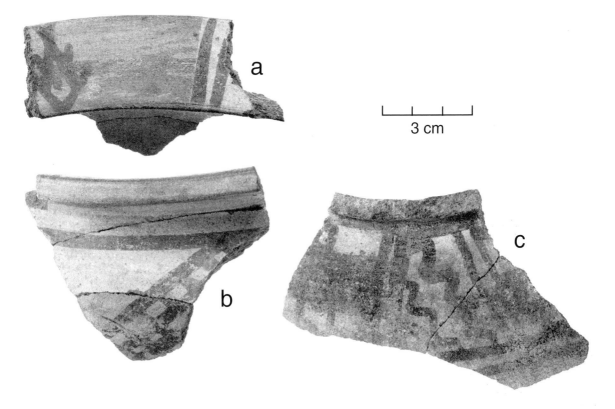

Figure 4.23. Pingüino Buff sherds from Feature 6, Structure D. *(a, b)*: globular jar with wide mouth, painted on the exterior of the body and the interior of the rim in black and white, with some areas left natural buff. *(a)*: interior surface of rim; *(b)*: exterior of shoulder; *(c)*: body sherd from globular jar, painted black and white.

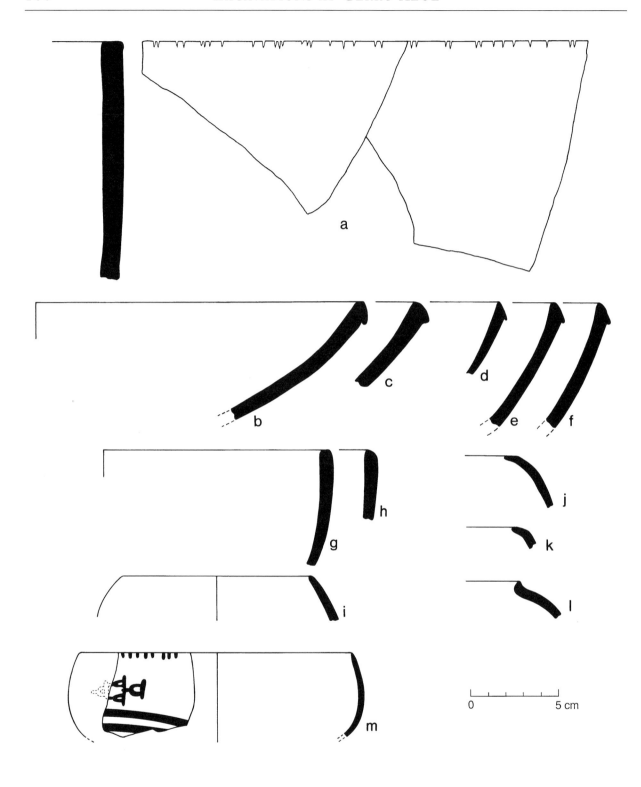

Figure 4.24. Pingüino Buff vessels from Feature 6, Structure D. *(a)*: large bowl (rim diameter greater than 50 cm) with rim ticking on the exterior; smoothed on the exterior over a wash of the same Pingüino clay; wiped on the interior (with no wash); *(b–f)*: bowls with cambered rim, burnished on both surfaces over a wash of the same Pingüino clay; *(g, h)*: hemispherical bowls, burnished on both surfaces; *(i)*: incurved-rim bowl; *(j, k)*: small bowls with incurved rim; *(l)*: rim from small bowl or jar with upturned, incurved rim; *(m)*: hemispherical bowl, slipped white on the exterior and painted black on white with "school of fish" motif.

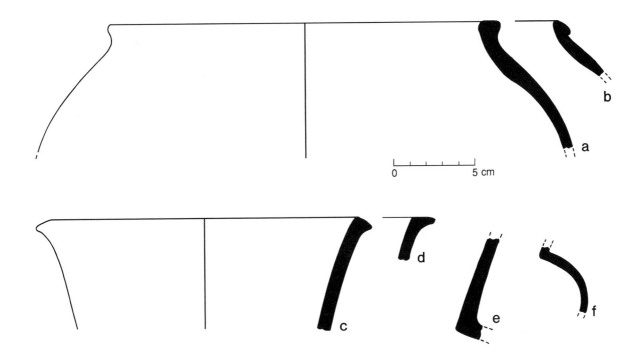

Figure 4.25. Ceramics from Feature 6, Structure D. (*a*): globular jar with rolled rim, more like Pingüino Buff than anything else, but with atypically coarse temper; traces of white paint or wash on exterior; (*b*): Pingüino Buff jar with rolled rim, painted black/white/red, but eroded; (*c, d*): funnel necks from Pingüino Buff jars with everted rims; (*e*): Pingüino Buff jar neck with white paint on exterior; (*f*): sherd from Pingüino Buff globular jar with wide mouth, painted black and white on exterior; design eroded.

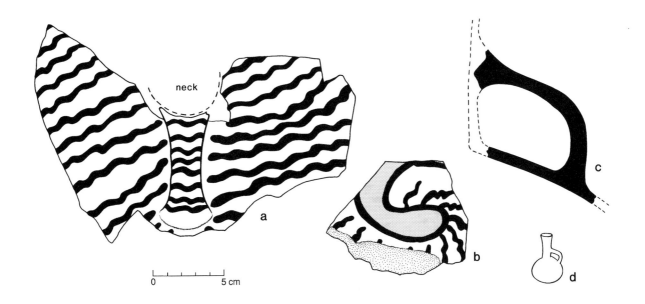

Figure 4.26. Unusual Pingüino Buff vessel from Feature 6, Structure D. This vessel appears to have been a tall-necked jar with a strap handle linking the neck and body. It has been painted black and white, with zones of burnished natural buff left unpainted. (*a*): top view, showing position of handle and neck; (*b*): basal sherd, showing raised modeled area with black-and-white paint, curving around a natural buff area; (*c*): side view of strap handle; (*d*): artist's reconstruction of vessel shape.

Figure 4.27. Sherds from an unusual Pingüino Buff vessel from Feature 6, Structure D. This jar was painted in black and white, with zones of burnished buff left unpainted.

Small bowls, incurved rim: 3 painted rims
Painted rims, small: 2
Miscellaneous painted body sherds: 20
Tiny handle from miniature jar: 1
Fragments of rectangular box-like vessel, painted black and white: 2 (Figure 4.28d)
Rims of hemispherical bowls: 6 (Figure 4.24g, h)
Rims of incurved rim bowls: 2 (Figure 4.24j–l)
Body sherd of large jar, painted black and white in band on shoulder and black/white/red on body: 1 (Figure 4.29a)
Jar body sherds, painted black and white: 2
Hemispherical bowl rim, slipped white on exterior only, painted in black and white with "school of fish" motif: 1 (Figures 4.24m, 4.29c)
Worked sherd, painted black: 1

Trambollo Burnished Brown (Figure 4.30)
Hemispherical bowls with cambered rim: 6 rims
Hemispherical bowls with plain rim: 5 rims
Hemispherical bowls with incurved rim: 6 rims
Hemispherical bowls: 8 basal sherds
Strap handle fragment: 1
Possible jar sherds (?): 2

Unusual or unique sherds
Jar sherds with shallow parallel grooving: 5 (Figure 4.28a)
Sherds with Pingüino Buff-like paste, painted design of zigzag nested chevrons in black/white/red (red is 10 R 4/6); very neat execution of painting: 3 (Figures 4.28b, 4.29e, f)

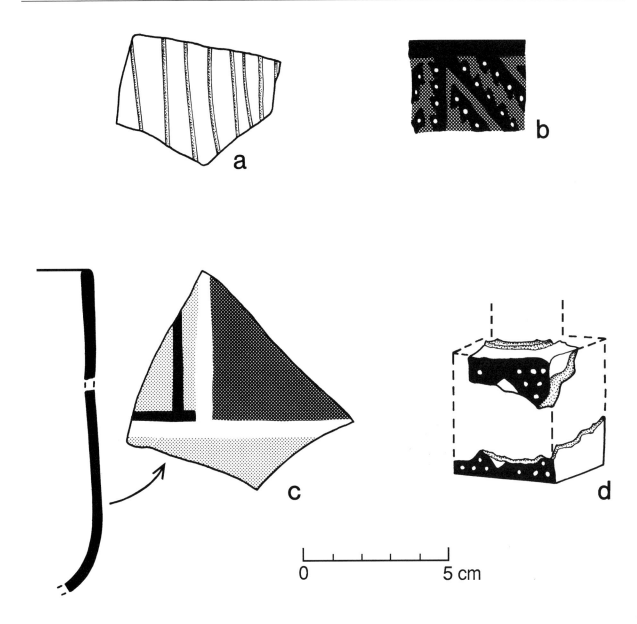

Figure 4.28. Unusual sherds from Feature 6, Structure D. *(a)*: sherd from small jar with parallel grooving, and paste resembling that of Trambollo Burnished Brown; *(b)*: body sherd with paste resembling that of Pingüino Buff, painted with an unusual "nested zigzag chevron" design in black/white/red; *(c)*: bowl sherd with design in black/white/red over natural brown; *(d)*: box-like Pingüino Buff vessel, painted black and white.

Sherds from bowls not unlike some Trambollo Burnished Brown specimens but with a redder paste; design painted over natural brown in black/white/red (red is 7.5 R 4/6): 2 (Figure 4.28c)

Sherds probably from a jar neck with a painted face on it, but on Camacho Reddish Brown paste rather than Pingüino Buff; faded black/white/red design: 2

Several coils of gray pottery clay stuck together, unfired, suggesting that some forming of vessels may have been done nearby

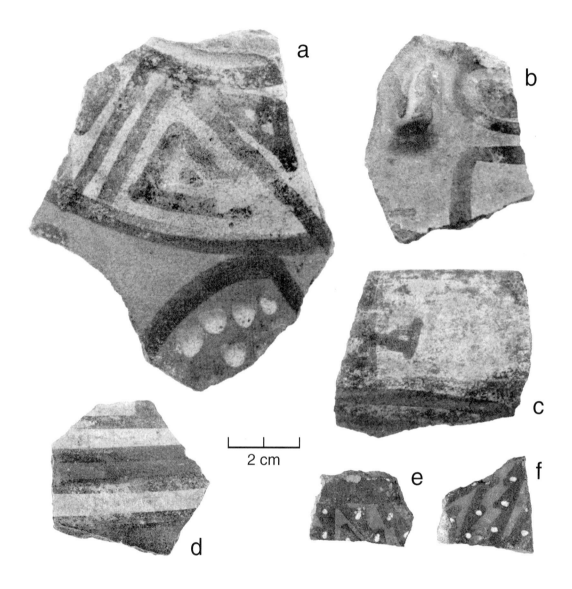

Figure 4.29. Miscellaneous Pingüino Buff (or Pingüino-like) sherds from Feature 6, Structure D. *(a)*: jar body sherd painted with a band of black-and-white geometric designs and an oval area of white dots on red paint; *(b)*: part of a human face painted in black/white/red; *(c)*: "school of fish" motif painted in black on white; *(d)*: horizontal striping in black/white/red; *(e, f)*: unusual sherds with Pingüino-like paste and "nested zigzag chevron" motif in black/white/red.

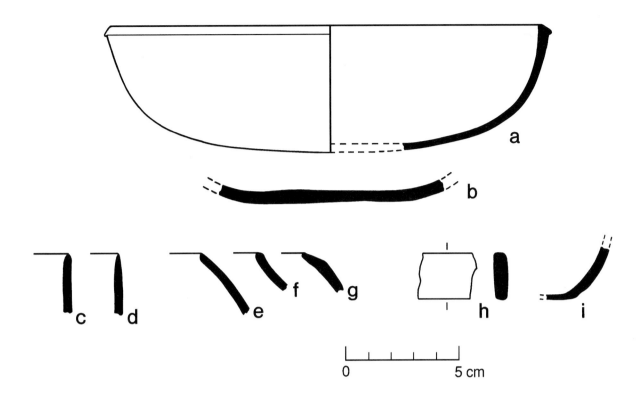

Figure 4.30. Trambollo Burnished Brown vessels from Feature 6, Structure D. *(a)*: hemispherical bowl with cambered rim; *(b)*: flattened base of bowl; *(c, d)*: plain rims from hemispherical bowls; *(e–g)*: incurved rims from hemispherical bowls; *(h)*: fragment of strap handle; *(i)*: possible jar sherd, showing angle between wall and base.

2. Undecorated body sherds

Camacho Reddish Brown
    407 sherds (by far the most abundant type in Feature 6)

Camacho Black (Standard Variety)
    10 sherds

Camacho Black (Highly Burnished Variety)
    20 sherds

Trambollo Burnished Brown
    25 sherds

Pingüino Buff
    59 sherds

Unclassified
    12 sherds

Radiocarbon dates for Feature 6

Charcoal from the Feature 6 midden was submitted to two different labs, Beta Analytic and Wisconsin. My expectation was that this refuse pile never got carried off to the quebradas of Cerro Camacho, because Structure D was abandoned when the Inka conquered Huarco in A.D. 1470. When calibrated using the OxCal 4.0 program (Bronk Ramsey 1995, 2001), the two-sigma ranges of both charcoal samples bracketed the Inka conquest.

Beta-10917 came out 340 ± 50 years B.P. The calibrated two-sigma range would be A.D. 1453–1645.

WIS-1936 came out 420 ± 70 years B.P. The calibrated two-sigma range would be A.D. 1405–1644.

I note that although both dates meet my expectations (in the sense that they bracket A.D. 1470), a calibrated two-sigma range is simply too wide to provide a precise date for a historic event. This is true for most of my calibrated dates.

LATER FLOORS BUILT IN THE SOUTHWEST CANCHÓN

Very late in the occupation of Structure D, fill was dumped into the Southwest Canchón, and a new series of walls and floors was built. To put these new floors in perspective, one can compare Figure 4.1 and Figure 4.31. It will be seen that the North Platform, whose original surface lay 2.79 m below datum, was covered first by (1) a slight-

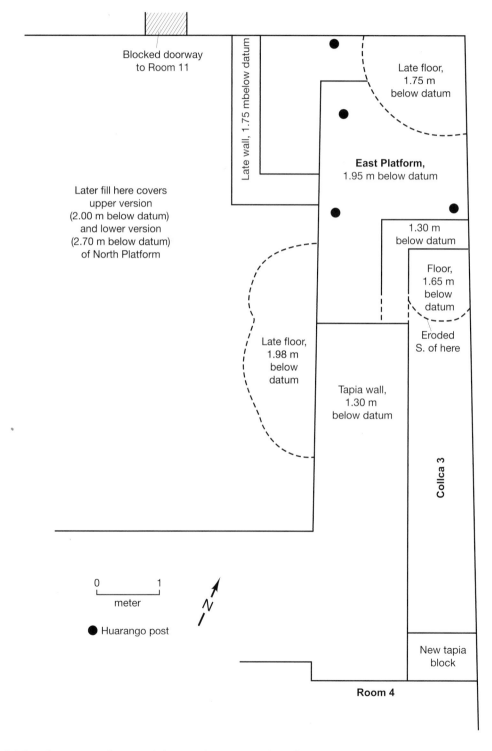

Figure 4.31. The eastern limits of the Southwest Canchón, Structure D, showing the superimposed walls, floors, and posts added above the original plan late in the occupation of the structure.

ly enlarged platform which was 9 cm higher, and then by (2) a later clay floor which lay only 1.98 m below datum. A remnant of that clay floor can be seen resting against the East Platform in Figure 4.31.

In the northeast corner of the Southwest Canchón, an L-shaped wall was built against the East Platform at 1.75 m below datum. The area so created was filled in with earth, completely burying the small stairway seen in Figure 4.1. Over the fill went a clay floor at 1.75 m below datum. Owing to later erosion, only a patch of this floor had survived in the extreme northeast corner. This patch can be seen both on the drawing (Figure 4.31) and in Figure 4.32, a photograph. Even later in time, a wattle-and-daub "squatters' house" was built in this corner; four of its wooden posts are shown in Figure 4.31. The posts were

Figure 4.32. The northeast corner of the Southwest Canchón, Structure D. The north arrow lies near a patch of whitish plaster floor at a depth of 1.75 m below datum. This floor was added at a very late stage in the use of Structure D. The earthen fill below it completely covered Collca 3 *(b)* and the rest of the East Platform, and obscured all but the uppermost third of the blocked corridor *(a)* that once led toward Room 7. (For a view of this same area following removal of the late floor, see Figure 4.14.)

of *huarango*, a generic term used by Quechua speakers to refer to leguminous trees of the genera *Acacia* and *Prosopis*.

It is possible that the floor shown at 1.75 m below datum in Figure 4.32 was built after Structure D had ceased to function as an elite residential compound. However, we doubt that the floor postdated the Late Intermediate period. It was built at a time when tapia was still the wall construction material of choice, and no clear Late Horizon ceramics were found in association.

In an effort to date these late constructions, we collected sherds from various contexts, both above and below them. The ceramics sealed *below* the upper floor shown in Figure 4.32 (and *above* the original East Platform) were a nondescript and largely redeposited collection; nevertheless, the sherds are all typical of the Late Intermediate period. The list is as follows:

Camacho Reddish Brown
    Body sherds from *tinajones*: 3
    Body sherds from jars: 18
    Worked sherd: 1

Camacho Black (Standard Variety)
    Jar body sherds (some accidentally refired): 4

Pingüino Buff
    Jar body sherds, plain: 2
    Jar body sherds, painted black and white: 5

Trambollo Burnished Brown
    Body sherds: 3

Next, let us examine a collection of diagnostic sherds found resting on the surface of the upper floor (1.75 m below datum) seen in Figure 4.32. Those sherds also appear to be Late Intermediate types and vessel shapes. The diagnostics are as follows:

Camacho Reddish Brown (Figure 4.33a–d)
    Large jars, cambered rims: 2
    Small jar, cambered rim: 1
    Strap handles: 2
    Tinajones or very large storage jars: 4 rims

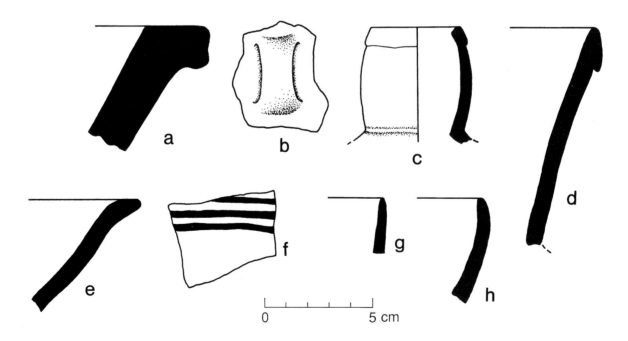

Figure 4.33. Selected sherds from the uppermost (most recent) floor, stratigraphically above the platforms in the Southwest Canchón, Structure D. Sherds *a–d* are Camacho Reddish Brown. *(a)*: rim of *tinajón*; *(b)*: strap handle; *(c)*: neck from small jar with cambered rim; *(d)*: cambered rim from large jar; *(e)*: Camacho Black (standard variety) rim from jar or amphora. Sherds *f–h* are Pingüino Buff. *(f)*: jar sherd, painted black and white; *(g)*: rim of small hemispherical bowl; *(h)*: rim of large hemispherical bowl.

Camacho Black (Standard Variety) (Figure 4.33e)
    Jar or amphora rims: 2

Pingüino Buff (Figure 4.33f–h)
    Jar neck, white painted: 1
    Jar body sherds, painted black and white: 2
    Large hemispherical bowl: 1 rim
    Small hemispherical bowl: 1 rim

Finally, let us look at a collection of diagnostic sherds associated with the wattle-and-daub "squatters' house" whose *huarango* posts are shown in Figure 4.31. This small collection is not particularly informative. It contains only types known from the Late Intermediate, as follows:

Camacho Reddish Brown
    Jar body sherd: 1 (fire-blackened)

Camacho Black (Standard Variety)
    Large jar or amphora body sherd: 1

Pingüino Buff
    Jar body sherds: 4

OTHER DIAGNOSTIC SHERDS FROM THE LATE FILL IN THE SOUTHWEST CANCHÓN

Figure 4.34 shows four more diagnostic sherds from later fill in the Southwest Canchón. The three from general fill are as follows:

Pingüino Buff (Figure 4.34a–c)
    Hemispherical bowl rim, given a white slip on the interior and exterior, then a red wash on the interior, painted in black and white on the exterior: 1
    Jar with everted rim, painted white on natural: 1
    Body sherd from a globular jar with wide mouth, painted black and white on the interior of the rim, black and white on the exterior of the shoulder and body: 1
    Hollow effigy vessel with thin white slip or wash; fragment of possible arm: 1 (this sherd, shown in Figure 4.34d, is from a possible effigy vessel and was found under a small patch of late floor above the East Platform)

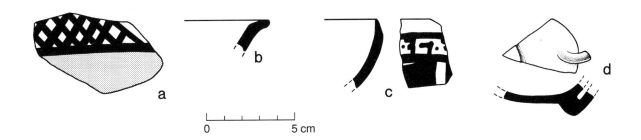

Figure 4.34. Pingüino Buff sherds from various provenances in the Southwest Canchón, Structure D. Sherds *a–c* are from general fill. *(a)*: sherd from globular jar, painted black and white on natural buff with a cross-hatched triangle motif; *(b)*: everted jar rim, painted black and white on natural on the rim interior; *(c)*: rim of hemispherical bowl, slipped white on interior and exterior, given a red wash on the interior, and painted black and white on the exterior; *(d)*: sherd from some sort of effigy vessel, found under a very late floor in the extreme northeast corner of the canchón, stratigraphically above the East Platform.

ROOM 4

At some point in the occupation of Structure D, the building's residents decided that they needed an additional room next to the Southwest Canchón. By adding a new L-shaped tapia wall, as shown in Figure 4.35, they created Room 4 in the southeast corner of the canchón. This new L-shaped wall was inferior in quality to the earlier walls nearby. The earlier walls had smooth, well-

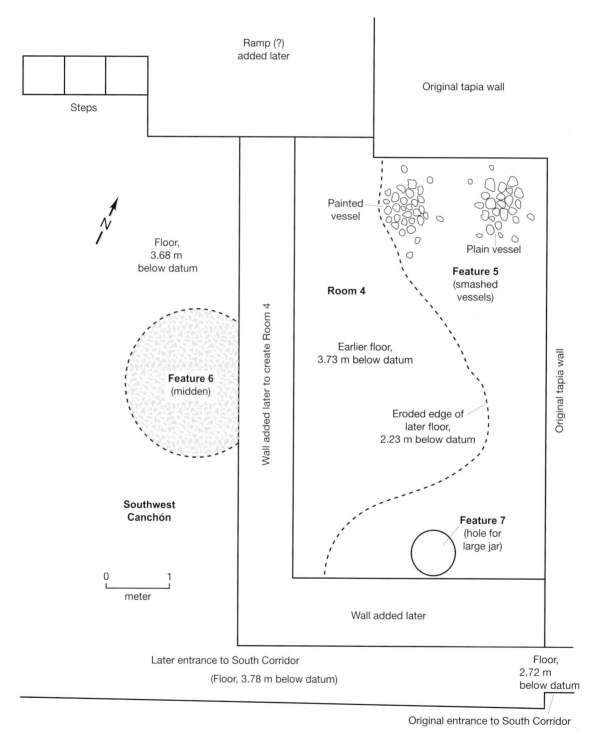

Figure 4.35. Room 4 and its surroundings, Structure D. It appears that the space occupied by Room 4 was originally part of the Southwest Canchón. At some point, an L-shaped tapia wall was added to create Room 4. This wall increased the length of the South Corridor as shown.

finished clay surfaces; the L-shaped wall was cruder, with clay surfaces that were more pockmarked.

The interior dimensions of Room 4 were roughly 6.67 × 4.03 m. Its floor (which was part of the original floor of the Southwest Canchón) lay at 3.73 m below datum (Figure 4.36). It seems almost certain that Room 4 was designed for storage, since its walls were more than 1.5 m high yet had no doorway. Entry would probably have been achieved via ladder from what appeared to be a low ramp (now greatly eroded), added to the old stair-and-wall access to the East Platform (Figure 4.35). The storage capacity of Room 4 at the time of its creation would have been more tphan 40 m³.

It is worth noting that the new L-shaped wall did more than create Room 4. As can be seen in Figure 4.35, its east–west arm added 4.85 m to the length of the South Corridor.

Figure 4.36. Alberto Barraza sweeps the original (lowest) floor of Room 4. His back faces the wall that was added in order to create Room 4 out of an area of the Southwest Canchón. (Since the room's original floor had once been part of the floor of that canchón, it occurred at roughly the same depth, 3.73 m below datum.) The tapia block marked *a* is the south jamb of the original doorway to the South Corridor (see Figure 4.1).

Room 4, like many parts of Structure D, had suffered earthquake damage to its floor and walls. We took advantage of this damage to open a small sounding below the room's original floor. The purpose of this sounding was to see whether any earlier construction lay stratigraphically below the floor of the Southwest Canchón. We removed a cracked but largely intact patch of floor at 3.73 m below datum and continued down to 4.73 m. No earlier floors or walls were encountered, but the fill below 3.73 m below datum did contain a few sherds. These sherds probably constitute the oldest collection from Structure D, at least in the stratigraphic sense. They are as follows:

Camacho Reddish Brown
    Body sherds from *tinajones*: 8
    Body sherds from jars: 16

Camacho Black (Standard Variety)
    Typical amphora neck with modeled human
        ear from a face: 1 (Figure 4.37)
    Body sherds: 4

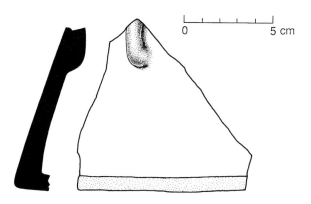

Figure 4.37. Sherd from amphora neck with modeled human ear, Camacho Black (standard variety). This sherd was found in the deep sounding in Room 4, Structure D, which probably produced the oldest collection of ceramics from Structure D. Depth, 3.73-4.73 m below datum.

Pingüino Buff
    Body sherds from jars, plain: 8
    Body sherds from jars, white paint or wash:
       10

Based on this small sample from below the floor, we still have no evidence that the construction sequence of Structure D went back to a time before the Late Intermediate period.

A radiocarbon date from 3.9 m below datum

We recovered chunks of charcoal below the original floor of Room 4 at a depth of 3.9 m below datum. The charcoal was submitted to Beta Analytic.

    Beta-10913 came out 340 ± 50 years B.P. The calibrated two-sigma range would be A.D. 1453–1645. My only real expectation for this date was that it should antedate the arrival of the Inka.

Later use of Room 4

At a later stage of occupation, Room 4's function seems to have changed. No longer was it used as a 40-m^3 storage room. Some 1.5 m of fill were shoveled into the room and then carefully leveled so that a new clay floor could be laid at 2.23 m below datum (see Figure 4.35). Two interesting discoveries, Features 5 and 7, were made on this floor.

Before discussing Features 5 and 7, however, let us examine the 1.5 m of fill below the later floor. While most of this fill was earth, it did contain ceramics. We present those ceramics in chronological order, from earliest (= deepest) to latest (= shallowest).

First, let us look at the sherds from the fill just above the original floor, 3.73 m below datum or 1.5 m below the floor on which we discovered Features 5 and 7 (Figures 4.38–4.40). Those sherds are as follows:

Camacho Reddish Brown (Figure 4.38)
    Jars with cambered rims: 16 rims
    Jar shoulders: 3
    Cooking pots with restricted orifice and
        horizontally set strap handles: 5 rims
        (fire-blackened)
    Jar sherd with modeled, punctate human
        arm: 1
    Body sherds: 23

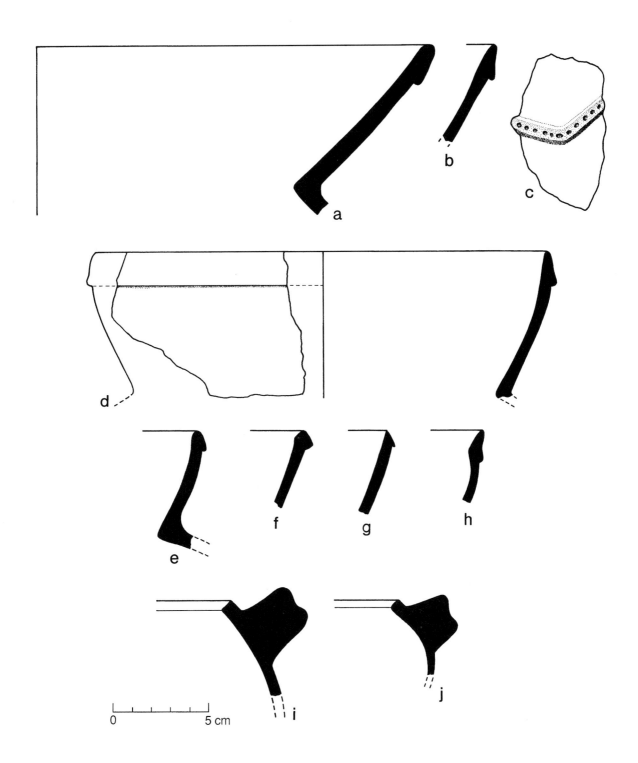

Figure 4.38. Camacho Reddish Brown vessels from the fill 1.5 m below the floor on which Feature 5 lay, Room 4, Structure D. *(a, b, d–h)*: jars with cambered rims; *(c)*: jar body sherd with what may be a modeled, punctate human arm on the exterior (based on more complete specimens); *(i, j)*: cooking pots with restricted orifice and strap handles; fire-blackened on the exterior.

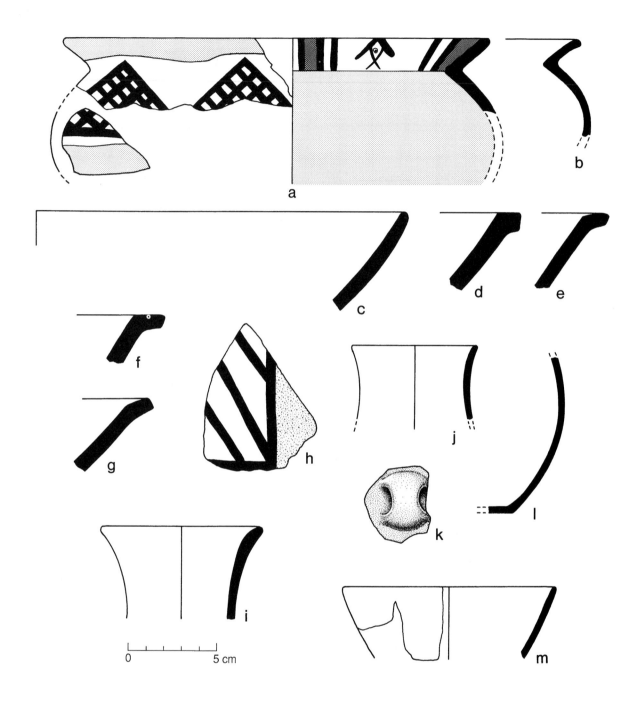

Figure 4.39. Ceramics from the fill 1.5 m below the floor on which Feature 5 lay, Room 4, Structure D. Sherds *a–e* are Pingüino Buff. *(a, b)*: globular jars with wide mouth; *a* is painted black and white over natural buff on the exterior and black/white/red on the interior of the rim; the red is 2.5 YR 5/4 (reddish brown); *(c)*: large hemispherical bowl, given wash or "self slip" of same clay as the paste; *(d, e)*: slightly everted rims from large jars; *(f, g)*: everted rims of large jars in atypical orange ware which looks superficially like Pingüino Buff, but has coarser temper; *(h)*: Pingüino Buff jar body sherd painted black, white, and faded muddy brownish gray (?); *(i)*: jar or amphora rim, Camacho Black (standard variety). Sherds *j–m* are Camacho Black (highly burnished variety). *(j)*: small jar rim; *(l)*: small jar base; *(k)*: strap handle from jar; *(m)*: hemispherical bowl.

Camacho Black (Standard Variety) (Figure 4.39i)
  Jar or amphora rim: 1

Camacho Black (Highly Burnished Variety) (Figure 4.39j–m)
  Small jars: 2 rims, 3 body sherds (1 is a base), 1 strap handle
  Hemispherical bowls: 3 rim sherds
  Plain body sherds: 5

Pingüino Buff (Figures 4.39a–e, h, 4.40)
  Globular jar with wide mouth, painted black/white/red on interior of rim, and black and white on exterior, rims: 4

Shoulders of globular jars with wide mouth: 5
Slightly everted rims, large jars: 3
Strap handle from large jar: 1
Neck, large jar, painted white: 1
Jar body sherds, painted black/white/red: 3
Large hemispherical bowls: 2 rims
Body sherds, unpainted: 10
Body sherds, traces of white paint: 11

Atypical Orange Variety of Pingüino Buff (superficially similar to standard Pingüino Buff, but with coarser temper) (Figure 4.39f, g)
  Slightly everted rims from large jars: 2

3 cm

Figure 4.40. Two views of a Pingüino Buff globular jar with a wide mouth, found in the fill 1.5 m below the floor on which Feature 5 lay, Room 4, Structure D. Sherd *a* shows the "fish motif" painted on the inside of the rim in black/white/red; *b* shows the "mountain motif" painted on the jar shoulder in black and white over natural buff.

Trambollo Burnished Brown
    Hemispherical bowl: 1 body sherd

A radiocarbon date from just above the original floor

We encountered charcoal in the fill just above the original floor, 3.73 m below datum or 1.5 m below the floor on which we discovered Features 5 and 7. This charcoal was submitted to Beta Analytic.

> Beta-10914 came out 370 ± 50 years B.P. The calibrated two-sigma range would be A.D. 1445–1637. My only expectation for this date was that it should antedate the arrival of the Inka.

Next, let us turn to the sherds found in the fill roughly half a meter above the original floor, or about 1.0 m below the floor where Features 5 and 7 were found (Figures 4.41, 4.42). These sherds are as follows:

Camacho Reddish Brown (Figure 4.41a–j)
    Jars with cambered rim: 7 rim sherds
    Jars with everted and bolstered rims: 4 rims
    Jars with plain rim: 2 rim sherds
    Jars with beveled rim: 2 rim sherds
    Other jar rims (including groove on top): 2
    Jar shoulders: 2
    Large bolstered rim, possibly from a *tinajón*: 1
    Cooking pot with restricted orifice and strap handle set horizontally: 2

Camacho Black (Highly Burnished Variety) (Figure 4.42a–e)
    Hemispherical bowl: 1 rim
    Hemispherical bowl, eccentric rim (kidney-shaped): 1 (pinkish paste)
    Hemispherical bowl with miniature maize-cob lug: 1 rim
    Hemispherical bowl with rim lug, possibly from kidney-shaped bowl (since it also has pinkish paste): 1 rim
    Miniature jar with rolled rim: 1 rim
    Body sherds: 6

Pingüino Buff (Figure 4.41k–q)
    Globular jar with wide mouth, painted black/white/red on interior of rim, and black/white (and red?) on exterior of body, rims: 2
    Rim of globular jar with strap handle: 1
    Shoulder of globular jar with black/white paint: 2
    Rim of relatively large, shallow hemispherical bowl: 1
    Body sherds from jars, painted with black/white geometric designs: 10
    Unpainted basal sherds from globular jars: 5

Trambollo Burnished Brown (Figure 4.42f–h)
    Small jar with funnel neck and strap handle: 1
    Miniature jar: 1 body sherd
    Rectangular sherd, possibly head of un-slipped figurine?: 1

Now let us turn to the sherds from the fill at 2.25 m below datum, directly below the floor on which Features 5 and 7 were found (Figures 4.43, 4.44). These sherds are as follows:

Camacho Reddish Brown (Figure 4.43b–g, and possibly h)
    Rims of jars, everted, plain: 3
    Rim of jar, everted, painted black and red; clearly part of a face on a jar neck with facial paint; reminiscent of Pingüino Buff, but the surface treatment, color, and temper are like Camacho Reddish Brown: 1 (Figure 4.43h)
    Rim of jar, cambered, with strap handle: 1 (fire-blackened)
    Jar shoulders, plain: 2 (fire-blackened)
    Jar shoulder, appliqué nipple: 1
    Cooking pots with restricted orifice: 3 (1 is fire-blackened)
    Body sherds of very large crude vessels with traces of red wash: 2

Camacho Black (Standard Variety) (Figure 4.43a)
    Amphora neck and rim: 1
    Jar or amphora shoulders: 2

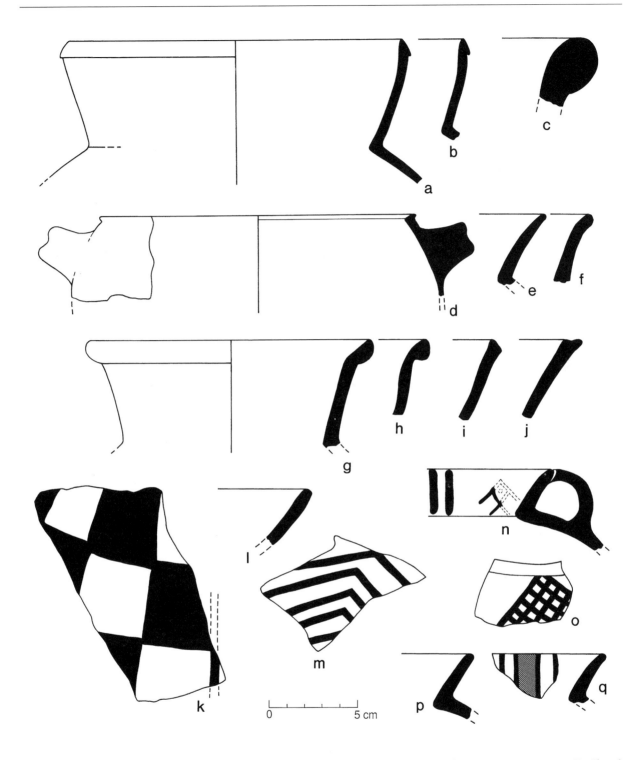

Figure 4.41. Ceramics from the fill 1.0 m below the floor on which Feature 5 lay, Room 4, Structure D. Sherds *a–j* are Camacho Reddish Brown. *(a, b)*: jars with cambered rims; *(c)*: large bolstered rim, possibly from *tinajón*; *(d)*: cooking pot with restricted orifice and strap handles; *(e, f)*: jar rims; *(g, h)*: jars with bolstered everted rims; *(i)*: beveled jar rim; *(j)*: grooved-on-top jar rim. Sherds *k–q* are Pingüino Buff. *(k)*: jar body sherds, painted black and white in squares; *(l)*: rim of large, shallow hemispherical bowl; *(m)*: jar body sherd with black chevrons painted on white slip; *(n–q)*: globular jars painted on the exterior and on the interior of the rim; sherds *n* and *o* are painted in black and white, and *q* is painted black/white/red. The motif on *p* is too eroded to draw.

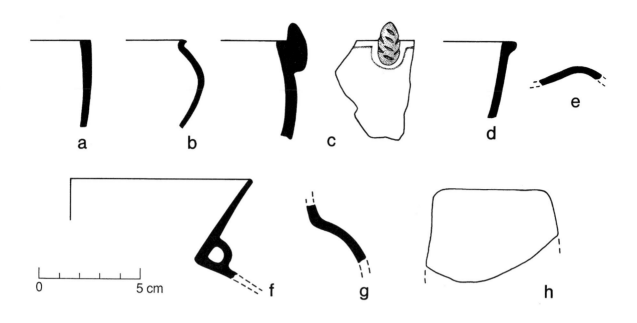

Figure 4.42. Ceramics from the fill 1.0 m below the floor on which Feature 5 lay, Room 4, Structure D. Sherds *a–e* are Camacho Black (highly burnished variety). *(a)*: hemispherical bowl, "graphite" surface; *(b)*: miniature jar with rolled rim; *(c)*: two views of hemispherical bowl with maize cob lug on rim; *(d, e)*: side and top views of hemispherical bowl with eccentric rim. Sherds *f–h* are Trambollo Burnished Brown. *(f)*: small jar with funnel neck and strap handle; *(g)*: shoulder of miniature jar; *(h)*: rectangular sherd, possibly an unslipped figurine head (?).

Pingüino Buff (Figures 4.43i–l, 4.44)

Small globular jar with wide mouth, painted black and white on interior of rim, black and white on exterior of body, with strap handle: 1 (Figure 4.43i)

Jar with rolled rim, painted black and white on exterior and rim: 1 (Figure 4.43k, l)

Neck and shoulder of jar with fish and mountains painted in black and white on natural buff (Figure 4.44)

Large bowl with restricted orifice, slipped white on exterior: 1

Strap handle from large jar, painted black: 1

Body sherds of jars, painted black: 3

Rare sherds

One aberrant sherd from a bucket-shaped bowl that might be from a different time period or a different region is shown in Figure 4.43m. This sherd is old and worn and may have been accidentally introduced into Structure D in fill dug up elsewhere. It is painted with opposing step-fret designs in a style atypical for Cerro Azul. Broadly similar vessels have been assigned to Ica 3C by Menzel (1976:Fig. 4.44).

For the most part, the vast majority of the sherds from the fill separating the earliest and latest floors within Room 4 fit comfortably in the Late Intermediate of Cerro Azul. To be sure, there are a few anomalous-looking sherds (Figures 4.41k, 4.43i, m); nevertheless, it is not clear whether they are anomalous because they are trade pieces from other regions or because they are from earlier periods within the same region.

Features 5 and 7

The later clay floor of Room 4—2.23 m below datum—had once filled the entire room. By 1984, however, its western, or seaward, side had been

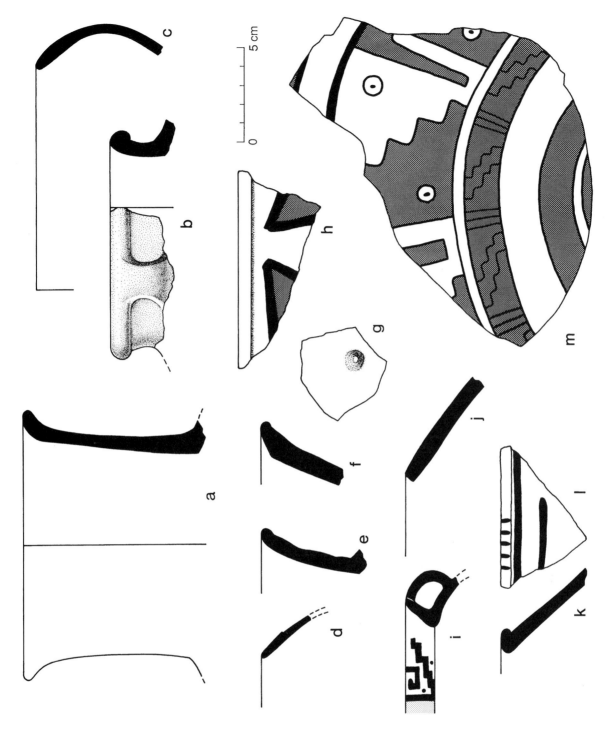

Figure 4.43. Ceramics from the fill immediately below the floor on which Feature 5 lay, Room 4, Structure D. (*a*): amphora neck of Camacho Black (standard variety). Sherds *b–g* are Camacho Reddish Brown. (*b*): small jar with cambered rim and strap handle; (*c*, *d*): cooking pots with restricted orifice; (*e*, *f*): jar rims; (*g*): jar shoulder with appliqué nipple; (*b*): jar rim, painted in black and red in a style usually seen on Pingüino Buff, but with Camacho Reddish Brown paste, temper, and surface treatment. Sherds *i–l* are Pingüino Buff. (*i*): globular jar with wide mouth, painted black and white on the exterior and on the interior of the rim; (*j*): large bowl with restricted orifice, white slip on exterior; (*k*, *l*): jar with rolled rim, painted black and white on exterior and rim; (*m*): aberrant sherd, either from another region or an earlier time period; it is painted in red (10 R 4/6) and white (10 YR 8/4) but appears worn and old.

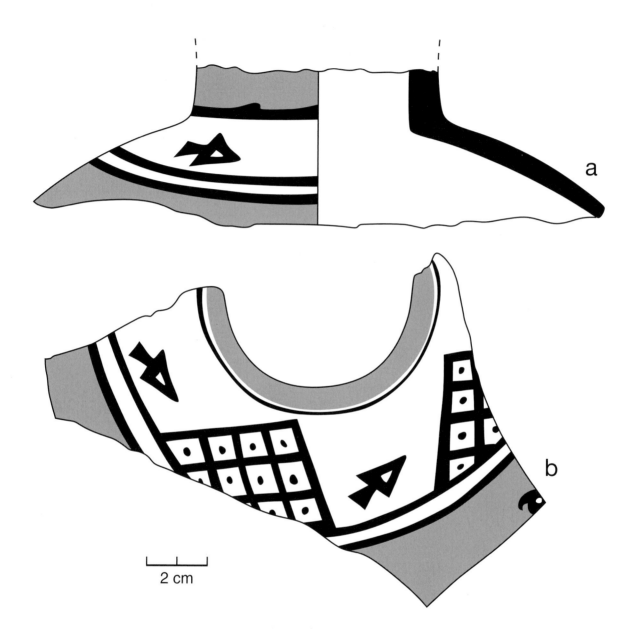

Figure 4.44. Neck and shoulder from Pingüino Buff jar, painted black and white over natural buff (shown as gray screen). Found in Room 4, Structure D, in the fill immediately below the floor on which Feature 5 lay. Motifs include fish and checkerboard mountains. (*a*): side view; (*b*): top view.

partially eroded (Figure 4.35). Near its southern limit we found Feature 7, a circular depression made in the floor in order to keep a large globular jar sitting upright. The jar was no longer present.

Near the northern limit of the floor we discovered a mass of sherds, most of them coming from two vessels that had collapsed in situ under the weight of the overlying earth (Figure 4.35). One of these vessels was a partially restorable Pingüino Buff globular jar with two effigy lugs in the shape of maize cobs. The other was a Camacho Black amphora. A length of coarse rope, evidently used as a harness around the Pingüino Buff jar, was found among the sherds (Figure 4.45). Large numbers of Camacho Reddish Brown jar sherds were also found in this mass of pottery.

We designated this deposit of collapsed vessels Feature 5. Since it appeared to be a primary deposit—vessels left in situ on a floor, where they eventually broke under their own weight and that of the overburden—Feature 5 provided us with useful data on the average size of sherds from primary contexts (see the final section of Chapter 3). A random sample of 100 Camacho Reddish Brown jar body sherds from Feature 5 weighed 4.7 kg. A random sample of Camacho Black amphora body sherds (standard variety) weighed 4.65 kg.

Figure 4.45. Room 4 of Structure D had a stratigraphic sequence of superimposed floors; the uppermost occurred at a depth of 2.23 m below datum. As Alberto Barraza began uncovering this floor, he discovered a cluster of partially restorable vessels and a length of coarse rope. In this mass of sherds—designated Feature 5—one could see the remains of a large Pingüino Buff jar with maize-cob-shaped lugs and an elaborate painted design.

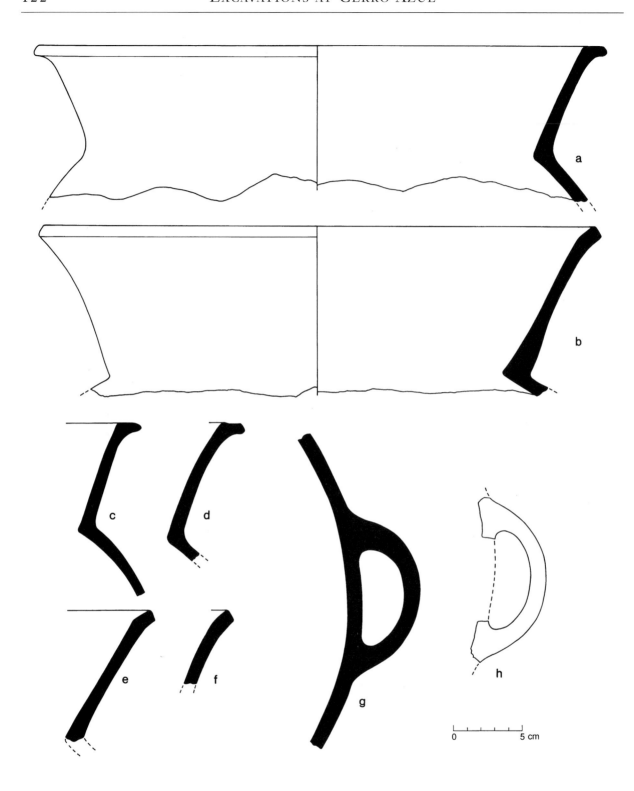

Figure 4.46. Vessels found in Feature 5, Structure D. *(a, c, d)*: Camacho Reddish Brown jars with everted rims. *(b, e, f)*: Camacho Black (standard variety) amphorae with slightly beveled rims; *(g, h)*: Camacho Black (standard variety) strap handles from large amphorae.

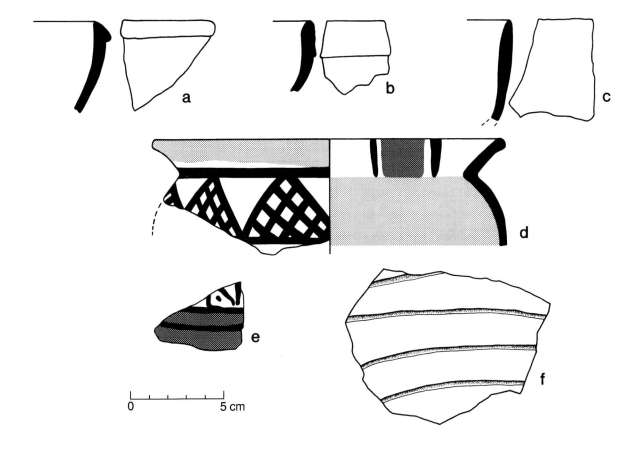

Figure 4.47. Vessels from Feature 5, Structure D. *(a, b)*: Camacho Reddish Brown cambered rims, probably from jars; *(c)*: rim sherd from Pingüino Buff hemispherical bowl, with atypical gray firing clouds and an atypical gray core to the paste. Sherds *d–f* are Pingüino Buff. *(d)*: globular jar, painted black and white on the exterior and black/white/red on the interior of the rim; the white is 2.5 Y 8/2 (white); the black is 7.5 R 3/0 (very dark gray); the red is 10 R 5/2 (weak red). *(e)*: jar sherd painted black/white/red on the exterior; the red is 10 R 4/6 (red). *(f)*: jar sherd, burnished and shallowly grooved on the exterior.

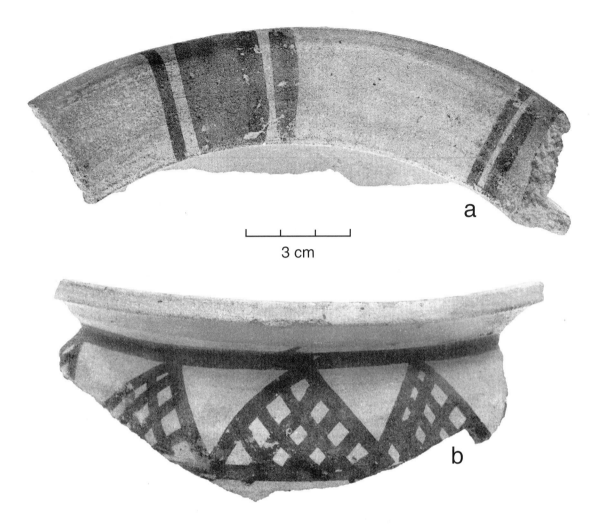

Figure 4.48. Two views of a Pingüino Buff globular jar with a wide mouth from Feature 5, Structure D. Sherd *a* shows the inside of the rim, painted in black/white/red; *b* shows the "mountain motif" painted on the jar shoulder in black and white.

Figure 4.49. Pingüino Buff jar sherd, burnished and shallowly grooved on the exterior, found in Feature 5, Structure D. This may be a sherd from a "fat skeleton" effigy vessel.

A representative sample of ceramics from Feature 5 is illustrated in Figures 4.46–4.51. This is perhaps the largest sherd sample from primary context we recovered in Structure D, and it is prototypically Late Intermediate. Its Camacho Reddish Brown storage jars, Camacho Black amphorae, and Pingüino Buff globular jars with the crosshatched "mountain motif" are all common at Cerro Azul. So is the grooved sherd shown in Figure 4.49, which may depict the ribs of a "fat skeleton" (see Chapter 3). Finally, the partially restorable Pingüino Buff globular jar shown in Figures 4.50 and 4.51 combines many elements we found elsewhere in Structure D: maize-cob effigy lugs, painted flocks of birds, and checkerboards with dots or geometric motifs. Had the western half of the upper floor of Room 4 not eroded away, we suspect we would have recovered all of this vessel.

The complete list of sherds from Feature 5 is as follows:

1. Diagnostic sherds

Camacho Reddish Brown (Figures 4.46a, c, d; 4.47a, b)
   Jar rims, cambered: 2
   Jar rims, everted: 14
   Jar necks: 4
   Jar shoulders: 14
   Jar bases: 2

Camacho Black (Standard Variety) (Figure 4.46b, e–h)
   Amphorae with beveled rim: 28 rim sherds
   Amphora necks (including rim): 1
   Amphorae (or jar) shoulders: 16
   Strap handles or handle fragments: 11

Pingüino Buff (Figures 4.47c–f, 4.48, 4.49)
   Globular jars with wide mouth; painting in white, black and/or red: 1 rim
   Globular jars with wide mouth; painting in white, black and/or red: 2 sherds

   Jar with shallow parallel grooves on body: 1 sherd
   Hemispherical bowl, unusual in having a gray core: 1 rim

Partially restorable Pingüino Buff globular jar with funnel neck, painted in white/black/red and bearing 2 effigy maize-cob lugs (Figures 4.50–4.51)
   Rim sherds: 3
   Neck sherd: 1
   Shoulder sherds: 6
   Painted body sherds: 25
   Note: In the Munsell color system, the colors of this vessel are as follows:
   Natural areas: 2.5 YR 5/6 (red) 5 YR 6/6 (reddish yellow), and fire-blackened in places
   Paste: 10 R 6/6 (light red)
   White paint: 10 YR 8/3 (whitish yellow)
   Black paint: 10 YR 3/1 (very dark gray)
   Red paint: 10 R 4/6 (red)

2. Body sherds

Camacho Reddish Brown
   Body sherds: 364

Camacho Black (Standard Variety), mostly amphora body sherds
   Body sherds: 415

Camacho Black (Highly Burnished Variety), "graphite-like" surface
   Body sherd: 1

Pingüino Buff
   Body sherds, plain, mostly from the globular pot in Figures 4.50 and 4.51: 62
   Body sherds, white paint/slip: 21
   Body sherds, painted black and white: 6

Unclassified Burnished Brown
   Body sherds: 3

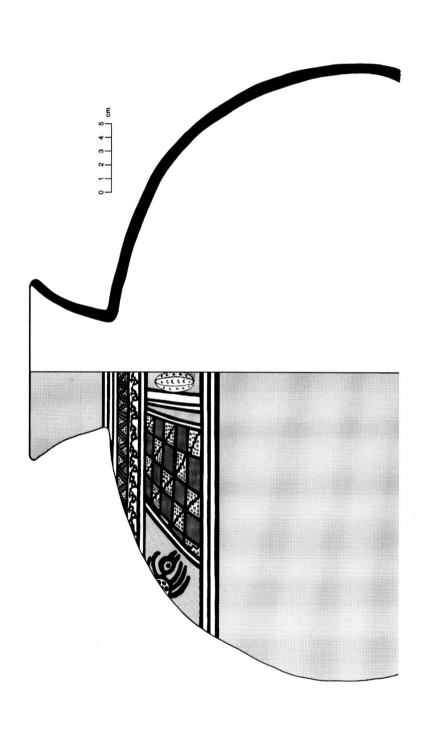

Figure 4.50. Partially restorable Pingüino Buff globular jar with funnel neck, Feature 5, Structure D. The vessel is painted on the exterior in black/white/red over natural buff and has two lugs in the form of maize cobs. The natural buff areas are 2.5 YR 5/6 (red) to 5 YR 6/6 (reddish yellow) and fire-blackened in places. The clay body (paste) is 10 R 6/6 (light red). The white paint is 10 YR 8/3 (whitish yellow); the red paint is 10 R 4/6 (red); and the black paint is 10 YR 3/1 (very dark gray).

Figure 4.51. Partially restorable Pingüino Buff globular jar with funnel neck, Feature 5, Structure D. The vessel is painted on the exterior in black/white/red over natural buff and has two lugs in the form of maize cobs.

ROOM 8

One more room appeared to be closely associated with the Southwest Canchón. This was Room 8, which lay immediately west of the North Platform (see Figure 4.1). Room 8 measured roughly 3.8 × 3.92 m and had no door, making it likely that it had been designed as a storage unit. Its floor was found at 4.30 m below datum. Its best-preserved wall (the east wall) suggests that Room 8 had been at least 1.5 m deep when built. That would have given it a storage capacity greater than 22 m³.

There is little doubt about the function of Room 8: it was for the storage of dried fish, primarily anchovies and sardines but occasionally larger fish as well. We can reconstruct the drying process as follows. First, hundreds of small fish would be dried in the sun, probably on a stretch of cobble beach. Then a layer of fine, clean sand was laid on the floor of Room 8. Over this went a single layer of dried sardines and anchovies. A second layer of sand would be placed over the fish; then came a second layer of dried fish; then a third layer of sand, and so on. The hygroscopic properties of the sand drew the last of the moisture out of the fish, completing the drying process. However, wherever the fish accidentally touched the clay floor or walls of Room 8, patches of skin and scales stuck to the clay. It was also the case that a few dried fish disintegrated over time, leaving their bones in the sand.

We suspect that one of the main products exported from Cerro Azul to other communities in the Kingdom of Huarco was dried fish. The location of Room 8 (Figure 4.52) makes it likely

Figure 4.52. Structure D seen from Structure C at a relatively early stage of excavation. Part of the South Corridor and the Southwest Canchón have been exposed, and Feature 6, an important midden, has been left on a pedestal so that it can be excavated later with small tools and fine screens. Room 8 has been exposed only to the level of the fine sand with fish remains. Rooms 9, 10, and 11 have not yet been excavated. In the distance can be seen the terraces of Cerro Camacho and the ruins of Structure H.

that, under the supervision of the administrator assigned to the North Platform, large quantities of dried sardines and anchovies would periodically have been removed from Room 8 and loaded onto the backs of the llamas that were led into the Southwest Canchón.

When we discovered Room 8, it still had more than a meter of sand in it (Figures 4.52, 4.53). We

Figure 4.53. Room 8 of Structure D, a sand-filled room used for storage of dried fish. *(Top)*: Edalio Aguidos has just finished sweeping the surface of the room's tapia walls. *(Bottom)*: Cirilo Cruz and Ramón Landa are passing the sand from the room through fine carburetor mesh, in a search for fish remains.

assigned four workmen to pass the contents of the room through our finest mesh sieves and collect the fish remains. Those remains will be discussed in a future volume.

There were sherds in the sand of Room 8, but none appear to be from in situ vessels stored in the room. Rather, the collection consists almost entirely of sherds from large storage and cooking vessels, probably tossed into Room 8 at a time when its function as a storage unit was near an end. Since many of the sherds conjoin, the number of vessels involved is probably small. The list of sherds is as follows:

Camacho Reddish Brown
> Jars with flaring rim: 2 rim sherds
> Jars with cambered rim: 4 rim sherds (2 are fire-blackened)
> Cooking pot with restricted orifice (brushed exterior) with rolled rim: 3 rims
> Cooking pot with restricted orifice and vertically set strap handle: 1 rim (fire-blackened)
> Jar with bowl shaped neck: 1 rim (unusual)
> Jar with narrow neck, plain rim, strap handle linking neck to shoulder: 1 (fire-blackened)
> Body sherds: 8 (fairly large)

Pingüino Buff
> Large jar with flaring rim, painted white on natural: 2 rims
> Large strap handle from large jar, fitting with several large body sherds: 1 (white on natural)
> Large painted white-on-natural body sherds: 6 (all from same jar)
> Globular jars with wide mouth, painted black and white on rim, black and white on exterior of body: 2 rims (1 with strap handle, 1 without)
> Jar neck with "swellings" pushed out from the interior: 1
> Cylindrical jar neck, highly burnished on exterior, not on interior: 3 rims from same vessel

> Open bowl, highly burnished on interior and exterior: 1 rim
> Burnished body sherds, fairly large: 5

THE SOUTH CORRIDOR

I conclude my discussion of the southwest quadrant of Structure D with the South Corridor. This single-file passageway led from the Southwest Canchón to the interior of the building. The South Corridor was deliberately kept narrow in order to restrict access to the interior and was laid out to be L-shaped so that no one standing in the Southwest Canchón could even see where it led.

As Figure 4.1 shows, the South Corridor was originally designed to run for a little more than 7 m west to east and then to make a sharp left turn and run south to north for another 3.36 m, ending in the patio we called "Room 2." The east–west arm of the corridor varied between 1.0 m and 0.97 m in width; the north–south arm was only 0.57 m wide. The corridor also had to slope uphill on its way to the interior of the building, since the canchón floor near the corridor's west entrance was 2.72 m below datum, while the floor of "Room 2" was only 1.45 m below datum.

Originally, both the west and north entrances to the South Corridor were given tapia thresholds. That changed when an L-shaped wall was added to create Room 4 (Figure 4.35). This new wall added 4.85 m to the length of the corridor, and the new entrance was given no threshold. Figure 4.54 provides a view down the east–west arm of the South Corridor, showing the relationship between the old and new entrances. The letter *a* indicates the south jamb of the old entrance; to its left can be seen the tapia threshold. The photograph also shows how this stretch of corridor rises (from 3.78 m below datum near the new entrance to 2.72 m below datum near the old entrance).

This concludes our tour of the southwest quadrant of Structure D. In Chapter 5, we continue on through the South Corridor and examine the southeast quadrant.

Figure 4.54. The later entrance to the east-west arm of the South Corridor, seen from the Southwest Canchón. The point marked *a* is the south jamb of the original entrance (see Figure 4.1). In order to create Room 4, the later occupants of Structure D built a new wall that added 4.85 m to the length of the South Corridor.

CHAPTER 5

Structure D:
The Southeast Quadrant

We now continue our tour of Structure D by passing through the South Corridor into "Room 2," the largest unit of the building's southeast quadrant. I have put quotation marks around "Room 2" because we eventually decided that it was an interior patio rather than a room. This was not clear when its walls first began to emerge, but became evident as excavation proceeded.

SHERDS LEFT IN THE SOUTH CORRIDOR

Figure 5.1 presents an artist's conception of the southeast quadrant of Structure D. It shows how the L-shaped South Corridor would have led residents single file from the Southwest Canchón into the Room 2 patio. Figure 5.2 displays both of the original entrances to the corridor. The entrance

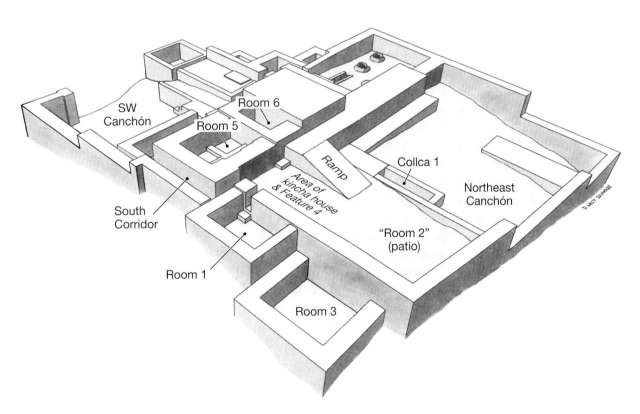

Figure 5.1. Artist's conception of the southeast quadrant of Structure D.

leading from Room 2 (Figure 5.2, top) had a raised threshold made from a large tapia block.

At some point—presumably late in the use of the South Corridor—someone left a large deposit of maize cobs on the floor of the corridor's east–west arm. One of the most interesting aspects of this mass of cobs is the lack of uniformity. Included are indurated, orange-kerneled maize, as well as the dark-kerneled variety called

Figure 5.2. The original entrances to the South Corridor. *(Top)*: The doorway from "Room 2" to the north–south arm of the corridor. *(Bottom)*: The original doorway from the Southwest Canchón to the east–west arm of the corridor; *(a)* marks the south jamb. Edgar Zavala sits at the point where the north–south and east–west arms converge.

maíz morado, used to make a beverage called *chicha morada*. This diversity strengthens our suspicion that maize was coming to Cerro Azul from several different localities, each growing its own race of maize. In the pile of maize cobs we also found burned willow branches (*Salix* sp.) that might represent fuel. We do not know why the cobs were left where we found them. We assume that the corridor would have been kept clean while Structure D was occupied, so it is likely that the cobs were dropped late in the building's history.

A small number of sherds were found in the mass of maize cobs and elsewhere on the floor of the South Corridor. Some of these sherds are illustrated in Figures 5.3 and 5.4, with the captions indicating which were found with the maize cobs and which were found elsewhere.

Sherds found with the pile of cobs are as follows:

Camacho Reddish Brown (Figure 5.3a, c, g)
　　Jar with everted rim: 1 rim
　　Jar with cambered rim: 1 rim (fire-blackened)
　　Cooking pots with restricted orifice and vertical strap handles: 2 rims (fire-blackened)
　　Body sherds: 2 (one fire-blackened)

Pingüino Buff (Figure 5.4b, d)
　　Jar neck sherds with human face modeled, painted: 2 (1 with ear; 1 with part of eye)
　　Body sherd from jar painted black and white: 1
　　Body sherd from jar showing birds painted in black and white: 1

Trambollo Burnished Brown (Figure 5.4e)
　　Hemispherical bowl rims: 2

Sherds found elsewhere in the South Corridor are as follows:

Camacho Reddish Brown (Figure 5.3b, d–f)
　　Large jar, beveled rim: 1 rim
　　Large jar, everted rim: 1 rim
　　Jar, cambered rim: 1 rim
　　Cooking pot with restricted orifice, vertical strap handle: 1 rim (fire-blackened)
　　Coarse base from jar: 1

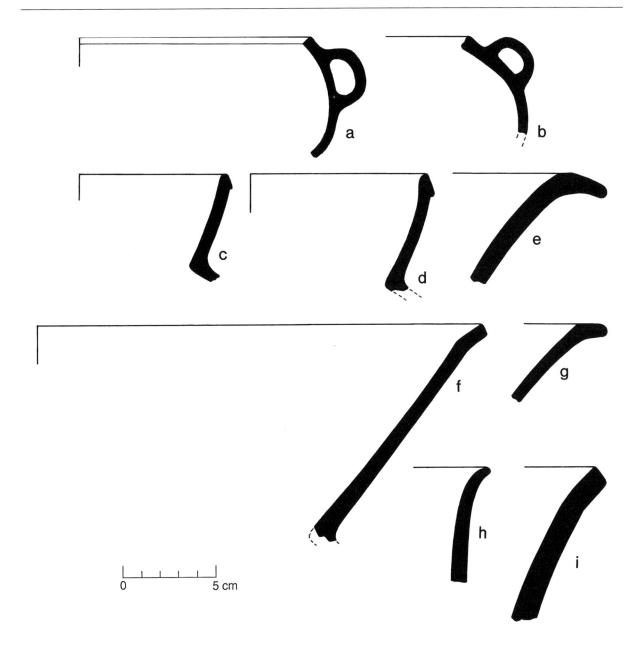

Figure 5.3. Ceramics from the floor of the South Corridor, Structure D. Sherds *a–g* are Camacho Reddish Brown. (*a, b*): cooking pots with restricted orifice and vertically set strap handles; (*c, d*): jars with cambered rims; (*e, g*): necks of large jars with everted rims; (*f*): neck of large jar with beveled rim. Sherds *h* and *i* are Camacho Black (standard variety). (*h*): amphora (?) with everted rim; (*i*): jar or amphora with beveled rim. (*a, c,* and *g* were found with a large pile of maize cobs.)

Camacho Black (Standard Variety) (Figure 5.3h–i)
  Jar or amphora neck sherds (1 beveled rim and 1 everted rim): 3

Pingüino Buff (Figure 5.4a, c)
  Jar funnel neck, human face with facial painting in black/white/red: 1 rim

Jar sherd, painted: 1 body sherd
Jar shoulder, plain: 1

Note that although these sherds presumably date to late in the history of Structure D, none would look out of place in the Late Intermediate. The collection includes none of the Late Horizon markers we found with Feature 4 (see below).

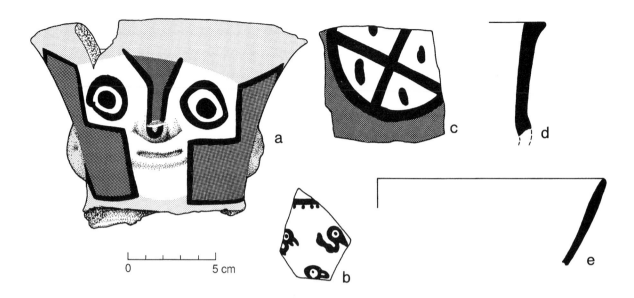

0   5 cm

Figure 5.4. Ceramics from the floor of the South Corridor, Structure D. Sherds *a–d* are Pingüino Buff. *(a)*: funnel neck from jar, painted black/white/red over natural buff. The facial paint resembles that used for figurines. The natural buff is 2.5 YR 6/6 (light red); the red paint is 7.5 R 3/6 (dark red). *(b)*: jar sherd with bird motif painted in black on white; *(c)*: jar body sherd painted in black/white/red (the red is 10 R 4/6); *(d)*: jar neck with painted and modeled human face; the eye has been pushed out from the inside. Sherd *e* is a Trambollo Burnished Brown hemispherical bowl. (*b*, *d*, and *e* were found with a large pile of maize cobs.)

Radiocarbon date

I submitted some of the carbonized willow branches found with the pile of maize cobs to the University of Wisconsin lab for dating. My expectation was that the cobs had been left in the corridor late in the building's history.

> WIS-1937 came out 520 ± 70 years B.P., or A.D. 1430 uncalibrated. The calibrated two-sigma range would be A.D. 1286–1612.

I note that while the uncalibrated date falls within one standard deviation of the Inka conquest of A.D. 1470, the calibrated two-sigma range is (as usual) too wide to provide a precise date for a specific event, such as the dropping of some maize cobs or the abandonment of Structure D.

"ROOM 2"

"Room 2" appears to be a private interior patio, flanked by two elite residential units (Rooms 1 and 3). We suspect that early in the history of Structure D, this complex of two rooms and a private patio was the living quarters of the compound's most important family (Figure 5.5). Unfortunately, as we will see below, earthquake damage later reduced the suitability of Rooms 1 and 2 for this purpose.

Before earthquake damage and erosion occurred, it appears that the Room 2 patio had been roughly 8.8 m wide north–south and 15.5 m long east–west. Some of its exterior walls were a meter or more in thickness. The patio had two superimposed clay floors, the uppermost of which (roughly 1.43–1.48 m below datum) was very badly eroded.

From Room 2, one could reach a series of smaller rooms to the west by means of a ramp, now badly eroded. The ramp had originally been about 6.16 m long east–west and 3.01 m wide north–south and was reinforced by *huarango* posts, some of which were round in cross section and others of which were square (Figure 5.5). It seems to take off from the uppermost floor of the patio, indicating that it dates to a later construction phase than the original patio floor. It rose to a height of about 84 cm below datum via four sloping tapia blocks.

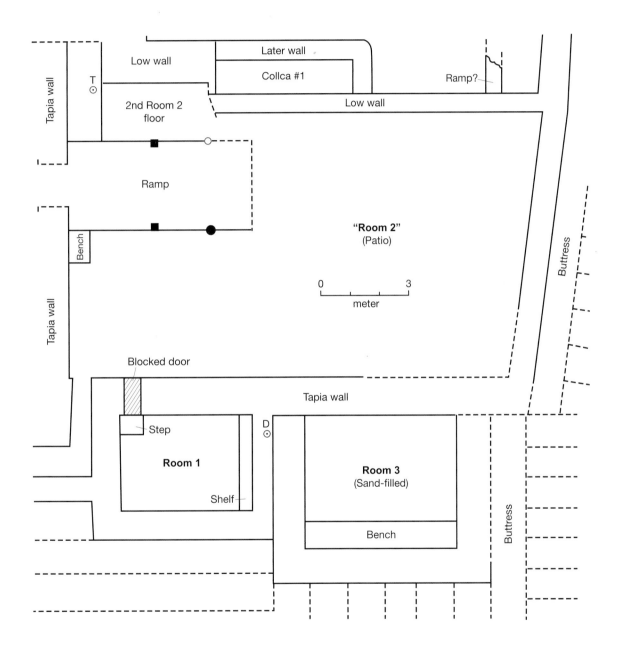

Figure 5.5. Plan of Rooms 1, 2, and 3 of Structure D.

While the ramp was accessible from the center of Room 2, it could also be reached by someone emerging from the South Corridor. Such a person could simply continue walking north from the corridor, step onto a tapia bench (1.08 m below datum) placed against the south wall of the ramp, and then step up to the top of the ramp.

Figures 5.6, 5.7, and 5.8 show the southern portion of Room 2, the bench, the ramp, and one of the square *huarango* posts in the north side of the ramp.

Figure 5.6. "Room 2" of Structure D, seen from the east. The Feature 4 midden has been removed, but several of the *huarango* posts (P) from the *kincha* structure associated with the midden remain (see also Figure 5.9).

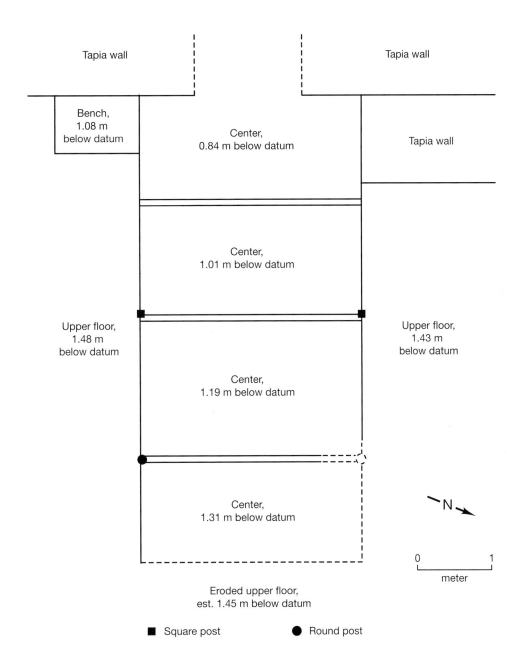

Figure 5.7. The ramp leading from "Room 2," Structure D, to the area of Room 6. The ramp was composed of four large tapia blocks which sloped down from 84 cm below datum to roughly 1.45 m below datum.

Figure 5.8. Two views of the ramp in "Room 2." *(Left)*: Alberto Barraza sweeps the floor of the Room 2 patio; his back is to the ramp. (Structure A can be seen in the background.) *(Right)*: A square wooden post set in the north side of the ramp. This ramp dates to the most recent construction phase of Structure D.

A radiocarbon date from the ramp

A piece of one of the *huarango* posts from the north side of the ramp was submitted to Beta Analytic for dating. My expectation for this post was that (as mentioned above) it would date to a later construction than the original floor of "Room 2."

> Beta-10916 came out 300 ± 60 years B.P. The calibrated two-sigma range would be A.D. 1447–1953. While A.D. 1447 would be an acceptable date, the calibrated two-sigma range is once again too wide to be very useful.

FEATURE 4

Because of the erosion suffered by both the upper and lower floors of the Room 2 patio, we found no sherds that we could confidently assign to that unit. Room 2 did, however, produce a post-occupation feature that was informative.

At some point after Structure D had ceased to function as an elite residential compound,

squatters had built a *kincha* house in the Room 2 patio. This wattle-and-daub house occupied the south half of the patio, that is, the area between the ramp and the entrance to the South Corridor (Figure 5.9). The construction involved a large number of small *huarango* posts, 13 of which could still be found in situ and others of which had eroded away with the patio floor. Figure 5.10 shows the way the floor had collapsed in places when the posts were driven through it. Judging by the fragments that had fallen to the patio floor, it appears that the walls of the "squatters' house" were of canes daubed with clay, while the roof was of matting made from *totora* or bulrushes (*Scirpus* sp.). The floor was a layer of fine greenish sand.

We do not know who the squatters were, but since their debris includes a local imitation of an Inka *aryballos*, it seems likely that the *kincha* house dates to the Late Horizon. The "squatters' house" eventually burned, scorching the tapia wall that formed the southern border of Room 2. This fire (and the associated roof collapse) evidently prevent-

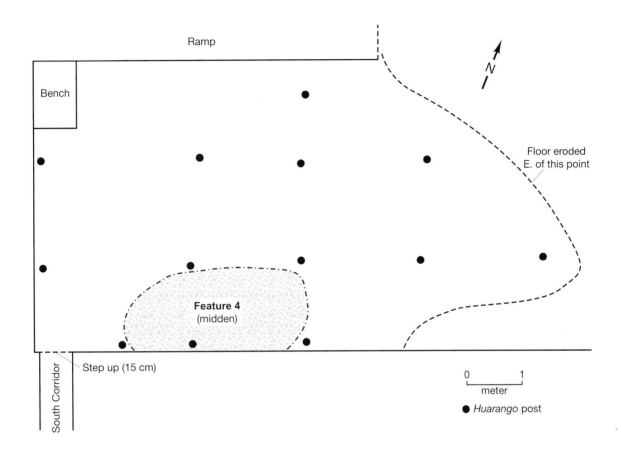

Figure 5.9. The southwest quadrant of "Room 2," Structure D, showing the Feature 4 midden and some 13 *huarango* posts from a possible Late Horizon *kincha* house associated with it.

ed the house's occupants from disposing of a pile of refuse left near the southern limit of the house. This refuse pile—essentially a midden 3 × 1.5 m in extent—was designated Feature 4 (Figure 5.9).

Since Feature 4 was one of our few Late Horizon proveniences, we screened it carefully. The various categories of material recovered will be reported in a future volume. Included in the ashy debris were fish bones, mollusk shells, complete dried anchovies, burned maize cobs, beans, lúcuma seeds, and a gourd bowl. In the nearby southwest corner of the house, we found spinning and weaving implements and the wooden arm of a small balance, the type sometimes used to weigh the portions of cotton or wool allocated to weavers. The variety of debris, in other words, suggests that the *kincha* house might have been occupied by a family (1) whose men were fishermen, (2) whose women were weavers, and (3) whose weavers received weighed amounts of cotton or

wool from an administrator of some kind. This range of activities and evidence of specialization would not be unusual for the Late Horizon.

As for the ceramics from Feature 4 (Figures 5.11–5.15), most are continuations of Late Intermediate types and vessel shapes. A few sherds, however, such as the aforementioned *aryballos* (Figure 5.15) and a unique effigy vessel (Figure 5.14d), suggest that the Feature 4 debris dates to the Late Horizon. The low frequency of sherds restricted to the Late Horizon does not surprise us, because we doubt that the Inka conquest of Huarco brought about an overnight change in ceramics.

The diagnostic sherds from Feature 4 are as follows:

Camacho Reddish Brown (Figures 5.11, 5.12)
 Hatun maccma: 1 rim (Figure 5.11d), 1
  shoulder

Figure 5.10. "Room 2" of Structure D seen from the west. In the foreground, one can see the dark circles left when the *huarango* posts of a later *kincha* structure broke through the original floor of this unit, which was actually an interior patio rather than a room. (Surviving posts are indicated by the letter "P.") Structure H can be seen in the distance.

Large storage jars, only slightly smaller than *hatun maccma*: 2 shoulders

Fire-blackened cooking pot with rim flange and restricted orifice: 1 rim (Figure 5.11g)

Fire-blackened cooking pot with bolstered rim and restricted orifice: 1 rim (Figure 5.12d)

Bowls with cambered rim: 5 rims (Figure 5.11o–q)

Jars with cambered rim: 8 rims (Figure 5.11h, k–m)

Jars with plain rim: 6 rims (Figure 5.11f, i–j)

Jars with everted rim: 4 rims (Figure 5.12a)

Jars with wide everted rim: 2 rims (Figure 11a, b)

Strap handles from jars: 5

Jars with rolled rim: 4 rims (Figure 5.12b, c)

Jar shoulder: 1

Jar with appliqué "nipples" on shoulder: 1 sherd (Figure 5.12e)

Conical base from amphora (or jar): 1 (Figure 5.11c)

Heavy, shallow "saucer" (possible pot stand or pot rest): 2 rim sherds (Figure 5.11e) (this vessel shape is unusual for the Late Intermediate and might have been more common in the Late Horizon)

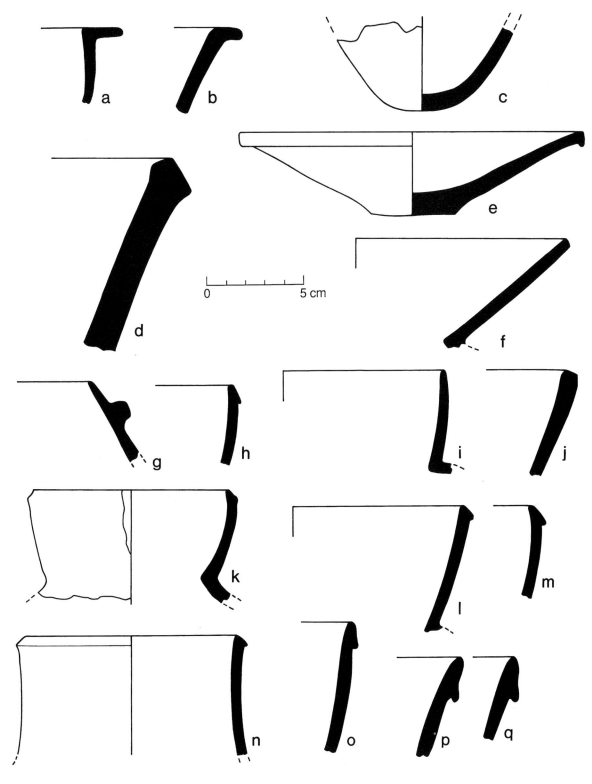

Figure 5.11. Camacho Reddish Brown vessels from Feature 4, Structure D. *(a, b)*: jars with wide everted rim; *(c)*: conical base from amphora; *(d)*: rim of *hatun maccma*; *(e)*: saucer-shaped vessel, possibly a pot rest; *(f)*: jar with plain rim, atypically burnished on the exterior; *(g)*: cooking pot with restricted orifice and rim flange; *(h, l, m)*: cambered rims from jars; *(i, j)*: jars with plain rims; *(k)*: small jar with slightly cambered rim; *(n)*: unusual jar neck with cambered rim; *(o–q)*: unusual cambered rims which, since they are burnished on the interior, might be from bowls rather than jars.

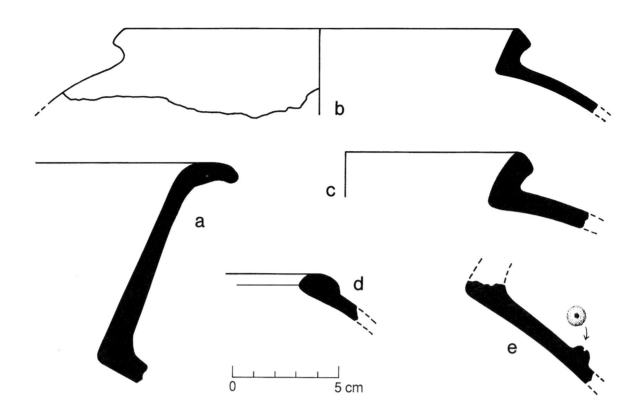

Figure 5.12. Camacho Reddish Brown vessels from Feature 4, Structure D. *(a)*: jar with everted rim; *(b, c)*: jars with rolled rims; *(d)*: cooking pot with restricted orifice and bolstered rim; *(e)*: jar shoulder with appliqué nipples placed 5 cm apart.

Camacho Black (Standard Variety) (Figure 5.13a–i)
> Refired rims from jars/amphorae: 2 (Figure 5.13b, c)
>
> Everted rims from jars or amphorae: 2 (Figure 5.13d, e)
>
> Neck from small amphora with loop handles: 1 (Figure 5.13a)
>
> Strap handle, jar or amphora: 1
>
> Tall jar neck with 2 loop handles from small amphora (?): 1
>
> Conical bases from standard amphorae: 2 (Figure 5.13i)
>
> Circular flat base from well-made amphora: 1 (Figure 5.13h)
>
> Jar or amphora necks with modeled human faces featuring "coffee-bean" eyes: 2 (Figure 5.13f, g)

Camacho Black (Highly Burnished Variety) (Figure 5.13j)
> Globular jar with restricted orifice and rolled rim: 1

Pingüino Buff (Figures 5.14, 5.15)
> Jar neck, traces of dark wash: 1
>
> Everted-rim fragment from jar: 1
>
> Fragment of strap handle from large jar, plain: 1
>
> Possible lug from jar shoulder: 1 (Figure 5.14b)
>
> Fragment of large jar with strap handle, painted black/white/red: 1 (Figure 5.14c)
>
> Fragment of jar neck, modeled (perhaps in the form of a human face): 1
>
> Jar shoulder, traces of white-on-natural paint: 1
>
> Painted body sherd from jar, too small to show design: 1
>
> Body sherd from a jar, traces of white paint: 1
>
> Body sherd from a jar, traces of white and red paint: 1
>
> Globular jar, painted black/white/red on exterior, black and white on interior of rim; strap handles: 1 rim (Figure 5.14a)

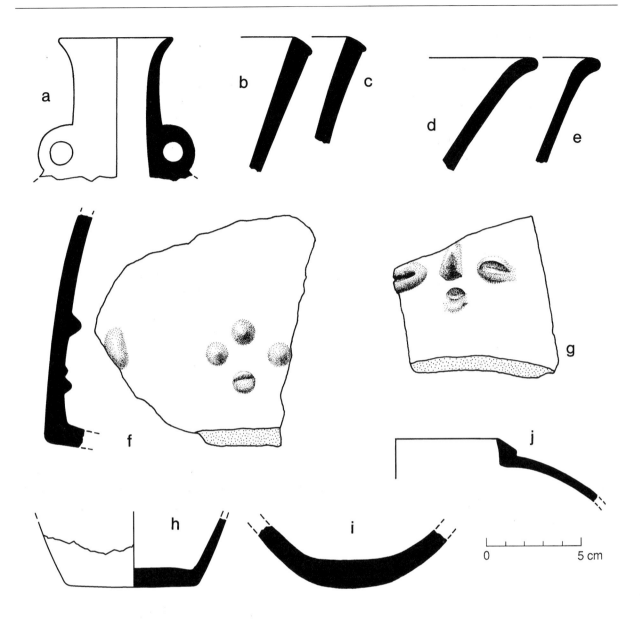

Figure 5.13. Ceramics from Feature 4, Structure D. Sherds *a–i* are Camacho Black (standard variety). *(a)*: tall neck from small amphora with two loop handles; *(b, c)*: refired rims from jars or amphorae; *(d, e)*: everted rims from jars or amphorae; *(f, g)*: modeled faces from the necks of jars or amphorae; *g* has "coffee-bean" eyes; *(h, i)*: bases from amphorae; *(j)*: Camacho Black (highly burnished variety) globular jar with rolled rim; a similar vessel was found in the upper fill of Room 5.

Locally made version of Inka *aryballos*, fragment: 1 (Figure 5.15)

Unique effigy (Figure 5.14d)
Burnished fragment of a hollow human figure that is incised, modeled, and painted black/white/red. Made on a paste with a black core and an oxidized buff layer near the surface, atypical for Pingüino Buff.

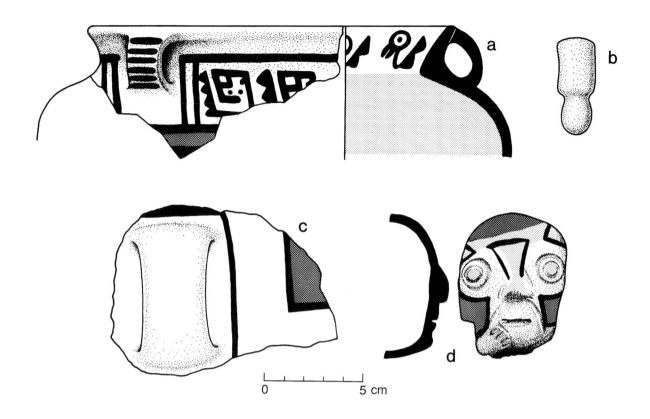

Figure 5.14. Pingüino Buff vessels from Feature 4, Structure D. *(a)*: globular jar with strap handles, painted black and white on the interior of the rim and black/white/red on the exterior; *(b)*: possible lug from a jar shoulder; *(c)*: sherd from large jar with strap handle, painted back/white/red; *(d)*: effigy head from unknown vessel, painted black/white/red over natural buff.

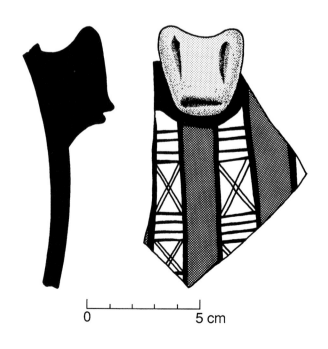

Figure 5.15. Sherd from a local imitation of an Inka *aryballos*, Feature 4, Structure D. The vessel is Pingüino Buff, painted black/white/red on natural buff. The white is 2.5 Y 8/4 (pale yellow); the red is 10 R 4/3 (weak red); the natural buff is 2.5 YR 6/6; and the black is more like a very dark brownish gray.

A radiocarbon date from Feature 4

One of the *huarango* posts from the *kincha* house associated with Feature 4 was submitted to Beta Analytic for dating. My expectation for this house was that it should date to very early in the Late Horizon, perhaps A.D. 1470–1490. At the same time, I knew that the *huarango* post might have been "borrowed," or reused from an earlier structure, rather than having been freshly cut and trimmed.

Beta-10918 came out 570 ± 80 years B.P. The calibrated two-sigma range would be A.D. 1273–1455. If one considers that the post may have been reused wood from an older structure, A.D. 1455 may not be far from the true date of the *kincha* house.

ROOM 1

As seen in Figure 5.1, both Room 1 and Room 3 lay adjacent to the Room 2 patio. Room 1 had originally been connected to the patio by a 64-cm-wide door with a sill and a step. Exactly how one would have entered Room 3 is less clear, owing to later erosion of its walls. We suspect that Room 3 would originally have been accessible from Room 1. If that is so, then Rooms 1 and 3 would have constituted a two-room residential apartment, with Room 3 the more private room and Room 1 providing access to the Room 2 patio.

Figure 5.16 shows how these rooms appeared before excavation. In the photograph, one can see that the wall separating Rooms 1 and 3 had been so broken down and eroded that one could no

Figure 5.16. The southeast corner of Structure D seen from the east, with Rooms 1 and 3 outlined but still unexcavated. Work is in progress on the South Corridor. This view shows some of the massive tapia buttresses that were added to the exterior of Structure D, presumably to stabilize it after an episode of seismic damage.

longer determine how the two rooms might have been connected.

Figure 5.17 gives the plan of Room 1 as we encountered it. The room measured 4.48 × 3.30 m, and its final floor lay 1.95 m below datum (before suffering earthquake damage). Because this floor was half a meter lower than the floor of the adjacent patio (Room 2), anyone entering Room 1 would have had to step down into it. As shown in Figure 5.17, a tapia step had been placed just inside the door to facilitate this; the surface of the step was 1.58 m below datum, just 37 cm above the final floor of the room.

At the east end of Room 1 was a bench 1.40 m below datum, 46 cm wide and running the length of the wall. Later damage had exposed enough of the construction in this area so that the following sequence of events could be inferred: (1) at one point the bench would have been high enough to serve as a shelf for the storage of important items, but (2) at a later point a new floor

was constructed at a higher level, leaving the bench only 55 cm above the floor and hence low enough to be a sleeping bench.

One of the most interesting features of Room 1 is the decoration of its north wall. As shown in Figures 5.18 and 5.19, the lower 90 cm of that wall had what appears to be a decorative arrangement of green adobe bricks (50 × 25 × 10 cm on average) set in tapia clay. The upper and lower rows of adobes present their short axes (22–28 cm), while the middle row present their long axes (50 cm). As Figure 5.19 shows, the green adobes continue behind our putative sleeping bench, suggesting that the bench had been a later addition rather than part of the original room. This wall features the only use of adobes in Structure D, leading me to suspect that their purpose was to decorate the room for an important family.

The sherds found in the fill above the floor of Room 1 are as follows:

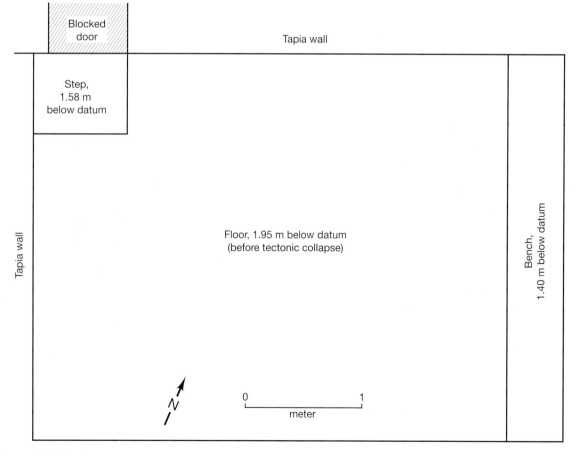

Figure 5.17. Plan of Room 1, Structure D, as it would have looked before the walls and floor were split by tectonic movement.

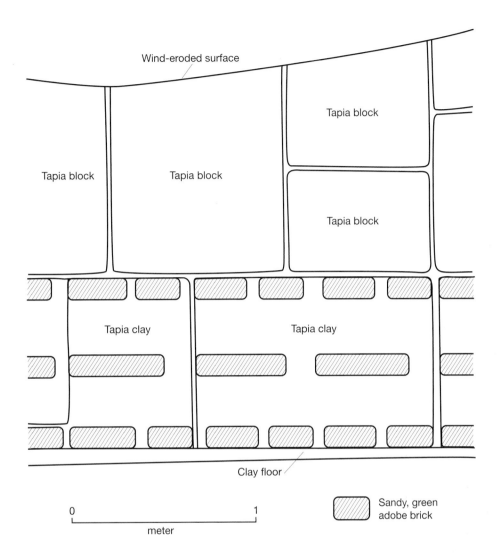

Figure 5.18. A portion of the north wall of Room 1, Structure D, showing the combination of adobe and tapia construction. The upper wall is composed of tapia blocks, like most rooms in the building. The lower 90 cm of the wall have what appear to be a decorative arrangement of green adobes set in tapia clay. The upper and lower rows of adobes show their short axes (22–28 cm), while the middle row show their long axes (50 cm).

Camacho Reddish Brown (Figure 5.20d–i)
    Large jars, slightly everted rims: 3
    Jar rim, grooved and everted: 1
    Jar shoulders: 2
    Cooking pot with restricted orifice: 12 rims
        (all fire-blackened)
    Cooking pot with horizontal strap handles:
        2 rim sherds
    Body sherds: 83 (25 are fire-blackened)

Camacho Black (Standard Variety)
    Jar shoulder sherds: 2

Camacho Black (Highly Burnished Variety) (Figure 5.20c)
    Hemispherical bowls, slightly cambered
        rims: 2
    Hemispherical bowls, body sherds: 2
    Jar shoulder (?): 1
    Other body sherds: 2

Pingüino Buff (Figure 5.20k–n)
    Jars, everted rims: 3
    Jar necks, painted black/white/red: 2
    Jar necks, plain: 2

Figure 5.19. Room 1 of Structure D, showing details of the adobes interdigitated with tapia blocks in the north wall.

Jar body sherds, painted black/white/red?: 5
Strap handle from jar: 1
Rim, possibly from bowl: 1 (burnished on
   interior)
Jar body sherds, plain: 15

Atypical Orange Variety of Pingüino Buff (Figure 5.20j)
These are superficially like Pingüino Buff but with coarser temper, like that of Camacho Reddish Brown
   Jar rim, everted: 1
   Jar shoulder: 1
   Jar body sherds: 3

Trambollo Burnished Brown (Figure 5.20a, b)
   Small hemispherical bowls: 1 rim, 2 body
      sherds
   Large shallow dishes: 8 rims, 6 body sherds

Unusual sherd: 1 (Figure 5.21)
   This unusual, possibly early sherd was
   found on the floor of Room 1. It is from
   the base of a hemispherical bowl, made on a
   paste similar to Trambollo Burnished
   Brown, and with a similar orange-brown
   surface. Unlike Trambollo Burnished
   Brown, however, it is very neatly painted on
   the interior in black and white, in a style

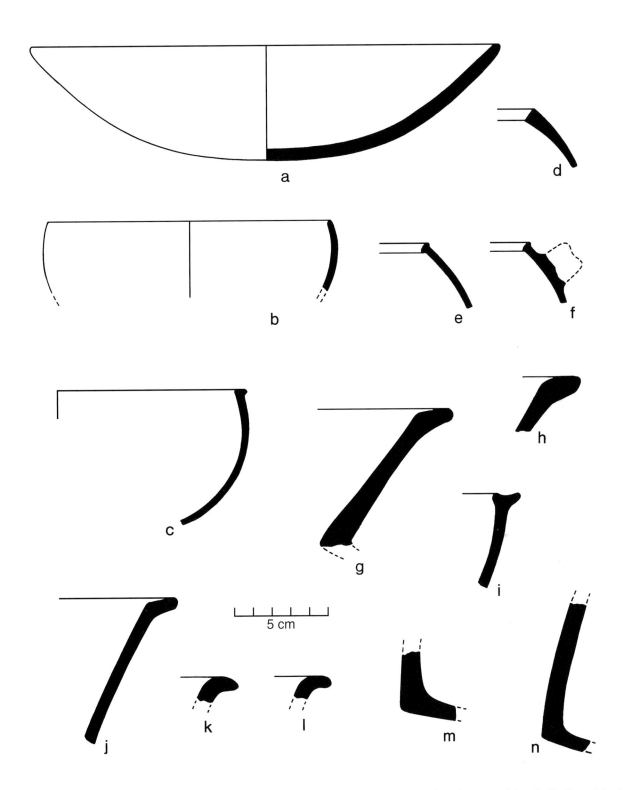

Figure 5.20. Sherds from the fill above the floor of Room 1, Structure D. Sherds *a, b* are Trambollo Burnished Brown. *(a)*: large shallow dish, reconstructed from 14 sherds. The pattern of wear suggests that this dish was used as the pot stand or pot rest for a round-bottomed jar (?) that was turned constantly, rubbing the upper 4 cm of the dish all while leaving the inner base unworn. *(b)*: small hemispherical bowl; *(c)*: Camacho Black (highly burnished variety) hemispherical bowl with slightly cambered rim. Sherds *d–i* are Camacho Reddish Brown. *(d–f)*: rims of cooking pots with restricted orifice, some fire-blackened; *f* had strap handles; *(g, h)*: slightly everted rims from large jars (rim diameters would have been close to 50 cm); *(i)*: grooved and everted jar rim; *(j)*: jar with everted rim, atypical orange variety of Pingüino Buff. The surface color ranges from 2.5 YR 6/8 to 2.5 YR 6/4. Sherds *k–n* are Pingüino Buff. *(k, l)*: everted rims from jars; *(m, n)*: jar necks.

reminiscent of the earliest ceramics from our deepest levels in the quebradas of Cerro Camacho (see Figure 3.19, Chapter 3).

It may be that the architects who originally laid out Room 1 felt that its isolated location—at the southeast extreme of Structure D—would provide its elite occupants with privacy.

Unfortunately, it also left the room more vulnerable to earthquake damage than would have been the case had they placed it closer to the center of the building. Figures 5.22 and 5.23 show what happened when an earthquake finally struck. Figure 5.22 shows a long, irregular crack running east–west through Room 1, splitting the floor, the step in front of the door, and the sleeping bench

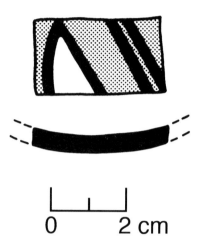

Figure 5.21. Rare sherd from the fill above the floor of Room 1, Structure D. The sherd is from a hemispherical bowl with a design painted on the interior of the base in black and white over natural burnished brown. The draftsmanship is neat, which is characteristic of pottery from the deepest levels of our quebrada excavations. The white is virtually pure white; the natural brown is 2.5 YR 5/6.

Figure 5.22. Room 1 of Structure D had been so damaged by an earthquake that its doorway was blocked off, and its function was changed from elite residence to dried fish storage. Note the massive crack running from the door step (*bottom*) to the sleeping bench or shelf (*top*). The white arrow points north.

Figure 5.23. Two views of seismic damage to Room 1, Structure D. *(Left)*: We see how a massive crack split the sleeping bench or shelf into north *(a)* and south *(b)* halves and dropped the latter into a depression. *(Right)*: We see how the door step *(c)* broke off the threshold, dropped with a section of the floor, and broke in two. The doorway was later blocked with tapia *(d)*.

or shelf along the east wall; the northern part of the floor then dropped 25–30 cm. Figure 5.23 shows in detail how the sleeping bench (*a*, *b*) and door step (*c*) were split in half. At this point, Room 1 became unsuitable for occupancy by an elite family. Its door was blocked with tapia (Figures 5.17, 5.23d), and it was filled with sand and converted to a fish storage room.

ROOM 3

Room 3, immediately adjacent to Room 1, had also suffered earthquake damage. As the photograph on the left in Figure 5.23 shows, the massive crack that destroyed Room 1 extended through the intervening wall and into Room 3, obliterating any evidence of a door between the two rooms.

Room 3 measured 5.20 × 4.45 m and, like Room 1, it had been converted from elite residential quarters to fish storage after being severely damaged. Figure 5.24 shows two stages in the ex-

cavation of Room 3. On the left, we see the thick layer of sand added to the room late in its history. We passed this sand through three sizes of screen in order to recover any remaining traces of fish. Eventually, at depths ranging from 3.69 m to 3.79 m below datum, we reached what was left of the original floor, now badly deteriorated (Figure 5.24, right). We estimate that in its damaged condition, Room 3 might have accommodated roughly 69 m^3 of sand and fish.

As Figure 5.24 (right) shows, Room 3 had a 25-cm-high tapia sleeping bench along its east wall, reminiscent of the bench in Room 1. However, Room 3 lacked the decorative use of green adobes seen in Room 1.

Just above the floor of Room 3, we encountered a 25-cm layer of daub chunks with cane impressions. No *kincha* structure was found in the room, however; rather, the daub chunks appear to have been laid on the floor just to the level of the sleeping bench, providing a level surface on which to dump the first layer of sand.

Figure 5.24. Two stages in the excavation of Room 3, Structure D. *(Left)*: The southeast corner of the room, excavated to the level of the layer of sand used for storage of dried fish (Cirilo Cruz serves as scale). *(Right)*: The same corner, after the removal of the sand (Alberto Barraza as scale). Fragments of the original floor and a sleeping bench are visible. Room 3 had originally been residential in function, but was converted to fish storage after suffering seismic damage.

Suspecting that some of the sherds in this *kincha* layer might have come from the original floor, we treated them as a collection in their own right, separate from and stratigraphically below the sand. This collection of sherds, coming from a depth of roughly 3.45–3.70 m below datum, is as follows:

Camacho Reddish Brown (Figure 5.25)
  Hatun maccma, rim sherd: 1 (Figure 5.25h)
  Amphora neck with face modeled on it: 1
    (has "coffee-bean" eyes) (Figure 5.25a)
  Everted rim from large jar: 1 (Figure 5.25b)
  Strap handle (discolored) from large jar or
    amphora: 1
  Jar shoulders: 4
  Cambered rims from jars: 3 (Figure 5.25c, d)
  Cooking pots with restricted orifice: 3 rims
    (Figure 5.25e–g)

Strap handle from rim of cooking pot: 1
Body sherds: 6

Camacho Black (Highly Burnished Variety) (Figure 5.26h–o)
  Small jars or amphorae, cambered rims: 5
    (Figure 5.26j)
  Small jars, shoulder sherds: 2
  Small jars, basal sherds: 2
  Small jars, body sherds: 8
  Hemispherical bowls, plain rims: 4 (Figure
    5.26h, i)
  Small bowls, cambered rims: 4 (Figure
    5.26k, l)
  Incurved rim bowls with horizontally set
    loop handles: 3 sherds (Figure
    5.26m–o)
  Small bowl body sherds: 8

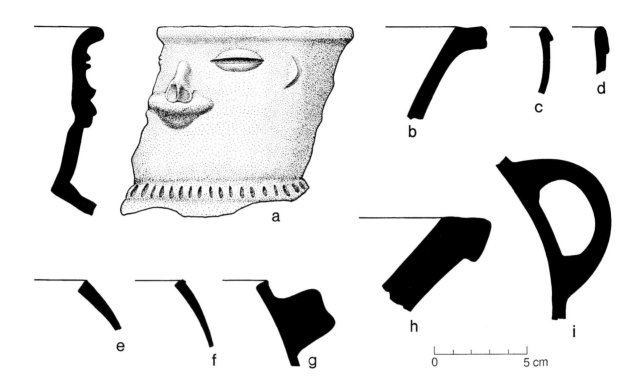

Figure 5.25. Camacho Reddish Brown vessels from the *kincha* fill above the original floor of Room 3, Structure D. *(a)*: amphora neck with modeled face on it, featuring "coffee-bean" eyes and a necklace of vertical slashes; *(b)*: everted rim from large jar; *(c, d)*: jars with cambered rims; *(e–g)*: rims from cooking pots with restricted orifice; *g* has a horizontally set strap handle; *(h)*: rim of *hatun maccma*; *(i)*: strap handle from large jar or amphora.

Pingüino Buff (Figures 5.27, 5.28)
  Jar neck with modeled face, painted black/white/red: 1 (Figure 5.27)
  Globular jars with wide mouth, painted black/white/red on interior of rim, black and white on exterior: 2 (one with a strap handle) (Figure 5.28b)
  Large globular jars painted black and white in zoned bands on the exterior: 4 sherds (Figure 5.28a)
  Body sherds of large globular jars, painted black/white/red: 30 (Figure 5.28d)
  Body sherds of large globular jars, plain: 15
  Strap handle of large globular jar: 1 (Figure 5.28c)
  Miniature loop handle: 1

Trambollo Burnished Brown (Figure 5.26a–g)
  Hemispherical bowls: 9 rims (Figure 5.26c–e)

Small bowls: 10 incurved rims (Figure 5.2a, b)
Bowl body sherds: 6
Small jar: 1 cambered rim (Figure 5.26f)
Tall spout or jar neck with strap handle: 1 (Figure 5.26g)
Small jars: 2 shoulder sherds, 5 body sherds

Unusual items
  Very thin bowl painted white outside: 1 body sherd
  Tiny sherd with geometric incising, atypical: 1 (Figure 5.26p)

Let me now make a few observations on this collection of ceramics, which lay stratigraphically below the sand fill of Room 3. To be sure, it is possible that some of these sherds were introduced into the room with the chunks of daub. However, it is equally possible that some of these

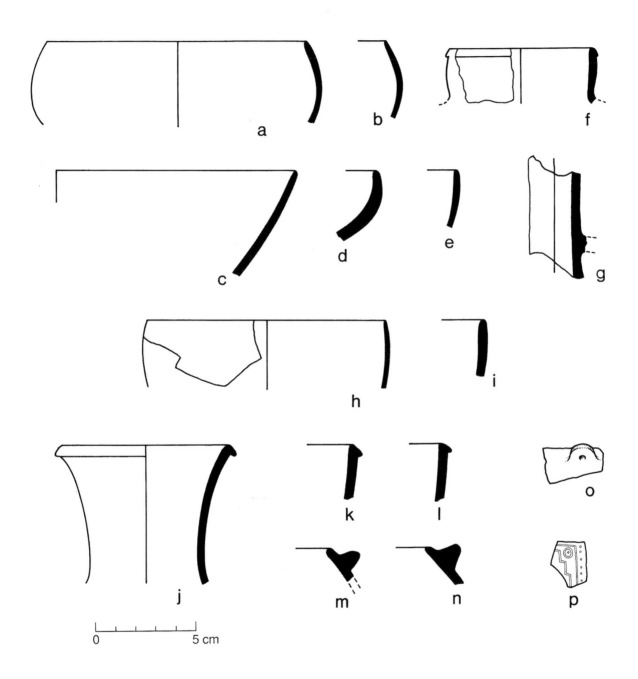

Figure 5.26. Ceramics from the *kincha* fill above the original floor of Room 3, Structure D. *(a–g)*: Trambollo Burnished Brown. *(a, b)*: small bowls with incurved rims; *(c–e)*: hemispherical bowls; *(f)*: small jar with cambered rim; *(g)*: fragment of tall spout or jar neck with strap handle. Sherds *h–o* are Camacho Black (highly burnished variety). *(h)*: hemispherical bowl with "graphite" finish; *(i)*: hemispherical bowl with atypically pinkish paste; *(j)*: neck of small amphora; *(k, l)*: bowls with cambered rims; *(m, n)*: bowls with incurved rims and horizontally set loop handles; *(o)*: side view of *n*; *(p)*: unusual incised sherd, type unknown.

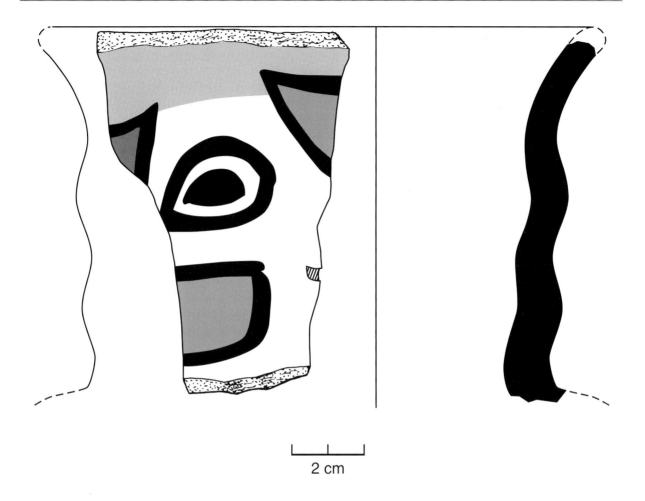

2 cm

Figure 5.27. Pingüino Buff jar neck with human face painted in black/white/red over natural buff or reddish brown (shown as light screen). Found in the *kincha* layer above the original floor of Room 3, Structure D. Some facial features have been modeled in relief, and the mouth has been cut out.

ceramics were present on the floor of the room when its function was still residential and were simply left there when it was decided that the room was to be filled with sand.

Several aspects of the collection reinforce the latter possibility. (1) First of all, there is almost no utilitarian cooking or storage ware present. There are only 21 sherds of Camacho Reddish Brown, and no sherds at all of the standard variety of Camacho Black. (2) Camacho Black is represented only by its highly burnished variety, which is present in unusually high numbers (36 sherds). Such high numbers are usually associated with elite refuse or elite burials. (3) The collection is dominated by Pingüino Buff (53 sherds). (4) The number of Trambollo Burnished Brown sherds

(33) is unusually high for a collection this size. We associate high frequencies of small Trambollo jars and hemispherical/incurved-rim bowls with the serving of individual meals for elite individuals, while lower-status individuals were more likely to use gourd vessels.

In other words, if I were asked to predict what the ceramic assemblage from an elite residential unit might look like, this collection from just above the floor of Room 3 would fit my prediction: lots of painted Pingüino Buff, lots of individual serving vessels in Trambollo Burnished Brown, lots of small vessels in the highly burnished ("graphite") variety of Camacho Black, and very few jars and cooking pots in Camacho Reddish Brown.

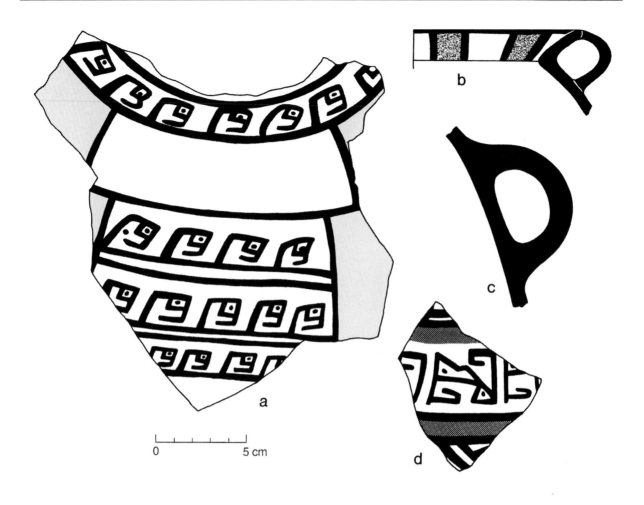

0   5 cm

Figure 5.28. Pingüino Buff vessels from the *kincha* layer above the original floor of Room 3, Structure D. *(a)*: portion of jar, painted on the exterior in black and white on natural, with some areas of natural buff given a weak red wash. The white is 5 YR 8/4 (pink); the red wash is 10 R 5/6 (red); the natural buff is 2.5 YR 5/4 (reddish brown). *(b)*: rim of globular jar with wide mouth and strap handle, painted black/white/red on the rim and black and white on the exterior; *(c)*: strap handle from large jar; traces of white paint on exterior. *(d)*: jar sherd with painted design in black/white/red in horizontal bands. The red is 10 R 4/3 (weak red).

The sand fill of Room 3

Stratigraphically above the *kincha* layer covering the floor of Room 3 was a thick deposit of sand with occasional fish bones. It is clear that this layer of sand had resulted from the conversion of the room to a fish storage unit.

A modest number of sherds were recovered from the sand layer (Figures 5.29, 5.30). The source of these sherds is unknown. We doubt that any of them would have been added to the sand deliberately. Some may have entered the room accidentally when dried fish were being added to or removed from storage. The diagnostic sherds are as follows:

Camacho Reddish Brown (Figure 5.29h–n)
    Slightly everted rims from large jars: 3
        (Figure 5.29h–j)
    Large jar shoulder: 1
    Strap handle from large jar: 1 (Figure 5.29l)
    Cambered rim from medium-size jar: 1
        (Figure 5.29k)
    Cooking pot with restricted orifice: 1 rim
        (Figure 5.29m)

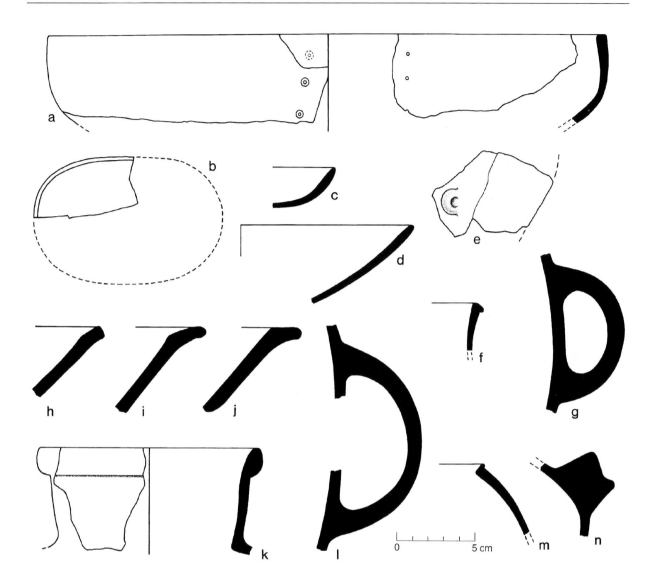

Figure 5.29. Ceramics from various levels of the upper fill in Room 3, Structure D. *(a)*: unusual Camacho Black bowl (highly burnished variety) with drill holes covered with blobs of resin, found in upper fill. Sherds *b–d* are Trambollo Burnished Brown bowls from sand fill above floor. *(b, c)*: plan and cross section of oval bowl; *(d)*: shallow open bowl. Sherds *e–g* are Camacho Black vessels from sand fill above floor. *(e)*: fragments of small amphora with loop handle (highly burnished variety); *(f)*: cambered rim of small jar (highly burnished variety); *(g)*: strap handle from large amphora (?) (standard variety). Sherds *h–n* are Camacho Reddish Brown vessels from sand fill above floor. *(h–j)*: slightly everted jar rims; *(k)*: jar with cambered rim; *(l)*: strap handle from large jar; *(m)*: restricted orifice of cooking pot; *(n)*: horizontally set strap handle. All these ceramics would have entered the room after it was converted to fish storage.

Strap handle from cooking pot like that listed above: 1 (fire-blackened) (Figure 5.29n)

Camacho Black (Standard Variety) (Figure 5.29g)
Strap handle from large amphora (?), strangely vitrified surface: 1

Camacho Black (Highly Burnished Variety) (Figure 5.29e, f)
Jar neck with cambered rim, small: 1 (Figure 5.29f)
Jar neck sherd: 1
Small amphora with loop handle: 2 body sherds (Figure 5.29e)

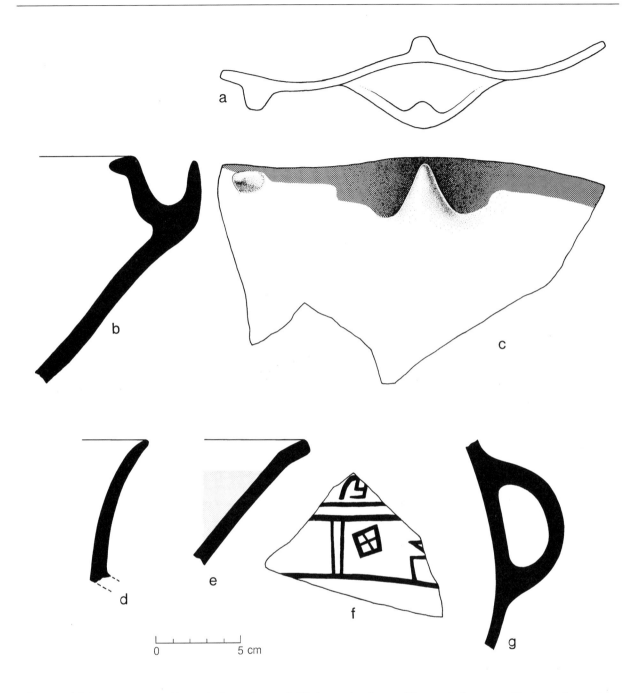

Figure 5.30. Pingüino Buff vessels from the sand fill above the floor of Room 3, Structure D. *(a–c)*: three views of unique bowl with eccentric rim, two lugs, and an appendage shaped like a turtle's tail; *(d)*: funnel neck from jar with white wash or paint on exterior; *(e)*: slightly everted rim from large jar, painted white on natural on interior and exterior; *(f)*: jar body sherd, painted black on natural; *(g)*: strap handle from large jar; traces of white paint on natural buff. All these ceramics would have entered the room after it was converted to fish storage.

Pingüino Buff (Figure 5.30)
    Funnel neck from jar, white wash or paint
        on exterior: 1 (Figure 5.30d)
    Slightly everted rim, large jar, band of white

paint at rim on interior and exterior: 1
    (Figure 5.30e)
Strap handle from large jar, painted white
    on natural: 1 (Figure 5.30g)

Jar body sherds, painted black on natural: 2
   (Figure 5.30f)
Unique vessel (presumably a bowl) with an eccentric rim that makes it kidney-shaped; has a handle like a turtle's tail, and 2 lugs like spikes, 1 on interior, 1 on exterior; given a red wash on interior, and on the exterior of the rim: 2 sherds (Figure 5.30a–c)

Trambollo Burnished Brown (Figure 5.29b–d)
   Hemispherical bowl, oval in plan: 1
   Shallow, subhemispherical open bowl: 1

The upper fill of Room 3

The sand layer in Room 3 was not the uppermost stratigraphic unit found. Above the sand was a layer of fine, soft room fill, mainly the weathering product of tapia. This upper fill had entered the room after it ceased to be used for fish storage. We kept the sherds from this layer of upper fill separate for purposes of analysis, since they were the last to enter Room 3. The diagnostic sherds are as follows:

Camacho Reddish Brown
   Cooking pots with restricted orifice: 2 rims
      (1 fire-blackened)
   Large jars, plain or slightly everted rims: 2 rims
   Large jar with cambered rim: 1 rim

Camacho Black (Highly Burnished Variety) (Figure 5.29a)
   One unique vessel with "graphite" appearance: a bowl, oval in plan, hemispherical in section, with 3 drill holes in it, either for suspension or repair; the holes are larger on the exterior, smaller on the interior, and covered with blobs of resin on the exterior

Pingüino Buff
   Small jar shoulders, painted black and white: 2
   Strap handle, painted white: 1
   Large jars, plain rims: 2
   Jar neck sherd, painted and modeled (probably part of a face or neck): 1

Trambollo Burnished Brown
   Hemispherical bowl rim: 1
   Bowl body sherd: 1

I have described the internal stratigraphy of Room 3 in detail because it illustrates the changes in room function that could occur during the course of occupation. Room 3 was originally part of an elite residential apartment. Later, after suffering damage, it was converted to fish storage. Finally, it was abandoned and left to fill up with disintegrated tapia.

ROOM 5

As Figure 5.1 shows, the ramp in the Room 2 patio leads west to what would once have been the highest rooms in Structure D. Ironically, because of the way wind erosion at Cerro Azul operates, there were few standing walls left in this area. The ocean wind and salt fog had reduced the building's uppermost walls to tapia powder, which then flowed downslope to cover and protect many of the lower walls.

Figure 5.31 shows this central point of the building. Rooms 5 and 6 could be mapped, but had been eroded down almost to their floors. It is likely that the area marked "earthen floor," just north of Room 6, was part of a third room whose walls had completely eroded away prior to our arrival.

The history of Rooms 5 and 6 was the reverse of that documented for Rooms 1 and 3. Whereas Rooms 1 and 3 had been converted from residential to storage, Rooms 5 and 6 appear to have been converted from storage to residential. Perhaps because of their central location within Structure D, they do not appear to have suffered earthquake damage. In fact, given their convenient proximity to the ramp leading from Room 2, it is even possible that Rooms 5 and 6 may have been remodeled to accommodate the former residents of Rooms 1 and 3.

Room 5 measured approximately 5.23 × 3.6 m and had no doorway, making it likely that it had originally been designed for storage. On two later occasions, however, it was given what appear to be sleeping benches or platforms.

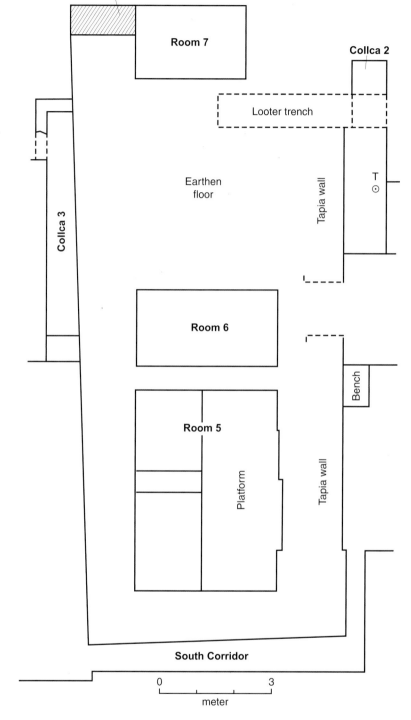

Figure 5.31. Plan of Rooms 5, 6, and 7 of Structure D. The dot marked with a "T" is the place where the alidade was set up.

Figures 5.32 and 5.33 show the earliest and latest stages of Room 5. In Figure 5.32, we see that it was divided into a number of storage cells by an east–west crosswall. To the north of the crosswall was an early floor, 1.44 m below datum. In the northeast corner of that floor was a small bench (1.02 m below datum) which may have served as a step by which the room could be entered from above. To the south of the crosswall was an early floor (1.58 m below datum) and a storage bench or shelf of almost equal size, 1.34 m below datum.

At a later stage, a tapia platform was built along the east wall of the room (Figure 5.31), and

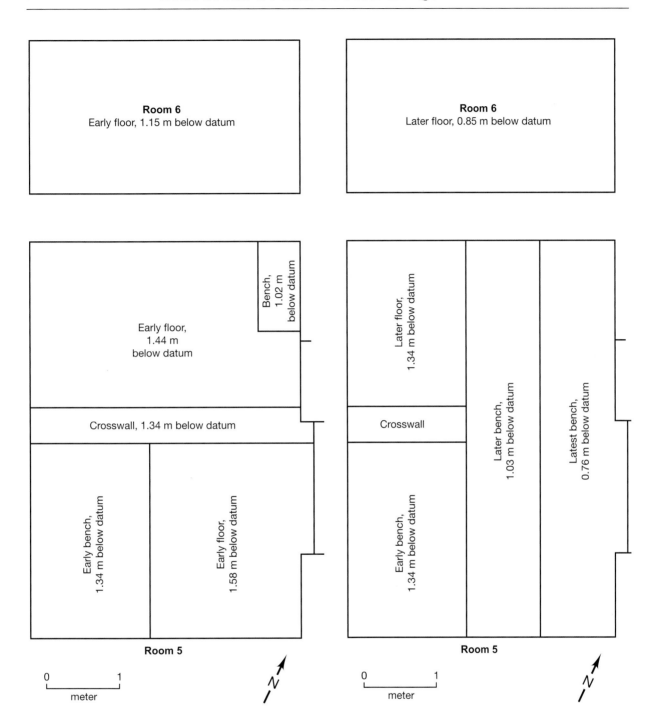

Figure 5.32. Rooms 5 and 6 of Structure D as they might have looked early in the history of the building.

Figure 5.33. Rooms 5 and 6 of Structure D as they might have looked late in the history of the building. In the case of Room 5, the early bench is a survival from the first stage of construction. The later bench filled the eastern half of the room during a later stage of construction; the latest bench was superimposed on the latter during the final stage of construction.

a high floor (1.34 m below datum) was built in the northwest quadrant. The platform essentially incorporated the former bench in the northeast corner of the room. We believe that at this point, the room had been converted to a residential unit.

Finally, as shown in Figure 5.33, Room 5 was modified again. A new bench, half the size of the platform, was built along the east wall, some 76 cm below datum. This gave the room a long, narrow floor at 1.34 m below datum; a "later" sleeping bench at 1.03 m below datum; and a "latest" sleeping bench at 0.76 m below datum. The photograph in Figure 5.34 shows the eroded remnants of the "early," "later," and "latest" stages of Room 5. By observing the workman sitting on the

latest bench, one can estimate how many occupants could have slept comfortably in the room.

Room 5 did not yield many ceramics, but we kept the sherds from each stage of construction separate. Let us begin with the seven sherds trapped in the fill between the "early" floor and the "later" floor in the west half of the room. They are as follows:

Camacho Reddish Brown (Figure 5.35c)
    Plain rim from jar: 1
    Slightly everted rim from jar: 1
    Jar body sherd: 1
    Restorable cooking pot with 2 strap handles: 1

Figure 5.34. Rooms 5 and 6 of Structure D, seen from the north, showing their later configuration (refer to Figure 5.33 for details). Edgar Zavala squats on the "Latest bench" of Room 5 (0.76 m below datum).

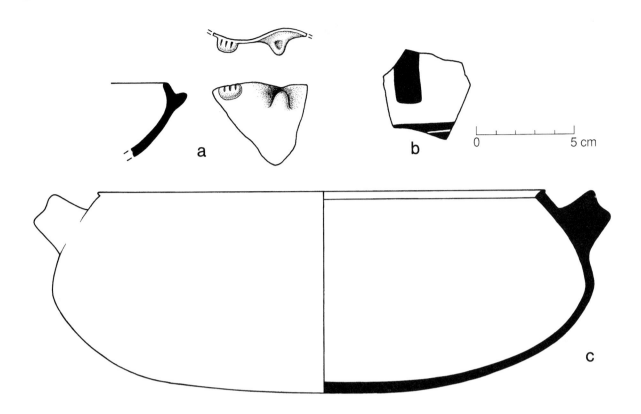

Figure 5.35. Ceramics found between the "early" and "late" floors of Room 5, Structure D. This collection antedates the sleeping bench. *(a)*: three views of Trambollo Burnished Brown sherd from a small bowl with a "turtle tail" lug and a "turtle foot" rim eccentricity; *(b)*: Pingüino Buff jar sherd, painted black on natural; *(c)*: Camacho Reddish Brown cooking pot with restricted orifice and two horizontally set strap handles, reconstructed from 50 to 60 fragments. The lower third of the exterior is fire-blackened.

Pingüino Buff (Figure 5.35b)
Body sherds from small jars, painted black on natural: 2

Trambollo Burnished Brown (Figure 5.35a)
Miniature version of the "turtle tail" vessel found in Room 3: 1

It is interesting that the fill trapped between the "early" and "late" floors contained a "turtle tail" vessel, reminiscent of the one found in the sand fill of Room 3 (see Figure 5.30a–c). This suggests that the conversion of Room 5 to a residential unit may have occurred broadly contemporaneously with the conversion of Room 3 to a fish storage unit. Thus, the possibility that the former occupants of Room 3 were moved to Room 5 cannot be ruled out on chronological grounds.

Next, let us look at the 12 sherds resting on the "later" sleeping bench on the east side of Room 5 (Figure 5.34). These sherds, some of which appear in Figure 5.36, are as follows:

Camacho Reddish Brown
Jar body sherds: 2

Camacho Black (Standard Variety) (Figure 5.36b)
Beveled rim from jar or amphora: 1
Body sherds, probably from jars: 3

Camacho Black (Highly Burnished Variety) (Figure 5.36a)
Small incurved-rim bowl: 1 rim

Pingüino Buff
Jar shoulder, traces of white paint: 1

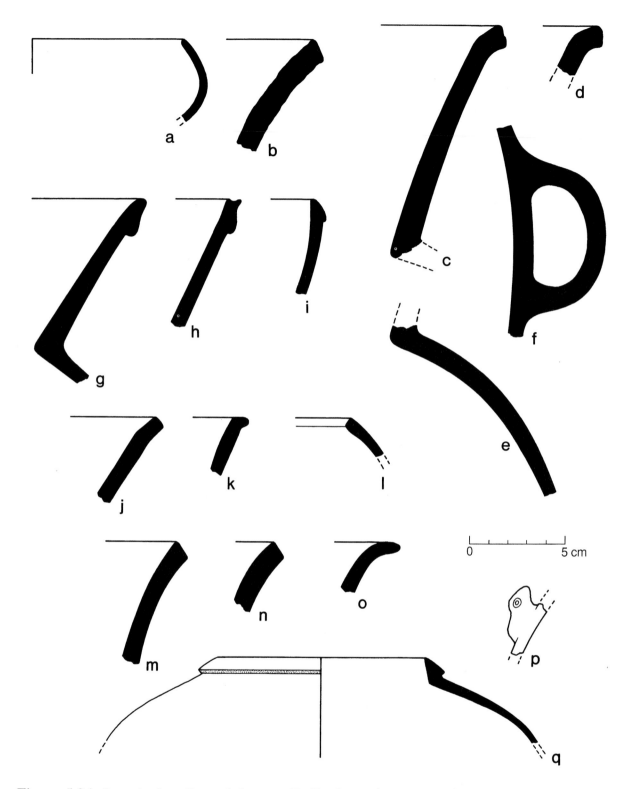

Figure 5.36. Ceramics from Room 5, Structure D. Sherds *a* and *b* are Camacho Black sherds, found on the "later" sleeping bench on the east side of the room. *(a)*: small incurved-rim bowl (highly burnished); *(b)*: beveled rim of jar or amphora (standard variety). Sherds *c–q* are from the room's upper fill; *c–f* are Pingüino Buff. *(c, d)*: jars with everted rims; *(e)*: jar shoulder with traces of white paint; *(f)*: strap handle from large jar. Sherds *g–l* are Camacho Reddish Brown. *(g–i)*: cambered rims from jars; *(j, k)*: slightly everted rims from jars; *(l)*: cooking pot with restricted orifice. Sherds *m–p* are all Camacho Black (standard variety). *(m, n)*: beveled rims from jars or amphorae; *(o)*: everted rim from jar; *(p)*: animal effigy lug from amphora; *(q)*: Camacho Black (highly burnished variety) globular jar with rolled rim and "graphite" surface finish.

Jar body sherd with traces of white paint: 1
Body sherd from jar with simple modeled
    lug: 2

Trambollo Burnished Brown
Body sherd from a bowl: 1

Finally, let us look at the ceramics found in the upper fill of Room 5, stratigraphically above the "latest" sleeping bench shown in Figure 5.34. Only diagnostic sherds were recorded from this overlying fill. They are as follows:

Camacho Reddish Brown (Figure 5.36g–l)
Jars with cambered rim: 12 rims (half are
    from 1 vessel)
Jars with slightly everted rims: 3 rims
Cooking pots with restricted orifice: 1 (fire-
    blackened)

Camacho Black (Standard Variety) (Figure 5.36m–p)
Jars or amphorae with beveled rim: 2 rims
Jar with everted rim: 1
Animal effigy lug from amphora: 1

Camacho Black (Highly Burnished Variety) (Figure 5.36q)
Globular jar with tightly rolled rim: 2 rims
Jar body sherds, almost certainly from glob-
    ular jars like those above: 13
Other body sherds: 3

Pingüino Buff (Figure 5.36c–f)
Jars with everted rims: 4 rims (one is white-
    painted)
Strap handle from large jar: 1
Jar shoulder with white paint: 1

Trambollo Burnished Brown
Bowl body sherd: 1

It is worth noting that this collection from the uppermost fill of Room 5 contains a highly burnished Camacho Black globular jar with a tightly rolled rim, not unlike one found in the Feature 4 midden (see Figure 5.13j). I consider Feature 4 a likely Late Horizon component and believe that the globular jar with a tightly rolled rim in highly burnished Camacho Black may be a relatively late vessel form. Thus it is possible that Room 5 was abandoned sometime around the transition from Late Intermediate to Late Horizon—perhaps as a result of the Inka conquest of Huarco—and gradually filled with debris after that.

ROOM 6

Room 6 lay adjacent to Room 5 (Figure 5.31) and was probably related to the latter during most of its history. Like Room 5, it had no door. While Room 6 did not undergo the complex remodeling of Room 5, it did present us with a succession of two floors.

Originally, Room 6 measured 3.68 × 2.06 m and had a clay floor 1.15 m below datum (Figure 5.32). Later in its history, fill was added to Room 6, and it was given a higher floor at 85 cm below datum (Figures 5.33 and 5.34).

The fill between the lower and upper floors of Room 6 contained hundreds of chunks of cane-impressed daub from *kincha* houses. This deposit reminded us of the *kincha* chunks used to level the floor of Room 3 before it was filled with sand. There were sherds in the *kincha* fill between the upper and lower floors, which we hoped would shed some light on the date of the *kincha* house remains used as fill. The total sherd collection is as follows:

Camacho Reddish Brown (Figure 5.37a, b)
Jar with cambered rim: 1 rim
Jar shoulders: 3
Small strap handle (of the type usually
    found on cooking pots with restricted
    orifice): 1
Chipped and ground disk made on body
    sherd: 1 (diameter 6.5 cm)
Body sherds: 8 (several brushed)

Camacho Black (Standard Variety)
Jar body sherd: 1

Pingüino Buff (Figure 5.37d–f)
Small jar with rolled rim, burnished lightly
    over thin reddish wash: 1

Body sherds from globular jar, painted
    black and white on natural: 2
Body sherds from jar, painted black on exterior;
    white "Life Savers" painted over the black: 4
Plain body sherds: 8

Atypical Orange Variety of Pingüino Buff (Figure 5.37c)
    Slightly everted rim from jar, white paint
        inside: 1

Body sherd: 1

I conclude that the *kincha* chunks used as fill between Floors 1 and 2 came from a relatively early house. Included was a Pingüino Buff sherd with the "Life Saver" motif, reminiscent of those from deep stratigraphic levels in the quebradas of Cerro Camacho (see Figure 3.20, Chapter 3).

This concludes our tour of the southeast quadrant of Structure D.

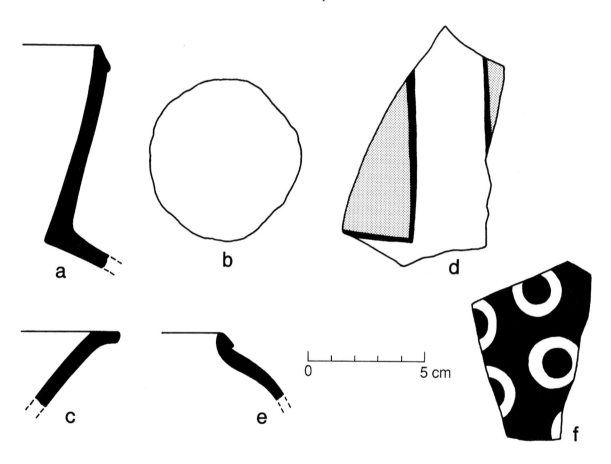

Figure 5.37. Ceramics found in the *kincha* fill between the lower and upper floors of Room 6, Structure D. Sherds *a, b* are Camacho Reddish Brown. *(a)*: jar with cambered rim; *(b)*: chipped and ground sherd disk. *(c)*: slightly everted rim from jar, atypical orange variety of Pingüino Buff. Sherds *d–f* are standard Pingüino Buff. *(d)*: jar body sherd, painted black and white over natural buff; *(e)*: small jar with rolled rim; *(f)*: jar body sherd, painted with the "Life Saver" motif in black and white.

CHAPTER 6

Structure D:
The Northeast Quadrant

In this chapter we continue our tour of Structure D by moving to the northeast quadrant. Figure 6.1 presents an artist's conception of that part of the building. Most of the northeast quadrant was taken up by the Northeast Canchón, a large walled area for outdoor activities.

Since there were no doorways in the walls surrounding this canchón, it would have been accessible only from the interior of the building. One possible entry would have been via a raised area just north of the "Room 2" ramp. This raised area would have provided access to a long, L-shaped bench which ran along the west wall of the Northeast Canchón. This bench was of a height appropriate for sitting and could have accommodated many individuals.

COLLCA 1

A tapia wall formed the southern border of the Northeast Canchón, separating it from the "Room 2" patio. A storage cell, designated Collca 1, had been created by adding an L-shaped tapia wall to the south wall of the canchón, as shown in Figure 6.1. Collca 1 could have been filled either from "Room 2" or from the Northeast Canchón.

Collca 1 measured 4.71 × 1.31 m (Figure 6.2). It was 1.05 m deep and had been given a smooth clay floor at a depth of 2.78 m below datum. Its storage capacity is estimated to have been about 6.48 m³. Figure 6.3 gives two views of this storage cell after all its contents had been removed.

We saw no evidence that Collca 1 had ever been used to store foodstuffs or fish. There was evidence for craft activity in the Northeast Canchón, and it is possible that Collca 1 served to store raw materials and artifacts for such activity. By the time we found the collca, however, it had long since been filled with what appeared to be debris from general housecleaning. To be sure, that debris includes a lot of remains from craft activity: spindles and spindle whorls, a weaving shuttle and other weaving implements, leftover cotton and camelid wool, textile fragments, and pieces of embroidered cloth. However, there are also other artifacts, such as a damaged crayfish trap, and fragmentary fishing nets of three different mesh sizes. Among the collca's other contents are a broken gourd vessel, sections of *caña brava* (*Gynerium* sp.), a small pottery figurine wearing a cloth skirt; fish spines and mollusk shells, maize cobs; and seeds of *Lucuma* sp.

There were also sherds in Collca 1, and although they were certainly not in primary context, they tend to be large sherds—the type one might pick up by hand and toss into a collca to get them out of the way. We found almost none of the tiny sherds that might have resulted from sweeping. The sherd collection from Collca 1 is as follows:

Camacho Reddish Brown (Figures 6.4a, c–g, 6.5b, c)
  Jar with cambered rim: 1 rim
  Jar with very simple plain rim and appliqué nipples on shoulder: 1 rim

169

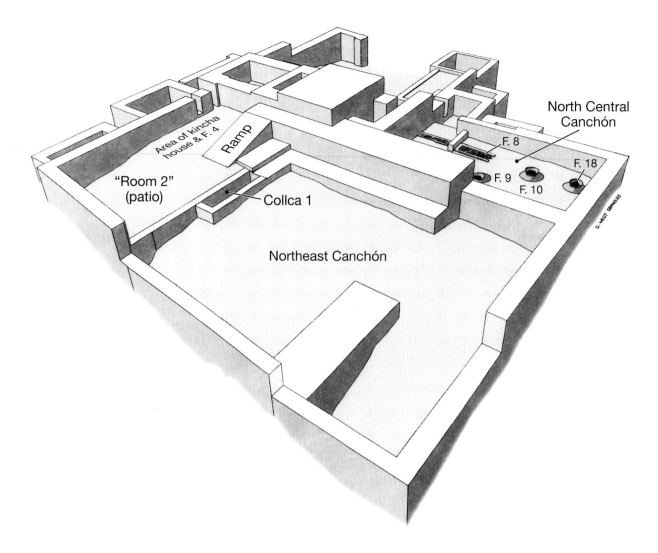

Figure 6.1. Artist's conception of the northeast quadrant of Structure D.

Jar rims, slightly flaring: 2 (fire-smudged)
Strap handle from jar: 1 (fire-smudged)
Hatun maccma rim sherd: 1
Cooking pots with restricted orifice and
    slightly bolstered rims: 2 (fire-blackened)
Unusual tall, teardrop-shaped cooking pot:
    1 (fire-blackened)

*Camacho Black (Standard Variety) (Figures 6.4h,
6.5g)*
    Beveled rim from large jar or amphora: 1
    Strap handle from small jar or amphora: 1

*Camacho Black (Highly Burnished Variety) (Figure
6.4i)*
    Miniature jar, body sherds: 2
    Fragment of miniature jar with loop handle: 1

Pingüino Buff (Figures 6.4b, 6.5a, d–f, h, j–k)
    Jar rim, plain: 1
    Jar with slightly everted rim (funnel neck?):
        1 rim
    Tiny loop handle from miniature vessel: 1
    Jar shoulders with band of black-and-white
        painted design: 2
    Large jar, body sherds: 2
    Large effigy appendage: 1
    Atypical tall bottle neck, with cross-hatched
        triangle motif on top of everted rim in
        black and white over a possible red
        wash. The neck is burnished in a
        streaky way (reminiscent of Trambollo
        Burnished Brown), and there is white
        paint at the juncture between neck and
        body: 1

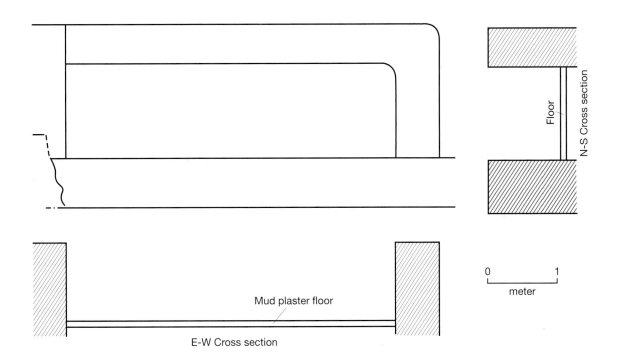

Figure 6.2. Plan and cross sections of Collca 1, a storage cell built between "Room 2" and the Northeast Canchón of Structure D. Its storage capacity was 6.48 m³.

Figure 6.3. Two views of Collca 1, Structure D. *(Left)*: César Francia squats in the east end, his back facing the L-shaped wall that was added to create this storage cell. *(Right)*: César squats in the west end, with his back against the north wall of "Room 2."

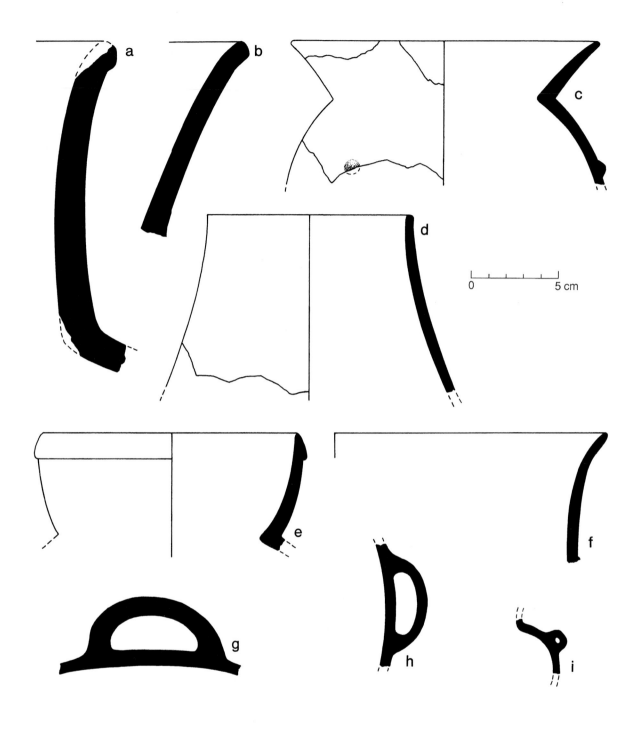

Figure 6.4. Ceramics from Collca 1, Structure D. Sherds *a* and *c–g* are Camacho Reddish Brown. *(a)*: rim of *hatun maccma*; *(c)*: jar with plain rim and appliqué nipples on shoulder; *(d)*: unusual tall, teardrop-shaped cooking pot (fire-blackened on exterior); *(e)*: jar with cambered rim; *(f)*: jar neck with slightly flaring rim; *(g)*: horizontally set strap handle from large jar. Sherd *b* is the plain rim from a large Pingüino Buff jar. *(h)*: vertically set strap handle from standard variety of Camacho Black jar or amphora; *(i)*: fragment of miniature jar with loop handle, highly burnished variety of Camacho Black.

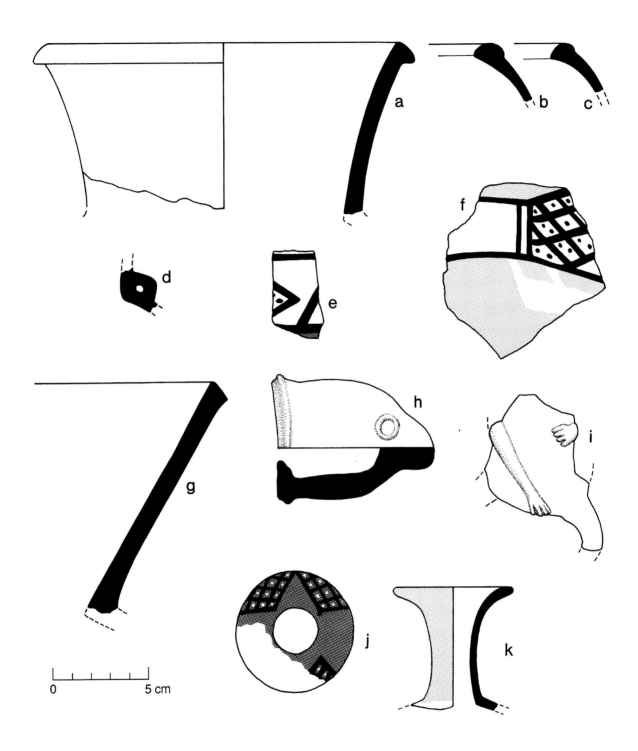

Figure 6.5. Ceramics from Collca 1, Structure D. Sherds *a, d–f, h,* and *j–k* are Pingüino Buff. *(a)*: discolored jar neck with bolstered or slightly everted rim; *(d)*: tiny loop handle from miniature vessel; *(e)*: jar shoulder sherd with band of black-and-white design, bordered with red; *(f)*: jar shoulder sherd with band of black-and-white design, and additional areas of white paint on natural buff; *(h)*: large hollow effigy appendage; *(j)*: top view of black/white/red painting on the rim of *k*, an atypical tall narrow bottle neck with white paint on the shoulder. *(b, c)*: Camacho Reddish Brown cooking pots with restricted orifice and slightly bolstered rim. *(g)*: beveled rim from large jar or amphora in standard variety of Camacho Black; *(i)*: hollow effigy done with reddish brown clay.

Atypical Orange Variety of Pingüino (paste is like Camacho Reddish Brown)
> Jar shoulder: 1

Effigy (Figure 6.5i)
> Hollow effigy of human (?) figure: 1 fragment (paste is somewhat like Camacho Reddish Brown)

All in all, the ceramics from Collca 1 appear to be a typical Late Intermediate collection. The only specimen that looks somewhat out of place—possibly a survival from earlier times or an import from another valley—is the atypical tall painted bottle neck shown in Figure 6.5j–k.

THE NORTHEAST CANCHÓN

The Northeast Canchón is the largest walled area within Structure D. Its north–south dimension is roughly 20.3 m, and its east–west dimension varies from 14.37 m (in the south) to 17.50 m (in the north). Because it functioned as an outdoor work area, no attempt had been made to give it a uniformly level floor, such as a room might have. Its floor varies from 2.68 m to 2.98 m below datum along the west wall, but slopes down to 3.43 m below datum near the center of the canchón. It descends even farther as it runs north and east from the center, reaching a low of 6.33 m below datum in the extreme northeast corner.

As shown in Figure 6.1, the Northeast Canchón appears to have been divided by a thick tapia bench or work platform extending in from its east wall. However, this bench is so eroded that its full length could not be traced. The floor of the canchón is also badly eroded, especially in the north and east. This erosion made it difficult to detect features in the floor, which affected our interpretation of activities in the canchón.

Both in the Northeast Canchón and in Collca 1, we found evidence for at least two activities—spinning and weaving. Spindles, spindle whorls, textile fragments, and weaving implements were among the evidence. There were also traces of post molds, possibly where posts had been set to which backstrap looms had been tied. Unfortunately, owing to the erosion of the floor, this evidence must be considered suggestive rather than conclusive.

The erosion of the floor also reduced our sample of sherds from good contexts. We were largely limited to sherds found in ash-filled hollows in the surviving patches of intact floor, mainly in the northwest corner of the canchón. The following collection of sherds comes from those ash-filled hollows:

Camacho Reddish Brown (Figure 6.6)
> Jar with cambered rim: 1
> Sherd from jar shoulder: 1
> Fragment of atypical jar, made on Camacho Reddish Brown paste, but painted black/white/red with a "school of fish" motif and a modeled human arm: 1 (usually such a pot would be on Pingüino Buff paste)

Camacho Black (Standard Variety) (Figure 6.7)
> Rim of large jar, plain rim: 1
> Rim of amphora, everted rim: 1
> Small amphora with loop handle: 1

Camacho Black (Highly Burnished Variety)
> Body sherd from bowl: 1

Pingüino Buff (Figure 6.8)
> Large jar, plain rim: 1
> Jar with rolled rim: 1
> Jar neck, everted rim, painted black and red, the design probably part of a face with the usual facial paint: 1
> Jar body sherd with black-on-white geometric motif (triangle filled with dots, inside a rectangular box), set off by burnished buff: 1

This sample (which is unfortunately our best from the Northeast Canchón) seems to reflect an ordinary Late Intermediate work area; it shows little in the way of ceramics that might be associated with elite individuals.

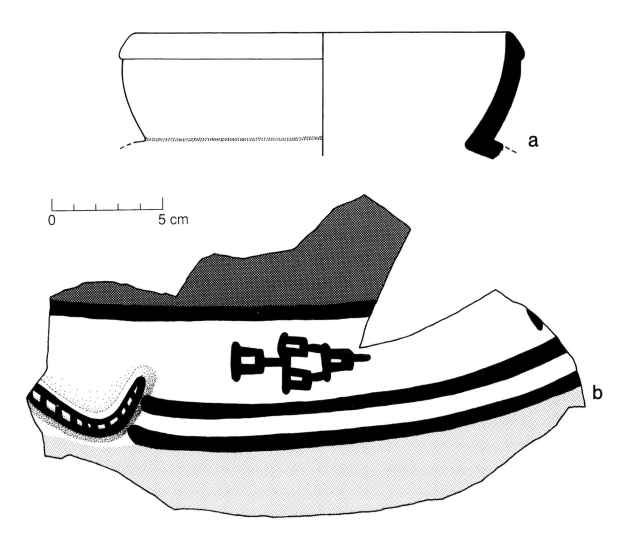

Figure 6.6. Ceramics from ash-filled hollows in the northwest corner of the floor, Northeast Canchón, Structure D. *(a)*: Camacho Reddish Brown jar neck with cambered rim. *(b)*: portion of large jar with painted design in black/white/red. This jar was atypical in having Camacho Reddish Brown (rather than Pingüino Buff) paste. The natural surface is 2.5 YR 5/4 (reddish brown). The red paint is 10 R 3/4 (dusky red).

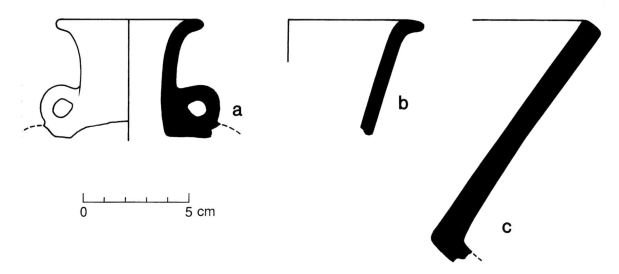

Figure 6.7. Camacho Black (standard variety) vessels from ash-filled hollows in the northwest corner of the floor, Northeast Canchón, Structure D. *(a)*: small amphora with loop handles; *(b)*: everted rim from amphora; *(c)*: plain rim from large jar.

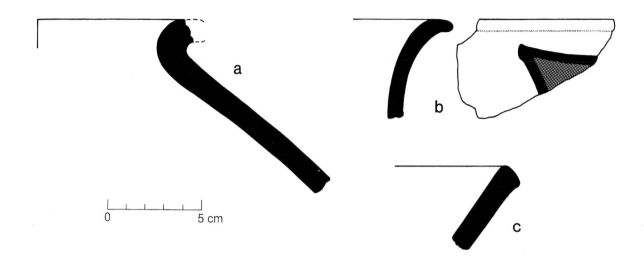

0　　　　　　　5 cm

Figure 6.8. Pingüino Buff vessels from ash-filled hollows in the northwest corner of the floor, Northeast Canchón, Structure D. *(a)*: jar neck with rolled rim; *(b)*: jar neck with everted rim, painted in black and red on natural; the red is 10 R 4/4 (weak red); the design was probably a human face with facial paint; *(c)*: plain rim from large jar.

THE LATER FILL IN THE NORTHEAST CANCHÓN

After the Northeast Canchón fell into disuse, it began slowly to fill with the decomposition products of tapia walls. Additional Late Intermediate sherds turned up in this fill from time to time. For example, the following three sherds were found in the upper 20 cm of the fill:

Camacho Black (Standard Variety) (Figure 6.9a)
　　Amphora or jar neck with modeled human
　　face, coffee-bean eyes and mouth: 1

Pingüino Buff
　　Small jar with a zoned band of black-on-

red decoration, apparently the "flock of birds" motif: 1 body sherd (Figure 6.9b)
Jar body sherd, painted black and white
　　over a buff surface that has been given
　　a reddish wash: 1 (Figure 6.10)

Finally, an unusual Pingüino Buff sherd (shown in Figure 6.11) was found on the surface of the Northeast Canchón fill, after sweeping but before excavation began.

Pingüino Buff
　　Rim from a hemispherical bowl with a like-
　　ly rim diameter of 16 cm, bearing on its
　　interior a screen pattern with black
　　lines over a red wash (10 R 4/6), with
　　white dots in the screen: 1

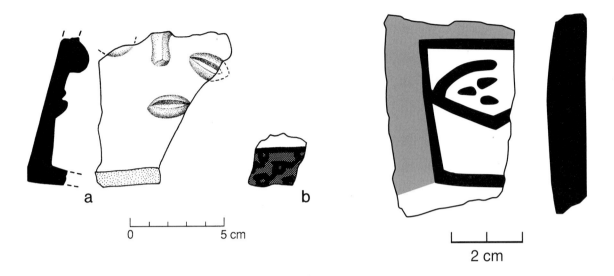

Figure 6.9. Sherds from a depth of 0–20 cm in the Northeast Canchón, Structure D. *(a)*: neck from Camacho Black jar or amphora (standard variety) with human face modeled on it; the eye is "coffee-bean" type; *(b)*: small Pingüino Buff jar body sherd with motif painted in black over a red wash.

Figure 6.10. Pingüino Buff jar body sherd, painted black and white over a natural buff that has been given a reddish wash (shown in gray). Found in the fill of the Northeast Canchón, Structure D.

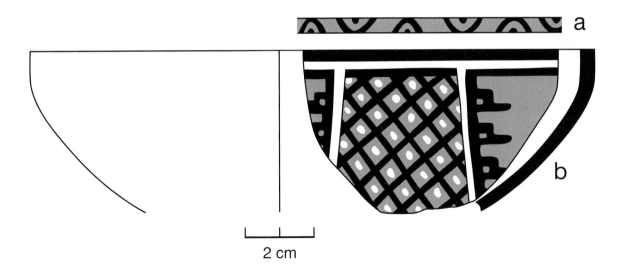

Figure 6.11. Fragment of unusual, probably nonlocal hemispherical bowl, found on the surface of the fill in the Northeast Canchón, Structure D. This bowl has been painted in black and white over a natural reddish brown surface (shown in gray). Both surfaces had been lightly burnished, and the interior surface had been made slightly redder by the addition of a red wash prior to burnishing. *(a)*: the top of the rim; *(b)*: the wall.

SUMMARY

The northeast quadrant does not provide as much detailed information as the other quadrants of Structure D. It does, however, tell us where a lot of the women's activities were carried out. Among the activities conducted in the Northeast Canchón were spinning, weaving (probably on backstrap looms), and embroidery. The Northeast Canchón was an open-air venue where there would have been abundant sunlight for these activities, and at the same time, it was far enough into the interior of the building that elite women would have had both protection and privacy.

CHAPTER 7

Structure D:
The Northwest Quadrant

Our tour of Structure D concludes with the northwest quadrant, a three-dimensional view of which can be seen in Figure 7.1. Our evidence suggests that that quadrant had once been dominated by two canchones, only one of which had survived to be excavated. The survivor was the North Central Canchón, an apparent kitchen/brewery that contributed some of our most interesting data.

The second canchón, about which we have only minimal information, is the Northwest Canchón. Its outer tapia walls had been essentially destroyed by time and nature, so eroded that we cannot even give the canchón's original dimensions. We found enough patches of clay floor to suggest that two small adjacent rooms (Rooms 9/10 and 12) were later additions; the preexisting surface of the Northwest Canchón had served as their floor.

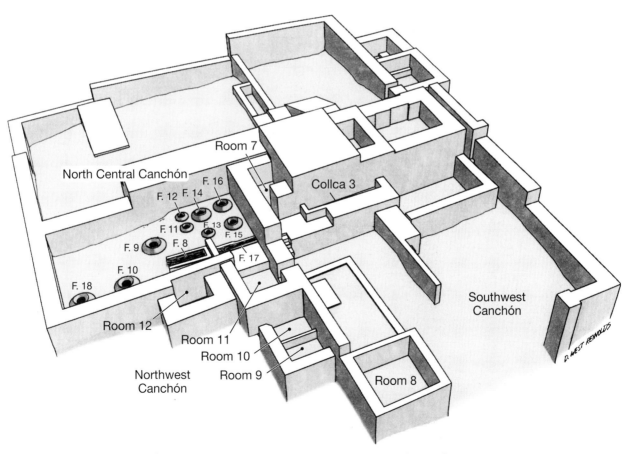

Figure 7.1. Artist's conception of the northwest quadrant of Structure D.

179

We assigned two other rooms to the north-west quadrant. The placement of Room 11 suggests that it might have been a pantry or store-room for the North Central Canchón. One could have entered this room from the Southwest Canchón via a doorway, later blocked with tapia (see Figure 4.16, Chapter 4). From Room 11, one could reach the southern part of the North Central Canchón through a gap in its west wall (Figure 7.2).

The final room assigned to this quadrant is Room 7. It appears to have been a storage room, originally reached from the Southwest Canchón via a small stairway and a narrow corridor, both of which were later blocked with tapia (Figure 4.13, Chapter 4).

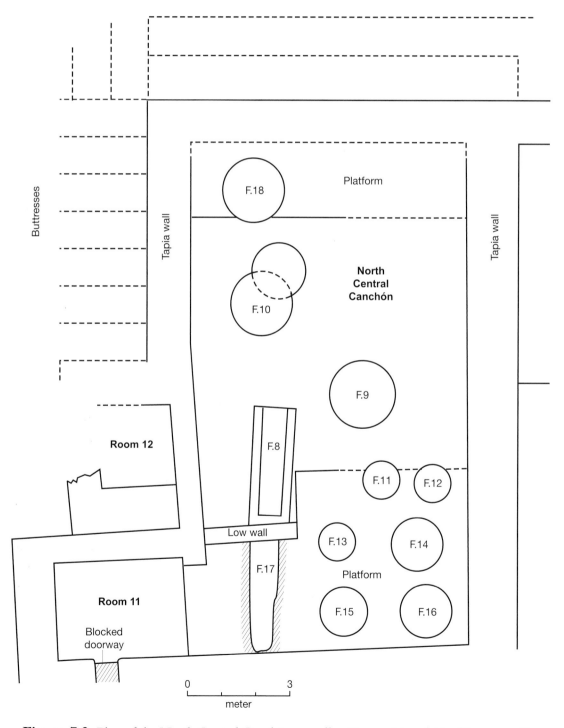

Figure 7.2. Plan of the North Central Canchón as well as Rooms 11 and 12 of Structure D.

THE NORTH CENTRAL CANCHÓN

The North Central Canchón measures roughly 14 × 7.8 m (Figure 7.2). The depth of its irregular floor runs from roughly 3.14 m to 3.40 m below datum. At the south end of the canchón we found a raised work platform, 2.70 m below datum. At the north end of the canchón was a smaller work platform that may once have been 2.80 m below datum; it was unfortunately too eroded for an accurate measurement.

The North Central Canchón had a very high density of features. Included were two hearth trenches (Features 8 and 17) and the cavities left by at least nine storage vessels that had been set in the floor (Features 9–16 and 18). In addition to these cavities, there were at least half a dozen impressions in the floor made by the round bases of smaller pots (Figure 7.3).

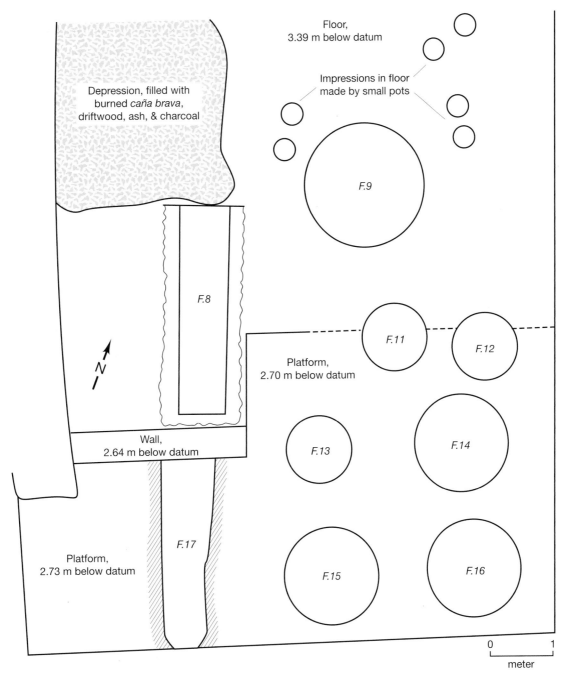

Figure 7.3. The south half of the North Central Canchón, Structure D, showing the location of Features 8, 9, and 11–17.

Feature 8

Let us begin with the hearth trenches. Feature 8 was the best made and appears to have been one of the original features in the canchón. Its interior dimensions are 2.98 m in length and 0.7 m wide, and its depth is 2.64 to 3.14 m below datum (Figure 7.4). Its walls had been constructed of tapia chunks and an occasional green adobe identical to those used as decoration in Room 3 (50 × 25 × 10 cm). The interior of Feature 8 had been given a smooth lining of clay.

A whole series of pots could have been set in sequence on Feature 8. When discovered, it was

Figure 7.4. Plan and cross section of Feature 8, a hearth trench in the North Central Canchón, Structure D.

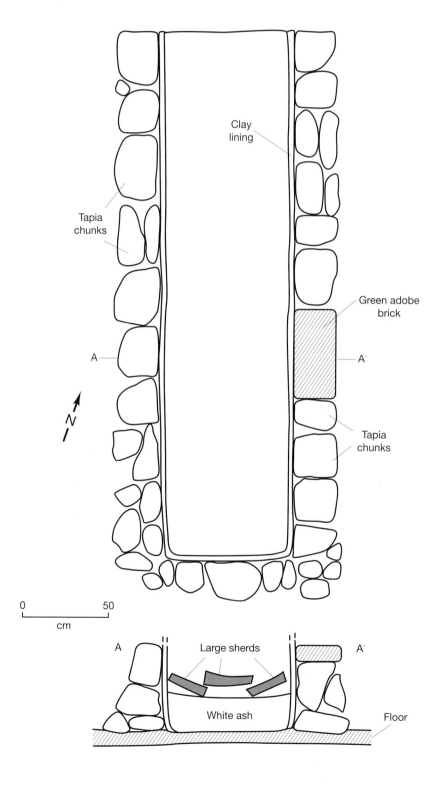

Figure 7.5. Two stages in the excavation of Feature 8, a hearth trench in the North Central Canchón, Structure D. (*Left*): The feature seen from the north, before the removal of any ash. (*Right*): The same feature after removal of ash from the north half.

partially filled with white ash (Figure 7.5) and yielded occasional large jar sherds. The fuel that was used apparently consisted of whatever discarded wood or cane happened to be available— for example, *caña brava* (*Gynerium* sp.), driftwood from the beach, a broken weaving shuttle, and some broken wooden posts that appear to be willow (*Salix* sp.).

Immediately to the north of Feature 8 was a large depression in the floor, filled with ash, charcoal, driftwood, and burned *caña brava*; this deposit likely represents refuse from the repeated use of Feature 8.

Feature 17

Feature 17, the second hearth trench, was less well made. My impression is that it had been hastily prepared in order to increase (perhaps even double) the boiling capacity of the canchón. Feature 17 had no formal walls or clay lining; it was simply a long, narrow trench, dug down 70 cm through the platform at the south end of the canchón (Figures 7.6, 7.7). Its interior dimensions

are 3.0 m in length and 0.8 m wide, and its depth is 2.73 m to 3.43 m below datum; its northern and southern limits had been determined by preexisting tapia walls. When discovered, this hearth trench was filled with alternating layers of white and gray ash, plus occasional large sherds. Included among these sherds were basal portions of very large Camacho Reddish Brown jars, one of which still bore the residue of *jora* (sprouted maize kernels, used as the basis for *chicha* or maize beer).

A radiocarbon date from Feature 17

A piece of charcoal from the gray ash inside Feature 17 was submitted to Beta Analytic for dating.

Beta-10915 came out 620 ± 50 years B.P., or A.D. 1330 uncalibrated. The calibrated two-sigma range would be A.D. 1284–1410.

I consider Beta-10915, whether calibrated or uncalibrated, to be one of the most satisfactory ^{14}C dates we obtained from Structure D. It suggests

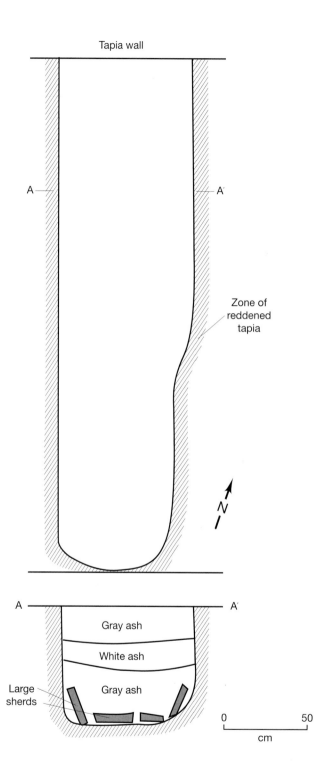

Figure 7.6. Plan and cross section of Feature 17, a hearth trench cut 70 cm into the solid tapia platform at the base of the North Central Canchón, Structure D.

that the activities of the North Central Canchón were in full swing during the fourteenth century A.D., meeting our expectations for "Late Cañete" culture. Even a date of A.D. 1410, near the upper limit of the calibrated two-sigma range, would have been acceptable.

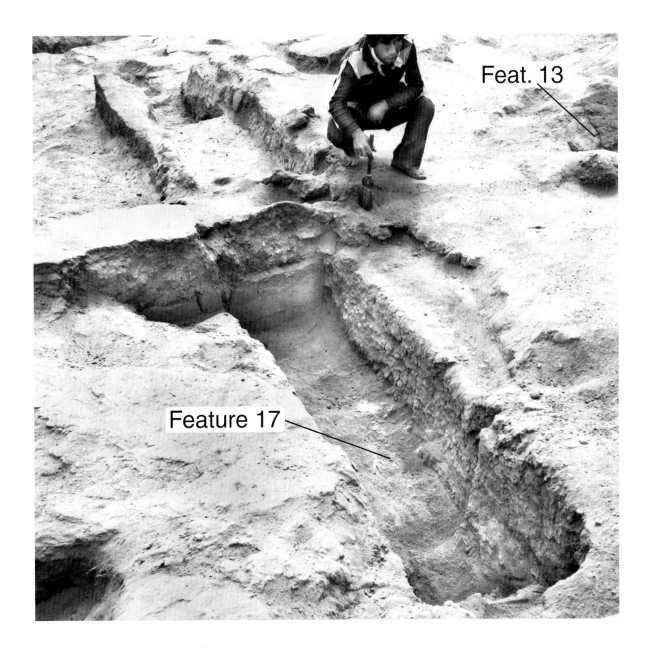

Feat. 13

Feature 17

Figure 7.7. Feature 17, a hearth trench in the North Central Canchón, seen from the south. This view shows how Feature 17 was laid out with its north end touching a preexisting tapia crosswall. Also visible are Feature 8 (another hearth trench) and Feature 13, the impression of a large storage vessel once buried in the floor of the canchón. José Aguidos serves as scale.

The Importance of *Chicha* Brewing

While we cannot rule out the possibility that meals were also prepared in the North Central Canchón, we believe that its major function was as a *chichería* or brewery for maize beer. Our conclusions are based partly on its similarity to breweries at other Peruvian sites—for example, Huánuco Pampa (Morris 1979; Morris and Thompson 1985), Manchán (Moore 1989), and Cerro Baúl (Moseley et al. 2005).

In addition to our evidence for *jora*, the North Central Canchón yielded two discarded *maraykuna* or *batanes* (grinding slabs) and three *tunaukuna* (handstones for grinding), which could have been used to prepare maize for brewing. We also found a likely "stirring stick" for agitating the *chicha* during heating, and cavities in the floor for a series of *chicha* storage vessels in four modal sizes (see below). Allowing for the possibility that this work area had multiple functions, I will simply describe the North Central Canchón as a "kitchen/brewery."

It should come as no surprise that there would be a brewery in an elite residential compound. In the Andes, native leaders used liberal amounts of *chicha* as an incentive for work crews of commoners (Morris 1979, 1982; Murra 1960, 1980; Rostworowski 1977; Rowe 1946). As in other parts of the ancient world (see Barth 1959: 77–79), such elite "hospitality" masked the hierarchical relationship involved. In 1551, the Spanish chronicler Juan de Betanzos reported that if native leaders in Jequetepeque "did not give drink to the Indians to work and to others to plant the fields of the community to pay tribute, they would not cooperate or come together to do it" (Betanzos 1968:72–73). In the case of Cerro Azul, elite families may well have supplied beer to the fishermen who filled their storerooms with sardines and anchovies. In addition to the daily consumption of *chicha* which characterized many Andean communities, Cerro Azul's elite may also have used *chicha* to entertain visitors from other compounds, or even from inland communities that supplied them with products they could not produce at Cerro Azul.

Rostworowski (1977:242) reports that much of the prestige that a coastal lord enjoyed result-ed from his generosity, including his ability to supply his subjects with beer. "When leaving his palace," she says, "a local lord would take with him an entourage of bearers who carried jars of *chicha*, and wherever the lord's litter would stop, everyone would be provided beer at his expense."

The storage features of the North Central Canchón

Among the most informative features of the North Central Canchón are the traces of nine large storage vessels that had been set deeply into the floor, so deeply that their shoulders were virtually at floor level. It seems clear that they had been set deep into the ground because, once they had been filled with liquid, their own weight might have caused them to break without the additional support of the surrounding earth. Each of the largest vessels was found to have had a flat beach cobble placed directly beneath its conical base. This was presumably done to prevent the vessel from digging itself more deeply into the ground under the weight of the liquid.

Some of these nine features consist mainly of the impression of the vessel in the ground, accompanied by a few sherds left behind when the vessel broke. In other cases, such as Feature 9, most of the vessel was still in situ; only the neck had been broken off, presumably because it projected above the floor. It appears that most of the breakage had taken place after the canchón had ceased to function as a kitchen/brewery, a time when people were no longer being careful where they stepped. Evidence that the vessels might have been fired in situ includes the impressions of multiple parallel grooves in the earth, reflecting coils of clay that had never been smoothed. This strongly suggests that many vessels had been formed and fired in place, with only the interior having been smoothed.

We cleaned and measured these features carefully and decided to estimate their cubic capacity while backfilling them. The way we did this was to assign each member of the backfilling crew an empty 18-liter cooking oil tin. We kept a record of how many of these tins of backdirt it took to backfill each feature. The results suggest that there were four modal sizes of storage jars. The two largest (Features 9 and 10) would have held almost

2000 liters; the second largest (for example, Feature 16) held about 700 liters; the third largest (for example, Feature 15) about 500 liters; and the smallest (for example, Feature 13) about 125 liters. We suspect that these four modal sizes correspond to four known Quechua categories of storage vessels. The largest of the latter were called *hatun maccma* or *maccma*; the next largest, *urpu*; the next, *iteco*; and the smallest, *puyñu* (Ravines 1978:180).

Had all the storage vessels in the North Central Canchón been in use simultaneously, their total volume would have been at least 5000 liters. If, on the other hand, only half of the vessels were filled at any time, their capacity would have been 2500 liters, making the Cerro Azul brewery's volume similar to the 1800-liter capacity of the Cerro Baúl brewery (Moseley et al. 2005:17267). Most of the vats in the Cerro Baúl brewery had a capacity of roughly 150 liters, similar to the smallest of the four vessel sizes set into the floor of the North Central Canchón at Cerro Azul.

We can perhaps offer a general estimate of how many people the Cerro Azul brewery could have served by referring to Gillin's (1947) ethnographic study of the town of Moche. Gillin (1947: 46) estimates that each person there probably consumed 3 liters of *chicha* at a given beer-drinking event. If we apply this figure to Cerro Azul, it suggests that the elite living in Structure D at Cerro Azul could have entertained somewhere between 800 people (if the half-capacity 2500 liters were produced) and 1650 people (if the full-capacity 5000 liters were produced).

We do not know whether Structure D was the only large compound at Cerro Azul producing *chicha* in volume, or if the other nine large compounds had similar breweries. The *chicha* produced in Structure D could have been used to entertain visiting elites from other compounds at Cerro Azul or from neighboring communities, as well as to reward the countless fishermen who filled up the fish-storage rooms in Structure D (Marcus 1987a, 1987b; Marcus et al. 1999).

Unfortunately, there is no accurate way to determine how many of the storage vessels in Structure D were filled to capacity for a given event. The fact that four different sizes of vessels were present suggests that different events may

have required different quantities of beer. As for who might have done the brewing at Cerro Azul, we can only point to Rostworowski's (1977:241) observation that while women were the primary brewers of beer in the highlands, men were often the *chicha*-makers on the coast.

Figures 7.2, 7.3, and 7.8 give the layout of the North Central Canchón and the location of each of the nine storage vessels. Figures 7.9, 7.10, and 7.11 provide photos of several of the best-preserved features, as well as some of the shallow impressions of small pots in the floor near Feature 9. The reader can refer to these figures as we discuss the dimensions of each feature in numerical order.

Feature 9 (Figure 7.9) was a *hatun maccma* with a storage capacity of roughly 1944 liters. Its maximum diameter was 2 m, and its conical base had rested on a flat beach cobble. At least half a dozen smaller vessels had evidently rested in concave impressions on the floor near Feature 9 (Figure 7.8); they may have been used to dip *chicha* from the larger vessel as needed.

A great deal of the actual *hatun maccma* remained in place in the case of Feature 9. Over time, stray sherds (and even a partially restorable vessel) had fallen into, or been thrown into, the cavity of the vessel. They are as follows:

Camacho Reddish Brown (Figure 7.12b)
  Everted rim from the neck of a *hatun maccma*: 1

Unusual Painted Vessel (Figure 7.12a)
  Sherd from a jar featuring light brown paint over gray paste, painted in black/white/red: 1

"Fat Skeleton" Vessel (Figure 7.13)
  Partially restorable effigy vessel with Pingüino Buff-like paste but atypical brown wash, depicting a skeletonized person: 1 (this vessel appears to have been used for cooking, something for which effigy vessels were rarely used)

Feature 10 (Figure 7.10, top), like Feature 9, had been a *hatun maccma* with a maximum diameter of 2 m and a storage capacity close to 2000 liters. Aside

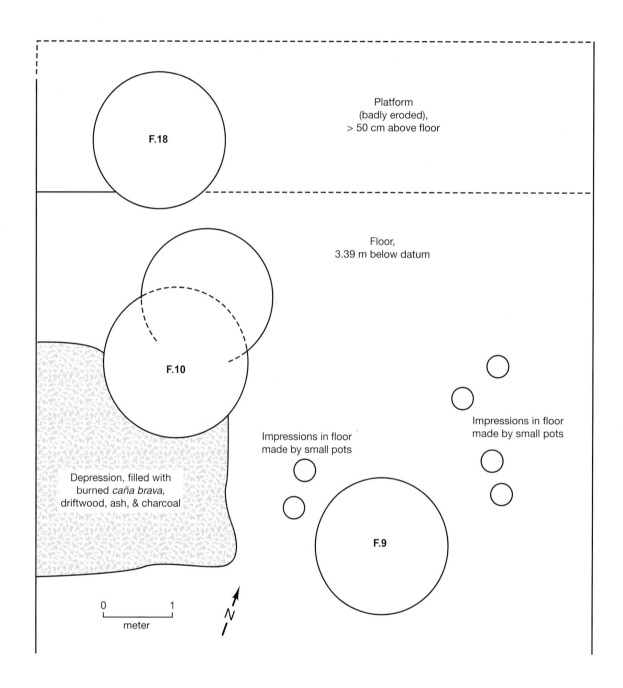

Figure 7.8. The north half of the North Central Canchón, Structure D, showing the location of Features 9, 10, and 18.

Figure 7.9. Stages in the excavation of Feature 9, a *hatun maccma* with a storage capacity of nearly 2000 liters, which had been buried in the floor of the North Central Canchón. (*Left*): César Francia begins the excavation. (*Right*): Alberto Barraza sweeps the circular beach cobble on which the conical base of the giant vessel once rested.

from a few sherds, only the impression in the ground survived. As the upper half of Figure 7.10 shows, that impression bears the parallel grooves of a vessel unsmoothed on the exterior. Feature 10 had probably been formed and fired in place.

Feature 10's conical base, like Feature 9's, rested on a flat beach cobble. Three *tunaukuna* or hand-held grinding stones had either fallen, or been discarded, into the cavity of Feature 10. They were the kind of stones we would expect to have been used to grind the maize used for *chicha*.

A number of sherds were found in Feature 10 as well. Based on its thickness, color, and paste, we suspect that one of those sherds might have been from the very *hatun maccma* for which the Feature 10 cavity had been created. An artist's reconstruction of the vessel is shown in Figure 7.14.

Three other rims of large *chicha* storage vessels had fallen into the Feature 10 cavity. They are illustrated in Figure 7.15. While similar in overall design, they appear to be from three different vessels.

As Figure 7.8 suggests, the Feature 10 jar appears to have been sunk into an area previously used for another vessel, to which no feature number was assigned because its cavity had been filled in.

Feature 11 (Figure 7.10, bottom) is the impression of a vessel about half the size of Feature 10; its maximum diameter is roughly 1.0 m. A doughnut-shaped beach cobble (which might once have been an artifact) had been placed beneath its conical base. A *batán* or grinding slab had been discarded in Feature 11; it appears to be the kind of slab on which the grinding stones found in Feature 10 might have been used.

Feature 12 (Figure 7.3) lay near Feature 11; it had a maximum diameter of about 1.16 m.

Feature 13 (Figures 7.3 and 7.11, top) is one of four storage jars placed near the center of the tapia platform east of Feature 17. Its diameter was only 90 cm, making it one of the smallest vessels, with a capacity of roughly 126 liters.

Features 14, 15, and 16 (Figures 7.3 and 7.11, top) were set in the same tapia platform as Feature 13. Features 14 and 15 had diameters close to 1.4 m

Figure 7.10. The impressions of large vessels buried in the floor of the North Central Canchón. (*Top*): Feature 10 seen from the east, showing the beach cobble placed below the conical base of the vessel, presumably to provide support. (*Bottom*): José Aguidos sweeps between Feature 11 (*left*) and Feature 9 (*right*). Feature 9 had been located but not yet excavated at this point.

Figure 7.11. Features in the floor of the North Central Canchón. (*Top*): Features 13, 15, 16, and 17. (*Bottom*): Shallow impressions in the floor made by small pots. The north arrow is marked in both centimeters (*right side*) and inches (*left side*).

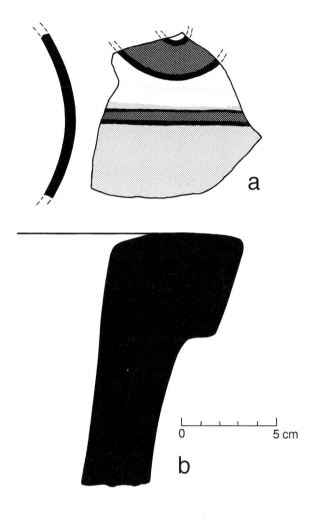

a

b

(LEFT):

Figure 7.12. Sherds found inside Feature 9, Structure D. (*a*): unusual jar sherd featuring light brown paint over gray paste. A design has been painted over the brown surface in black/white/red. The red paint is 7.5 R 3/4 to 4/4 (weak red to dusky red). Similar sherds were found elsewhere in the North Central Canchón. (*b*): everted rim from the neck of a *hatun maccma*. The vessel was made of extremely coarse clay with temper particles up to 5 mm in diameter. Its paste is 2.5 YR 6/6 (light red) and the exterior surface is 5 YR 6/3 (light reddish brown). The part of the vessel that would have been above ground has been given a light wash of the same reddish clay.

Top view

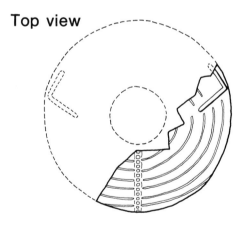

Side view

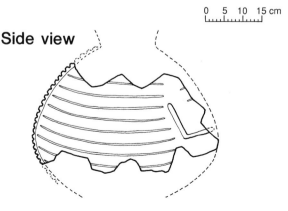

(RIGHT):

Figure 7.13. Partially restorable vessel that fell (or was thrown) into Feature 9, Structure D. This jar depicts a "fat skeleton." A human spinal column runs up the back, with grooves coming off the spine at intervals to represent ribs. On each side is a spindly arm, and there was probably a face on the neck. The paste resembles Pingüino Buff's, but the surface seems to have a brown wash on it which would be atypical for Pingüino vessels. The lower third of the vessel is fire-blackened or smudged. Where not blackened, the surface color is 10 R 4/4 to 2/5 YR 4/2 (weak red).

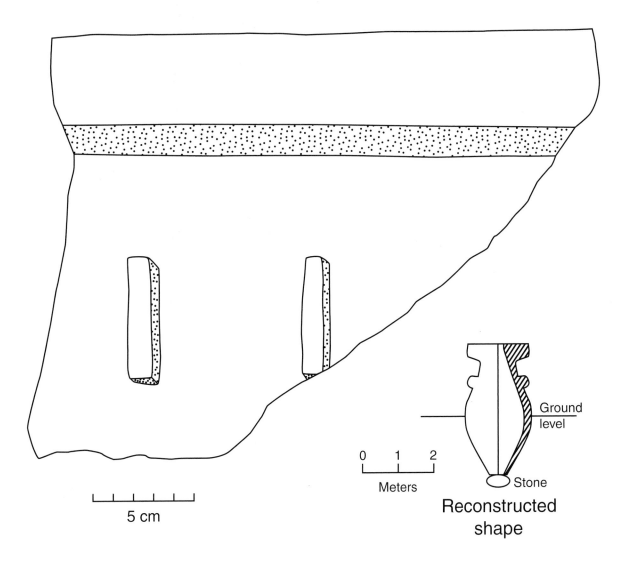

Figure 7.14. Rim sherd from *hatun maccma* that had fallen into Feature 10 of the North Central Canchón. The two protuberances on the vessel wall are stubs from a broken horizontally set handle. At lower right is an artist's reconstruction of how the vessel was set in the ground, with its base deliberately resting on a stone.

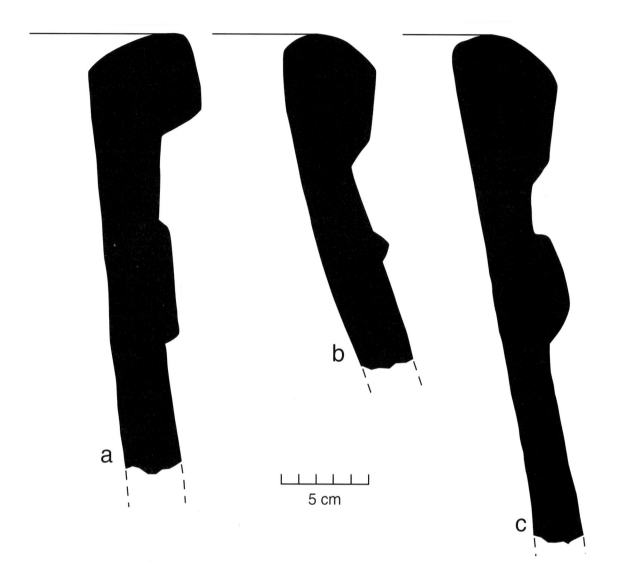

Figure 7.15. Rims of *hatun maccma*, or large *chicha* storage vessels, that had fallen into Feature 10 of the North Central Canchón. All vessels had rim diameters in the range of 1.6 m. The protuberance on the wall of *a* is the stub of a broken handle; that on the wall of *b* is a "pinched point" decoration; that on the wall of *c* is a large decorative adornment.

and capacities close to 500 liters. Feature 16 had a maximum diameter of 1.6 m and an estimated capacity of about 700 liters, making it a candidate to be an *urpu*. Only the cavities of Features 14, 15, and 16 remained; there were no sherds left.

Feature 18 (Figure 7.8) had been set into the tapia platform at the northern end of the North Central Canchón. Its diameter was about 1.7 m, and discarded inside it we found a patinated wooden stick of the type traditionally used to stir batches of *chicha*.

Ceramics from the floor of the North Central Canchón

A number of sherds were found on the floor of the North Central Canchón. Because we knew that many different activities had been carried out on that floor, we kept the ceramics from various sectors separate in case the makeup of the sherd samples reflected different tasks.

Scattered throughout the canchón were rim sherds broken off the large storage vessels that had been set in the floor. Figure 7.16 presents a sample of these rim sherds, whose diameters ranged from 60–70 cm to more than 1.0 m.

Some 22 diagnostic sherds were found on the floor near the two hearth trenches, Features 8 and 17. Not surprisingly, 10 of these are from Camacho Reddish Brown cooking pots and storage jars. The remaining sherds are from Pingüino Buff jars of the type we suspect were used to store or transport liquids. No Camacho Black diagnostics were found in this collection of sherds, which is as follows:

Camacho Reddish Brown (Figure 7.17a–d)
Jars with everted rims: 3 rims
Cooking pots with restricted orifice (fire-blackened): 2 rims with horizontal strap handle; 5 plain rims

Pingüino Buff (Figure 7.17e–i)
Jars with everted rim: 1 unpainted rim
Jars with everted rim, painted white on natural: 3 rims (white band at rim)
Jar neck, painted white and black: 1
Jars with everted rim, black tick marks on rim over white background: 3 rims

Funnel neck with face painted in black and red: 1 rim
Jar body sherd painted black over a red wash: 1
Jar body sherds painted black/white/red: 2

A collection of nine diagnostic sherds came to light as our workmen cleaned the floor near Features 11–16, which were storage jars set in the canchón floor. This collection consists entirely of Pingüino Buff jars and bowls. These vessels, which might have been used for transporting *chicha* from the storage jars to thirsty guests, are as follows:

Pingüino Buff (Figure 7.18)
Large jar painted white on natural, showing modeled ear from a face: 1 rim
Everted rim of jar, painted on rim with black-and-white ticking: 1
Large strap handle from jar: 1
Large shallow bowl painted black/white/red on interior: 2 rims, 2 body sherds
Large jar shoulder, painted white on natural: 1
Large jar body sherd, possibly showing modeled arm: 1

Finally, an additional 17 diagnostic sherds were found scattered around the canchón floor, not near any of the features (Figure 7.19). Six of these sherds are from Camacho Reddish Brown jars and include an effigy maize cob lug that may have been a symbolic reference to the jars' contents: *chicha*. Nine more sherds are from Pingüino Buff jars of the type we suspect were for storage or transportation of liquids. The two remaining sherds are from unusual items, of whose function we are unsure. The whole collection is as follows:

Camacho Reddish Brown (Figure 7.19a–c)
Jar with everted rim: 1 rim (fire-blackened)
Jar with thickened rim: 1 rim
Jar with cambered rim decorated with cane-end punctations: 1 rim (fire-blackened)
Strap handles: 2 (1 large, 1 small)
Modeled "ear of maize" lug from a huge jar, possibly a *tinajón*: 1 lug

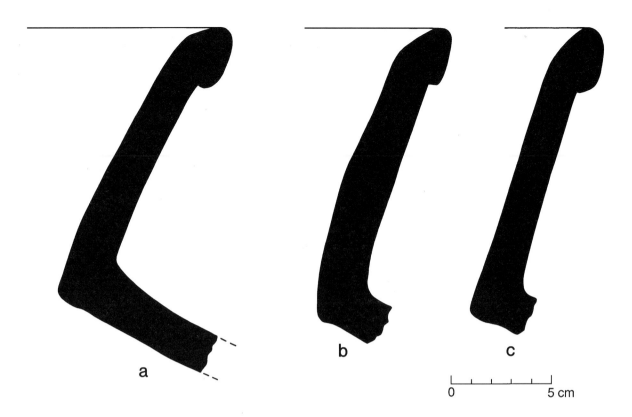

Figure 7.16. Rim sherds from *hatun maccma*, found resting on the floor of the North Central Canchón, Structure D. The rim diameters of the complete vessels are estimated to have ranged from 60–70 cm to more than 1.0 m.

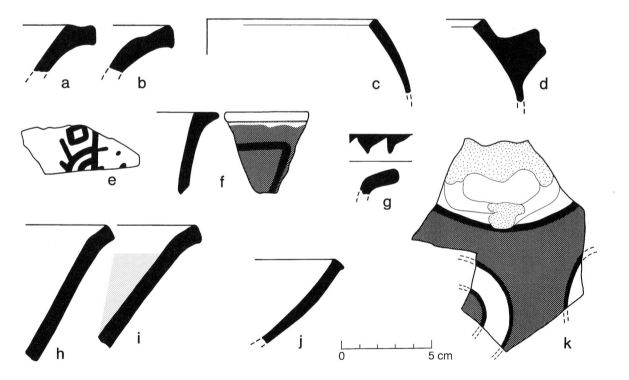

Figure 7.17. Diagnostic sherds from various proveniences in the North Central Canchón, Structure D. Sherds *a–d* are Camacho Reddish Brown. (*a, b*): everted rims from large jars; (*c, d*): cooking pots with restricted orifice and horizontally set strap handles; fire-blackened. Sherds *e–j* are Pingüino Buff. (*e*): jar body sherd with design painted in black over a red wash; (*f*): funnel neck with face painted in black and red; (*g*): everted jar rim, painted with black rim ticking over a white background; (*h*): everted rim of jar, plain; (*i*): everted rim of jar, painted white-on-natural; (*j*): rim of subhemispherical bowl with fugitive light red slip; (*k*): unusual jar shoulder sherd with gray paste, modeled figure on shoulder; cream slipped; painted black/red/cream.

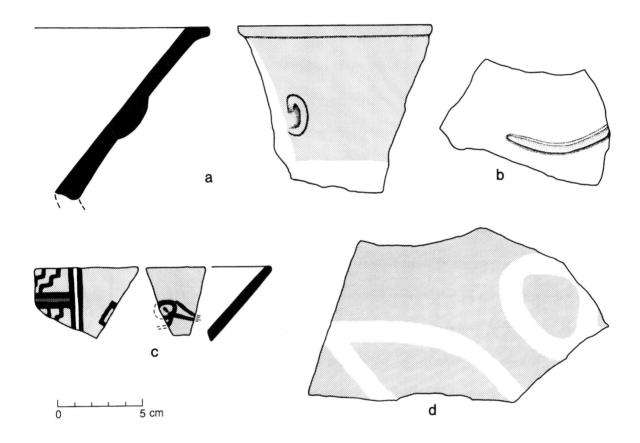

Figure 7.18. Pingüino Buff vessels found while cleaning around Features 11–16 in the North Central Canchón, Structure D. (*a*): large jar with modeled left ear from what is presumably a face, painted white on natural; (*b*): body sherd from large jar, showing what may be a modeled arm; (*c*): two sherds from large shallow bowl, painted on the interior in black/white/red; (*d*): sherd from shoulder of large jar, painted white on natural.

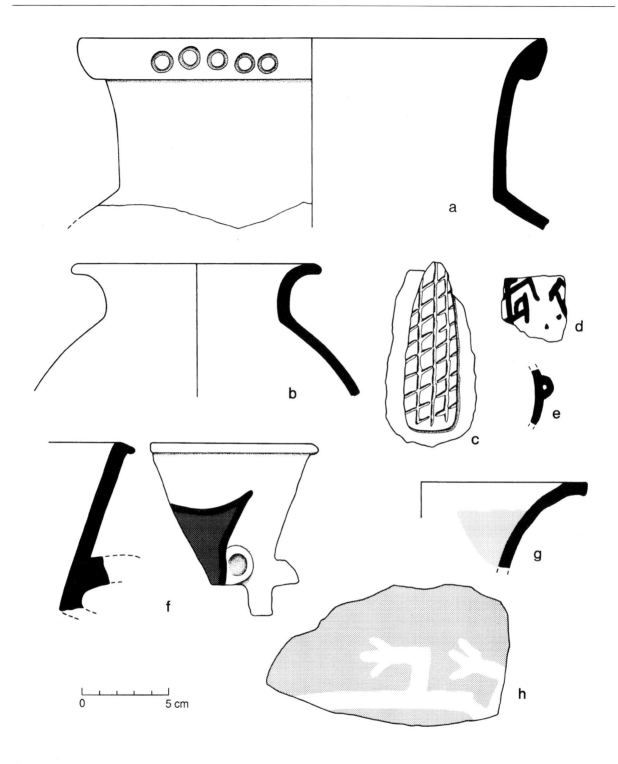

Figure 7.19. Ceramics from the floor of the North Central Canchón, Structure D. Sherds *a–c* are Camacho Reddish Brown. (*a*): jar with cambered rim, decorated with cane-end punctations in groups of five; (*b*): fire-blackened jar with everted rim; (*c*): maize-cob lug modeled on large jar; (*d*): sherd from gray-paste jar, painted black on white; (*e*): unusual jar body sherd with gray paste and white-on-black painting; (*e*): loop handle from miniature pot, Trambollo Burnished Brown (?). Sherds *f–h* are Pingüino Buff. (*f*): funnel neck from jar with modeled human head showing facial paint; there was a strap handle behind the ears (the red paint is 10 R 6/8 and is outlined in black); (*g*): jar with everted rim, painted white on natural on the interior; (*h*): jar body sherd painted white on natural.

Pingüino Buff (Figure 19f–h)
> Jar with funnel neck, everted rim, ear mod-
> eled in it, typical zoned red facial paint;
> strap handle on back of head: 1 rim
> Large jar with everted rim, painted white
> on natural inside: 1 rim
> Jar shoulder with strap handle, painted
> white on natural: 1
> Jar body sherds, painted white on natural: 2
> Strap handles from large jars, plain: 2
> Body sherd painted black and white: 1
> Large plain body sherd: 1

Unusual items
> Body sherd from gray-paste jar, painted
> black on white: 1
> Loop handle from a miniature pot, possibly
> Trambollo Burnished Brown: 1

Pottery from the fill of the North Central Canchón

After Structure D was abandoned, the North Central Canchón gradually began to fill with dust, sand, and the disintegration products of tapia. We suspected that the lower levels of this fill might still contain sherds related to *chicha*-making activities, so we continued to keep our ceramic collections separate.

Twenty-six sherds were found in the fill near the Feature 8 hearth trench. Included were vessels not usually found lying directly on the floor—for example, Camacho Black amphorae, and some unusual painted jars that could be from another region. Their concentric swirl motif resembles that seen on one of the sherds from Feature 9 (see Figure 7.12a). We therefore concluded that many of the sherds from the lower fill had entered the canchón after its abandonment, rather than belonging to the original occupation. The entire collection is as follows:

Camacho Reddish Brown (Figure 7.20e, f)
> Jar rims, everted: 2
> Jar shoulder, appliqué nipple: 1
> Cooking pot with restricted orifice, verti-
> cally set strap handle: 1 rim (fire-black-
> ened)

Camacho Black (Standard Variety) (Figure 7.20g, h)
> Slightly everted rim, jar or amphora: 1
> Neck of amphora with head modeled on it:
> 1 (coffee-bean eye)
> Amphora sherd with strap handle: 1

Pingüino Buff (Figure 7.20c)
> Jar neck/shoulder sherds: 2
> Strap handle from jar: 1
> Jar rim, everted, painted black and white: 1

Unusual sherds (Figure 7.20a, b, d)
> Sherd from possible cucurbit effigy,
> Pingüino Buff paste, dark gray paint: 1
> Jars, gray paste, painted black/white/red
> with concentric swirl on exterior of
> base: 14 sherds from 2 jars

In the fill along the east wall of the canchón, we found more sherds from the same jar with concentric swirls of red paint whose fragments had been found inside Feature 9 (Figure 7.12a) and in the fill near Feature 8 (Figure 7.20a, b). The paste of these sherds, as usual, is gray. The sherds seem to come from a jar shoulder with a human effigy modeled on it (Figure 7.17k).

In the same area of fill, we found the following:

Pingüino Buff
> Jar body sherd, painted with white "Life
> Savers" against a black background: 1 (a
> similar sherd came from Room 6; see
> Figure 5.35f)
> Open (subhemispherical) bowl with fugitive
> light red slip (7.5 YR 6/8), burnished on
> interior and exterior: 1 rim sherd
> (Figure 7.17j)

Elsewhere in the general fill of the North Central Canchón, we found the interesting sherd seen in Figure 7.21. It is a Pingüino Buff jar sherd with nested chevrons painted in black/white/red, very similar to a specimen found in the fill of Room 11 (see Figure 7.29, later in this chapter). The two sherds are so similar that they could have

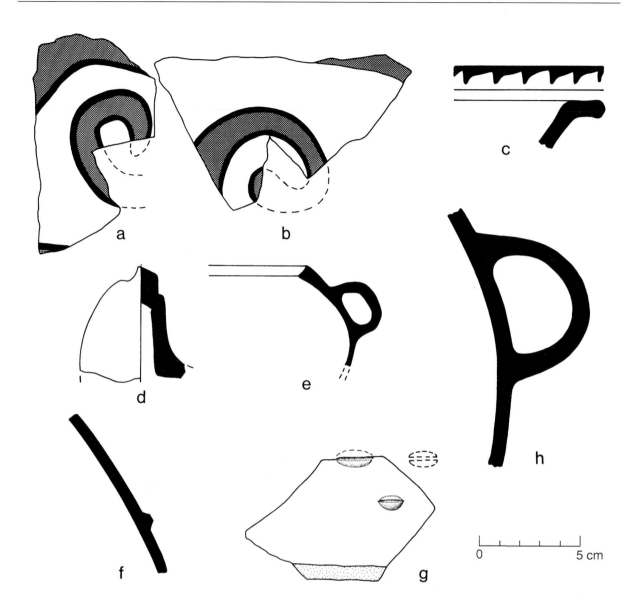

Figure 7.20. Ceramics from the fill of the North Central Canchón, Structure D, near Feature 8. (*a, b*): unusual jar sherds with gray paste, painted black/white/red with concentric swirls; the red is 7.5 R 4/4 (weak red); (*c*): everted rim from Pingüino Buff jar, painted white on the exterior, painted black on the rim as shown; (*d*): sherd from possible cucurbit effigy. Sherds *e* and *f* are Camacho Reddish Brown. (*e*): cooking pot with restricted orifice and strap handle, fire-blackened; (*f*): jar sherd with appliqué nipple. Sherds *g* and *h* are Camacho Black (standard variety). (*g*): amphora sherd with appliqué "coffee-bean" eye and mouth; (*h*): amphora sherd with strap handle.

come from the same vessel, suggesting that both Room 11 and the North Central Canchón had filled in during roughly the same time period.

Very late fill in the North Central Canchón

The North Central Canchón clearly had filled with dust, sand, and debris in stages, over a long period

of time. Resting on the surface of the fill were three sherds that we regard as Late Horizon (at the earliest) to Early Colonial (at the latest) (Figure 7.22). These sherds have a brick red paste and a well-applied cream slip that do not match any of our Late Intermediate types. One sherd is from a ring base, which we have already singled out as a late attribute (see Figure 3.34 of Chapter 3). The other two

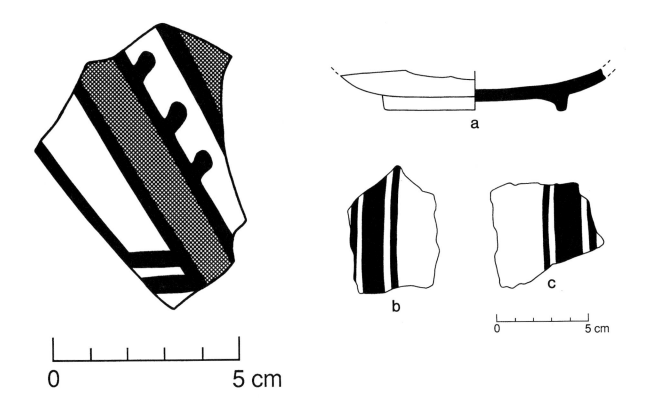

Figure 7.21. Pingüino Buff jar sherd from the fill of the North Central Canchón. The vessel was painted black/white/red on the exterior with the same chevron motif seen on sherds from the fill of Room 11 (see Figure 7.29).

Figure 7.22. Ceramics found resting on the surface of the fill in the North Central Canchón, Structure D. This collection appears to be very late Late Horizon at the earliest, and perhaps even Colonial. (Its closest ties are to material from a late feature on Cerro del Fraile.) All specimens have a brick red paste and a cream slip. (*a*): vessel with a ring base, unknown in the Late Intermediate period; (*b, c*): black-on-cream painted body sherds.

sherds have black-on-cream stripes and resemble vessels from Late Horizon/Early Colonial deposits elsewhere at Cerro Azul (Figure 7.22b, c). These sherds, therefore, may have been left on the surface well after the canchón filled in.

ROOM 7

Also assigned to the northwest quadrant of Structure D is Room 7, a small room on the opposite side of the south wall of the North Central Canchón (Figure 7.23). Room 7 measures 2.89 × 1.99 m, and early in the history of the building had been connected to the East Platform of the

Southwest Canchón by a narrow corridor. At a later time, that corridor was blocked with tapia (see Figures 4.13 and 4.14 of Chapter 4). Access to Room 7 may have been blocked because it suffered severe earthquake damage (Figure 7.24).

The floor of Room 7 was encountered at 1.98 m below datum. Only one sherd was found lying on the floor of the room, as follows:

Pingüino Buff (Figure 7.25)
    Hemispherical bowl, given a white wash on the interior and exterior, then painted with a very fine-line black-on-white design. Rim diameter, ca. 18 cm.

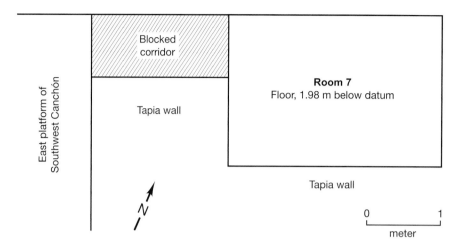

South wall of North Central Canchón

Blocked corridor

East platform of Southwest Canchón

Tapia wall

Room 7
Floor, 1.98 m below datum

Tapia wall

N

0   1
meter

Figure 7.23. Detail of Room 7, showing the corridor that had once connected it to the Southwest Canchón. At a later stage of the building's occupation, the corridor was blocked with tapia.

Figure 7.24. Room 7, Structure D, seen from the east. Earthquake damage is evident on the south and west walls. The floor had also collapsed in the northwest corner, where Edalio Aguidos is sweeping.

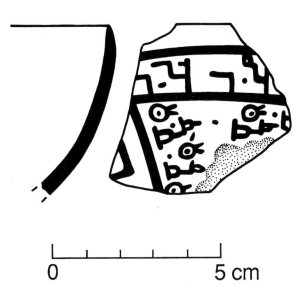

Figure 7.25. Pingüino Buff sherd found on the floor of Room 7, Structure D. The sherd is from a hemispherical bowl with a white wash on the interior and exterior, painted on the exterior in black and white.

0   5 cm

It appears that at some point, perhaps after Room 7 had suffered damage and its access blocked, it became a place to dump refuse. In addition to the usual windblown dust and sand, its fill contained midden-like material not unlike that found in Feature 6 of the Southwest Canchón (see Chapter 4). The complete collection of sherds from the fill of Room 7 is as follows:

Camacho Reddish Brown (Figure 7.26i–p)
　Jars with cambered rim: 4 rims
　Jars with simple everted rim: 5 rims
　Jars with everted and bolstered rim: 3 rims
　Jar shoulder sherds: 7
　Strap handle from very large jar: 1
　Cooking pots with restricted orifice and
　　vertically set strap handle: 3 rim sherds
　　(fire-blackened)
　Strap handle from cooking pot like that listed above: 1 (fire-blackened)
　Body sherds: 22 (half of them fire-blackened)
　Several *hatun maccma* sherds were thrown
　　in above the room fill; one example is
　　shown in Figure 7.26q.

Camacho Black (Standard Variety) (Figure 7.26d)
　Jar shoulder: 1
　Hemispherical bowl rim: 1
　Body sherds: 6

Camacho Black (Highly Burnished Variety) (Figure 7.26b, c)
　Incurved-rim bowl, miniature: 1 rim
　Modeled human face from jar neck?: 1
　Body sherds: 2

Trambollo Burnished Brown (Figure 7.26g, h)
　Fragment of miniature jar with some kind
　　of plastic decoration: 1
　Small incurved-rim bowl: 1
　Body sherds: 2

Pingüino Buff (Figure 7.26a, e, f)
　Funnel neck from jar with modeled human
　　ear: 1
　Jar neck with everted rim, black ticking
　　painted on interior of rim: 1
　Jar shoulder with traces of white-and-red
　　paint: 1
　Body sherds from jars with traces of white
　　paint: 2
　Plain jar body sherds: 8
　Hemispherical bowl rims: 2 (atypical in
　　paste; 1 is white-slipped)

My suspicion is that although I have assigned Room 7 to the northwest quadrant of Structure D, its post-occupation fill is more likely to have come from the Southwest Canchón than from the North Central Canchón. The only sherds that seem out of place in Southwest Canchón debris

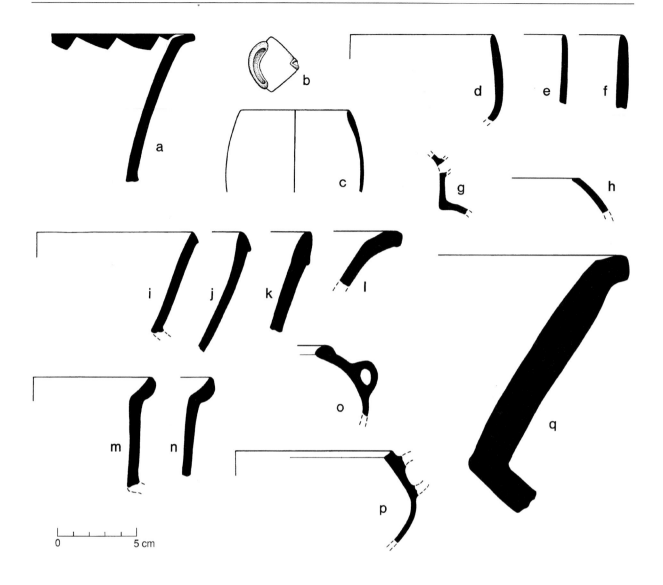

0　5 cm

Figure 7.26. Ceramics from the fill of Room 7, Structure D. (*a*): Pingüino Buff jar neck with everted rim and black rim ticking on interior. Sherds *b* and *c* are Camacho Black (highly burnished variety). (*b*): fragment of modeled human face (ear and part of eye) from jar neck (?); (*c*): miniature incurved-rim bowl. Sherds *d–f* are hemispherical bowl rims; *d* is Camacho Black (standard variety); *e* and *f* are Pingüino Buff with a somewhat atypical paste. Sherds *g* and *h* are Trambollo Burnished Brown. (*g*): miniature jar with plastic decoration; (*h*): small incurved-rim bowl. Sherds *i–p* are Camacho Reddish Brown. (*i–k*): cambered rims from jars; (*l*): simple everted rim from jar; (*m, n*): everted and bolstered rims from jars; (*o, p*): cooking pots with restricted orifice and vertically set strap handles; (*q*): rim of *hatun maccma* tossed into Room 7 late in its history. Surface color 10 R 4/8 (red) to 2.5 YR 6/8 (light red).

are the fragments of Camacho Reddish Brown *hatun maccma*, and stratigraphically speaking, they appear to have been the last sherds thrown into the room.

ROOM 11

As mentioned earlier in this chapter, Room 11 appears to have served originally as a pantry or storage room for the North Central Canchón. Supplies for the kitchen/brewery could have been carried directly from unloaded llamas in the Southwest Canchón, through a doorway and into Room 11 (Figure 7.27). At a late stage of occupation, that doorway was blocked (Figure 7.28, bottom).

Room 11 measures 3.74 × 2.70 m, and its floor lies at a depth of 3.41 m below datum. The passageway coming from the Southwest Canchón slopes upward so that it enters Room 11 some 45 cm above the floor, which is not atypical for rooms designed for storage.

Our small sample of sherds from Room 11 all come from post-occupation fill. Only 13 of the sherds are diagnostic, and they are as follows:

Camacho Reddish Brown (Figure 7.29d–g)
  Jars with everted rim: 4 rims
  Jars with cambered rims: 1 rim

Trambollo Burnished Brown
  Jar body sherd: 1

Pingüino Buff (Figure 7.29a–c)
  Large hemispherical bowls: 2 rims
  Large jars painted black/white/red on exterior: 3 body sherds (note similarity to sherd in Figure 7.21)
  Medium-sized jar with everted rim: 1 rim (red wash on rim)

Atypical Orange Variety of Pingüino Buff (with grit similar to Camacho Reddish Brown)
  Jar with flaring rim: 1 rim (Figure 7.29h)

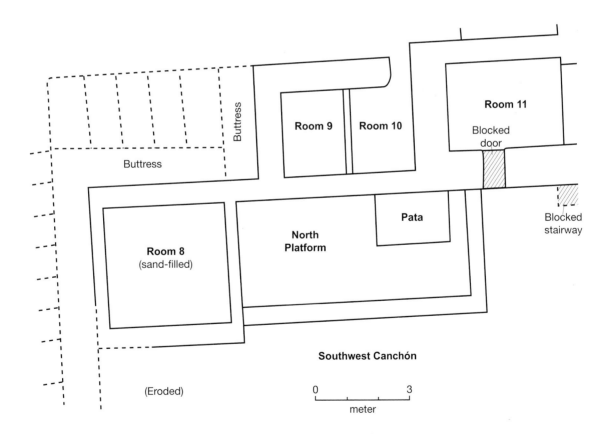

Figure 7.27. Plan of Rooms 8, 9, 10, and 11 of Structure D.

Figure 7.28. Excavation of Rooms 9, 10, and 11. (*Top*): Alberto Barraza cleans the narrow wall separating Rooms 9 and 10 (view from the north). (*Bottom*): Cirilo Cruz cleans the southwest corner of Room 11 (view from the northeast). Rooms 9 and 10 appear in the background. To the left of Cirilo is a blocked doorway which formerly allowed one to enter Room 11 from the Southwest Canchón.

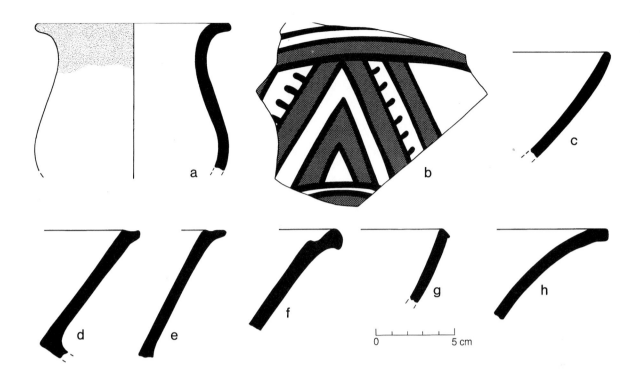

Figure 7.29. Ceramics from the fill of Room 11, Structure D. Sherds *a–c* are Pingüino Buff. (*a*): jar with everted rim and weak red wash extending 3 cm down the neck; (*b*): body sherd of large jar, painted black/white/red on the exterior; the red is 10 R 4/3 (weak red); (*c*): rim of large hemispherical bowl (rim diameter, 40 cm). Sherds *d–g* are Camacho Reddish Brown. (*d–f*): everted rims from large jars (the rim profile of *f* results from pinching the everted rim between thumb and index finger while turning the vessel); (*g*): cambered rim from jar. (*h*): flaring rim from large jar, made on an atypical orange version of Pingüino Buff; the gritty temper is like that of Camacho Reddish Brown.

ROOMS 9 AND 10

Immediately west of Room 11 lay Rooms 9 and 10 (Figure 7.30; see also Figure 7.28, top). Although two numbers were assigned to them, it was clear that we were dealing with a single original room, later divided into two.

Early in the occupation of Structure D, the architects had laid out a room 4.18 m long east–west and 2.70 m wide north–south (Figure 7.31). Its floor lay at roughly 4.20 m below datum. A small doorway with a threshold 64 cm wide led from the northeast corner of the room to our postulated Northwest Canchón. At a later date, this room was divided into two by the addition of a crude narrow wall of tapia blocks (Figures 7.31, 7.32). This wall was about 15 cm thick and 70 cm high; it originally had a central doorway, but that was later blocked with tapia fragments, as shown in Figure 7.32.

We designated the western room of the two new units Room 9; the eastern room became Room 10. Room 9, which measures 2.70 × 2.02 m, had a 10- to 15-cm thick layer of guinea pig dung pellets mixed with matted grass on its floor. Room 10, which measures 2.70 × 1.99 m, had on its floor a layer of maize stalks, leaves, and loose kernels; grass; and a variety of small, leafy herbs which might have served as food for guinea pigs. We conclude that at some point in its history, this space had been turned into a *cuyero*, or guinea pig nursery, consisting of two small rooms—one where the rodents were kept and one where their food and bedding were stored.

No ceramics were found on the floor of Rooms 9 and 10. The only sherds we found were in the later fill above the jerry-built dividing wall of narrow tapia blocks. The diagnostics, which probably represent sherds tossed into the rooms

Figure 7.30. Structure D, seen from Structure C, during excavation of the North Central Canchón. Rooms 9, 10, and 11 have all been excavated. Areas that were completed, drawn, and photographed early in the excavation of Structure D, such as the Southwest Canchón, have already been backfilled. This was done partly to discourage looting and partly to reduce the area that would have to be backfilled at the end of the project.

as they gradually filled with dust and sand, are as follows:

Camacho Reddish Brown (Figure 7.33a–g)
    Rims of *tinajones*: 3
    Large jars with cambered rim: 3 rims
    Jar with simple flaring rim: 1 rim
    Strap handle from large jar: 1
    Jar shoulders: 5
    Cooking pots with restricted orifice: 2 rims
        (fire-blackened)
    Rim of cooking pot, horizontally set loop
        handle: 1

Camacho Black (Standard Variety) (Figure 7.33h)
    Jar or amphora rim, everted: 1

Camacho Black (Highly Burnished Variety)
    Jar body sherd, "graphite" finish: 1

Trambollo Burnished Brown (Figure 7.33j)
    Hemispherical bowl: 1 rim sherd, 2 body sherds
    Jar body sherd: 1

Pingüino Buff (Figure 7.33k, l)
    Slightly everted rim from jar: 1

Large jar shoulder: 1
Jar body sherds painted in black and white over burnished natural buff: 3 (all from same vessel)
Jar body sherds, white slip: 2
Jar body sherd, white slip and grooved decoration: 1

Atypical sherd (Figure 7.33i)
Neck of small jar painted black and red on exterior: 1 (the color is orange brown, superficially like Pingüino Buff, but with coarse gritty paste and temper like that of Camacho Reddish Brown)

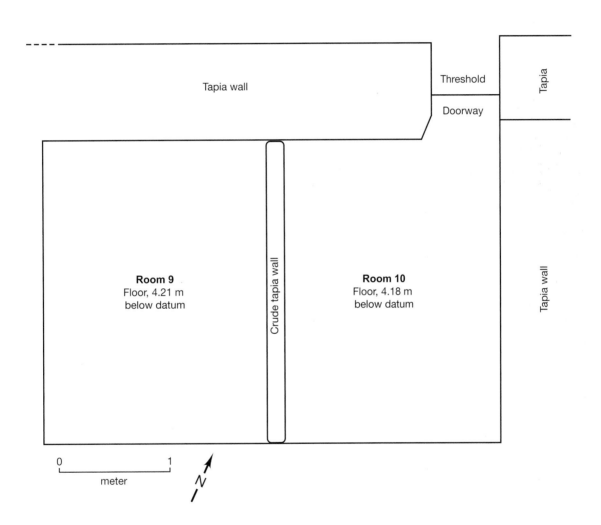

Figure 7.31. Plan of Rooms 9 and 10, Structure D. Later divided into two spaces by a crude tapia wall 15 cm wide and 70 cm high, these two rooms had originally been one. They shared a single floor (the difference in depth below surface is due to a 3-cm slope).

Figure 7.32. Rooms 9 (foreground) and 10 (background) seen from the southwest. These two rooms had been created by dividing a preexisting room into two smaller spaces with a narrow tapia wall. The new wall originally had a doorway, later blocked with large tapia fragments as seen here. Guinea pigs were then kept in Room 9, while Room 10 (which opened to the outside) was used for their stored bedding and food.

ROOM 12

Room 12 is a small room which, like Room 10, opened onto our putative Northwest Canchón. It had originally measured about 2.28 × 2.10 m but was very badly eroded. We found no ceramics that we could reliably associate with Room 12, and cannot specify a function for it.

SHERDS FROM CONSTRUCTION FILL IN THE BUTTRESSES OF THE WALL SEPARATING THE NORTHWEST AND NORTH CENTRAL CANCHONES

As we cleaned the badly eroded wall between the North Central Canchón and our putative Northwest Canchón, we found an area where

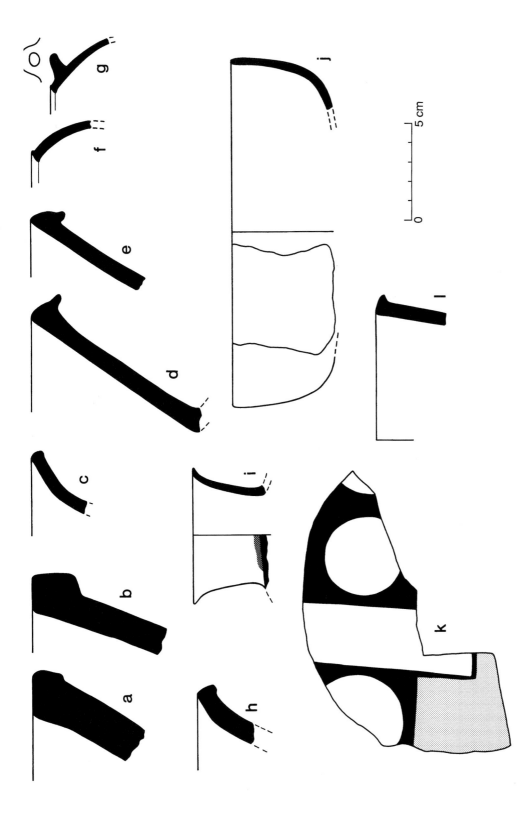

Figure 7.33. Ceramics found in the fill above the low wall separating Rooms 9 and 10, Structure D. Sherds *a–g* are Camacho Reddish Brown. (*a, b*): rims of 500-liter *tinajones*; (*c*): jar with simple flaring rim; (*d, e*): cambered rims from large jars; (*f, g*): cooking pots with restricted orifice; *g* has a horizontally set loop handle. (*b*): Camacho Black everted rim from jar or amphora; (*i*): atypical jar neck. The paste and temper resemble Camacho Reddish Brown's, but the surface color is pinkish orange like Pingüino Buff's, and the black-and-red paint on the exterior is also like Pingüino's. (*j*): Trambollo Burnished Brown hemispherical bowl. Sherds *k* and *l* are Pingüino Buff. (*k*): Three conjoining sherds from a jar body, showing white-on-black disks painted over burnished natural buff; (*l*): slightly everted rim from jar.

there were sherds included in the tapia of the wall's buttresses. This was an unusual discovery, since most of the tapia walls in Structure D are composed of clean, artifact-free clay. We decided to excavate part of the buttress to recover these sherds. Our reasoning was that since the buttresses presumably dated to the original construction of the canchón, this excavation might provide one of our earliest sherd samples. As it turned out, all the sherds looked to be typical Late Intermediate types. The whole collection is as follows:

Camacho Reddish Brown
    Basal sherds, all from the same conical-based, heavy amphora: 3

Camacho Black (Highly Burnished Variety)
    Rim of small bowl, probably with outleaned wall: 1
    Body sherd from thin hemispherical bowl: 1
    Body sherd from small jar: 1

Trambollo Burnished Brown
    Body sherd from small hemispherical bowl: 1

Pingüino Buff
    Jar body sherds, undecorated, mostly from the lower part of a jar: 17

FEATURE 3

Finally, we come to an isolated feature that cannot be associated with any quadrant of Structure D. Feature 3 was found while sweeping the surface of the structure prior to excavation; it appears to be part of an offering made long after the building had been abandoned and filled with dust and sand. This offering had been placed not far from the center of the building—in other words, in the area where we established our alidade station (Figure 4.1).

The offering consists of maize cobs, burned llama bones, and the funnel neck of a Camacho Black globular jar (standard variety). The remainder of the jar was never found. The neck is illustrated in Figure 7.34.

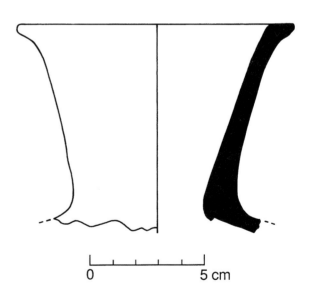

Figure 7.34. Funnel neck from globular Camacho Black jar (standard variety), found in Feature 3 of Structure D.

Structure 9

Having completed the excavation of one of Cerro Azul's ten major tapia compounds, I decided next to investigate one of the buildings called a "small ruin" by Kroeber. The nearest of these lay on a natural promontory not far to the southwest of Structure D. Designated Structure 9, this small ruin turned out to be a multiroom tapia structure, too eroded to measure with precision but covering roughly 290 m² (Figures 8.1–8.3).

We began work on Structure 9 during the first week of August 1984. Our first task was to sweep the surface with brooms until the tapia wall stubs began to emerge. Our crew then used trowels, whisk brooms, and dustpans to outline the walls by removing the first 10 cm of windblown dust that had filled the rooms. Once this was done, we drew a preliminary plan of the building and assigned room numbers. We first established a datum point from which all depth measurements could be taken. Then, early in the course of excavation, we discovered a level tapia surface where Charles Hastings could set up his alidade and plane table for mapping. This alidade station was 55 m from the alidade station on Structure D at an angle of 12.5° E of magnetic north. The shortest distance between the two buildings, however, was only about 22 m, from the northeast corner of Room 4 of Structure 9 to the southwest corner of the Southwest Canchón of Structure D.

In the course of sweeping the surface of Structure 9, we recovered a small collection of di-agnostic sherds (Figures 8.4–8.8). This collection, which suggests that Structures D and 9 were broadly contemporaneous, is as follows:

Camacho Reddish Brown (Figure 8.4)
Cambered rim from large jar: 1
Globular jar with low neck, bolstered rim, strap handle: 1 (fire-blackened)
Everted rim from jar: 1
Unusual restricted-orifice bowl with red slip (7.5 R 3/6) and a circular "swelling" pushed out from the interior: 1
Body sherds: 8

Camacho Black (Standard Variety)
Jar neck with coffee-bean eye from a face: 1

Pingüino Buff (Figures 8.5–8.8)
Jar with plain rim, white wash: 1 rim (Figure 8.7d)
Jar with cambered rim: 1 rim (Figure 8.7c)
Jar (?) with flaring rim; painted black over thin white wash; rim ticking: 1 rim (Figure 8.6b)
Large jar with flaring rim, painted white on natural: 1 rim (Figure 8.7b)
Funnel neck from jar with everted rim, corner of painted face (upper left cheek area), painted black and red on natural: 1
Neck from amphora or jar showing left cheek area of face, painted black/white/red: 1 (Figure 8.8)

Figure 8.1. Two views of Structure 9. *(Top)*: a view of Structures D and 9 from the north, showing their relationship. (Structure I can be seen in the distance.) *(Bottom)*: excavation beginning on Structure 9. This view shows the northeast corner of the building, with Rooms 3 and 4 partially exposed.

Jar shoulder showing black-and-white painting over natural buff: 1

Jar shoulder with white slip: 1

Jar sherd with raised arm (?) modeled on it: 1

Jar body sherd, painted black and white over natural buff with cream wash: 1 (Figure 8.5b)

Jar neck with eye of painted and modeled face; nose broken off; painted white on natural: 1 (Figure 8.5c)

Incurved-rim bowl with rolled rim and broken-off spout (?), highly burnished: 1 rim (Figure 8.5d)

Rim of neckless jar with cream slip, painted black on white with "school of fish" motif: 1 (Figure 8.6a)

Small strap handle from jar: 1

Jar body sherd, painted black and white: 1

Jar body sherd, painted black over cream slip, "school of fish" motif: 1 (Figure 8.6c)

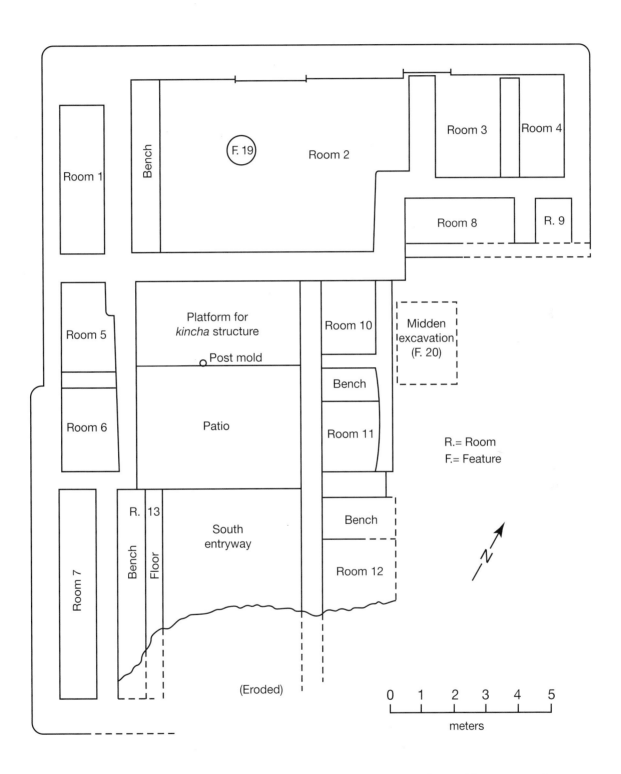

Figure 8.2. Plan of Structure 9, showing rooms and features from both earlier and later stages of occupation.

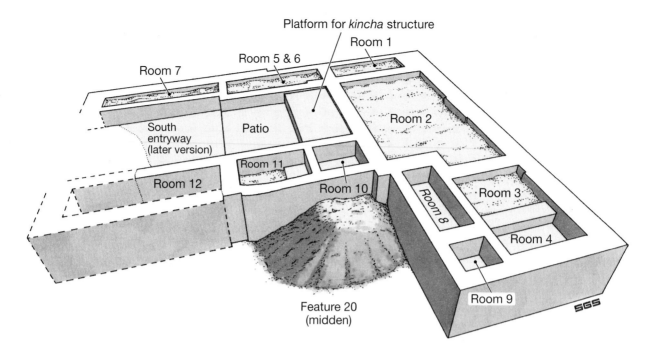

Figure 8.3. Artist's conception of Structure 9 during a late stage of occupation, when many of the rooms had been modified or converted to fish storage units.

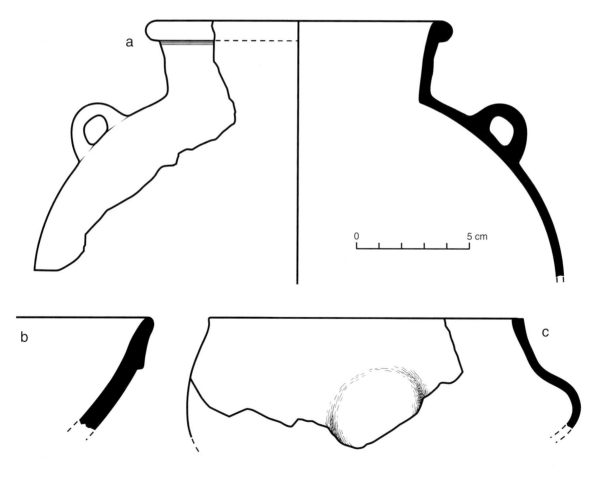

Figure 8.4. Camacho Reddish Brown sherds found on the surface of Structure 9 while the area of Rooms 3–5 was being swept prior to excavation. *(a)*: globular jar with low neck, bolstered rim, and vertically set strap handle; fire-blackened; *(b)*: cambered rim from large jar; *(c)*: unusual vessel with red slip; "swelling" pushed through from the interior.

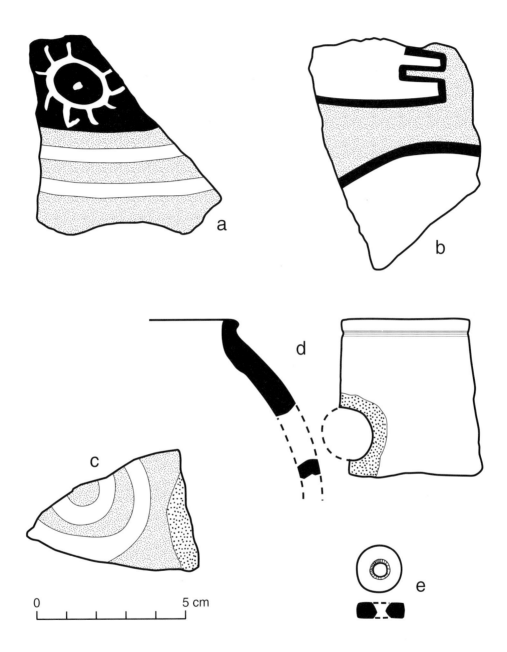

Figure 8.5. Miscellaneous sherds found on the surface of Structure 9 while it was being swept prior to excavation. (*a*): jar body sherd, paste similar to Pingüino Buff but not identical. An octopus motif is painted in white on a zone of chocolate brown wash; below are two stripes of white paint on natural buff (light stipple indicates natural buff). (*b*): Pingüino Buff jar body sherd, painted in black and white on natural. The white is a kind of cream wash (light stipple indicates natural buff). (*c*): Pingüino Buff jar neck sherd which bore a painted and modeled human face. The eye is painted in white on natural (light stipple indicates natural buff; coarse stipple shows where the nose broke off). (*d*): Pingüino Buff incurved-rim bowl with rolled rim and broken-off spout (?) of some kind; coarse stipple indicates broken surface. (*e*): drilled sherd disk made from a Pingüino Buff sherd, slipped cream white on one side; biconically drilled.

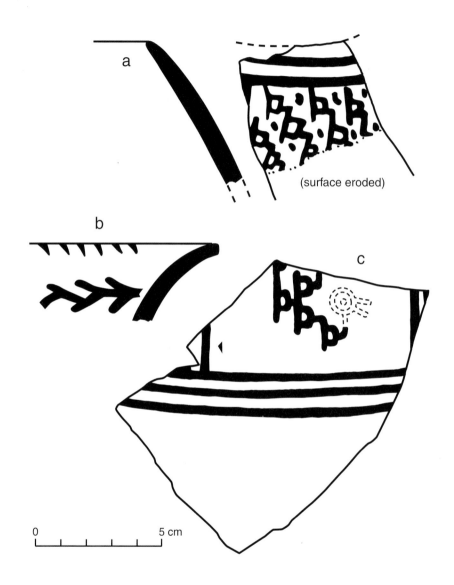

Figure 8.6. Eroded Pingüino Buff sherds found on the surface of Structure 9 while the west side was being swept prior to excavation. *(a)*: neckless jar with yellowish cream slip, painted in black on white with a "school-of-fish" motif (?); *(b)*: flaring rim of jar (?) painted in black over a thin watery white wash; *(c)*: jar body sherd with a yellowish cream slip on the exterior; design painted in black over that.

Jar body sherd, painted black/white/red (10
    R 3/2); octopus motif: 1 (Figure 8.7e)
Sherd from "fat skeleton," showing spine
    and incised ribs: 1 (Figure 8.7a)
Body sherds: 9

Atypical Sherd with Pingüino Buff-like Paste
Jar body sherd with zone of chocolate
    brown wash above natural buff, octo-
    pus motif in white paint: 1 (Figure
    8.5a)

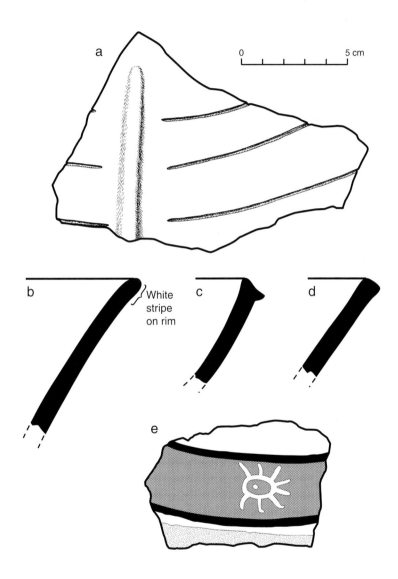

Figure 8.7. Pingüino Buff sherds found on the surface of Structure 9 while the area of Rooms 3–5 was being swept prior to excavation. *(a)*: body sherd from a "fat skeleton" pot, reminiscent of one found in Structure D (see Figure 7.13). The ribs are incised and run outward from a modeled spinal column which is not divided into individual vertebrae (fire-smudged on lower part). *(b)*: flaring rim of large jar, painted white on natural as shown; *(c)*: cambered rim from jar; *(d)*: plain rim from jar, given a white wash on the exterior and the top of the rim; *(e)*: jar body sherd with cream-white wash or slip above, natural buff (shown as light stipple) below; octopus motif painted in white over red band bordered with black.

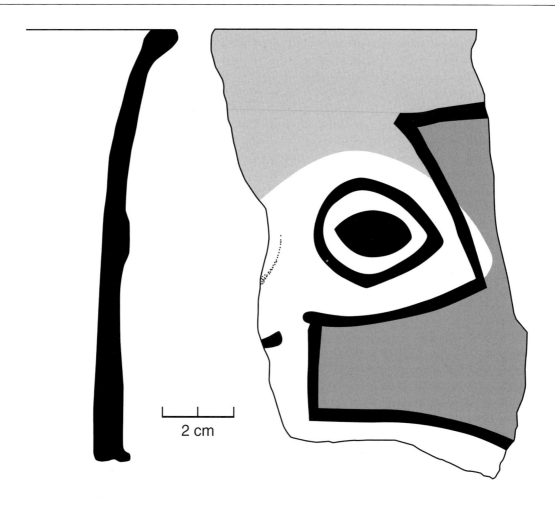

Figure 8.8. Pingüino Buff amphora (or jar) neck with human face modeled and painted on the exterior in black/white/red over natural buff (shown as light gray screen). Found on the surface above the South Entryway of Structure 9 while it was being swept prior to excavation. Both the nose and the eye are in raised relief.

THE LAYOUT OF STRUCTURE 9

Our sweeping revealed that Structure 9 had been divided into at least 15 spaces. The main point of entry had been from the south, which unfortunately was the most eroded part of the building. Complicating our efforts to reconstruct the building's layout was the fact that the plan had been modified during the occupation, possibly several times.

Figure 8.3 shows an artist's reconstruction of Structure 9 as seen from the east. Access would have been from the south, through an entryway flanked by a somewhat enigmatic unit we called Room 13 (Figure 8.2). Room 13 consisted of a long narrow tapia bench above an even narrower stretch of floor. The bench lay 117.5 cm below

datum, the floor 127 cm below datum, and the earlier version of the entryway 177 cm below datum (Figure 8.9, top). At a later stage of occupation, Room 13 and the earlier entryway were filled in, and a new clay floor was laid over them at a depth of 99 cm below datum. This new floor widened the entryway by covering Room 13 completely (Figure 8.9, bottom).

Once having traversed the entryway, a visitor entering Structure 9 would have reached a rectangular patio measuring 5.1 × 3.7 m. To the north of this patio was an elevated tapia platform 5.1 × 2.5 m in extent. There were signs that a *kincha* house had once sat on this platform, with its floor at a depth of 9.5 cm below datum. At least one post mold and multiple chunks of cane-im-

Figure 8.9. Two views of an earlier stage of the South Entryway (floor, 177 cm below datum), Structure 9. *(Top)*: view from the north. *(Bottom)*: view from the east. To the right of the workman, one can see the fill placed over the earlier floor and the bench of Room 13.

pressed daub from the house were found in association with the platform.

The elevated platform, patio, and elongated entryway seem to define the north–south axis of Structure 9. This linear sequence of structures allows us to divide the rest of the building into a north complex of rooms, a west complex of rooms, and an east complex of rooms.

Only a few sherds were found while exposing the entryway. During the course of sweeping the area prior to excavation, we found the neck of a Pingüino Buff amphora or jar, painted and modeled as a human face, with the usual zoned red facial painting (2.5 YR 3/4, dark reddish brown) (Figure 8.8). At a depth of 177 cm below datum, in association with the earlier stage of the entryway (Figure 8.9, top), we recovered a collection of 24 sherds, five of which are shown in Figure 8.10. The full list is as follows:

Camacho Reddish Brown (Figure 8.10a, b)
    Cambered rim from jar: 1

Cooking pot with restricted orifice: 1 rim
    (fire-blackened)
Body sherds of *tinajones*: 3
Body sherds: 5

Camacho Black (Standard Variety) (Figure 8.10c)
    Everted rim from jar: 1
    Strap handle from jar: 1
    Body sherds: 6

Pingüino Buff (Figure 8.10d–f)
    Bowl with cambered rim, weak white wash
        on exterior: 1 rim

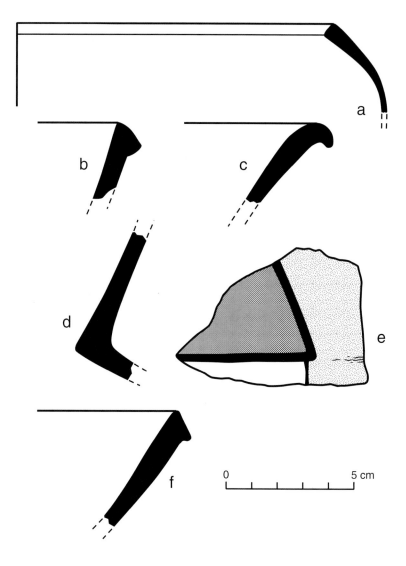

Figure 8.10. Ceramics found at a depth of 177 cm below the surface in the South Entryway of Structure 9. *(a)*: Camacho Reddish Brown cooking pot with restricted orifice, fire-blackened; *(b)*: Camacho Reddish Brown jar with cambered rim; *(c)*: Camacho Black (standard variety) jar with everted rim. *(d, e)*: Pingüino Buff jar with funnel neck, painted on the exterior in black/white/red; the design was probably a human face with facial painting. *(d)*: profile; *(e)*: exterior of sherd (medium screen indicates red; light stipple indicates natural buff); *(f)*: Pingüino Buff bowl with weak white wash on exterior; cambered rim.

Funnel neck from jar with facial painting in
   black/white/red: 1
Strap handle fragment (?): 1
Body sherds: 3

THE NORTH COMPLEX

At the north end of Structure 9 was a complex of six tapia-walled units: Rooms 1, 2, 3, 4, 8, and 9. Room 2 was the largest and may originally have

been residential in function, but like so many of the rooms in Structure D, it had later been converted to fish storage. We begin our tour of this complex on the west, with Room 1.

Room 1

Room 1 was roughly 1.4 × 4.4 m in extent and had suffered considerable earthquake damage (Figure 8.11). Whatever this room's original function, its floor had buckled so badly that it became suitable

Figure 8.11. Room 1 of Structure 9, seen from the north after all the sand had been removed. This photo shows the strong buckling of the floor caused by seismic activity. This damage led to Room 1 being converted to fish storage.

only for fish storage; accordingly, it had been filled with sand. We fine-screened the entire room and recovered a sample of fish bone, both from the sand itself and from places where fish skin and scales were adhering to the clay floor (Figure 8.12).

The buckling of Room 1 made it difficult to calculate its storage capacity for fish. For example, the floor at the south end of the room lay 100 cm below datum, while the north end of the floor had collapsed to 160 cm below datum. Our estimate of Room 1's potential fish storage capacity is roughly 0.67 m^3.

 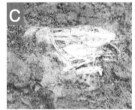

Figure 8.12. Fish remains from Room 1 of Structure 9. *(a)*: patch of fish skin and scales adhering to the clay floor; *(b)*: section of fish vertebrae incorporated into a sand layer; *(c)*: crushed anchovy skull adhering to clay floor.

Room 2

Room 2 was the largest in Structure 9, measuring 8.6 × 5.2 m (Figure 8.13). It presented us with a series of floors and some evident changes in function. Its earliest floor lay 141 cm below datum, and I suspect that the room was a residential unit at that time; it had a possible "sleeping bench" 90 cm wide running along its west wall, its surface 47 cm above the floor (Figure 8.2).

At some point this room's function had changed, and some 1.29 m of sand had been laid over the original floor. There were anchovy bones in this sand but virtually no sherds. We could detect no structural damage, such as cracks from earthquakes that would have necessitated Room 2's abandonment as a residential unit. It seemed possible, therefore, that its conversion was designed to increase the building's fish storage capacity by more than 50 m^3.

One possible scenario is that early in the building's history, Room 2 was the residence of its most important occupant. After the need for greater storage capacity was recognized, that occupant built himself a *kincha* residence on the platform immediately to the south and converted Room 2 to fish storage.

At a still later stage of occupation, the function of Room 2 changed again. A well-made clay floor was laid over the sand at a depth of 12 cm below datum. The most interesting feature found in association with this later floor was a large *tinajón* or conical storage vessel buried near the center of the room, its rim only 15–20 cm above the floor (Figure 8.14).

Designated Feature 19, this large storage vessel had broken during the intervening centuries but could be reconstructed (Figure 8.15). Both its shape and the way it had been buried reminded us of the *hatun maccma* or *chicha* storage vessels found in the North Central Canchón of Structure D (Chapter 7). This vessel was smaller than a *hatun maccma* and was made of Pingüino Buff rather than a coarse version of Camacho Reddish Brown. However, it had similar maize-cob effigy lugs, suggesting that it too might have been used to store *chicha*.

Figure 8.13. A view of Structure 9 from a terrace above Structure H, showing work in progress. The crew on the right is exposing Room 2. The crew on the left is completing excavation of the South Entryway.

Figure 8.14. Feature 19, a large vessel set in the uppermost floor of Room 2, Structure 9, as it was first encountered. View from the west. The two objects resting on the fill inside the vessel are beach cobbles.

Feature 19 was 60 cm high and had a rim diameter of 81 cm. The exterior had a sloppily applied, streaky white wash that extended down over the natural buff surface to a point roughly

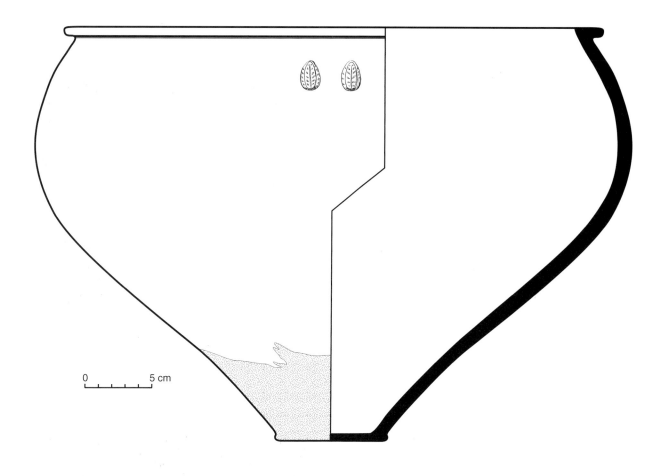

Figure 8.15. Reconstruction drawing of large Pingüino Buff *tinajón* designated Feature 19, found in Room 2, Structure 9. This large storage vessel had been buried in sand to within 15–20 cm of its rim. The vessel has an everted rim and appliqué lugs in the shape of maize cobs. The interior of the vessel is smoothed but unslipped. The exterior has a sloppily applied, streaky white wash which extends down to about 15 cm above the base (light stipple indicates natural buff). Rim diameter: 81 cm. Height: 60 cm.

15 cm from the base. The interior of the vessel was smoothed but unslipped. The best-preserved side had a pair of lugs in the shape of maize cobs, each 4.2 cm long and 1.7 cm wide (Figure 8.16). We assume that the other side of the vessel, which is not preserved, had a matching pair of lugs. Such paired lugs, set 3.5 cm apart, 5 cm below the rim, would have allowed the heavy vessel to be carried with a rope harness.

When Feature 19 was first discovered, it had two unmodified beach cobbles resting on the dust

and sand that had filled it after Structure 9 was abandoned. There is no evidence that these cobbles had been associated with the vessel during its use.

Little else of note was found with the most recent floor of Room 2. It is possible that during the later stages of occupation of Structure 9, an overseer or administrator living in the *kincha* house immediately to the south kept a good supply of *chicha* available in Room 2, perhaps to reward the workmen who filled or emptied the fish storage units in the rest of the building.

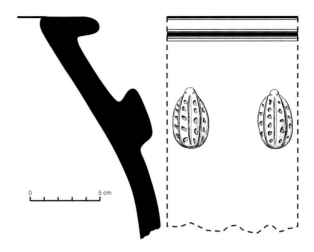

Figure 8.16. One large sherd of the Pingüino Buff *tinajón* designated Feature 19, found in Room 2, Structure 9. The drawing shows how two modeled lugs, incised and punctated to resemble maize cobs, were placed as a pair on the upper shoulder of the jar just below the everted rim. (It is assumed that a matching pair of lugs was placed on the opposite side of the vessel.) Like the entire upper portion of the jar's exterior, the lugs are covered with a white wash.

Room 3

Room 3 was one of a group of four small rooms to the east of Room 2. All four had probably been storage units of some kind. There were signs that some of these small rooms had been created from larger rooms by the addition of later walls. In particular, the tapia wall between Rooms 3 and 4 appears to have been a later addition (see Figure 8.2).

Room 3 measured 2 × 3 m; its floor lay an average of 68 cm below datum and sloped downward as it ran east. Its fill included greenish gray sand, presumably from an episode of fish storage. Among the most interesting contents of the room, however, are the remains of a destroyed *kincha* structure, including fragments of *caña brava* and chunks of cane-impressed daub. Since Room 3 seems a bit small to have contained a wattle-and-daub structure, it may be that this room simply became a convenient dumping place for the remains of the *kincha* house from the platform nearby.

Ceramics were recovered from two contexts in Room 3: (1) lying directly on the floor and (2) in the fill above the floor. Lying directly on the floor was a typical Pingüino Buff jar neck with a human face painted on it. Only the right side of the face is preserved, with black-outlined red facial paint over a black-and-white face. The Munsell color of the red is 7.5 R 4/4, "weak red."

The collection of pottery from the fill is only slightly larger, consisting of six sherds. A sample of these sherds can be seen in Figure 8.17, and the full collection is as follows:

Camacho Reddish Brown (Figure 8.17a)
   Cooking pot with restricted orifice: 1 rim (fire-blackened)

Camacho Black (Standard Variety) (Figure 8.17d)
   Everted rim from jar or amphora: 1

Pingüino Buff (Figure 8.17b, c)
   Funnel neck from jar, everted rim, painted white on natural: 1
   Body sherd from large jar, traces of black zoning line: 1
   Body sherd painted black on white, probably from globular jar: 1

Atypical sherd
   Body sherd of jar, with paste resembling that of Pingüino Buff; however, the paste shows an atypical gray sandwiched between pinkish buff layers; outside of vessel is highly burnished: 1

Our final discovery in Room 3 was an intrusive secondary burial in the northeast corner of the room. Designated Burial 10, this interment consists of the partial remains of two individuals, an adult and an infant, placed in the room when it was already two-thirds full of windblown sand, decomposed tapia, and fragments of wall collapse. The adult is represented by a skull (wrapped in coarse cloth), femur, tibia, and fibula. The infant is represented only by a pelvis. No ceramics or other offerings were included with Burial 10, which may be the reburied remains of individuals accidentally dug up elsewhere.

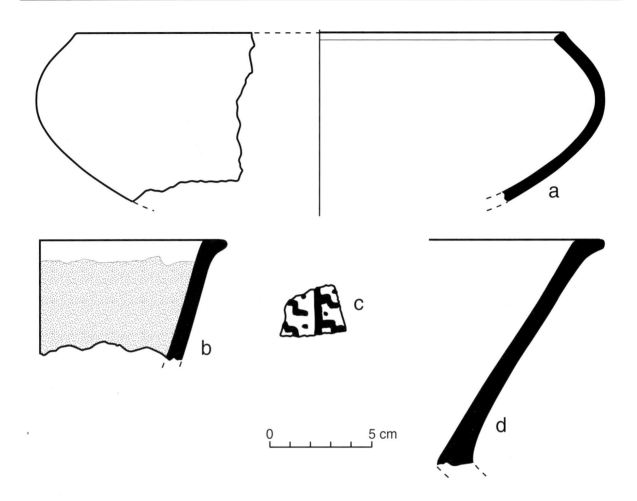

Figure 8.17. Ceramics found above the floor of Room 3, Structure 9. *(a)*: Camacho Reddish Brown cooking pot with restricted orifice; fire-blackened (this vessel may have had strap handles, but too little was found to confirm it). *(b)*: Pingüino Buff funnel neck from jar with everted rim; interior painted white on natural (light stipple indicates natural buff). *(c)*: Pingüino Buff sherd, probably from the shoulder of a globular jar; exterior painted black on white. *(d)*: Camacho Black (standard variety) everted rim from jar or amphora.

Room 4

Room 4, another small storage unit, measured 3 × 1.4 m. We found its original floor (now broken, buckled, and uneven) at a depth of roughly 78 cm below datum. We suspect that Rooms 3 and 4 had once been a single room, now divided by a later wall. The fact that the floor of Room 4 is now 10 cm lower than the floor of Room 3 can probably be blamed on seismic disturbance.

Room 4 contained greenish gray sand, as well as some brownish earth and maize cobs. We recovered 54 sherds from the floor, some of which are shown in Figure 8.18. The full collection is as follows:

Camacho Reddish Brown (Figure 8.18a–d)
    Jars with cambered rims: 3 rims

Jar shoulder: 1
Basal sherd from amphora or tapering jar:
    1
Body sherds, mostly from jars: 25

Camacho Black (Standard Variety)
    Body sherds, mostly from jars: 7

Pingüino Buff (Figure 8.18e–g)
    Everted rim, probably from jar with funnel
        neck: 1
    Neckless jar with rolled rim, painted black
        and white on natural: 1 rim
    Jar body sherd, black-and-white painting:
        1
    Body sherds, mostly from jars: 14

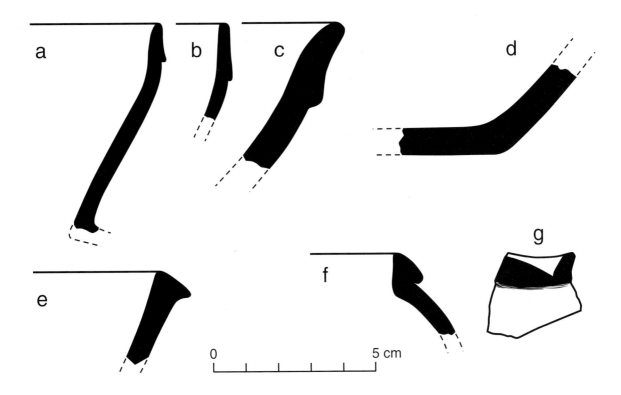

Figure 8.18. Ceramics found above the floor of Room 4, Structure 9. *(a–c)*: Camacho Reddish Brown jars with cambered rims; *(d)*: Camacho Reddish Brown jar or amphora base; *(e)*: Pingüino Buff everted rim, probably from funnel-necked jar; eroded, possibly painted white on natural. *(f, g)*: Pingüino Buff neckless jar with rolled rim, painted in black and white on natural on the top of the rim. *(f)*: profile; *(g)*: exterior of sherd.

Room 8

Room 8, immediately to the south of Room 3, measured 3.4 × 1.4 m; its floor was found 88 cm below datum. This room was filled with the remains of disintegrated tapia rather than sand.

The ceramic collection from Room 8 consists almost entirely of large, often partially restorable, storage and cooking vessels. Not only are the diagnostic sherds big, but even the body sherds could be fitted together into large vessel segments. My assessment of this collection is that even though it may be a secondary deposit, it had not been moved far from its original place of use.

Figures 8.19–8.24 illustrate many of the diagnostic sherds from Room 8. The full collection is as follows:

Camacho Reddish Brown (Figures 8.19–8.21)
    Jars with flaring rim: 2 rims
    Jars with cambered rim: 4 rims (2 are fire-blackened)

Cooking pots with restricted orifice, brushed exterior, rolled rim: 3 rims (fire-smudged below rim)
Jar with unusual bowl-shaped neck: 1 rim
Jar with narrow neck, plain rim, strap handles linking neck to shoulder: 1 neck (fire-blackened)
Cooking pot with restricted orifice and vertically set strap handle: 1 rim (fire-blackened)
Body sherds: 8 (fairly large)

Pingüino Buff (Figures 8.22–8.24)
    Large jar with funnel neck, painted white on natural: 2 rims (Figure 8.23a)
    Large strap handle from jar listed above, fitting with several large body sherds: 1 (Figure 8.22)
    Large body sherds painted white on natural: 6 (all from the same jar)

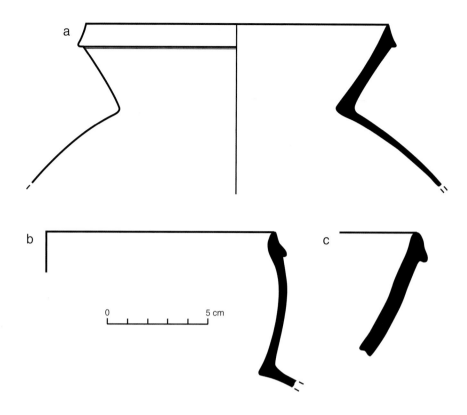

Figure 8.19. Camacho Reddish Brown vessels from Room 8, Structure 9. (*a*): jar with cambered rim, fire-blackened; (*b, c*): jars with cambered rims.

Figure 8.20. Camacho Reddish Brown vessels from Room 8, Structure 9. (*a*): un-usual jar neck, shaped like a bowl with a shallow horizontal groove encircling it; (*b*): flaring rim from jar.

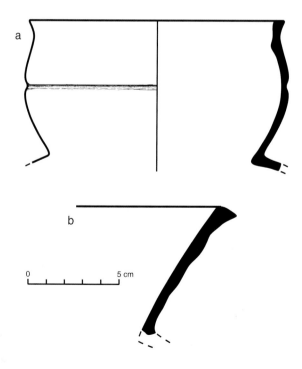

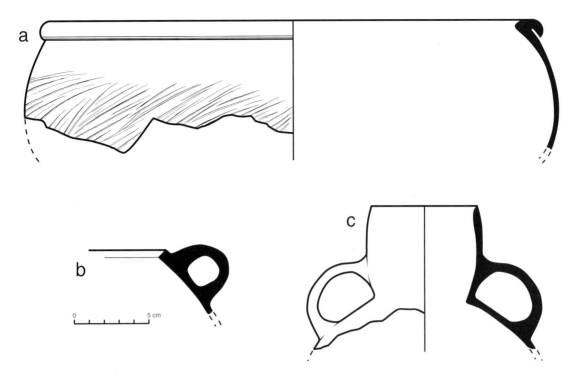

Figure 8.21. Camacho Reddish Brown vessels from Room 8, Structure 9. *(a)*: cooking pot with restricted orifice and rolled rim; brushed on the exterior; fire-smudged below the midsection; *(b)*: cooking pot with restricted orifice and vertically set strap handle; fire-blackened; *(c)*: jar with narrow neck, plain rim, and strap handles linking the neck and shoulder; fire-blackened.

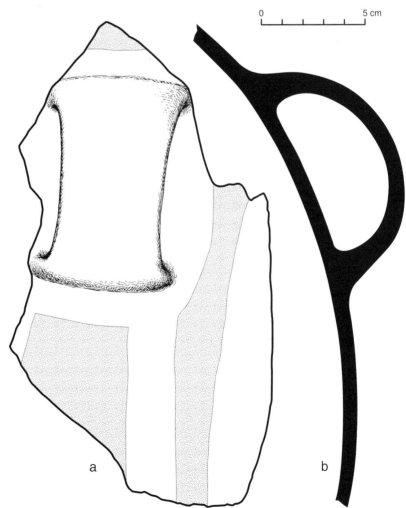

Figure 8.22. Pingüino Buff vessel from Room 8, Structure 9. *(a, b)*: Pingüino Buff jar body sherd with vertically set strap handle and sloppy white-on-natural painting. *(a)*: exterior of sherd; *(b)*: profile. Light stipple indicates natural buff.

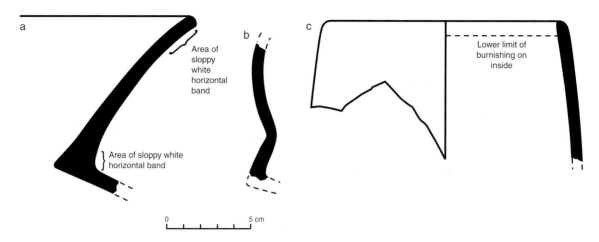

Figure 8.23. Pingüino Buff vessels from Room 8, Structure 9. *(a)*: rim from funnel-necked jar with sloppy white bands painted on the exterior as shown; *(b)*: jar neck with "swelling" pushed through from the interior; *(c)*: cylindrical jar neck, highly burnished on the exterior; burnished on the interior only to 1 cm below the rim, as shown by the dashed line.

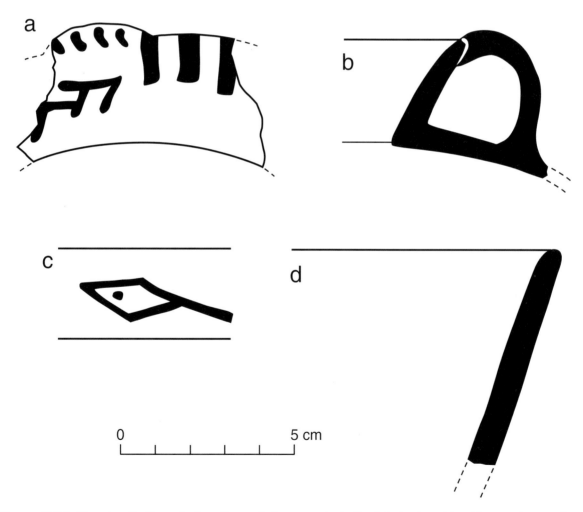

Figure 8.24. Pingüino Buff vessels from Room 8, Structure 9. *(a, b)*: globular jar with wide mouth, strap handle linking the rim to the shoulder; painted black and white on the interior of the rim. *(a)*: interior of rim, showing motifs; *(b)*: profile. What appears to be a bump on the upper margin of *a* is really the attachment of the strap handle shown in *b* (there are horizontal black-on-white stripes on the handle, not shown). *(c)*: reconstruction of eroded fish motif painted in black on white inside the rim of a second jar like the one shown in *a*; *(d)*: open bowl, burnished inside and out.

Globular jars with wide mouth, painted black and white on rim, black and white on exterior of body: 1 with strap handle, 1 without (Figure 8.24a–c)

Jar neck with "swelling" pushed through from interior: 1 (Figure 8.23b)

Cylindrical jar neck, highly burnished on exterior: 3 rims (from same vessel) (Figure 8.23c)

Open bowl, highly burnished on interior and exterior: 1 rim (Figure 8.24d)

Burnished body sherds: 5 (fairly large)

Room 9

Room 9 was the smallest of the four storage units to the east of Room 2, measuring only 1.1 × 1.4 m. Its floor was reached at 88–90 cm below datum. Nothing of note was found in Room 9, whose fill consisted mainly of drift sand, dust, and disintegrated tapia.

THE WEST COMPLEX

The West Complex consists of Rooms 5, 6, and 7—three storage units along the west side of the building—and Room 13, a somewhat enigmatic unit eventually covered up by a later version of the South Entryway (see above).

Room 5

As Figure 8.25 shows, Rooms 5 and 6 had once been a single long, narrow room. At some point during the occupation of Structure 9, a tapia crosswall had been added, dividing one room into

Figure 8.25. Rooms 6 (foreground) and 5 (background) of Structure 9, seen from the south after the removal of their sand contents. Cirilo Cruz serves as scale.

two. Both Rooms 5 and 6 had been used for the storage of small fish and contained thick layers of greenish gray sand.

Room 5 measures 2.7 × 1.6 m, and its walls are preserved to a height of 44 cm above the floor. (The floor itself was found at an average depth of 150 cm below datum.) We were able to fine-screen roughly 1.9 m³ of sand from this room. Compared with other storage units, Room 5 produced a great many sherds, significant faunal remains, and five grinding stones or *manos de batán*. This fact suggests to us that

after its main use as a storage room, Room 5 was used as a convenient place to dump trash.

There are two contexts in which ceramics occurred in Room 5: (1) in the greenish sand layer and (2) on top of it. The sherds in the sand layer (stratigraphically the earlier of the two collections) are as follows:

Camacho Reddish Brown (Figures 8.26–8.28)
 Jars with cambered rims: 15 rim sherds
 Jars with everted rims: 2 rim sherds

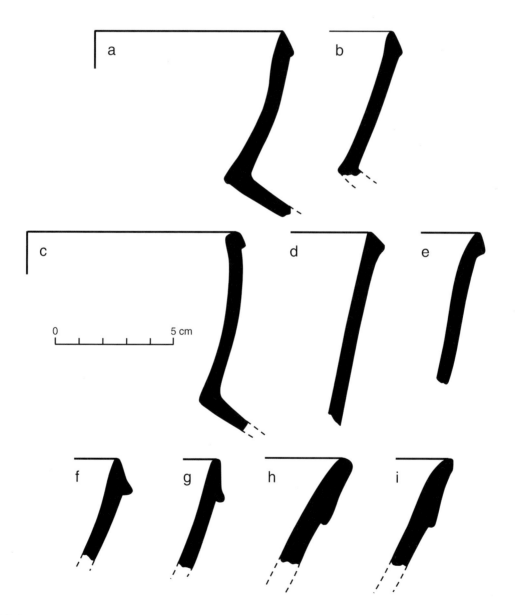

Figure 8.26. Camacho Reddish Brown vessels from the fill of Room 5, Structure 9. All specimens are jars with cambered rims; the drawing is intended to show the variety of rim forms. Two rims had the form shown in *a* and *b*; two had the form shown in *c*; one had the form shown in *d*; one had the form shown in *e*; three have the form shown in *f* and *g*; and two had the form shown in *h* and *i*.

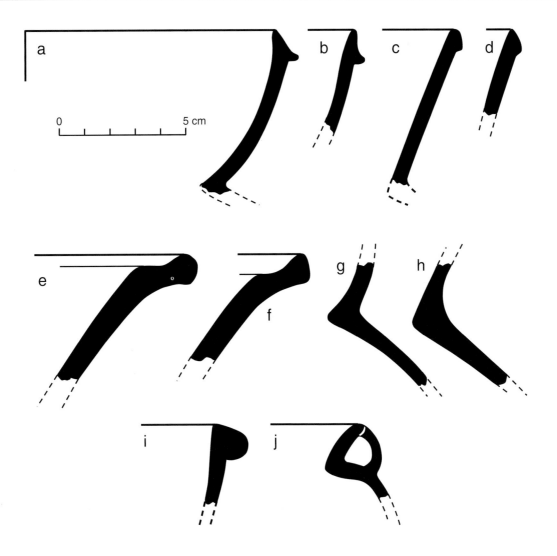

0   5 cm

Figure 8.27. Camacho Reddish Brown vessels from the fill of Room 5, Structure 9. All specimens are jars. Sherds *a–d* show varieties of cambered rims. Two specimens had the form shown in *a* and *b*; two more had the form shown in *c* and *d*. *(e, f)*: jars with everted rims; *(g, h)*: jar shoulders; *(i)*: jar with bolstered rim; *(j)*: small globular jar with strap handle linking rim and shoulder.

Jar shoulders: 7
Jar with bolstered rim: 1 rim
Jar with low neck, plain rim, strap handle linking rim and shoulder: 1 neck
Strap handles from jars: 4
Cooking pots with restricted orifice: 7 rims (fire-blackened)
Cooking pots with restricted orifice and horizontally set strap handle: 2 sherds
Body sherds, mostly from jars: 105

Camacho Black (Standard Variety) (Figure 8.29e–g)
Flaring rims from jars: 2

Small jar with strap handles linking neck and shoulder: 1 neck
Body sherds: 15

Camacho Black (Highly Burnished Variety) (Figure 8.29a–d)
Outleaned wall bowl: 1 rim sherd
Flaring rim from open bowl: 1
Neck of miniature bottle (?) with ear from modeled human face: 1
Jar body sherd from miniature vessel with modeled arm (?): 1
Small effigy vessel with incised flanges: 3 body sherds

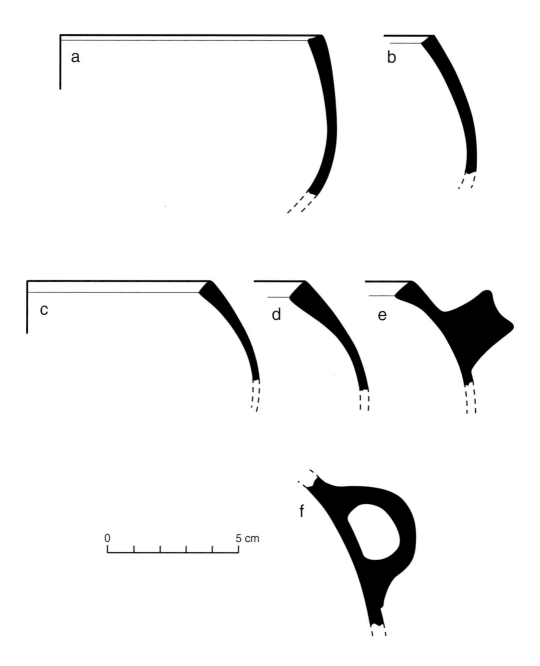

Figure 8.28. Camacho Reddish Brown vessels from the fill of Room 5, Structure 9. *(a–e)*: cooking pots with restricted orifice; the drawing is intended to show the variety of rim forms. Sherd *e* has a horizontally set strap handle; *(f)*: vertically set strap handle, possibly from a jar.

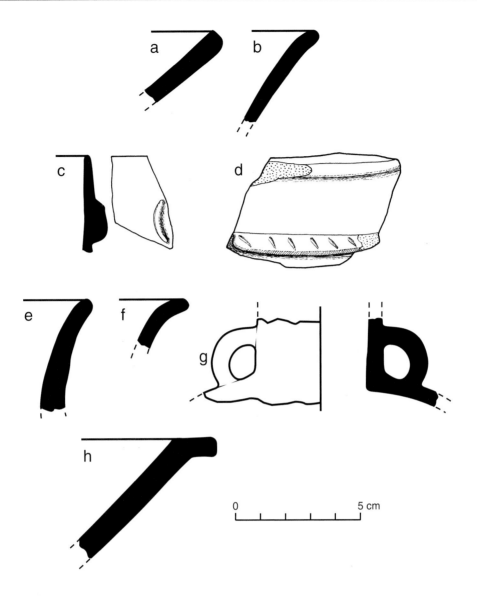

Figure 8.29. Vessels from the fill of Room 5, Structure 9. *(a–d)*: Camacho Black, highly burnished variety. *(a)*: outleaned wall of open bowl; *(b)*: flaring rim from open bowl; *(c)*: rim of small jar with modeled ear from human face; *(d)*: fragment of vessel with incised decorative flanges (stipple indicates damaged areas). *(e–g)*: Camacho Black, standard variety. *(e, f)*: flaring rims from jars; *(g)*: jar neck with strap handles linking neck and shoulder. *(h)*: atypical orange variety of Pingüino Buff, everted rim from jar.

Pingüino Buff (Figures 8.30, 8.31)
    Large funnel-neck jars with everted rim, face modeled on neck, painted white on natural: 2 rims, 2 neck sherds
    Large funnel neck from jar, burnished, painted red on shoulder: 2 neck sherds
    Funnel neck from jar, everted rim, face with black/white/red paint on neck: 1 rim

    sherd, 5 neck sherds
    Jar body sherds, pale white wash filling zone set off from burnished natural buff by black lines: 2
    Body sherds of jar, painted cream on natural, perhaps with modeled "arm": 2
    Jar body sherd, raised vertical band painted black and white, the rest natural buff: 1

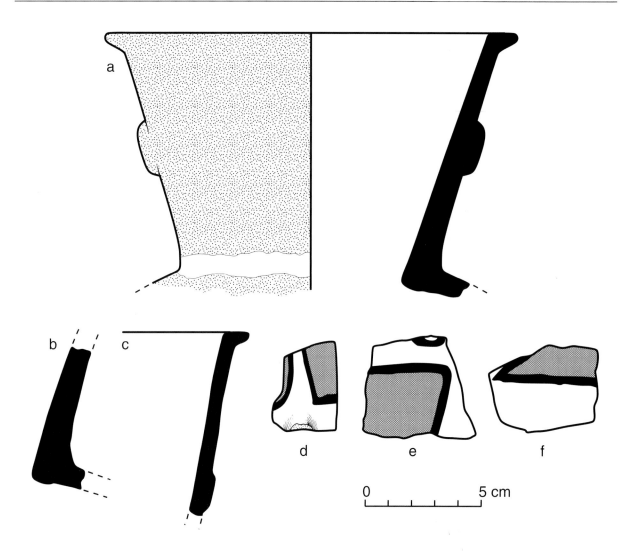

Figure 8.30. Pingüino Buff vessels from the fill of Room 5, Structure 9. *(a)*: funnel neck from jar with everted rim (reconstructed from one large sherd). This jar had a modeled human face on its neck, most of it now missing. The base of the neck had a horizontal white stripe (light stipple indicates natural buff). *(b)*: jar neck similar to *a*, but with a red stripe instead of a white one; *(c)*: everted rim of jar, with trace of modeled human ear and facial painting. *(d–f)*: sherds from jar necks with modeled and painted faces; the colors involved are cream white, black, and red (10 R 4/4), the latter shown by medium screen. Sherd *d* shows the bridge of the nose; *e* shows the eye and cheek; *f* shows the lower face.

Jar body sherds, painted black over cream
    wash: 2
Strap handles from jars: 2 fragments
Globular jar with wide mouth, painted
    black on natural on interior of rim,
    probably black and white on exterior of
    body: 1 eroded rim
Body sherds of globular jars with wide
    mouth, painted black and white: 2
Incurved-rim bowl, slightly bolstered rim
    (?): 1 rim

Miscellaneous fragments of small painted
    bowls: 5
Body sherds, mostly from jars: 40 (32 plain,
    8 white-painted)

*Atypical Orange Variety of Pingüino Buff (Figures
8.29h; 8.32a, b)*
    Jar with everted rim: 1 rim sherd
    Jar body sherd: 1
    Unusual cylindrical vessel which appears to
        be an effigy representation of a roll of

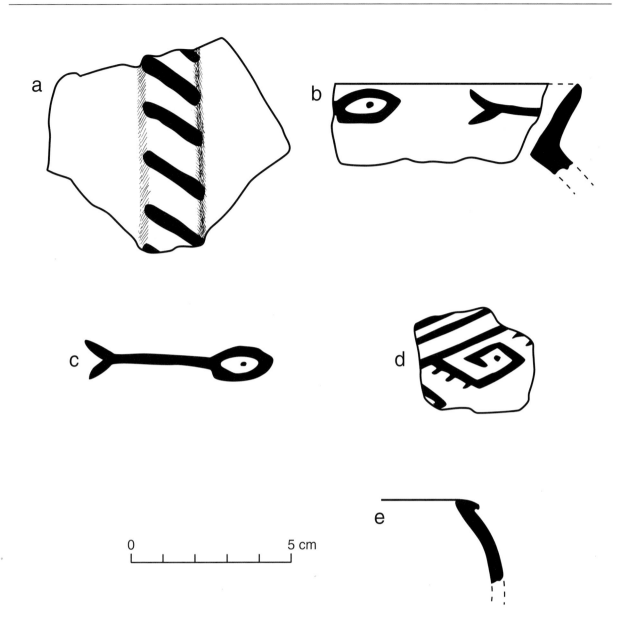

Figure 8.31. Pingüino Buff vessels from the fill of Room 5, Structure 9. (*a*): jar body sherd with raised vertical band painted black and white; natural buff to either side. (*b*): globular jar with wide mouth, painted black on natural on inside of rim as shown. The motif (reconstructed in *c*) is probably a fish, perhaps an anchovy. (*d*): jar body sherd, painted in black and white as shown; (*e*): small bowl with incurved and bolstered rim.

brown-and-white striped cloth, perhaps a funerary wrapping, with a small strap handle: 6 sherds (Figure 8.32a, b) [cream stripes = 10 YR 8/4; brown stripes = 10 R 3/2]

Sherds that do not fit into one of the previous categories (Figures 8.32, 8.33)
   Small jar with strap handle, slipped yellow-cream (7.5 YR 7/4–8/4), painted black and white with "school of fish" motif; paste is most like Trambollo Burnished Brown, but vessel is atypical: 2 sherds (Figure 8.32c)
Rim of jar with restricted orifice; pale brown surface and paste like Trambollo Burnished Brown, but eroded, unclassifiable: 1 (Figure 8.33a)
Hollow vessel appendage (leg?) with traces of white/black/red paint, unknown

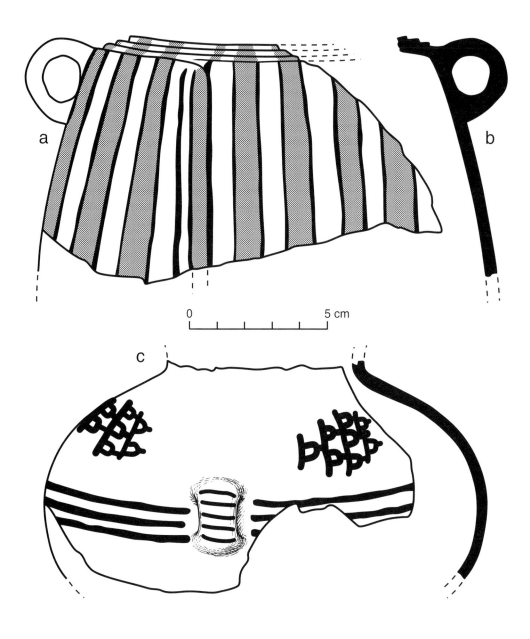

Figure 8.32. Ceramics from the fill of Room 5, Structure 9. *(a, b)*: unique vessel made in the atypical orange variety of Pingüino Buff. The vessel is painted in imitation of a typical Late Intermediate brown-and-white striped burial wrapping; it has loop handles. Sherd *a* shows the vessel exterior; *b* shows the profile. *(c)*: unique jar with vertically set strap handle, painted in black over a strong cream slip, featuring a "school of fish" motif.

sandy light brown paste: 1 (Figure 8.33b)

Jar body sherd with "hand" motif. Light brown, painted white and black; paste shows gray core sandwiched between reddish layers; fire-blackened on inside of jar: 1

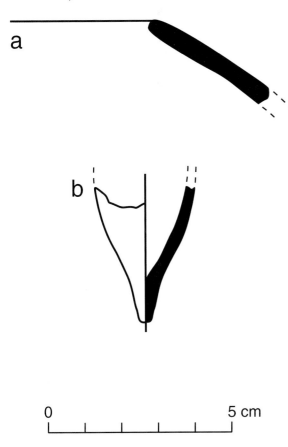

Figure 8.33. Unusual ceramics from the fill of Room 5, Structure 9. *(a)*: eroded rim of hole-mouth jar, unknown ware, with pale brown paste and surface; *(b)*: hollow appendage with traces of black/white/red paint, unknown ware.

Conclusions

The collection of ceramics from the sand fill of Room 5 includes many large sherds and partially restorable vessels, suggesting that it had not been moved far or often and could be considered a good secondary collection. The mix of types (including Pingüino Buff and the highly burnished variety of Camacho Black) is what we would expect to see in a residential room rather than a kitchen or work area. I wonder, therefore, if this collection might not be trash from the *kincha* house on the platform in the center of Structure 9.

The collection of sherds found above the sand fill (and hence stratigraphically later) is smaller and shows less variety. These sherds, some of which are illustrated in Figure 8.34, are as follows:

Camacho Reddish Brown (Figure 8.34a, b)
    Cambered rims from jars: 2
    Flaring rim from jar: 1
    Everted rim from jar: 1
    Body sherds: 13

Camacho Black (Standard Variety)
    Body sherd: 1

Pingüino Buff (Figure 8.34c–e)
    Everted jar rims, probably from funnel necks: 3
    Chipped sherd disk, painted white on natural: 1
    Jar body sherd, painted black and white on natural: 1
    Body sherds: 5 (4 plain, 1 white-slipped)

Room 6

Room 6, immediately to the south of Room 5, measures 2.6 × 1.7 m. Its walls are preserved to a height of 44 cm above the floor, giving the surviving room 1.94 m³ of storage capacity.

Room 6's history of use is somewhat different from that of Room 5, despite the fact that both were created by dividing the same earlier room into two units (see Figure 8.25). Room 6 was not used for fish storage immediately after its creation, and as a result, its lowest level of fill consisted mainly of tapia debris. Twenty sherds were found in this lower fill. Later, the room was filled with sand and used for the storage of small fish. No sherds were found in the sand layer.

Finally, late in the room's history, a group of 16 sherds was thrown on top of the sand layer. These sherds postdate both the original use of the room and its later conversion to fish storage. This late collection of pottery is still typically Late Intermediate in style and consists mainly of utilitarian vessels.

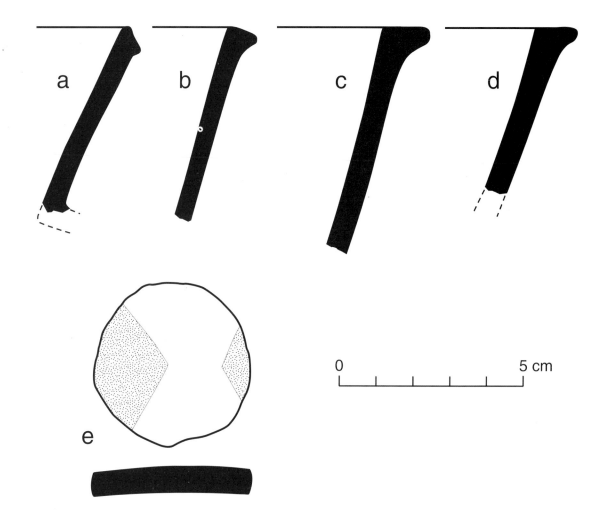

Figure 8.34. Ceramics found just above the sand layer in Room 5, Structure 9. *(a)*: Camacho Reddish Brown jar neck with cambered rim; *(b)*: Camacho Reddish Brown jar neck with everted rim. *(c, d)*: Pingüino Buff everted rims from funnel-necked jars; *(e)*: Pingüino Buff chipped sherd disk from vessel painted white on natural (light stipple indicates natural buff).

Let us begin with the oldest ceramics from Room 6, those found in the layer of tapia debris immediately above the floor (Figure 8.35). They are as follows:

Camacho Reddish Brown
    Jar with cambered rim: 1 rim (Figure
        8.35a)
    Jar body sherds: 10

Camacho Black (Standard Variety)
    Body sherd, large jar or amphora: 1

Camacho Black (Highly Burnished Variety)
    Triangular lug from effigy vessel: 1 (Figure
        8.35b)

Trambollo Burnished Brown (?)
    Body sherd of hemispherical bowl: 1

Pingüino Buff
    Neck of small jar, painted black and white
        on exterior: 1 (Figure 8.35e)
    Jar shoulder, large jar: 1 (Figure 8.35c)
    Body sherds, large jars: 3

Unclassified sherd
    Foot (?) from human effigy vessel of some
        kind (Figure 8.35d)

Next let us examine the smaller, later collection of sherds thrown into Room 6 after it had

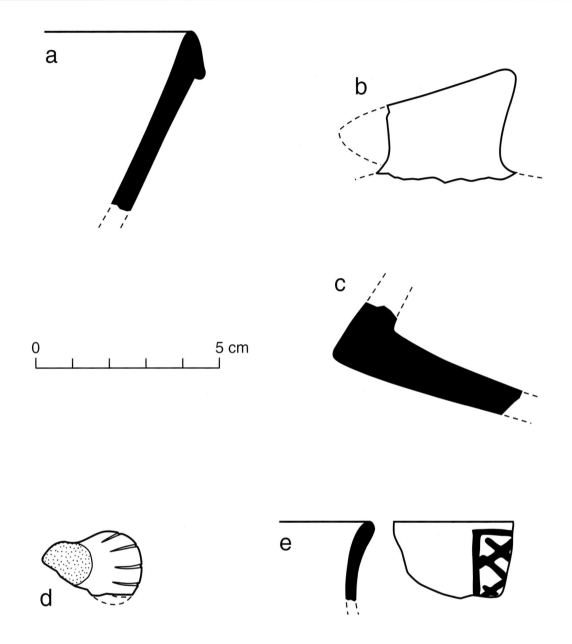

Figure 8.35. Ceramics from Room 6, Structure 9. All these sherds go with the period of the room's early use, before it was converted to fish storage. *(a)*: Camacho Reddish Brown jar with cambered rim; *(b)*: Camacho Black (highly burnished variety) triangular lug from jar; *(c)*: Pingüino Buff jar shoulder; *(d)*: foot (?) from effigy vessel, unclassified pottery type; *(e)*: Pingüino Buff neck of small jar, painted black and white on exterior.

ceased to function as a fish storage unit (Figure 8.36). These sherds are as follows:

Camacho Reddish Brown
    Rim of large *tinajón*: 1 (Figure 8.36b)
    Plain rim from jar: 1 (fire-smudged) (Figure 8.36c)

Cooking pot with restricted orifice and vertically set strap handle: 1 rim (Figure 8.36a)
Jar body sherds: 5

Camacho Black (Standard Variety)
    Jar body sherds: 2

Pingüino Buff
    Hemispherical bowl, slipped white on interior and exterior, painted black and white on exterior: 1 rim (Figure 8.36d)
    Body sherds: 5

Room 7

Room 7, immediately to the south of Room 6, is long and narrow, measuring 6.3 m north–south and 1.1 m east–west. It appears to have been used for fish storage virtually from the start, and contained mostly sand with small fish bones.

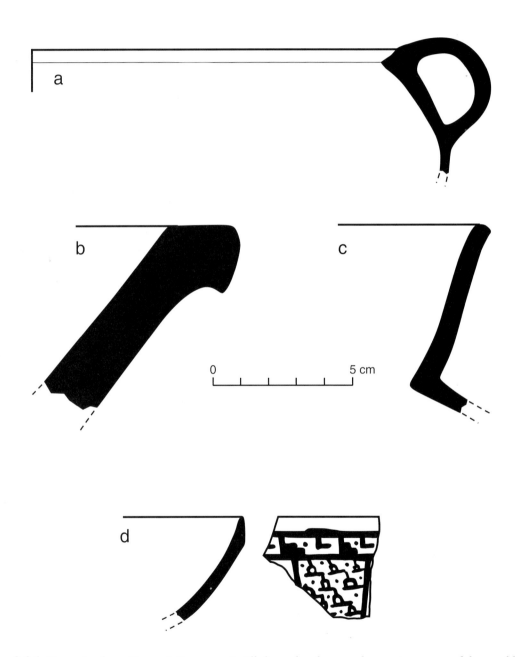

Figure 8.36. Ceramics from Room 6, Structure 9. All these sherds were thrown in on top of the sand layer used to convert the room to fish storage. Sherds *a–c* are Camacho Reddish Brown. *(a)*: cooking pot with restricted orifice and vertically set strap handle (fire-blackened); *(b)*: rim from large *tinajón*; *(c)*: jar rim. *(d)*: Pingüino Buff hemispherical bowl sherd, slipped white on interior and exterior, painted black on white on exterior.

After the room ceased to function as a fish storage unit, a small number of sherds were thrown in on top of the sand (Figure 8.37).

These sherds, all typically Late Intermediate, are as follows:

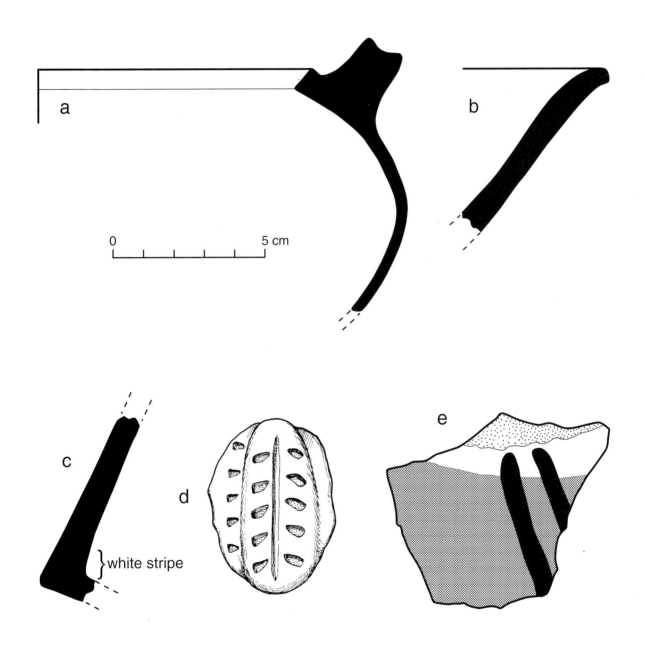

0   5 cm

Figure 8.37. Ceramics from Room 7, Structure 9. All specimens were found stratigraphically above the sand. *(a)*: Camacho Reddish Brown cooking pot with restricted orifice and horizontally set strap handle (fire-blackened); *(b)*: flaring rim from large Pingüino Buff jar; *(c)*: funnel neck from Pingüino Buff jar, painted white on natural (the area of a horizontal white stripe is indicated); *(d)*: maize-cob-shaped lug from a large *tinajón*, superficially resembling Pingüino Buff, but with atypically coarse temper; *(e)*: body sherd from a Pingüino Buff jar, painted in black and white over a weak red wash (10 R 4/4); the light stipple indicates natural buff, the dense screen red wash.

Camacho Reddish Brown
> Cooking pot with restricted orifice, horizontally set strap handle: 1 rim (Figure 8.37a)
> Jar body sherds: 3
> Body sherd of large *tinajón*: 1

Pingüino Buff
> Base of funnel neck from jar, painted white on natural: 1 (Figure 8.37c)
> Strap handle fragment: 1
> Jar shoulder with red wash, painted black and white: 1 (Figure 8.37e)
> Flaring rim from large jar: 1 (Figure 8.37b)
> Body sherds: 3

Atypical sherds
> Maize-cob lug from large *tinajón*, Pingüino-like paste and white wash, but temper much too coarse to be Pingüino: 1 (Figure 8.37d)
> Body sherd, similar paste to the lug from the *tinajón*: 1
> *Comment*: The *tinajón* sherds and the maize-cob lug suggest vessels intended to store *chicha*. They are reminiscent of Feature 19, the large storage vessel buried in Room 2 of the North Complex.

Room 13

Room 13 could as easily have been lumped with the South Entryway as with the West Complex. Precise dimensions for this room cannot be given, because the room was damaged by erosion and eventually covered up by modifications to the South Entryway. As shown in Figures 8.2 and 8.9, Room 13 was long and narrow and featured a bench (or step?). I report no sherds from Room 13, because the degree of disturbance and erosion in this part of the building is so great that I could not be convinced any sherd was reliably associated with the room.

THE EAST COMPLEX

The East Complex is a series of small rooms running north–south along the eastern edge of Structure 9. Included are Rooms 10, 11, and 12 (see Figures 8.2 and 8.3). The shapes of these rooms differ from those of the West Complex, presumably because their original functions had been different. Rooms 11 and 12 both had tapia benches.

Room 10

Room 10 measures 2.2 × 1.7 m; its floor was encountered 80 cm below datum. Whatever its original use may have been, it contained only tapia disintegration products and windblown dust when we excavated it.

Room 11

Room 11 measures 3.1 × 1.7 m. Its original purpose was probably not for fish storage; rather, it seems to have been designed for some other kind of "walk-in" storage. A tapia bench occupied the northernmost meter of the room, its surface resting 76 cm below datum. The southern part of the room had a much lower floor (155 cm below datum).

Like so many other rooms in Structure 9, however, Room 11 had eventually been converted to fish storage and filled with greenish gray sand. This sand, in fact, filled the surviving room so completely that we only discovered the tapia bench after we had sieved the upper part of the fill for fish bones (Figure 8.38). Most of the fish remains consist of anchovies (*Engraulis ringens*), but there were also traces of sardines (*Sardinops sagax*) and even larger fish such as corvina (*Sciaena gilberti*) and bonito (*Sarda sarda*). When our workmen reached the floor, they found many identifiable fish bones stuck to it because, in spite of the hygroscopic properties of the sand, the tapia floor had remained damp from the salt fog of the coast (Figure 8.39). These fish remains will be discussed in a future volume.

Room 12

Room 12 was more than 1.7 m wide. Its total length (north–south) could not be determined owing to

Figure 8.38. Room 11 of Structure 9, a sand-filled room used for storage of dried fish. Workmen are screening the sand through fine brass carburetor mesh to remove the fish bone. This room produced abundant remains of anchovies and occasional remains of sardines, corvina, and bonito.

Figure 8.39. Fish remains stuck to the sandy floor of Room 11, Structure 9. *(a)*: head of anchovy (*Engraulis ringens*); *(b)*: remains of small fish (mostly anchovies and sardines); *(c)*: three vertebrae of a larger fish.

erosion, but it was apparently greater than 2.3 m (Figure 8.2). The northernmost 1.2 m of Room 12 was occupied by a tapia bench whose surface lay 125 cm below datum. The floor to the south of the bench was about 30 cm lower than that.

Room 12 had never been converted to fish storage; its room fill consisted of tapia disintegration products and windblown dust. Two partially restorable vessels (one Camacho Reddish Brown, the other the standard variety of Camacho Black) lay on the floor, looking as if they might actually have been left behind there. There were also four Pingüino Buff jar body sherds that might have been tossed into the room as it slowly filled with dust. Based on the utilitarian nature of the ceramics, it is possible that Room 12 had been used for domestic storage of some kind.

The total sherd count from Room 12 is as follows:

Camacho Reddish Brown
Jar shoulder, brushed exterior finish: 1
Jar body sherds, brushed exterior: 7 (probably the partial remains of 1 fire-blackened vessel)

Camacho Black (Standard Variety) (Figure 8.40)
Globular jar with wide mouth and plain rim, partially restorable:
Rim sherds: 1
Shoulder sherds: 2
Body sherds: 20 (as is the case with the Reddish Brown jar listed above, all these remains probably came from one use-worn, eroded vessel)

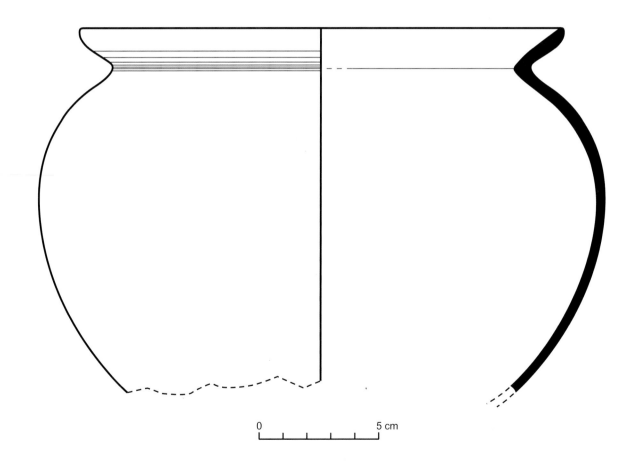

Figure 8.40. Camacho Black (standard variety) globular jar with wide mouth and plain rim, from fill of Room 12 in Structure 9 (reconstructed from several large sherds).

Pingüino Buff
    Jar body sherds: 4 (from several different
        vessels)

FEATURE 20

As luck would have it, the best single sherd sample from Structure 9 came not from the rooms inside the building, but from an outdoor trash midden banked up against its east wall. My artist's reconstruction of this midden is shown in Figure 8.3; it was piled up in the angle between Room 8 and Room 10. My suspicion is that the midden represents domestic debris from the *kincha* residence in the center of Structure 9, and that it had been dumped against the east wall of the building pending removal to one of the quebradas of Cerro Camacho. When Structure 9 was abandoned, this debris may simply have been left behind.

The Feature 20 midden was too large to excavate completely in the time we had, since we felt we needed to fine-screen it all through carburetor mesh, as we had Feature 6 of Structure D (Chapter 4). We therefore sampled Feature 20 by excavating an area 2.0 × 2.5 m (Figure 8.2). The midden proved to be only 50 cm deep; it lay on a clay floor that flanked the building and sloped downhill along one of the structure's external tapia buttresses. Our total sample of Feature 20, therefore, was 2.5 m^3.

As we excavated Feature 20, it occurred to me that we were being presented with an interesting opportunity: the chance to compare Feature 6, a midden from an elite residential compound, with Feature 20, a midden in what we were beginning to suspect was a storage facility staffed by commoners. Our in-the-field impression was that Feature 20 contained lots of anchovies, but fewer fish in the corvina, róbalo, and bonito size range than we had recovered in Feature 6. The occupants of Structure 9 seem also to have eaten lots of small mussels (*Perumytilus* sp., *Semimytilus* sp.), but fewer large clams (*Mulinia edulis*) and chanques (*Concholepas concholepas*) than the occupants of Structure D. The plants in Feature 20 included maize, beans, squash, peanuts, and cotton, but seemed to be lacking in many of the coveted tropical fruits we had found in Feature 6.

While our comparative analyses of Features 6 and 20 are ongoing, we have published some preliminary results of the vertebrate faunal analyses (Marcus et al. 1999). It would appear that the elite occupants of Structure D had greater access to large, prestigious fish species than did the commoners of Structure 9. Both middens had anchovy and sardine bones, but Feature 6 had twice as many sardines. Both middens had the bones of drums (family Sciaenidae), but Feature 6 had twice as many members of medium-to-large species, while Feature 20 had mainly small drums like *Menticirrhus* sp. and *Stellifer* sp. Most notably, Feature 20 produced 113 fragments of sea catfish (*Galeichthys peruvianus*), a fish of low prestige, while Feature 6 had none at all. Both middens had camelid bone, but the elite of Structure D seem to have had greater access to whole animals, while the commoners of Structure 9 got mostly the kinds of bones that would have been included in portions of *charqui* or dried meat. We will have more to say about the differences between Features 6 and 20 in future volumes.

A radiocarbon date from Feature 20

A piece of charcoal from the Feature 20 midden was submitted to the University of Wisconsin lab for dating. My expectation was that Feature 20 might represent a pile of refuse that never got carried away to the quebradas of Cerro Camacho, because Structure 9 was abandoned when the Inka conquered Huarco in A.D. 1470.

> WIS-1939 came out 480 ± 60 years B.P., or A.D. 1470 uncalibrated. The calibrated two-sigma range would be A.D. 1305–1623.

The uncalibrated date of A.D. 1470 meets my expectation too perfectly to be more than a coincidence, but it is encouraging nonetheless. As usual, the calibrated two-sigma range is too wide to fix precisely a historic event like the conquest of Huarco.

The ceramics from Feature 20

The Feature 20 midden produced some 258 sherds. As with the fish bone mentioned above, our impression was that the Feature 20 sherd sample lacked many of the elite elements found in Feature 6 of Structure D. For example, Feature 20 yielded only one possible sherd of the highly burnished variety of Camacho Black, and no Trambollo Burnished Brown serving bowls at all. Feature 20 also lacked the extensive list of unusual, possibly foreign wares seen in Feature 6.

I am reluctant to push the contrast between these two middens too far, since the sherd sample from Feature 6 is much larger. Even allowing for possible sampling error, however, it is hard to escape the impression that the Feature 20 collection is composed largely of commoner refuse.

Figures 8.41–8.51 present examples of the ceramics from Feature 20. The full, screened sherd sample is as follows:

Diagnostic sherds

Camacho Reddish Brown (Figures 8.41, 8.42a–e)
   Jars with cambered rims: 4 rims (Figure 8.41a–c)
   Jars with flaring rims: 2 rims
   Jars with slightly everted rims: 3 rims (Figure 8.42a, b)
   Jar shoulders: 8 (plain or brushed) (Figure 8.42d)

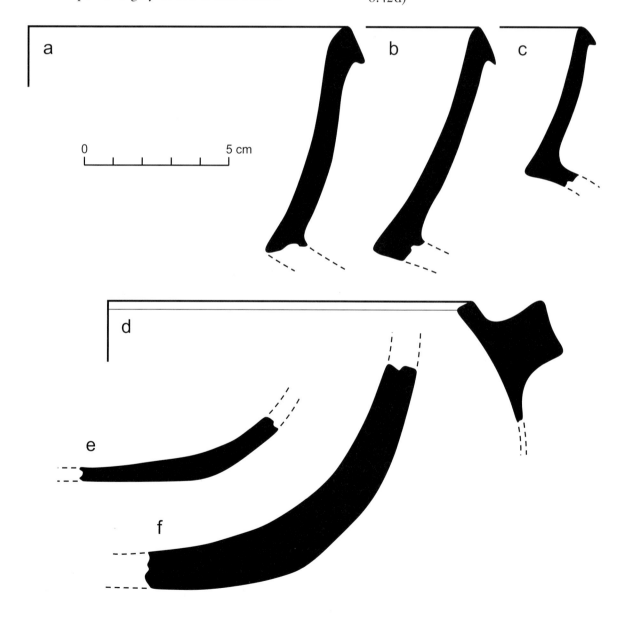

Figure 8.41. Camacho Reddish Brown vessels from Feature 20, Structure 9. *(a–c)*: cambered rims from jars; *(d)*: cooking pot with restricted orifice and horizontally set strap handle (fire-blackened); *(e, f)*: bases from jars.

Jar shoulder with 2 appliqué "nipples": 1 (Figure 8.42e)

Jar basal sherds: 2 (Figure 8.41e, f)

Large *tinajón*: 1 rim (Figure 8.42c)

Cooking pot with restricted orifice, horizontally set strap handle: 1 rim (Figure 8.41d)

Camacho Black (Standard Variety) (Figure 8.42f–h)

Cambered rims from jars: 3 (Figure 8.42h)

Flaring rims from jars: 3 (Figure 8.42g)

Body sherds: 20

Camacho Black (Highly Burnished Variety?) (Figure 8.42f)

Neckless jar with rolled rim: 1 rim

Pingüino Buff (Figures 8.43–8.50)

Globular jars with wide mouth, painted black and white over cream slip inside rim: 3 rims, 2 shoulders (Figure 8.43a)

Globular jars with wide mouth, unpainted: 7 rims (1 with strap handle), 3 shoulders (Figure 8.43b)

Thin-walled jars with low flaring neck: 2 rims (Figure 8.43c)

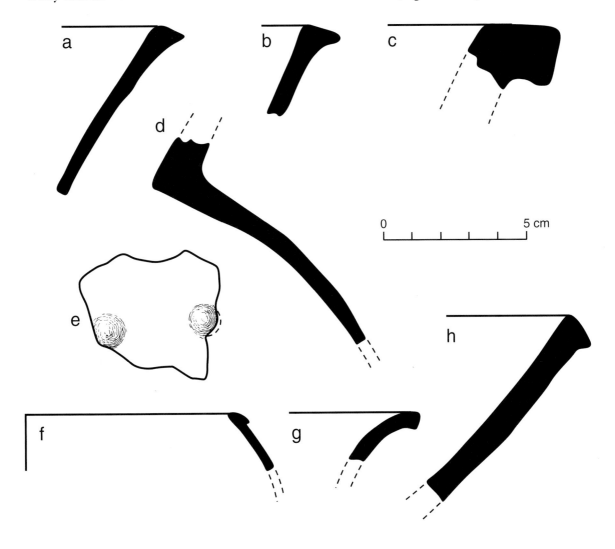

Figure 8.42. Ceramics from Feature 20, Structure 9. Sherds *a–e* are Camacho Reddish Brown. *(a, b)*: slightly everted rims from jars; *(c)*: rim from large *tinajón*; *(d)*: jar shoulder; *(e)*: fragment of jar shoulder with appliqué "nipples." Sherds *f–h* are Camacho Black. *(f)*: small, burnished, neckless jar with rolled rim (heavily pitted and eroded, but probably the highly burnished variety); *(g)*: flaring rim from jar (standard variety); *(h)*: cambered rim from jar (standard variety); interior surface only roughly finished.

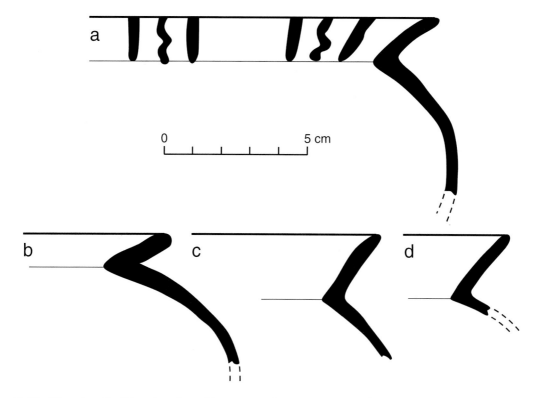

Figure 8.43. Pingüino Buff jar rims from Feature 20, Structure 9. *(a)*: globular jar with wide mouth, given a cream-white slip and painted in black and white on the interior of the rim (the exterior of the vessel is eroded); *(b)*: globular jar with wide mouth, unslipped and unpainted; *(c)*: thin-walled jar with low flaring neck; *(d)*: thin-walled jar with low flaring neck, highly burnished.

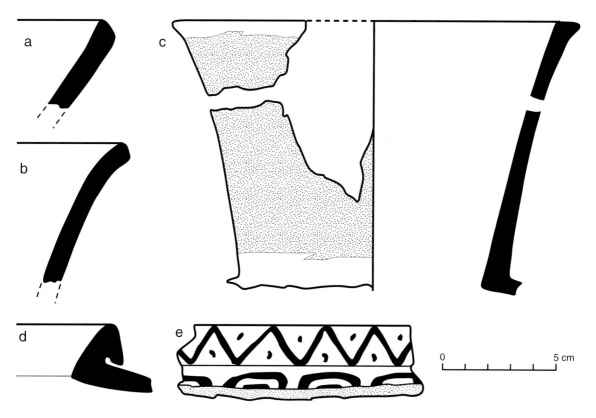

Figure 8.44. Pingüino Buff vessels from Feature 20, Structure 9. *(a)*: plain rim from jar; *(b)*: flaring rim from large jar; *(c)*: funnel neck from jar, painted white on natural (light stipple indicates natural buff; sloppy white bands appear above and below); *(d)*: rim profile of large low-necked jar with rolled rim; *(e)*: exterior of sherd shown in *d*, covered with white wash and painted in black and white (coarse stipple indicates broken edge of sherd).

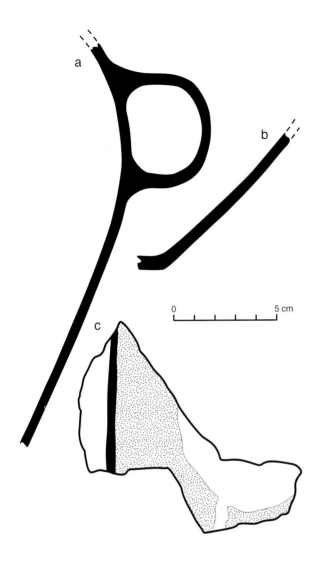

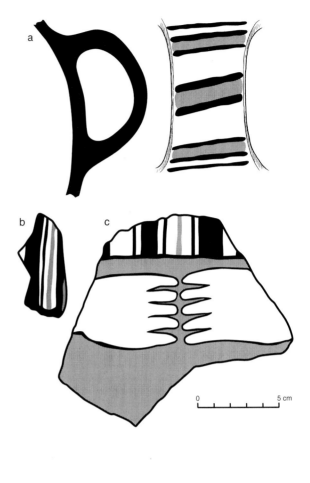

Figure 8.45. Pingüino Buff vessels from Feature 20 midden, Structure 9. *(a)*: amphora or conical jar with strap handle; *(b)*: jar base and lower wall; *(c)*: jar body sherd with both black-on-white and white-on-natural painting on exterior (light stipple indicates natural buff).

Figure 8.46. Pingüino Buff vessels from Feature 20, Structure 9. *(a)*: strap handle from large jar, vertically set, painted in black and red over a sloppy white wash; the red (indicated by medium screen) is specular hematite, 10 R 3/4; *(b)*: jar body sherd painted in black and red over a white slip; *(c)*: jar sherd with areas of white slip and red slip (the latter is 10 R 4/6), highly burnished and painted in black and red on white (red is indicated by medium screen).

Thin-walled jars with low flaring neck, highly burnished: 2 rims (Figure 8.43d)
Plain rims from large jars: 3 (Figure 8.44a)
Flaring rims from large jars: 3 (Figure 8.44b)
Slightly everted rims from large jars: 1
Funnel neck from jar, painted white on natural: 2 rims, 2 neck sherds from same vessel (Figure 8.44c)
Large neckless jar with rolled rim, given white wash and painted black and white on rim and shoulder: 1 rim (Figure 8.44d, e)

Amphora or conical jar: 2 bases (Figure 8.45b)
Amphora or conical jar with strap handle: 1 sherd (Figure 8.45a)
Strap handle from large jar, painted black and red over white wash: 1 sherd (Figures 8.46a, 8.49a)
Jar body sherds, painted black and red on white: 8 (Figure 8.46b, c)
Jar body sherds, painted black and white on natural buff or white on natural: 4 (Figures 8.45c, 8.48b)

Large bowl, plain rim, burnished on interior and exterior: 1 rim (Figure 8.47d)

Shallow bowl, burnished on interior: 3 rims (Figure 8.47a)

Hemispherical bowl with eccentric rim (appliqué bumps), slipped red on the interior; painted black and white over that:

5 rims, 5 body sherds, all from the same vessel (Figures 8.47b, 8.48a)

Rim of "ashtray," similar to the hemispherical bowl above, but painted white on red: 1

Miscellaneous painted bowl sherds, mostly black and white: 5

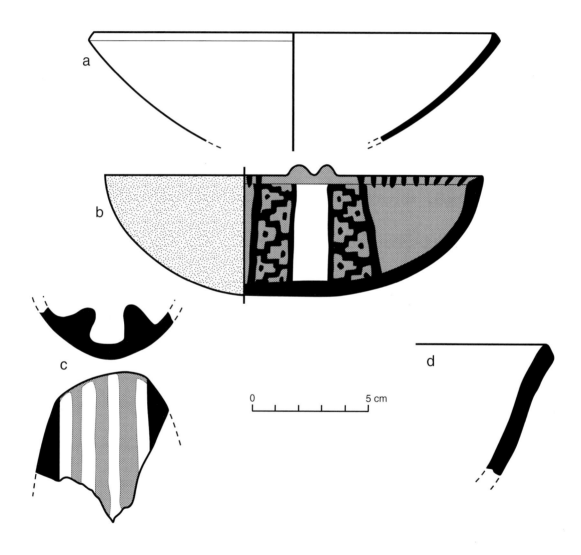

Figure 8.47. Pingüino Buff vessels from Feature 20 midden, Structure 9. *(a)*: shallow bowl, burnished on interior (reconstructed); *(b)*: hemispherical bowl with eccentric bumps on rim, slipped red on the interior, painted in black and white over that; the red is 7.5 R 4/6 (in this reconstruction, based on four sherds, red is represented by medium screen and natural buff by light stipple); *(c)*: unique ceramic "tongue" with modeled teeth on one side *(top)*, painted in black and white over a red slip on the other side *(bottom)*; (d): rim of large bowl.

Figure 8.48. Pingüino Buff sherds from Feature 20, Structure 9. *(a)*: two conjoining sherds from a hemispherical bowl with eccentric bumps on the rim, slipped red on the interior, painted in black and white over that; *(b)*: jar body sherd with both black-on-white and white-on-natural painting on the exterior.

Unique "tongue-shaped" sherd with conical
  modeled teeth on one side, painted
  black and white on red on the other
  side: 1 (Figures 8.47c; 8.49b, c)
Large jar with wide, plain rim, horizontally
  set strap handles, painted white on nat-

ural: 3 rims, 4 shoulders, 17 body sherds
  from the same vessel (Figure 8.50)

Atypical Orange Variety of Pingüino Buff (Figure 8.51)
  Cambered rim of jar: 1
  Jar shoulder with white wash: 1

Figure 8.49. Pingüino Buff sherds from Feature 20, Structure 9. *(a)*: strap handle from large jar, vertically set, painted black and red over white wash; *(b, c)*: both sides of a unique ceramic "tongue" with modeled teeth on one side and black-and-white stripes painted over a red slip on the other side.

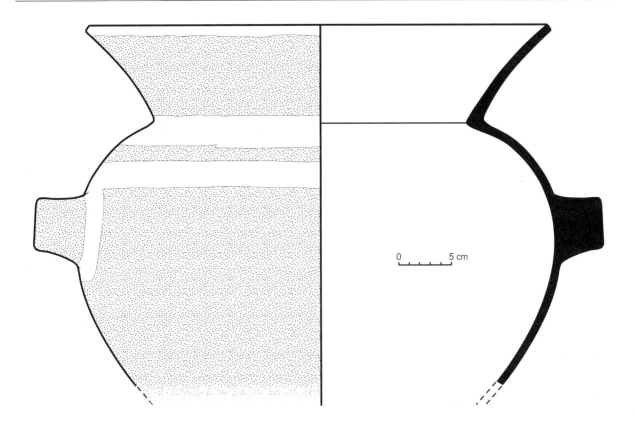

Figure 8.50. Large Pingüino Buff jar from Feature 20 midden, Structure 9 (reconstruction drawing based on 24 sherds). The jar has horizontally set strap handles. It is painted white on natural on the exterior, with one white stripe at the rim, two on the shoulder, and another encircling each strap handle. The natural buff is 2.5 YR 5/4 (reddish brown), while the white paint is a yellowish cream color (2.5 Y 8/2 to 2.5 Y 8/4).

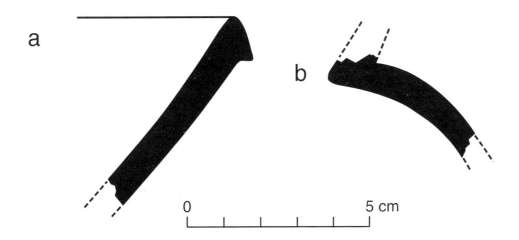

Figure 8.51. Sherds from Feature 20 midden, Structure 9. Both belong to the atypical orange variety of Pingüino Buff. *(a)*: cambered rim from jar, coarse temper, pinkish-orange; *(b)*: jar shoulder with white wash on the exterior; temper too coarse to be typical Pingüino Buff, surface color too orange.

Body sherds

Camacho Reddish Brown: 115

Camacho Black (Standard Variety): 20

Camacho Black (Highly Burnished Variety): 0

Pingüino Buff: 110

Atypical Orange Variety of Pingüino Buff: 0

Trambollo Burnished Brown: 0

An assessment of Structure 9

As we excavated Structure 9, we were drawn to the conclusion that it had been built originally as a small storage facility of some kind, perhaps built by the same family who built Structure D. Many of the rooms along its western and eastern sides appear to be storage units. Entry into the building appears to have been from the south side. Room 2, a large room with a sleeping bench, seems likely to have been designed originally as a residential unit, located at the northern extreme of the building. Presumably it would have been occupied by Structure 9's administrator and his family. All the evidence provided by the refuse in the building suggests that this family was not of elite descent; most likely the administrator was a trusted commoner.

Structure 9 shows two trends seen earlier in Structure D: (1) a steadily increasing need for more fish-storage capacity, and (2) changes in room function necessitated by earthquake damage. Room 1 had clearly suffered seismic damage, after which it was used to store fish in sand layers. Several rooms had been subdivided into smaller units by the addition of later walls; Rooms 3/4 and 5/6 are examples of this process.

Perhaps the most dramatic evidence of the need for increased fish-storage capacity is provided by Room 2. Once a residential space measuring 8.6 × 5.2 m, it was later converted to 50 m³ of fish storage. Our suspicion is that when this happened, the administrator of the building moved from Room 2 to a wattle-and-daub house on a platform to the south. While this house had a small patio adjacent to it, it represents a significantly reduced residential area.

Structure 9 lacks many of the features seen in Structure D, such as spacious canchones, a kitchen/brewery, and facilities for keeping guinea pigs. It did, however, have a possible *chicha* storage vessel (Feature 20) buried in the sand of Room 2, suggesting that workers were rewarded with maize beer (Marcus 2008).

It could legitimately be asked whether Structure 9 was built as a storage annex to Structure D, or by a corporate group of fishermen (something like an *ayllu*). For various reasons, I favor the former interpretation. My suspicion is that at the beginning of Cerro Azul's occupation, most fish storage would have been assigned to buildings like Structure 9, rather than being included in the elite family's residence itself. It is only the gradually escalating need for storage that caused more and more rooms to be devoted to dried fish over time. Seismic damage to residential space may have influenced decisions about which rooms would be converted to fish storage, but in and of itself it is insufficient to explain the steady increase in storage features over time. I do not doubt that there were commoner *ayllus* at Cerro Azul, but I suspect that their members lived in the *kincha* houses for which there is evidence both in the quebradas and in the spaces between tapia compounds. The fact that Structure 9 was built of the same tapia architecture as nearby Structure D provides persuasive evidence that its construction was ordered by the same elite family. In the final analysis, of course, the exact relationship between the elite families, their commoner staff, and any *ayllus* of fishermen could be the subject of further research at Cerro Azul.

An unanswered question is: To what extent was Structure 9 typical of Kroeber's "small ruins?" Some of the other small ruins at the site appear superficially similar to Structure 9, but others do not. Several of the unexcavated small ruins, in fact, appear to have been built of beach cobbles rather than tapia; it seems unlikely that those buildings had the same function as Structure 9. Unfortunately, our time and money were insufficient to explore the full range of small ruins.

CHAPTER 9

The Quebradas of Cerro Camacho

Cerro Camacho overlooks the site of Cerro Azul from a height of 86 m above sea level. Descending from its crest are quebradas that deepen and widen as they run toward the sea. Those that lead toward the tapia compounds were designated Quebradas 4 through 8 by Kroeber (1937). Two of them bifurcate in such a way that Kroeber numbered them 5/5a and 8/8a (see Figures 2.1 and 2.2, Chapter 2).

The quebradas of Cerro Camacho are terraced virtually to the summit of the hill. Kroeber was naturally curious about the nature of the terraces. He knew that they could not be agricultural terraces, since there is insufficient rainfall at Cerro Azul and no evidence that anyone had tried to deliver freshwater to the terraces. Another possibility was that the terraces might have been designed to support the *kincha* houses of fishermen and other commoners. Kroeber (1937:244) pointed out, however, that "these terraces are of insufficient width to contain buildings." Based on his discovery of cist tombs in several quebradas, he concluded that the terraces "probably represent the result of efforts to construct tombs on the hill side" (1937:244). Such tombs would have been impossible to construct outside the matrix of the terraces, since "there is nothing that could be called genuine soil on the cerro slope. Where the surface is not bare rock it is disintegrated rock, with more or less windblown sand mixed in" (Kroeber 1937:244).

While the quebradas do, in fact, contain numerous burial cists, my own excavations there suggest that the history and function of the terraces are even more complex than their mortuary role would suggest. Very early in the history of the site, the quebradas of Cerro Camacho seem to have become the final resting place for domestic trash from the large tapia compounds—a kind of prehistoric landfill. Hundreds of linear meters of the terraces are little more than middens, consolidated and held in place with rocks from the scree-covered slopes of the hill. This process began so early, I believe, that some of the site's earliest ceramics can be found in the deepest stratigraphic levels of the oldest terraces. I have already mentioned this possibility in Chapter 3, where I comment that our smallest sherds (on average) are the ones from the quebrada terraces, a prototypical tertiary context.

If, as Kroeber says, most terraces were too narrow to support residences, some were not too narrow to support storage units. Later in this chapter we examine Structure 11, a small tapia storage building on the south side of Quebrada 5. In contrast to the sand-filled fish storage rooms of Structures D and 9, Structure 11 seems to have been used to store plant foods. It seems that the quebradas might have been just far enough inland to protect vegetables from the salt fog.

One other feature of Quebrada 5 should be mentioned: in its mouth one can see traces of a tapia wall that may once have been used to close off, or at least control access to, the quebrada. It is possible, therefore, that any storage units in Quebrada 5 were considered private, perhaps

259

controlled by the elite family occupying nearby Structure F (see Figure 2.2, Chapter 2).

As the terraces of Cerro Camacho grew deeper over time, their relatively soft midden matrix became a good place to hide burials. Most of the burials we found come from multiperson funerary cists, whose walls were constructed of beach cobbles and loose stones from the slopes of Cerro Camacho. A number of these cists had been discovered by looters prior to our arrival (for example, Structure 12, which I discuss later in this chapter).

Kroeber excavated a total of seven oval or circular tombs at Cerro Azul. These tombs often contained several individuals, in some cases perhaps entire extended families. Some tombs were packed with as many as 12 or 18 mummies (Tomb 4 at the mouth of Quebrada 8/8a contained 6 adults and 6 children, while Tomb 1 in Quebrada 2 included 4 adults plus 14 children and infants [Kroeber 1937:264–265]). Some individuals were clearly elite, buried with fine textiles and with silver or copper objects placed in their mouths (Kroeber's Tombs 1 and 4); others (Kroeber's Tomb 3) apparently had no objects with them. We, too, found tombs with elite individuals in them; their grave goods will be presented in a future volume (see also Marcus 1987a:Figs. 42–65).

It is interesting that at least some of the Cerro Azul elite were hidden in the midden-filled terraces of the quebradas, rather than buried below the floors of compounds like Structure D (assuming that Structure D was typical). Such a burial program contrasts with that of Late Intermediate Chan Chan, where huge burial platforms were incorporated into the elite compounds. Such burial platforms gave living descendants a location to practice royal ancestor worship. It is possible that the difference between Chan Chan and Cerro Azul might have resulted from concerns with theft and disturbance. Conrad (1982:116) mentions that the fear of theft was a Chimú preoccupation and that "the degree of looting and relooting of the [burial] platforms is in itself mute testimony to the vast quantities of high-status artifacts they once contained" (Conrad 1982:99). The elite families of Cerro Azul may have felt that by hiding their elite burials in the midden-filled terraces of the quebradas, they reduced the chances of grave robbing. What they could not have anticipated was the dogged determination of twentieth-century *huaqueros*.

HOW THE TERRACES FORMED

Let us now look at the way the terraces of Cerro Camacho were formed. Figures 9.1–9.4 present a long north–south panorama of the hill, beginning in the north with Quebrada 5 and ending in the south with Quebrada 7. Figure 9.1 shows the tapia wall that may once have closed off the mouth of Quebrada 5.

The creation of terraces may have been suggested by the conformation of Cerro Camacho itself. Figure 9.5a shows how the bedrock descends in a series of natural steps. In many cases, it appears that the Late Intermediate trash-dumpers had taken advantage of these natural steps, making each the core of a new terrace. In order to prevent the trash from sliding downhill as it grew beyond the natural step, the creators of the terrace built simple retaining walls, using readily available loose stones from the scree of the hill (Figure 9.5b).

I decided to test-excavate a series of terraces in Quebradas 5, 5a, and 6. To do this, I needed a way to record relatively small excavation units on the slopes of a very large hill. I decided to keep Kroeber's original designation for each quebrada, and within each quebrada I numbered all the terraces in order, beginning at the summit of Cerro Camacho and working downward. Our excavation units were 1 × 1 m squares, oriented magnetic north–south. In those cases where the results encouraged us to expand beyond our original square, we considered that initial square to lie near the center of a grid of 1 × 1 m units, allowing us to expand in any direction we chose.

Because of the large numbers of burial cists in the terraces, and the resultant threat of future looting, I had to take precautions in the quebradas that I did not need to take elsewhere on the site. After excavation we not only backfilled, but also swept the terrace with brooms until no trace of our excavation could be seen. I also decided not to publish the locations of our quebrada discoveries on any map that might be seen by potential looters. This was an extreme measure that I have not had to use elsewhere.

Figure 9.1. Part 1 of a photo panorama of Cerro Camacho, beginning in the north with Quebrada 5. At the base of the quebrada, one can see traces of the tapia wall that may originally have controlled access to it.

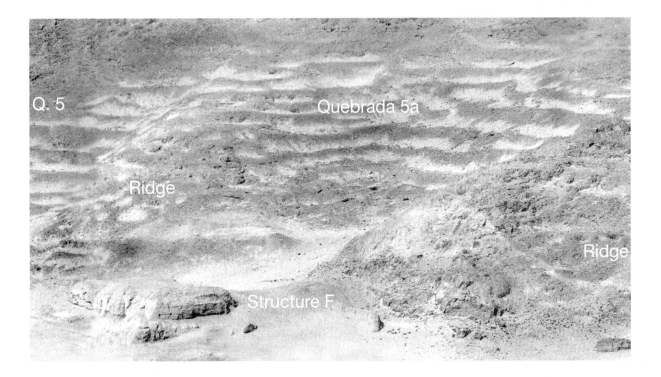

Figure 9.2. Part 2 of a photo panorama of Cerro Camacho, moving south to Quebrada 5a.

Figure 9.3. Part 3 of a photo panorama of Cerro Camacho, moving south to Quebrada 6.

Figure 9.4. Part 4 of a photo panorama of Cerro Camacho, ending in the south with Quebrada 7.

Figure 9.5. The creation of terraces on Cerro Camacho. *(a)*: a rocky ridge adjacent to Structure H, showing the way the bedrock descends in natural steps. Such steps often formed the cores of terraces. *(b)*: a terrace in Quebrada 6, showing how rough retaining walls of natural scree were used to extend terraces and keep them level.

Excavations in Quebrada 5, Terrace 16

I decided to test Terrace 16 of Quebrada 5 because (1) it had no signs of looting, and (2) no bedrock outcrops could be seen, leading me to suspect that its deposit might be relatively deep. Fortunately, my suspicions were correct; the excavation went more than 2.2 m deep and gave us a good look at the deposits making up the terrace.

Our test covered 2 × 2 m (Figure 9.6) and was subdivided into four 1 × 1 m squares designated

Figure 9.6. Quebrada 5, Terrace 16. Work has just begun on a 4-m² excavation. This view is from Terrace 15, above and to the northwest.

M6, N6, M7, and N7. By beginning our alphanumeric grid near the middle of the alphabet, we could expand in any direction we chose.

At least 10 "natural" or "cultural" strata could be recognized in the excavation (Figure 9.7). At the bottom is a nearly sterile layer of cinnamon-colored earth which we call Zone G. This stratum appears to be an indurated layer of windblown dust that overlies bedrock. The first evidence for the dumping of refuse on Terrace 16 is provided by Zone F, a 50-cm-thick layer of soft gray ash with abundant sherds. Above this is Zone E, a sloping deposit of gray ash and cinnamon-colored earth that becomes thicker as it runs south.

Above Zones E and F, as shown in Figure 9.7, the deposit changes. Zone D is a layer of ashy mid-den up to 55 cm thick in places. It is divided into an upper member (Zone D1) and a lower member (Zone D2) by a layer of *salitre* or salty crust. The presence of this crust suggests to us that the process of dumping ashy midden debris on Terrace 16 had been interrupted for a while, and that during this hiatus the upper surface of Zone D2 had been repeatedly moistened by salt fog until a layer of *salitre* had formed. Salt fog, or *garúa*, is most common during the Andean winter.

Overlying Zone D1 is a layer of discarded mussel shells. The mussels, at an average depth of 1.06 m below the surface, had lain exposed for so long that they seem partially cemented to each other in places. It looks as if the dumping of these shells had been a one-time event.

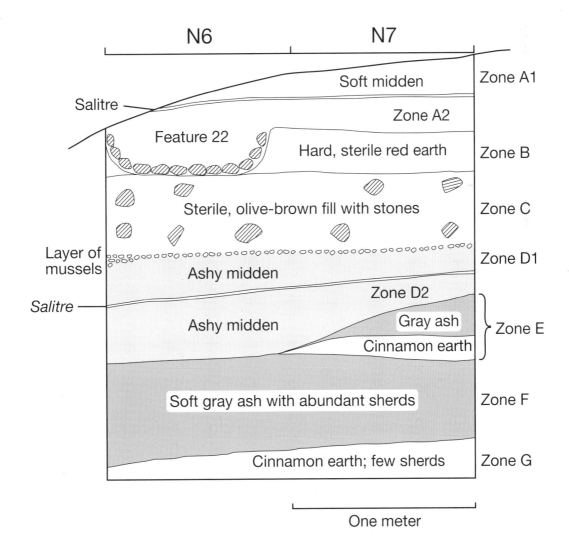

Figure 9.7. Quebrada 5, Terrace 16: a profile of the east wall of Squares N6 and N7.

It appears that following the deposition of Zone D1 and the mussels, activity ceased for a time on Terrace 16. Zone C, the layer immediately above the mussel shells, is a 40-cm-thick deposit of olive-brown windblown fill with occasional stones. This deposit is completely sterile; it appears to consist of natural decomposition products from Cerro Camacho. Zone B, the layer immediately above Zone C, is also sterile. It consists of hard red earth, seemingly a somewhat darker-colored version of the sterile cinnamon earth that overlies bedrock in Zone G. This is the kind of indurated, windblown deposit that we would expect to form during a long period of time without human activity on Terrace 16.

The most interesting cultural feature we found on Terrace 16 had been cut down into the hard sterile earth mentioned above. This is Feature 22, a stone-lined, basin-shaped hearth (Figure 9.7). Feature 22 is oval in outline (90 cm north–south and more than 1.0 m east–west) and had been excavated 22 cm into the red earth below. This hearth had been used to roast a sea lion (*Otaria byronia*) over heated stones. Sea lion bones (and miniscule amounts of smaller fauna) were found in Zone A2, the layer of refuse associated with Feature 22.

Following this episode of sea-lion roasting, Terrace 16 was abandoned for long enough that another layer of *salitre* formed above Zone A2. This layer of salty crust, roughly 24 cm below the surface, is taken to be a natural division between the upper member (Zone A1) and lower member (Zone A2) of stratigraphic Zone A. Zone A1 is a layer of soft midden that seems to represent the last stage of refuse dumping on Terrace 16 (Figure 9.7).

What we learned from our excavations on Terrace 16 is that the process of terrace development had gone on for a considerable length of time but was frequently interrupted. There had been periods of repeated dumping of ashy refuse, followed by periods of abandonment and sterile layer formation. At least twice, the terrace surface had been exposed long enough for *salitre* to form. At least once, during a period when refuse was not being dumped, the terrace had been used as a place to roast a sea lion in a stone-lined hearth.

Having established the stratigraphy of Terrace 16, let us now look at the ceramic collections from the excavation. We proceed in order of age, from oldest (Zone F) to youngest (Zone A).

Ceramics from Terrace 16

Zone F

Zone G is nearly sterile, yielding only a few unclassifiable body sherds. Zone F, the oldest layer of true midden debris, produced a collection of 137 sherds, some of which are illustrated in Figure 9.8. The collection is dominated by jar sherds of Camacho Reddish Brown and contains no sherds of Camacho Black at all. The total sherd count is as follows:

Camacho Reddish Brown (Figure 9.8a, b, h)
    Jars with very low necks: 3 plain rims (from at least 2 vessels)
    Jar shoulders: 2
    Jar body sherds, perforated 1–2 times each by drilling through from the exterior: 8
    Jar body sherds, plain: 112

Trambollo Burnished Brown (Figure 9.8c–f)
    Rims of small carinated bowls: 2 (thin)
    Shoulder of small, thin-walled jar, painted white and purple (5 R 3/2, "dusky red"): 1

Pingüino Buff (Figure 9.8g)
    One bird effigy from bridge spout (?) vessel: 1
    Body sherds: 3 plain, 5 with cream slip on exterior
    Comment on Zone F: Two attributes of this collection suggest that it dates to an earlier stage of the Late Intermediate than the bulk of Structure D. One is the total lack of standard variety Camacho Black. The other attribute is the painting of a thin Trambollo Burnished Brown jar in purple and white, which reminds one of the ceramics at earlier sites like Cerro del Oro. It would be interesting to know from which of the tapia compounds this layer of soft gray ash had been brought.

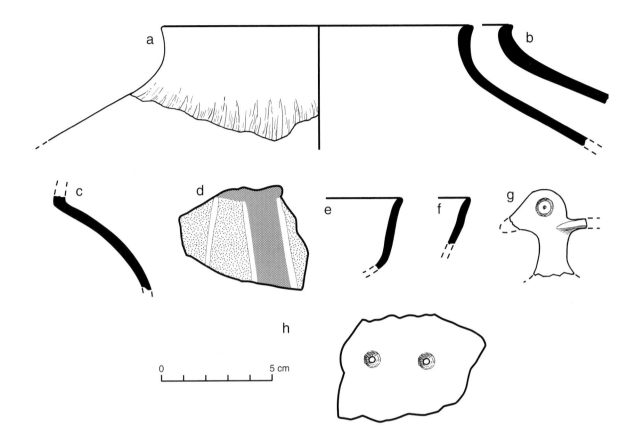

Figure 9.8. Sherds from Zone F of Terrace 16, Quebrada 5. *(a, b)*: Camacho Reddish Brown jars with very low necks and plain rims. The bodies are brushed below the neck. *(c, d)*: Trambollo Burnished Brown thin-walled jar, painted white and purple over natural buff; *(c)*: profile; *(d)*: exterior surface of sherd. Light stipple indicates natural buff (2.5 YR 5/6); medium screen indicates purplish red (5 R 3/2); the white is light cream (2.5 Y 8/4). *(e, f)*: Trambollo Burnished Brown, small carinated bowls; *(g)*: Pingüino Buff bird effigy bridge spout; *(h)*: Camacho Reddish Brown, jar body sherd with two holes drilled from the exterior of the vessel.

Another interesting feature of the Zone F collection is the group of eight drilled body sherds (Figure 9.8h), some of which show sawing and cutting marks as well as drill holes. One possibility is that these sherds are waste products from the process of creating net weights from body sherds. At least one fine-mesh fishing net from Cerro Azul was found with an 11-g worked sherd tied on as a weight (Marcus 1987a:Fig. 47A).

Zone E

Zone E, a layer of gray ash and cinnamon earth that only partially filled our excavation, yielded only 10 sherds. As with Zone F, Camacho Black is absent, and there is at least one painted vessel whose style suggests that it was relatively early.

This is a Pingüino Buff bowl, painted black and yellow on both the interior and exterior (Figure 9.9a, b). Like the black-and-yellow painted bowls discussed earlier in Chapter 3 (Figure 3.19), this choice of color and design on the interior of a bowl reminds one of earlier sites like Cerro del Oro. The full sherd collection is as follows:

Camacho Reddish Brown (Figure 9.9d, e)
  Slightly flaring rim from jar: 1
  Jar shoulder, fire-blackened: 1
  Jar body sherd, drilled from exterior: 1
  Jar body sherds (mostly blackened): 4

Pingüino Buff (Figure 9.9a–c)
  Rim of bowl, nearly hemispherical, burnished inside: 1

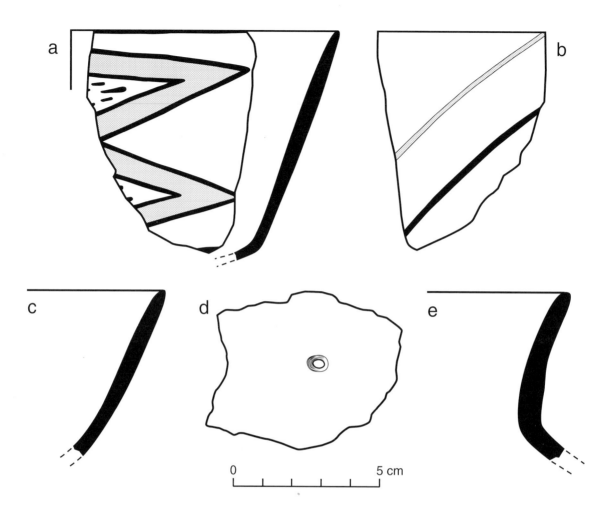

Figure 9.9. Sherds from Zone E of Terrace 16, Quebrada 5. *(a, b)*: Pingüino Buff bowl, painted black and yellow on both exterior and interior. Yellow paint (2.5 Y 8/6) is indicated by light screen. *(a)*: interior of vessel; *(b)*: exterior. *(c)*: rim of Pingüino Buff bowl, nearly hemispherical. *(d)*: Camacho Reddish Brown jar body sherd, drilled through from the exterior; *(e)*: Camacho Reddish Brown, slightly flaring rim from jar.

Rim of bowl, evidently with carinated basal angle or convex base; painted on exterior with yellow and black on natural; "self-slipped" on interior, painted in black and yellow; burnished on both surfaces: 1

Body sherd, possibly from the same carinated bowl: 1

Zone D

Zone D, the ashy midden deposit below the layer of mussel shells, produced a collection of 49 sherds. As mentioned above, a layer of *salitre* divides this zone into upper (D1) and lower (D2) members. However, most of the diagnostic sherds come from D2, while D1 has predominantly un-

decorated body sherds. In the interest of sample size, therefore, we have combined all the sherds from Zone D into one collection. The sherd count is as follows:

Camacho Reddish Brown (Figure 9.10a–d)
    Flaring rims from jars: 6
    Jar shoulders: 2
    Jar body sherds, drilled through from exterior: 2
    Body sherds: 15

Pingüino Buff (Figure 9.10j–o)
    Neckless jar rims, slipped cream on exterior: 2

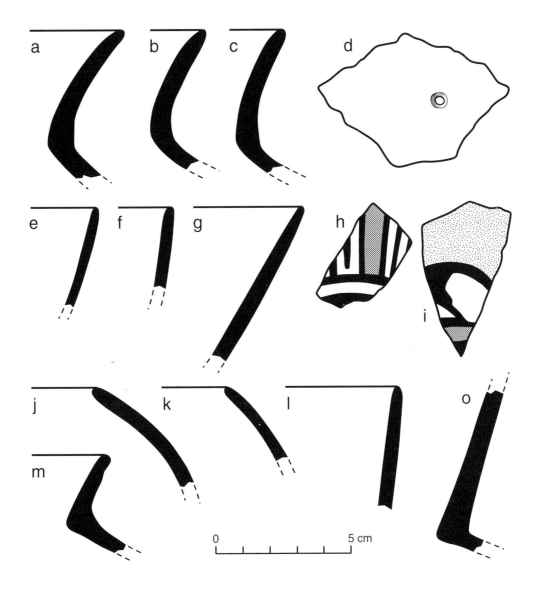

Figure 9.10. Sherds from Zone D of Terrace 16, Quebrada 5. *(a-c)*: Camacho Reddish Brown, flaring rims from jars; *(d)*: Camacho Reddish Brown jar body sherd, drilled from the exterior of the vessel; *(e, f)*: Trambollo Burnished Brown, rims from hemispherical bowls; *(g):* Trambollo Burnished Brown, rim from open bowl; *(h, i)*: Trambollo Burnished Brown, bowl body sherds, painted black/white/red on the interior of the base (light stipple indicates natural brown; medium screen indicates red); *(j, k)*: Pingüino Buff rims from neckless jars, slipped cream white on the exterior; *(l)*: Pingüino Buff rim from hemispherical bowl, discolored in firing; *(m)*: Pingüino Buff rim from globular jar with wide mouth; *(o)*: Pingüino Buff sherd from funnel-necked jar, painted white on natural.

Globular jar with wide mouth, plain: 1 rim
Funnel neck sherd, painted white on
    natural: 1
Jar body sherd, traces of black-and-white
    painting: 1
Hemispherical bowl rim: 1
Body sherds: 12

Trambollo Burnished Brown (Figure 9.10e–i)
    Hemispherical bowl rims: 3
    Open bowl rim: 1
    Bowl body sherds, painted black/white/red
        on interior of base: 2
    Comment on Zone D: Like the collection
        from Zones F and E, these ceramics

look early, relative to the bulk of the pottery from Structure D. The absence of Camacho Black and the relative abundance of Trambollo Burnished Brown are once again striking. In particular, the Trambollo Burnished Brown bowls painted in three colors on the inside of the base remind one of earlier sites like Cerro del Oro.

I conclude that the whole of Terrace 16 below the layer of mussel shells (that is, the deepest 1.1 m of our excavation) probably accumulated before the bulk of the occupation at Structures D and 9. Assuming that this lower deposit is refuse from tapia compounds, it suggests that some compounds at Cerro Azul go back to an earlier stage of the Late Intermediate, perhaps to the period A.D. 1100–1300.

Zone A

Zones C and B in Terrace 16 are sterile deposits, suggestive of a hiatus in refuse dumping on that particular terrace. Activity resumes with the digging of Feature 22 (a stone-lined pit used to roast a sea lion), which is associated with Zone A2 (Figure 9.11). Zone A2 is the lower member of a zone divided in two by a layer of *salitre*. Because Zones A1 and A2 look very similar, and produced only 21 diagnostic sherds between them, their sherds have been combined for analytical purposes.

A glance at Figure 9.12 shows that this collection is contemporaneous with the occupation of Structure D. The strap-handled, restricted-orifice cooking pots in Camacho Reddish Brown are prototypical; so are the Pingüino Buff jars with funnel necks or slightly everted rims. Camacho Black, standard variety, is also present. The full list of diagnostic sherds is as follows:

Camacho Reddish Brown (Figure 9.12a–e)
  Flaring rims from jars: 2
  Rim sherds from cooking pots with restricted orifice, fire-blackened outside: 4 (2 with horizontal strap handles, 2 without)

Camacho Black (Standard Variety)
  Fragment of large strap handle: 1

Pingüino Buff (Figure 9.12h–l)
  Everted rims from funnel-neck jars: 2
  Neck sherd from funnel-neck jar: 1
  Everted rims from jars: 2 (thin)

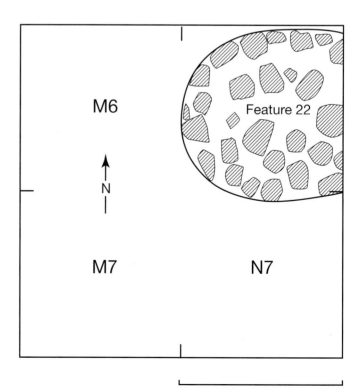

Figure 9.11. Quebrada 5, Terrace 16. Plan of Squares M6–N7 at the level of Zone A2. Feature 22 was a basin-shaped hearth filled with fire-cracked rocks, ash, and sea lion bones.

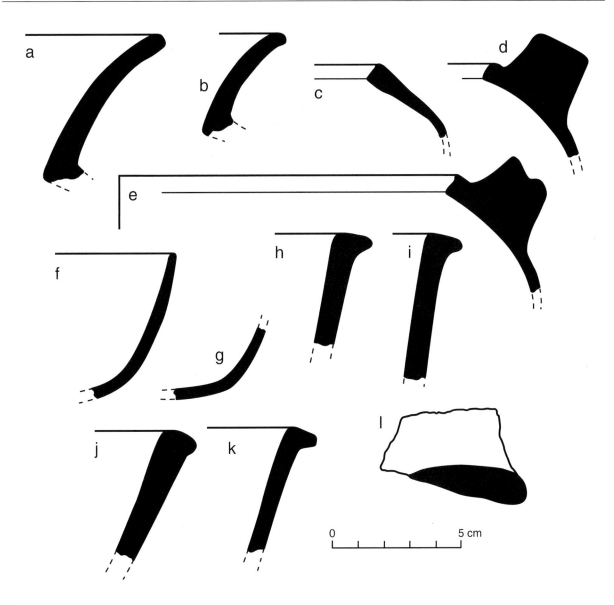

Figure 9.12. Sherds from Zone A of Terrace 16, Quebrada 5. *(a, b)*: Camacho Reddish Brown, flaring rims from jars; *(c–e)*: Camacho Reddish Brown, cooking pots with restricted orifice, fire-blackened. Sherds *d* and *e* have horizontally set strap handles. *(f, g)*: Trambollo Burnished Brown, sherds from hemispherical bowls; *(h, i)*: Pingüino Buff, everted rims of funnel-necked jars; *(j)*: Pingüino Buff, slightly everted or bolstered rim of thick jar; *(k)*: Pingüino Buff everted jar rim, discolored; *(l)*: Pingüino Buff bowl body sherd with glossy black paint on interior.

Slightly everted rims from thick jars: 4
Fragment of strap handle from jar: 1
Jar body sherd, painted black and red on
    natural buff: 1
Bowl body sherd, painted on interior with
    glossy black paint: 1

Trambollo Burnished Brown (Figure 9.12f, g)
    Hemispherical bowl: 1 rim sherd, 1 body
        sherd

The Implications of Terrace 16, Quebrada 5

Terrace 16 is relatively deep (Figure 9.13) and shows two phases of activity. Early in the Late Intermediate period (perhaps A.D. 1100–1300), it was used for the dumping of refuse from one or more tapia compounds. Then came a period of disuse, during which sterile deposits formed on the terrace. At a later stage of the Late Intermediate, perhaps A.D. 1300–1470, Terrace

Figure 9.13. Quebrada 5, Terrace 16. Pedro Manuel Zavala stands in the excavation, which has now reached a depth of 1.5 m.

16 was used as a place to roast a sea lion and renew the dumping of refuse. One of the most interesting implications of the sequence in Terrace 16 is that one or more of the tapia compounds at Cerro Azul might be older than Structure D.

QUEBRADA 5-SOUTH

As Quebrada 5 descends to the level of Structure F, it widens into the shape of a crescent whose arms enclose an oval depression (see Figure 2.2 in Chapter 2). This crescent-shaped area could be seen as having northern, central, and southern sectors. Figure 9.14 shows the oval depression in the mouth of the quebrada, a series of old looters' holes on the slopes of the northern sector, and our crew of workmen beginning an excavation in the southern sector.

Our attention had been drawn to Quebrada 5-south (as we designated this sector) by two features we could see from the surface. One was a stone-lined burial cist, partially exposed by looters, which we decided to salvage. The other, only 5 or 6 m to the east, was a tapia wall partially exposed by wind erosion. As can be seen in Figure 9.15, neither the tapia wall nor the looted cist occurs on a numbered terrace; both were buried in a talus of midden debris that had eroded down from terraces higher up on the south side of the quebrada.

Structure 11

We began our excavation with the tapia building, which we designated Structure 11. It turned out to be a long, narrow, multiroom storage structure, built directly against the rocky slope of the quebrada. We excavated three of its rooms but did not have the time or funds to work out its complete plan. It was clear that it continued to the east, but for how many meters is unknown.

Figure 9.16 shows the three rooms we exposed, and Figure 9.17 presents a north–south cross section through Structure 11. The building had at least two phases of construction and had lost its northern tapia wall to wind erosion. Our excavations revealed a line of small storage units, including Rooms 1 and 2, which continue beyond our excavation. Below and to the north of these small units is a much larger room—Room 3—of which we exposed an area 2.6 × 1.5 m. Figure 9.18 shows the surviving remnant of Room 1, and Figure 9.19 documents the exposure of Room 3. In the lower half of Figure 9.19, one can see bedding lines from post-abandonment wind erosion on the south wall of Room 3.

Figure 9.17 provides some insights into the construction history of Structure 11. The building was set against the stony slope of the quebrada, with any available loose stones used to fill in the irregular gaps between bedrock and the tapia walls. The downhill (north) wall of the building had been buttressed with tapia blocks. Artificial fill had been used to level the clay floors of Rooms 2 and 3. At some point, Room 3 had been given a second clay floor, 10 cm above the first. The space between the two floors had been filled with sand containing the bones of anchovies and sardines.

Figure 9.14. Quebrada 5, seen from a high point on Structure F. Work is in progress in Structure 11, on the south side of the quebrada. (Note the old looters' holes on the slope at the far left and the oval depression in the foreground.)

We fine-screened this sand layer and concluded that it was simply fill used to level the floor, rather than an attempt to store fish. In other words, at the time the later floor was laid down, someone leveled it with a few basketloads of sand from a fish storage room in one of the tapia compounds. One clue that this had been the source of the sand is the fact that the fish bone is very badly fragmented, as if it had been moved one or more times. There are no fish remains stuck to any of the clay floors in Structure 11, nor any other evidence that it had been used to store fish.

As for what *had* been stored in the line of storage units, it appears to have been plant foods.

There were desiccated beans and maize in Room 1, and in the corner of Room 2 was a deposit of *Phaseolus* beans still in their pods (see Figure 9.16). When questioned, our workmen told us that because the quebradas are farther from the ocean and its salt fog, they would have been better places to store vegetal foods than the tapia compounds nearer to the beach.

For its part, at least late in its history, Room 3 may temporarily have become residential; a *kincha* house was built in it. The evidence consists of (1) eight post molds, which we discovered along the west and south limits of the floor (Figure 9.16), and (2) several fallen chunks of clay daub

Figure 9.15. Quebrada 5-south, showing Structures 11 (a tapia-walled storage unit) and 12 (a looted burial cist) not long after their initial discovery. (At this point, only Room 1 of Structure 11 had been exposed.)

with cane impressions (Figure 9.20). In the later of the two clay floors, we also found four impressions left by convex-based ceramic vessels (probably jars) that had rested on the floor for some time. Like the *kincha* house in the center of Structure 9, this building may have been the residence of a lower-level administrator who oversaw the filling and emptying of the storage units.

Room 3 is the only part of Structure 11 that yielded ceramics. Some 18 fragments, mostly large sherds and sections of semi-intact pots as-

sociated with the *kincha* house, were recovered (Figures 9.21, 9.22). This ceramic collection appears to be a primary deposit, that is, a collection of cooking and storage wares left in Room 3 at the time of its abandonment, and eventually damaged by erosion and the weight of the overburden. It has the look of lower-status domestic pottery. The full collection of sherds is as follows:

Camacho Reddish Brown (Figures 9.21, 9.22a–c)
　　Jars with cambered rim: 4 rims

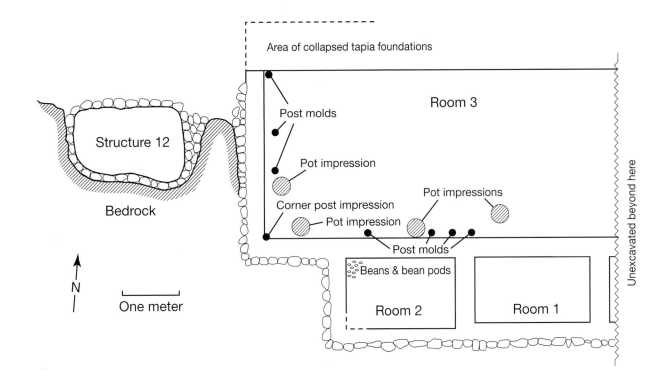

Figure 9.16. Quebrada 5-south: plan of Structures 11 (R) and 12 (L).

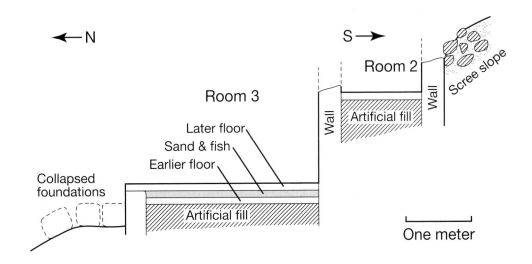

Figure 9.17. Quebrada 5-south. North–south cross section through Rooms 2 and 3 of Structure 11.

Figure 9.18. Two views of Room 1, Structure 11. *(Top)*: the room as seen from the northeast. *(Bottom)*: a view from the west.

Figure 9.19. Two views of Room 3, Structure 11. *(Top)*: workmen are exposing the floor of the room. *(Bottom)*: Iván Francia (with dust mask in place) sweeps below the south wall of Room 3. Bedding lines left by wind erosion show how the room slowly filled in with sand after abandonment.

Cooking pots with restricted orifice: 2 rims (fire-blackened)
Body sherds: 6

Camacho Black (Standard Variety)
Jar with tall neck and two strap handles linking neck and shoulder (still with cords running through handles): 1 large sherd
Jar body sherds: 4

Possible misfired Camacho Black? (Figure 9.22d)
Jar or amphora with tall neck and two strap handles linking neck and shoulder (the paste is light orange and the surface is dark orange, looking like an accidentally oxidized Camacho Black): 1 neck

Comment on Structure 11: Perhaps our most interesting discovery in Quebrada 5-south was that (along with all its other uses) it was a venue for the storage of plant foods. Maize still on the cob, beans still in the pod, and perhaps other crops, were evidently brought to Cerro Azul from the irrigated fields of inland communities and stored in the slightly drier quebradas of Cerro Azul until needed. At one point, these stored commodities may have been watched over by a lower-level administrator, perhaps a trusted commoner.

Figure 9.20. A chunk of cane-impressed daub from a *kincha* building placed in Room 3 of Structure 11.

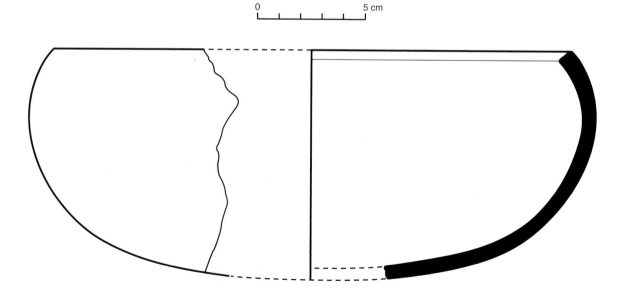

Figure 9.21. Vessel from the fill of Room 3, Structure 11, Quebrada 5-south. This is a Camacho Reddish Brown cooking pot with restricted orifice, fire-blackened and carbon-crusted over the entire exterior. Reconstructed from one large sherd, this vessel may have had strap handles on the missing portion.

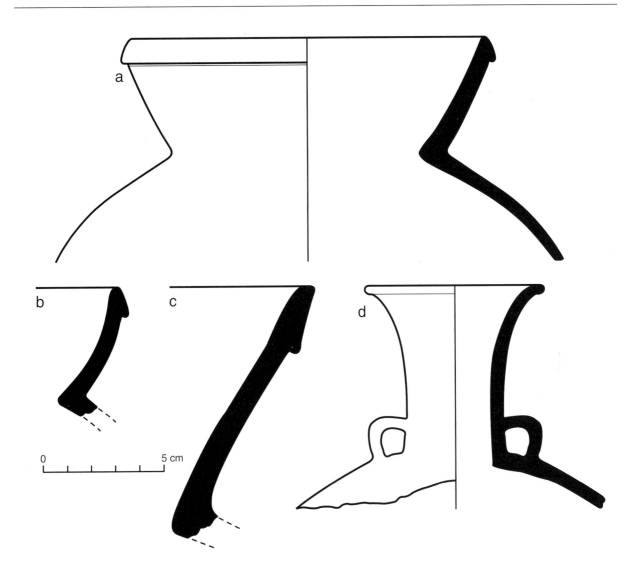

Figure 9.22. Sherds from the fill of Room 3, Structure 11, Quebrada 5-south. *(a–c)*: Examples of Camacho Reddish Brown jars with cambered rims; *(d)*: apparently misfired Camacho Black jar or amphora with paired handles connecting the neck and shoulder. The vessel shape is right for Camacho Black, but the jar seems to have been accidentally oxidized during firing, so that the paste came out pale orange (5 YR 7/6) and the exterior surface dark orange (2.5 YR 5/8).

Structure 12

Structure 12 is a typical Late Intermediate burial cist, found just to the west of Structure 11 (Figure 9.16). The cist is roughly 2 m wide east to west and an average of 1.4 m wide north to south (Figure 9.23a). Its creators had dug down through midden debris until they reached the bedrock of the quebrada, which (as described earlier in this chapter) descends in the form of natural steps (Figure 9.23b). At an average depth of 1.28 m below the surface, the builders laid in a clay floor to compensate for the irregularities in the bedrock.

As can be seen in Figure 9.24, the walls of the cist are composed of unmodified stones picked up from the slope of the quebrada and stacked carefully atop each other. Once stacked, the stones were held in place by a layer of clay plaster. How the cist had been roofed is unknown. It appears that over the centuries, the earth and midden debris concealing Structure 12 had eroded away to the point where the tops of the stone walls were exposed; this had attracted the attention of looters.

As has frequently happened at Cerro Azul, the looters (1) broke some of the burial offerings and

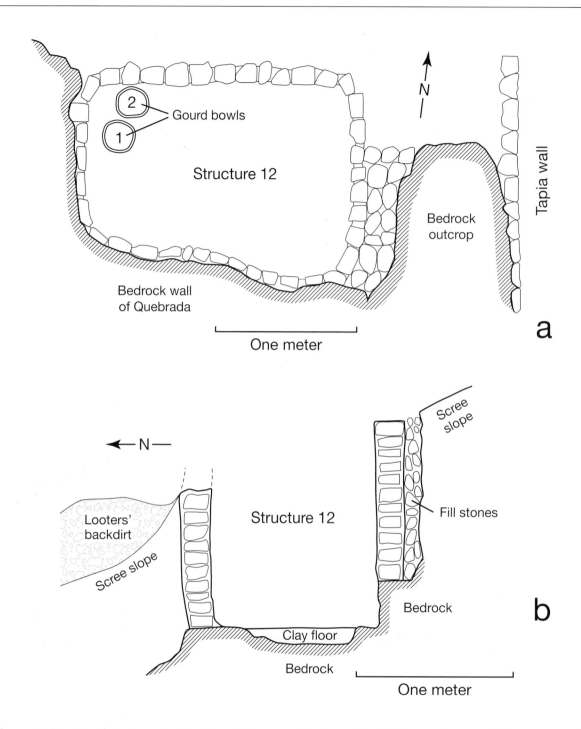

Figure 9.23. Quebrada 5-south. (*a*): plan of Structure 12, a looted burial cist to the west of Structure 11; (*b*): north–south cross section through Structure 12.

(2) did not empty the cist completely. Several large sections of broken vessels were found in the looters' backdirt pile, whose location is shown in Figure 9.23b. Hidden in the slumped debris covering the clay floor of the cist we discovered two hemispherical gourd bowls that had evidently held food offerings (including dried fish) for one or more of the burials (for location, see Figure 9.23a). We do not know how many individuals had been buried in Structure 12, but the human bones left by the looters show that at least one adult and one child had been present.

Figure 9.24. Two views of Structure 12, a looted, dry-laid stone masonry burial cist. *(Top)*: the southeast corner. *(Bottom)*: the west end. (Arrow points north and is marked in both centimeters and inches.)

Figures 9.25 and 9.26 present some of the larger sherds from the looters' backdirt. They include a badly eroded amphora (Figure 9.25), a black-and-white painted Pingüino Buff dish (Figure 9.26a, b), and a highly burnished Camacho Black "fat skeleton" vessel (Figure 9.26c).

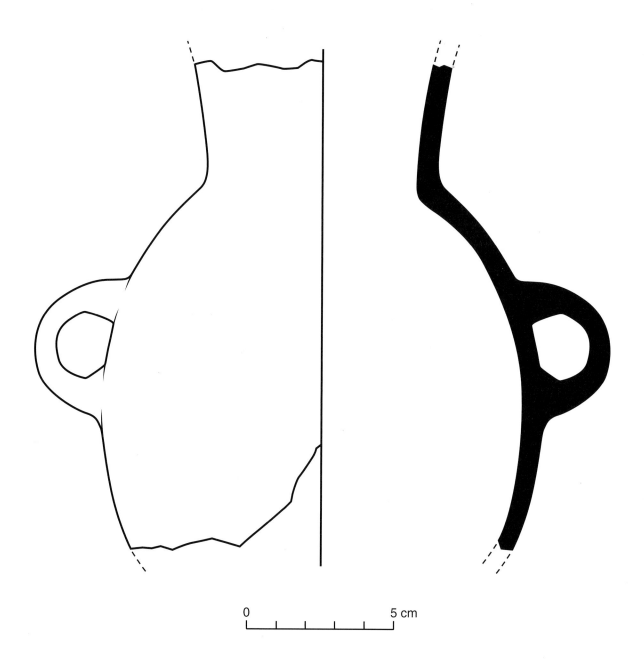

0   5 cm

Figure 9.25. Vessel from Structure 12 in Quebrada 5-south. This amphora, originally from Structure 12 but found in looters' backdirt, is too eroded to be classified. The paste is uniformly gray, but there are traces of burnished pinkish reddish surface in places (reconstruction based on partial vessel).

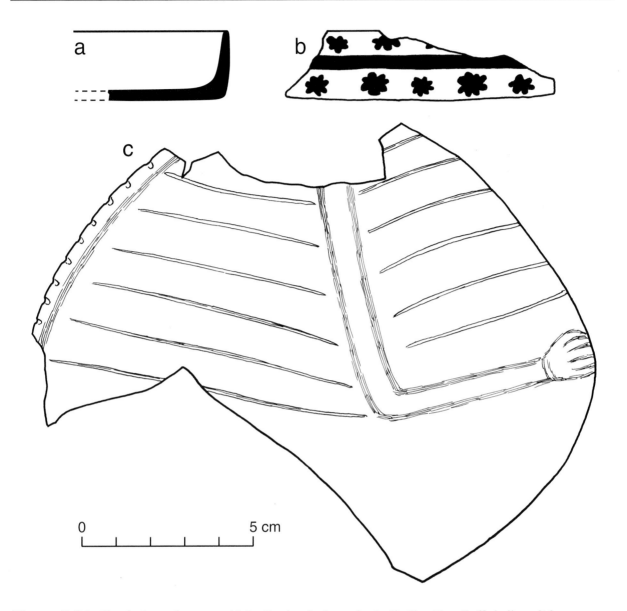

Figure 9.26. Sherds from Structure 12 in Quebrada 5-south. *(a, b)*: Pingüino Buff shallow dish or saucer, slipped cream white and painted in black and white on the exterior, left natural buff (and burnished) on the interior. *(a)*: profile; *(b)*: exterior of sherd. *(c)*: Camacho Black "fat skeleton" vessel with ribs and vertebral column indicated by modeling and incising. Highly burnished. Found in looters' backdirt; probably from a looted burial in Structure 12.

The midden deposit between Structures 11 and 12

In places, Structures 11 and 12 are separated by an outcrop of bedrock that projects north from the wall of the quebrada. In other places, they are separated by tightly packed midden debris. In Figure 9.23a, this midden deposit lies in the area occupied by the north arrow.

Since the source of this midden debris is uncertain (it is almost certainly a tertiary deposit), I decline to draw too many conclusions from it.

One sherd from this deposit, however, attracted my attention because it may date to an earlier stage of the Late Intermediate than the bulk of Structures D and 9. It comes from a hemispherical Pingüino Buff bowl, slipped white on both interior and exterior, and painted on the exterior in black and purplish gray (Figure 9.27). The use of purplish paint reminds us of some of the sherds with "Life Saver" motifs which come from deep levels in other quebradas (see Figure 3.20c, Chapter 3).

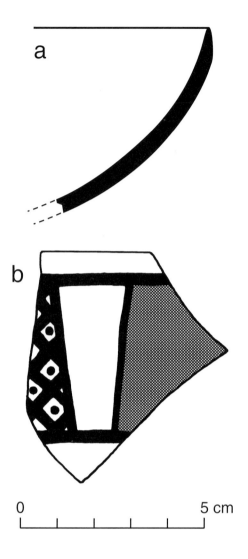

Figure 9.27. Pingüino Buff sherd from the midden deposit between Structures 11 and 12, Quebrada 5-south. The sherd is from a hemispherical bowl, slipped white on both interior and exterior, painted on the exterior in black and purplish gray over white. *(a)*: profile; *(b)*: exterior of sherd. Dark screen indicates purplish gray (5 R 3/1).

QUEBRADA 5A, TERRACE 9

Immediately to the south of Quebrada 5 lies Quebrada 5a, partially separated from the former by a rocky ridge high up near its point of origin (see Figure 2.2, Chapter 2). My attention was initially drawn to Quebrada 5a because it displayed abundant and distressing evidence of having been looted. Terrace 9 (the ninth from the top) was wide and deep enough so that it had become a suitable venue for burial cists. Local looters had discovered these cists and opened them rapidly and inexpertly, breaking many of the burial offerings and littering the hillside with discarded human bones. I decided to photograph and clean up the looted cists, salvage whatever information I could, and then have my crew collect all the human remains from the surface and give them a dignified reburial.

We discovered that the targets of looting included no fewer than four cists, which we designated Structures 4–7. A photograph of Structure 4 has been presented in an earlier publication (Marcus 1987a:Fig. 42); all of the cists and their surviving contents will be described in a future volume on the Cerro Azul burials. We found that the looters had missed a great deal and had even inadvertently hidden a number of intact mummy bundles under their own backdirt piles.

Most importantly from the perspective of this volume, it was on Terrace 9 of Quebrada 5a that we first discovered how some terraces of Cerro Camacho had gone from refuse dumps to cemeteries. Structures 4–7 had all been inserted into a deep midden deposit that predated their construction. It occurred to us that if we could find a space between burial cists, we might be able to put a deep sounding into that midden deposit and find out when it began to form. We laid out a rectangular excavation block 5 m on a side, designed to incorporate all the looted burial cists as well as any gaps among them. Eventually we found a gap to the north and west of Structure 4, where we could send down a shaft to the sterile stratum below the midden layers.

Figure 9.28 presents the north–south cross section of this sounding, which is 1.6 m wide and reaches a layer of sterile sand and stones at an average depth of 2.6 m below the surface of Terrace 9. We ended the excavation at this point, and while we presume that this deposit of stones and sterile sand overlies bedrock, we cannot guarantee it.

Zone A

The visible stratigraphy of the deep sounding in Terrace 9 is not overly complicated. We decided to designate the upper 1.2 m (which mainly featured burial cists and looters' pits) simply "Zone A." This layer appears to be Late Intermediate in age but is so disturbed that any sherds found in it had to be treated with caution. It occurred to us that we might be able to radiocarbon date some of the organic materials in the burial cists, such as the reed mats lining them, or one of the food-filled gourds left as an offering. We eventually settled on a litter pole associated with Burial 4, an interment that will be described in detail in a future volume.

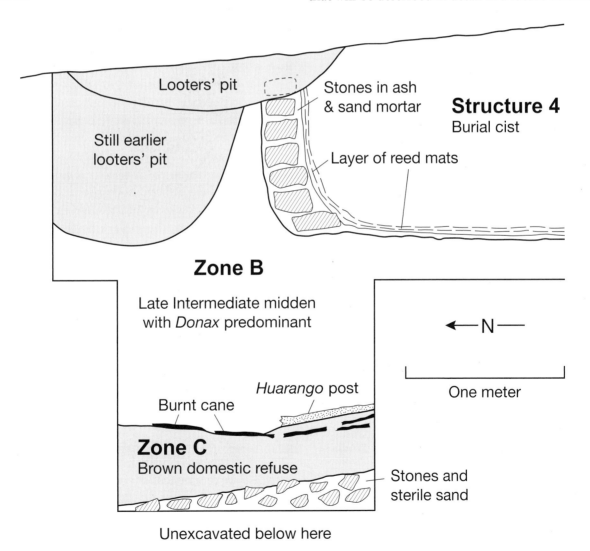

Figure 9.28. The north–south cross section of a deep sounding into Terrace 9 of Quebrada 5a, below the level of the Structure 4 burial cist.

A piece of this pole was submitted to Beta Analytic for dating.

> Beta-7797 came out 610 ± 70 years B.P., or A.D. 1340 uncalibrated. The calibrated two-sigma range would be A.D. 1276–1431.

This date is important because it places the final use of Terrace 9—the creation of burial cists in an earlier midden layer—in the Late Intermediate. The funerary offerings of the Zone A burials exemplify Kroeber and Strong's "Late Cañete culture." Like the date from Feature 17 of Structure D, Beta-7797 places that culture in the fourteenth century A.D. Even A.D. 1431, the upper limit of the calibrated two-sigma range, would have been an acceptable date.

Zone B

Below Zone A is an undisturbed Late Intermediate midden in which valves of the small coquina clam (*Donax obesus* [= *peruvianus*]) are extremely abundant. These clams are available in the sandy beach (or *playa*) zone of Cerro Azul bay (Marcus 1987a:Fig. 2A). This midden, more than a meter thick in places, was designated stratigraphic Zone B.

Zone C

Finally, the lower 30–40 cm of the sounding were filled with a layer of brown domestic refuse which we designated Zone C. There is a sharp disconformity at the meeting of Zones C and B. On the surface of Zone C lay what appear to be fragments of a destroyed *kincha* structure, including a post of *huarango* wood and half a dozen sections of burnt cane. It is not clear whether (1) a *kincha* structure had once stood nearby, or (2) the canes and wood had simply been discarded on Terrace 9.

Pottery from the Sounding

Zone C produced some of the earliest-looking sherds from our excavations at Cerro Azul. We begin with the sherds from this deepest stratum and proceed upward.

Lower Zone C

We divided Zone C into three approximately equal arbitrary levels, each of which was carefully screened. The lowest of these levels produced 42 sherds; four of the most interesting are illustrated in Figure 9.29. The total inventory is as follows:

Camacho Reddish Brown (Figure 9.29a, d)
> Flaring rim from jar, fire-blackened: 1
> Jar shoulder: 1
> Jar body sherd, perforated, with a knot from a cotton cord preserved inside the perforation: 1
> Body sherds, fire-blackened: 30

Unclassified thin ware with sandy reddish to brownish paste; fine temper with prominent white quartz grains; similar, but not identical, to Trambollo Burnished Brown
> Open bowl, slipped red on interior, painted with neat black lines over this; left light brown on exterior: 1 rim (Figure 9.29b)
> Jar body sherds, slipped in zones on exterior; zoning band yellow-cream; slipped red above band, purple below: 5 (Figure 9.29c)
> Hemispherical bowl body sherd, slipped red on interior and exterior: 1
> Hemispherical bowl body sherd, burnished light brown on interior and exterior: 1
> Thin jar sherd, shiny black paint over natural light brown on exterior: 1
> *Comment*: The bichrome/trichrome sherds of unclassified sandy reddish to brownish ware appear to me to date to an earlier stage of the Late Intermediate than the bulk of the occupation in Structures D and 9. This unclassified ware (paste 2.5 YR 5/6) looks like an earlier variety of Trambollo Burnished Brown. The slip/paint colors include red (10 R 4/6), purple (10 R 4/2), and yellow-cream (2.5 Y 7/4). The burnished natural brown surface varies from 5 YR 4/3 to 2.5 YR 5/4. Some painted bowls are reminiscent of pottery from earlier sites such as Cerro del Oro (Kroeber 1937).

Middle Zone C

The middle arbitrary level taken from Zone C yielded 48 sherds, three of which are illustrated in Figure 9.30. The total collection of sherds is as follows:

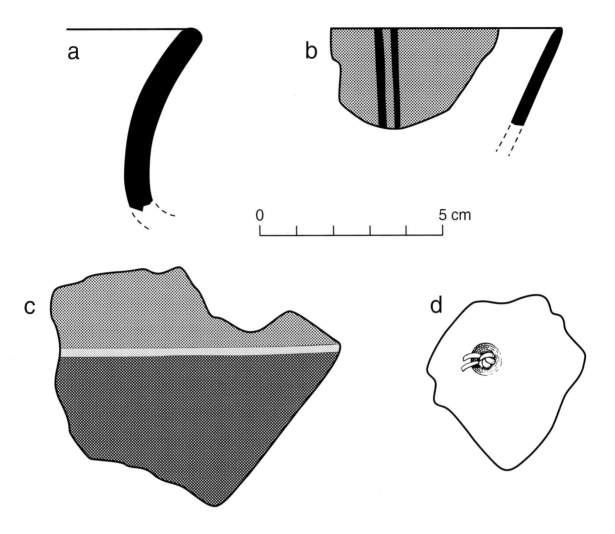

Figure 9.29. Sherds from Lower Zone C of the 5 × 5 m excavation block, Terrace 9, Quebrada 5a. *(a)*: Camacho Reddish Brown, flaring rim from fire-blackened jar; *(b)*: unclassified ware, thin-walled open bowl with sandy reddish clay body, slipped red (10 R 4/6) on the interior, then painted with vertical black lines; *(c)*: unclassified ware, thin-walled jar with polychrome painting on the exterior. A horizontal yellow-cream band crosses the sherd. Above the band, it is slipped red (10 R 4/6); below the band, it is slipped purple (10 R 4/2). *(d)*: Camacho Reddish Brown jar body sherd perforated for suspension, with cotton cord and knot preserved inside the perforation.

Camacho Reddish Brown
   Jar body sherds, fire-blackened: 35

Pingüino Buff (Figure 9.30b)
   Globular jar with wide mouth, unpainted: 1 rim, 1 shoulder
   Jar body sherds: 5

Same unclassified thin ware with sandy reddish to brownish paste mentioned in Lower Zone C
   Hemispherical bowl, slipped red on interior and exterior: 1 rim (Figure 9.30a)
   Open bowl, slipped yellow-cream on interior and exterior; painted "graphite" black on interior: 1 rim (Figure 9.30c)

   Jar shoulder, slipped white on exterior, with band of black paint encircling base of neck: 1
   Jar body sherds, painted "graphite" black on cream: 3
   Comment: This sherd collection, like the one from Lower Zone C, looks relatively early. In addition to the unclassified sandy reddish to brownish ware (which may be an early variety of Trambollo Burnished Brown), this second sample of Zone C does not contain a single sherd of Camacho Black.

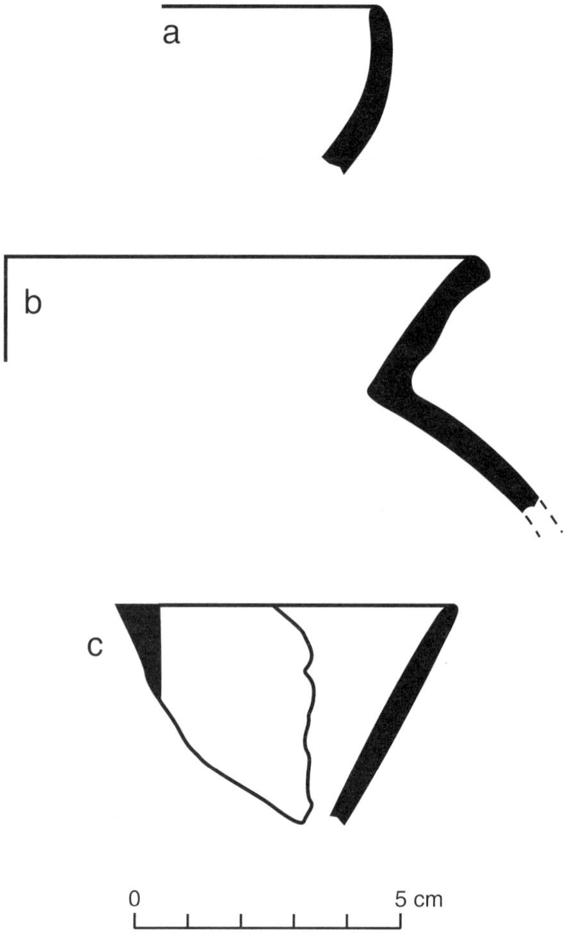

Figure 9.30. Sherds from Middle Zone C of the 5 × 5 m excavation block, Terrace 9, Quebrada 5a. *(a)*: unclassified ware, hemispherical bowl with sandy reddish clay body, slipped red (2.5 YR 3/6) on both exterior and interior; *(b)*: Pingüino Buff globular jar with wide mouth, apparently unpainted; *(c)*: unclassified ware, open bowl, clay body reddish brown with a gray core, slipped yellow-cream (7.5 YR 6/4) on both exterior and interior, painted "graphite" black on the interior.

Upper Zone C

The upper third of Zone C produced 46 sherds, four of which are illustrated in Figure 9.31. The total inventory is as follows:

Camacho Reddish Brown
 Jar body sherds, fire-blackened: 31

Pingüino Buff
 Jar body sherds with traces of yellow-cream paint: 2

Same unclassified thin ware with sandy reddish to brownish paste mentioned in Lower Zone C
 Open bowl with red wash on the interior: 1 rim (Figure 9.31a)
 Open bowl with reddish brown wash, burnished: 1 rim (Figure 9.31b)
 Jar body sherds, slipped shiny "graphite" black: 3 (one has a broken-off spout or tubular opening [Figure 9.31c])

Jar body sherd, "graphite" black paint over natural: 1 (Figure 9.31d)
Plain body sherds: 7
Comment: Sherds from the arbitrary lower, middle, and upper divisions of Zone C do not indicate significant chronological change during the deposition of the zone.

Two radiocarbon dates relevant to Upper Zone C

As Figure 9.8 shows, a *huarango* post was found lying on the upper surface of Zone C. Fragments of wood from this post were submitted to two different radiocarbon labs, Beta Analytic and the University of Wisconsin. My expectation was that these might be the oldest dates obtained from Cerro Azul. At the same time, I realized that the post could be "reused" from an earlier structure, possibly a *kincha* house. Good wooden poles are in such demand on the desert coast that many may have been saved, to be used over and over.

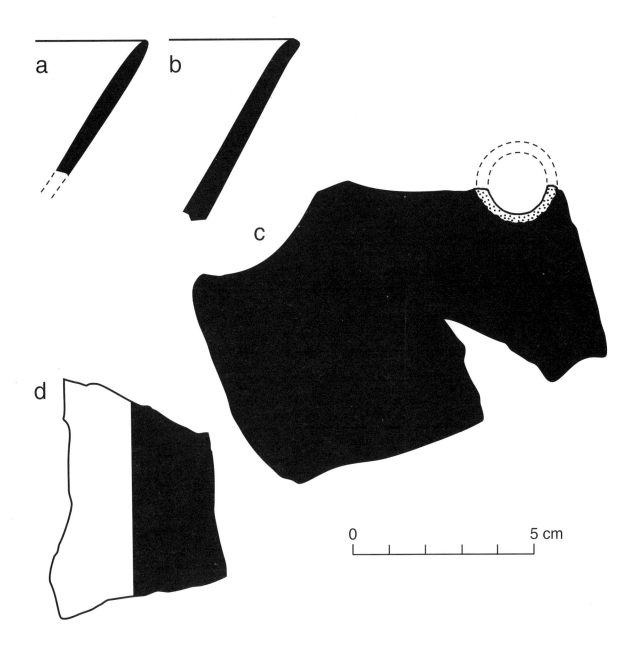

Figure 9.31. Sherds from Upper Zone C of the 5 × 5 m excavation block, Terrace 9, Quebrada 5a. *(a)*: unclassified ware with sandy reddish clay body, open bowl covered with red wash (10 R 5/6) on the interior; *(b)*: unclassified ware with fine reddish brown clay body, open bowl with reddish brown wash (2.5 R 4/4), burnished; *(c)*: unclassified ware with sandy reddish clay body, jar body slipped "graphite" black on the exterior; one area shows a broken-off spout or tubular opening 1.5 cm in diameter; the black slip is shiny, metallic, and almost purplish black; *(d)*: unclassified ware with sandy reddish clay body, jar body sherd with a zone of "graphite" black paint over natural brown exterior.

Beta-7796 came out 1650 ± 120 years B.P., or A.D. 300 uncalibrated. The calibrated two-sigma range would be A.D. 129–633.

WIS-1938 came out 1150 ± 70 years B.P., or A.D. 800 uncalibrated. The calibrated two-sigma range would be A.D. 694–1018.

The good news is that these are, as expected, our oldest dates from Cerro Azul. The bad news is that they seem *too* old. These are essentially Middle Horizon dates, and the pottery from Zone C, while certainly earlier than "Late Cañete," does not look to be as early as A.D. 300–800, uncalibrated. I would not have been surprised by a date of A.D. 1018, the upper limit of the calibrated two-sigma range for WIS-1938. I am, however, surprised by how old Beta-7796 is.

In addition to keeping my mind open, I am aware that we do not know the date at which the *huarango* post was cut and trimmed. Nor do we know how old the *huarango* tree was when cut, or which of its growth rings were sampled by the pieces of wood we submitted for dating. If we knew these things, the date might not be so surprising.

Zone B

Two kinds of sherd samples were taken from Zone B, a gray ashy Late Intermediate midden above Zone C (Figure 9.28). Those parts of Zone B that appeared undisturbed by intrusive burial cists were fully screened, and all sherds saved. When we were in doubt about the undisturbed nature of the midden, we saved diagnostic sherds but did not screen.

Let us begin with the screened sample from undisturbed context. It consists of 117 sherds, 10 of which are illustrated in Figures 9.32 and 9.33. The complete list is as follows:

Camacho Reddish Brown
    Rim sherd from a *tinajón* (500-liter size): 1 (Figure 9.32b)
    Jar shoulder, fire-blackened: 1 (Figure 9.32c)
    Jar body sherd, perforated, with knot from

cotton cord stuck in perforation: 1 (Figure 9.32d)
    Body sherds: 95

Camacho Black (Standard Variety)
    Neck from jar or amphora: 1 (Figure 9.33a)
    Body sherds: 5

Pingüino Buff
    Shoulder of large jar, plain: 1 (Figure 9.32g)
    Thin-walled jar sherds with purplish paint (10 R 4/2) on exterior; "Life Savers" painted in yellow-cream (2.5 Y 7/4) over purple: 2 (Figure 9.32f)
    Rim of open bowl; paste transitional between the unclassified reddish-to-brownish ware of Zone C and more typical Pingüino Buff: 1 (Figure 9.32e)
    Body sherds: 5

Trambollo Burnished Brown
    Small bowl with restricted orifice, painted black on natural: 1 rim (Figure 9.32a)

Unclassified fine, sandy paste ware with a gray core sandwiched between brown layers; surface brown (5 YR 4/3 to 5 YR 4/4)
    Jar body sherds with zones of "graphite" black paint: 2 (Figure 9.32h)

Unique sherd
    Body sherd with fine red paste, slipped yellow-cream and highly burnished on exterior; "Superman's S" motif painted in black and red over slip: 1 (Figure 9.33b)
    Comment: Zone B appears transitional between (1) the earlier Late Intermediate pottery complex seen in Zone C and (2) the more typical "Late Cañete" material of Structures D and 9. While some earlier ceramic attributes (such as "Life Savers" and purplish paint) are still present, the familiar complex of Camacho Reddish Brown, Camacho Black, Pingüino Buff, and Trambollo Burnished Brown is now present.

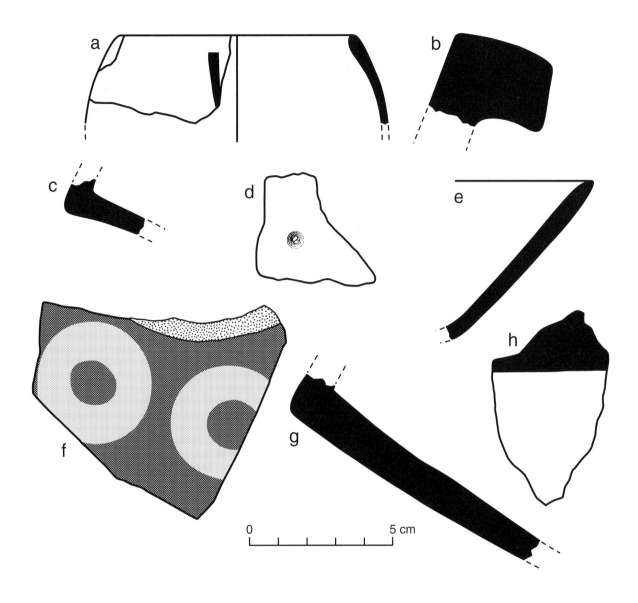

Figure 9.32. Sherds found in Zone B, a Late Intermediate midden below Structures 4 and 5, Terrace 9, Quebrada 5a. *(a)*: Trambollo Burnished Brown, small bowl with restricted orifice, painted black on natural on the exterior; *(b)*: Camacho Reddish Brown, bolstered rim from large storage jar; *(c)*: Camacho Reddish Brown jar shoulder, fire-blackened; *(d)*: Camacho Reddish Brown, body sherd from a jar with a hole drilled through from the exterior; a knot from a cord is still stuck in the hole; *(e)*: Pingüino Buff (?) open bowl; interior color 2.5 YR 4/6, exterior color 2.5 YR 5/4; *(f)*: Pingüino Buff jar shoulder, exterior covered with purplish paint (10 R 4/2); yellow-cream "Life Savers" have been painted over the purple, and light stipple shows the broken edge of the sherd; *(g)*: Pingüino Buff, shoulder of large jar; *(h)*: unclassified ware characterized by fine, sandy paste with a gray core between brown layers; this body sherd has a zone of shiny "graphite" black paint over natural brown, with the brown being 5 YR 4/3 in the Munsell system.

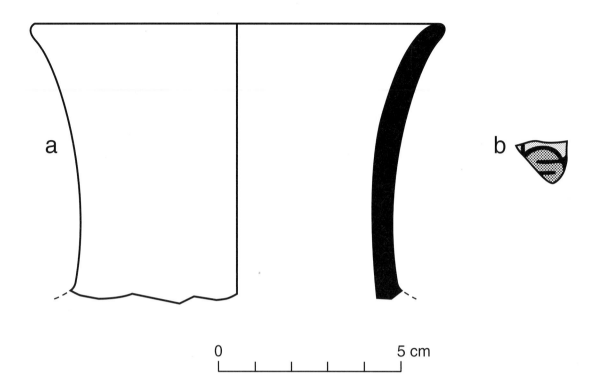

Figure 9.33. Sherds found in stratigraphic Zone B, a Late Intermediate midden below Structures 4 and 5, Terrace 9, Quebrada 5a. *(a)*: Camacho Black (standard variety) neck of jar or amphora; *(b)*: unique body sherd with fine red clay body. The vessel is slipped yellow-cream (2.5 Y 6/4) on the exterior, then painted in black and red (10 R 3/4) over the slip. (The finely executed motif looks like the "S" on Superman's chest.)

Additional Zone B sherds

Figure 9.34 presents two more sherds from Zone B; these are sherds from areas deemed too close to the burial cists to merit screening. One is a Trambollo Burnished Brown bowl rim, painted white on brown (Figure 9.34a). The other is an eroded sherd, possibly Pingüino Buff, painted white and black over a red slip (Figure 9.34b). Both sherds look to be a bit earlier than the bulk of the ceramics from Structures D and 9.

Sherds from the wall of Structure 5

As Figure 9.28 indicates, some of the burial cists on Terrace 9 had walls made of stone, set in a mortar composed of ash and sand. The interior of the cist was then lined with reed mats before the funerary bundles were set in place.

In the case of Structure 5, there are small sherds in the mortar, suggesting to us that Zone B might have been the source of the gray ash in which the stones were set. To test this possibility, we collected 76 sherds from a damaged section of Structure 5's wall. This sample of sherds reinforces our suspicion that the ash was from Zone B. The full inventory is as follows:

Camacho Reddish Brown
    Flaring rim from jar: 1
    Body sherds, many fire-blackened: 64

Camacho Black (Standard Variety)
    Flat base from jar or amphora: 1
    Body sherds: 3

Pingüino Buff
    Jar shoulder, painted in two horizontal zones separated by a yellow-cream band (2.5 Y 8/2); zone of red paint (10 R 4/3) with

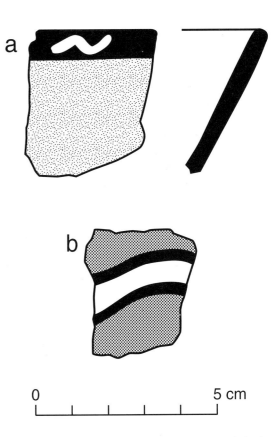

Figure 9.34. Additional sherds from Zone B of Terrace 9, Quebrada 5a. (These sherds were not part of the screened sample.) *(a)*: Trambollo Burnished Brown bowl sherd with plain rim, burnished on the interior, with a chocolate brown band (5 YR 3/2) painted on the rim and a cream-white "worm" motif painted over the band. The vessel exterior is plain; light stipple indicates natural brown. *(b)*: possible Pingüino Buff bowl body sherd, slipped red (10 R 4/4) on the interior and painted in white and black over that (red shown as medium screen). The exterior (too eroded to illustrate) had been slipped cream-white, then painted in black over that.

0   5 cm

yellow "Life Savers" above the band; zone of purple paint (5 R 3/1) with cream "Life Savers" below the band: 1 (this sherd is shown in Figure 3.20c, Chapter 3)

Sherd from base of jar, unpainted: 1

Jar body sherd with traces of black paint over natural buff: 1

Body sherds: 5

Sherds from Zone A

In general, Zone A of our 5 × 5 m excavation block was so disturbed by burial cists and looters' pits that no reliable sherd sample could be obtained. In the extreme northwest corner of the block, however, we found a small area that seemed to be relatively undisturbed. A cluster of 13 sherds appeared at a depth of 30 cm below the surface of the terrace; five of these sherds are shown in Figure 9.35. The full list of sherds is as follows:

Camacho Reddish Brown

Flaring rim from jar: 1 (Figure 9.35a)

Strap handle from cooking pot, fire-blackened: 1 (Figure 9.35c)

Amphora neck with everted rim, modeled human face with "coffee-bean" eyes: 1 (Figure 9.35e)

Body sherds: 8

Camacho Black (Standard Variety)

Loop handle from miniature jar: 1 (Figure 9.35d)

Pingüino Buff

Rim of open bowl, burnished on interior: 1 (Figure 9.35b)

Comment: If this sherd collection is, in fact, an undisturbed sample from Zone A, then that zone is broadly contemporaneous with the main occupation of Structures D and 9.

Broken vessels from Structure 4

As mentioned earlier, the *huaqueros* who looted Structure 4 broke numerous burial offerings and missed others in their haste. The still-intact offerings will be described in a later volume. Figure 9.36 illustrates two of the vessels the looters broke.

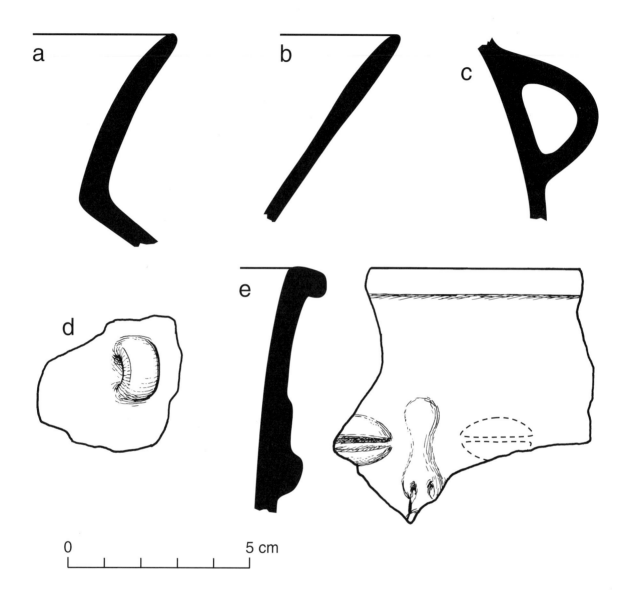

Figure 9.35. Sherds from 30 cm below the surface in stratigraphic Zone A of the 5 × 5 m excavation block, Terrace 9, Quebrada 5a. All sherds come from the northwest corner of the block. *(a)*: Camacho Reddish Brown, flaring rim from jar; *(b)*: Pingüino Buff, rim of wide, open, probably shallow bowl; *(c)*: Camacho Reddish Brown, strap handle from cooking pot; *(d)*: Camacho Black, loop handle from miniature jar; *(e)*: Camacho Reddish Brown, amphora with modeled human face just below the bolstered rim. The eyes (one of which had eroded away) were the appliqué "coffee-bean" type.

Figure 9.36a shows a small jar with two loop handles in the highly burnished ("graphite") variety of Camacho Black. Figure 9.36b shows a modeled and painted human face from the neck of a Pingüino Buff jar. The black/white/red facial paint is typical of the main period of occupation of Structures D and 9.

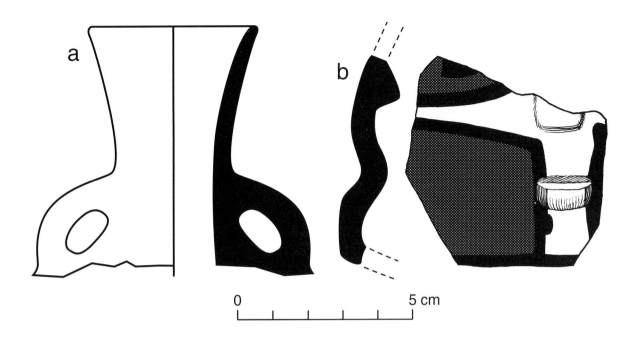

Figure 9.36. Sherds from vessels broken by the looters of Structure 4, Terrace 9, Quebrada 5a. *(a)*: Camacho Black ("graphite" variety), small jar with two loop handles; *(b)*: Pingüino Buff, jar neck with human face modeled on it, painted in black, white, and reddish brown (the latter shown as heavy screen).

Summary of Terrace 9

The first use of Terrace 9 would seem to have antedated the main occupation of Structure D. During the deposition of stratigraphic Zone C, trash was dumped in Quebrada 5a, and a *huarango* post yielding unexpectedly early ^{14}C dates was discarded.

Zone B represents domestic refuse (including coquina clam shells) that was dumped on Terrace 9 during the transition from an earlier stage of the Late Intermediate to the later stage reflected in the pottery of Structure D.

Zone A, as well as the burial cists excavated into it, displays the same ceramic complex seen in the main occupation of Structures D and 9. This complex matches Kroeber's "Late Cañete" pottery assemblage in all its details.

QUEBRADA 6, TERRACE 11

Quebrada 6 lies roughly 120 m to the south of Quebrada 5a (see Figure 2.2, Chapter 2). Structure H, one of Kroeber's large tapia compounds, sits directly in front of Quebrada 6 and can be considered a plausible source for the debris dumped in the quebrada (see Figure 2.7, top, in Chapter 2).

My attention was first drawn to Quebrada 6 while surface-collecting Structure H. As I looked up into the nearby quebrada, I saw a series of terraces that appeared to be almost coal black. The only coastal site where I had previously seen deposits that black was Huaca Prieta in the Chicama Valley. There, Junius Bird and various of his colleagues had surmised that the black color was the result of a high content of fish oil. I wondered if that same explanation would apply to the black terraces of Quebrada 6. If so, those terraces might contain an interesting sample of fish remains to supplement what we had found in Structures D and 9.

One of the blackest terraces in Quebrada 6 is the eleventh, counting down from the summit of the hill (Figure 9.37). We chose a relatively flat part of Terrace 11 on which to lay out a north–south grid of 1 × 1 m squares (Figure 9.38). We labeled the two initial squares M6 and N6, which (by placing us near the middle of the alphabet) would enable us to expand any direction we wanted. We eventually chose to expand south-ward into Squares M7, N7, M8, and N8.

The west profile of Squares M6 and M7 divides Terrace 11 into western and eastern halves.

Laying out the squares required the removal of a great many loose stones that had slid down from above. We stored these stones nearby (Figure 9.37, bottom center) so that we could backfill with

Figure 9.37. Two views of Terrace 11, Quebrada 6. *(Top)*: looking west out of the quebrada toward the light-house on Cerro Centinela. *(Bottom)*: looking southwest toward Structure H, the nearest residential compound and a plausible source for the midden material in Quebrada 6.

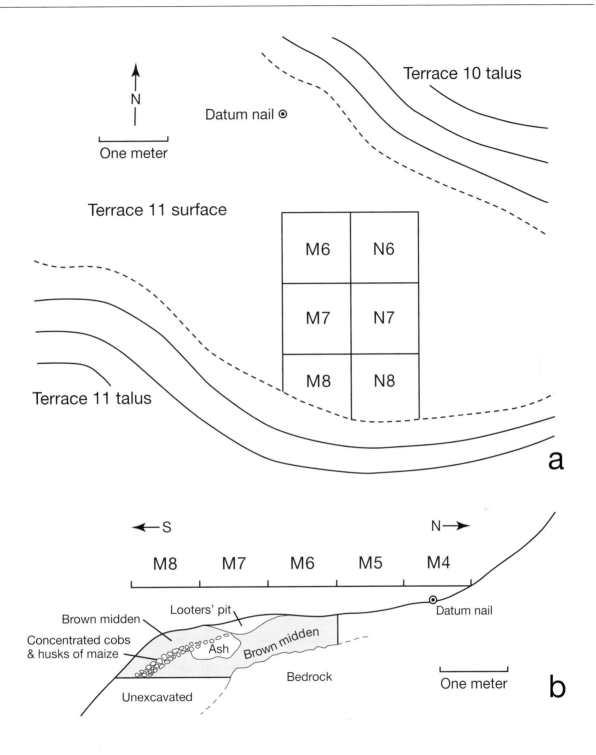

Figure 9.38. Excavation of Terrace 11, Quebrada 6. *(a)*: plan view of the terrace showing Squares M6-N8. *(b)*: profile of the west wall of Squares M6, M7, and M8.

them, as well as use them to prevent debris from falling back into the excavation.

The black matrix of Terrace 11 is extremely greasy, a condition caused by high levels of de-

composed organic material (Figure 9.39). The uppermost 10 cm of the deposit had been hardened by *salitre* until it resembled cement. Once we broke through this salty crust, we found ourselves

Figure 9.39. Excavation of Terrace 11, Quebrada 6. *(Top)*: Edgar Zavala and Alberto Barraza are removing the upper 20 cm of Squares M6 and N6. *(Bottom)*: sweeping the excavation before proceeding to the next level. Note the greasy black appearance of the debris, caused by high levels of organic material.

in a brown midden so soft and powdery that we had to supply the workmen with dust masks (Figure 9.39, bottom). The contents of this midden are reminiscent of Feature 6 in Structure D (Chapter 4), except that all the materials appear to have been broken into smaller particles during their transport from one of the tapia compounds. As Figure 9.38b shows, there were lenses of ash and layers of maize cobs in the midden. There were also abundant mussels, clams, beans, maize husks, canes, rushes, fish bones, and even pellets of llama dung like those we had found in the Southwest Canchón of Structure D. Indeed, a lot of the material looks like the kind of fine debris that might have been swept from the floor of a tapia compound. Where dry, the midden was dark brown; where dampened and hardened by salt fog at the southern limits of the terrace, it had turned the coal black color that attracted our attention.

Terrace 11 is not particularly deep. As shown in Figure 9.40, we eventually reached a series of stepped, irregular bedrock outcrops at the bottom of the excavation. We ended our investigation into Terrace 11 convinced that this "black terrace" was one of the places in which fine-fraction debris from the tapia compounds had reached its final resting place.

The pottery from Terrace 11

Sherds were small on average, but relatively abundant, in the midden deposits of Terrace 11. Because of significant irregularities in the depth of bedrock, our collection of pottery consists of a series of subsamples from varying depths. Deposits

Figure 9.40. Ramón Landa sweeps the bedrock outcrop found at the bottom of Terrace 11, Quebrada 6. Note the masses of plant fiber (mostly shredded canes and rushes of the types used for matting and basketry) in the dark brown midden deposit.

were deepest in Squares M8 and N8, where the midden had poured over the edge of Terrace 11 and slid down toward Terrace 12 (Figure 9.38b). Deposits were shallowest in Square N6, where bedrock was only 20 cm below the surface.

We begin our inventory of pottery with the deepest deposit, which comes from 30–50 cm below the surface in Squares M8 and N8. This deposit was screened and every sherd saved, no matter how small. Seven of those sherds are shown in Figures 9.41 and 9.42. The complete collection is as follows:

Camacho Reddish Brown
    Cooking pots with restricted orifice, fire-blackened, horizontally set strap handle: 2 rims (Figure 9.41)
    Same as above, but with vertically set strap handle: 1
    Neckless jar with everted rim: 1 (Figure 9.42e)
    Rim of *hatun maccma* (2000-liter size): 1 (Figure 9.42b)
    Plain rims from jars: 3 (Figure 9.42c, d)
    Bolstered rim from jar: 1 (Figure 9.42f)
    Flaring rim from jar: 1
    Cambered rim from jar: 1
    Jar shoulders: 3
    Body sherds: 12

Camacho Black (Standard Variety)
    Flaring jar neck with modeled face ("coffee-bean" eyes): 1 (Figure 9.42a)
    Strap handle fragment from large jar: 1
    Body sherds: 5

Pingüino Buff
    Jar body sherds with three black zoning lines on natural buff: 3

Comment: This collection dates to the main period of occupation in Structures D and 9. The fire-blackened Camacho Reddish Brown cooking pots and the Camacho Black modeled face with "coffee-bean" eyes are prototypical.

The second deepest sherd sample from Terrace 11 comes from Squares M6 and N6. It consists of all sherds discovered between the very irregular bedrock and a point 30 cm below the surface. Five of those sherds are shown in Figure 9.43; the entire collection is as follows:

Camacho Reddish Brown
    Rims from jars: 5 (Figure 9.43c–f)
    Jar shoulders: 2
    Small strap handles from jars: 2
    Jar body sherds: 19

Camacho Black (Standard Variety)
    Jar shoulder: 1
    Jar body sherds: 6

Pingüino Buff
    Rim from large jar: 1 (Figure 9.43b)
    Jar body sherd, upper part slipped yellowish cream and painted black and red; lower part left natural buff: 1 (Figure 9.43a)
    Body sherds: 4

Our next subsample consists of sherds found at a depth of 30 cm below the surface in Square M8. Many of these ceramics are shown in Figures 9.44 and 9.45. Some 54–57 of the sherds appear to have come from a single vessel, which is reconstructed in Figure 9.45. The complete inventory is as follows:

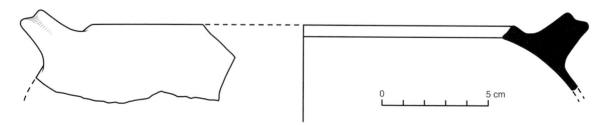

Figure 9.41. Reconstruction of a broken Camacho Reddish Brown vessel from 30–50 cm below the surface in Squares M8/N8 of Terrace 11, Quebrada 6. This is a cooking pot with restricted orifice and horizontally set strap handles; the vessel is fire-blackened.

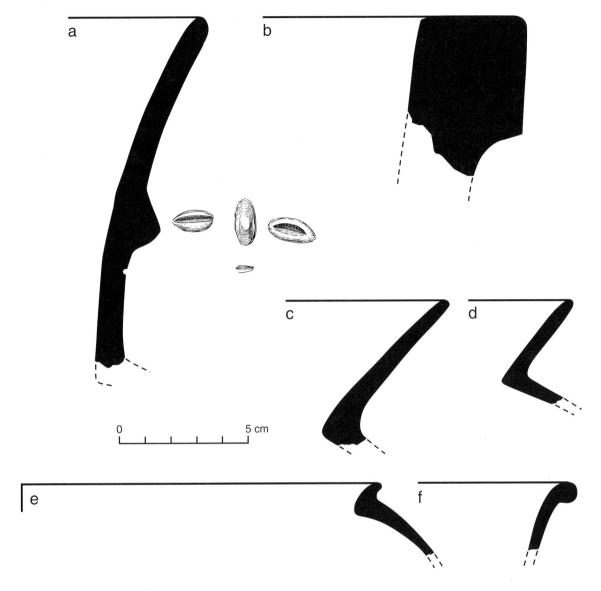

Figure 9.42. Sherds found at a depth of 30–50 cm below the surface in Squares M8/N8 of Terrace 11, Quebrada 6. *(a)*: Camacho Black jar neck with a human face modeled on the exterior; the face, with its "coffee-bean" eyes, is shown to the right of the profile. Sherds *b–f* are Camacho Reddish Brown. *(b)*: rim from *hatun maccma*. *(c, d)*: plain rims from jars; *(e)*: neckless jar with everted rim; *(f)*: jar with bolstered rim.

Camacho Reddish Brown
　　Jars with cambered rims: 4 rim sherds
　　　　(Figure 9.44a–c)
　　Jar with slightly flaring rim: 1 rim sherd
　　　　(Figure 9.44d)
　　Jar shoulder, fire-blackened: 1
　　Body sherds (mostly jars): 15

Camacho Black (Standard Variety)
　　Jar body sherd with large strap handle: 1
　　　　(Figure 9.44e)
　　Jar body sherds: 6

Pingüino Buff (?)
　　Badly eroded jar neck sherd with nose from
　　　　modeled face: 1 (Figure 9.44f)

Atypical Orange Variety of Pingüino Buff
　　Jar with a funnel neck and vertically set
　　　　strap handles, painted in black/
　　　　white/ dusky red with stripes and fish
　　　　motif: 1 complete neck, 3–4 shoulder
　　　　sherds, 50–52 body sherds (Figure
　　　　9.45)

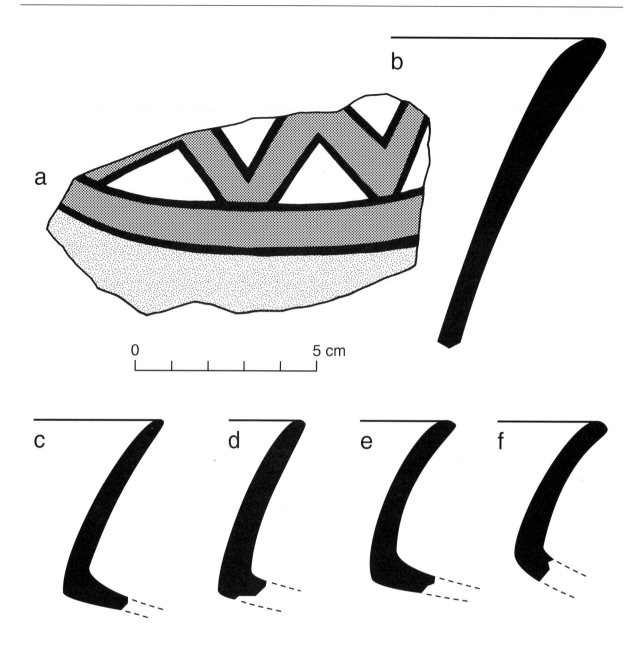

Figure 9.43. Sherds found from 30 cm below the surface down to bedrock in Squares M6/N6, Terrace 11, Quebrada 6. *(a)*: Pingüino Buff, jar body sherd left natural buff below, slipped yellowish cream (10 YR 7/4) above, with geometric designs painted over the slip in black and red (10 R 3/6). Medium screen indicates red; light stipple indicates natural buff. *(b)*: Pingüino Buff, rim from large jar. *(c–f)*: Camacho Reddish Brown, four examples of jar rims that vary from plain *(c)* to slightly flaring or outcurved *(f)*. Most are fire-blackened.

At a depth of 30 cm in Square M7 (immediately adjacent to the square mentioned above), we found the unusual vessel shown in Figure 9.46. The original vessel had been a large Camacho Black amphora (standard variety). At some point it broke, and its lower half had been reused as a cooking pot. The upper half was never found.

At a depth of 30 cm in Square N8 we found a cluster of 15 sherds, three of which are shown in Figure 9.47. The full list of sherds is as follows:

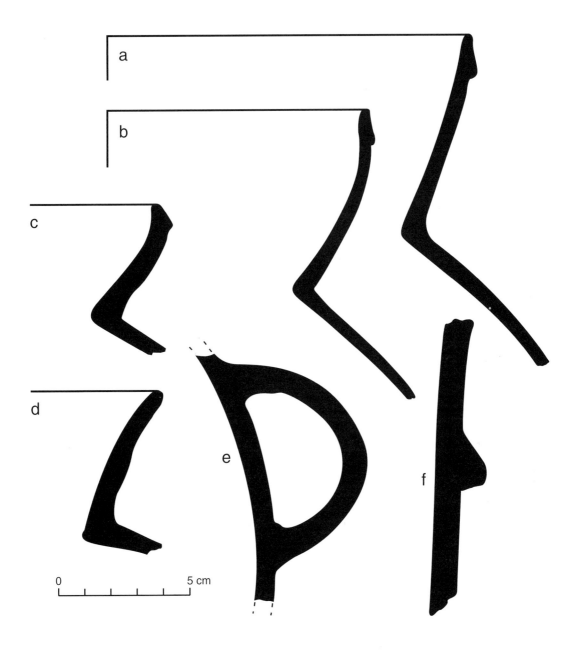

Figure 9.44. Sherds found at a depth of 30 cm in Square M8, Terrace 11, Quebrada 6. *(a–c)*: Camacho Reddish Brown, cambered rims from jars; *(d)*: Camacho Reddish Brown, slightly flaring rim from jar; *(e)*: Camacho Black (standard variety), jar body sherd with vertically set strap handle; *(f)*: Pingüino Buff (?) jar neck sherd with prominent nose from modeled human face; badly eroded.

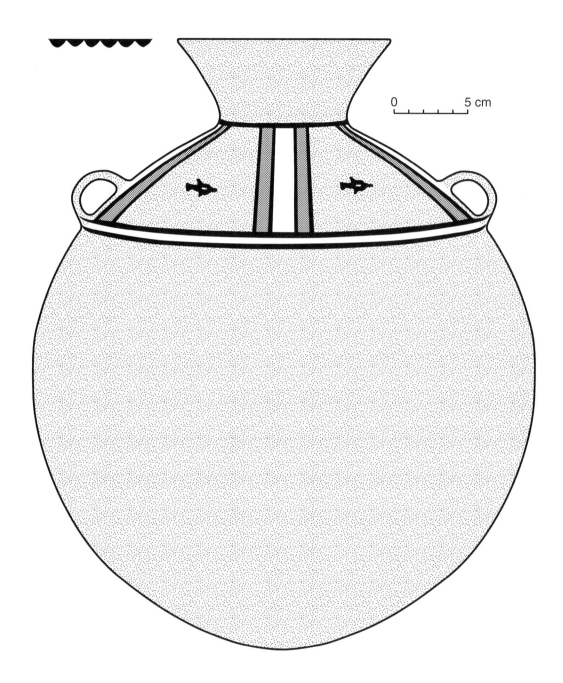

Figure 9.45. Reconstruction of a vessel in the atypical orange variety of Pingüino Buff, found broken at a depth of 30 cm in Square M8, Terrace 11, Quebrada 6. This is a jar with a lenticular body, flaring neck, and vertically set strap handles. The area covered by light stipple is natural buff. The shoulder of the vessel is divided into zones by painted stripes of black/white/dusky red (7.5 R 2/4-3/4); the red is shown as a medium screen. In the zones, simple fish motifs have been painted in black. A continuous band of black semicircles (shown to the left of the neck) runs around the rim interior.

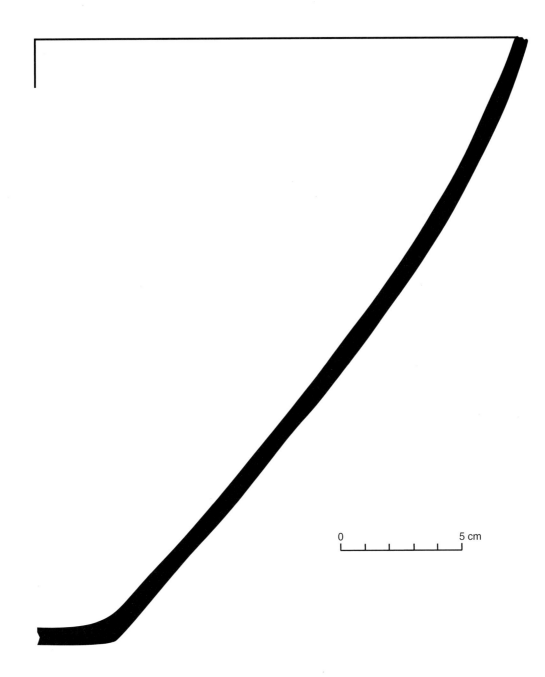

Figure 9.46. Reconstruction of a Camacho Black vessel found at a depth of 30 cm in Square M7, Terrace 11, Quebrada 6. The original vessel was an amphora. After it broke, its lower half was reused and is carbon-smudged from use as a cooking pot. The upper half was never found.

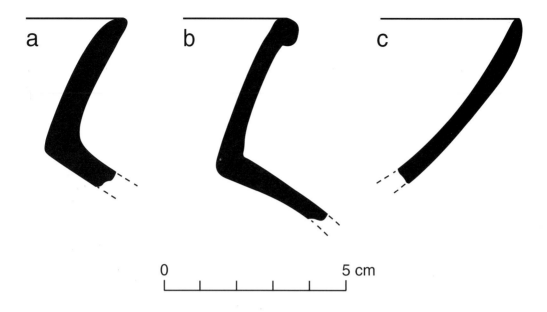

Figure 9.47. Sherds found at a depth of 30 cm in Square N8, Terrace 11, Quebrada 6. *(a)*: Camacho Reddish Brown, plain rim from jar; *(b)*: Camacho Reddish Brown, bolstered rim from jar; *(c)*: Pingüino Buff, open bowl rim, burnished and given a white wash on both interior and exterior (discolored).

Camacho Reddish Brown
 Jar with plain rim: 1 rim (Figure 9.47a)
 Jar with bolstered rim: 1 rim (Figure 9.47b)
 Body sherds: 9 (almost all fire-blackened)

Pingüino Buff
 Open bowl rim: 1 (discolored; burnished
  and white-washed on interior and exterior) (Figure 9.47c)
 Body sherds: 3

Finally, we come to two pottery samples from the uppermost 20 cm of Terrace 11. While these samples are not particularly large, they contain a few elements that I associate with the transition from Late Intermediate to Late Horizon at Cerro Azul. One of these elements is the Pingüino Buff open bowl with large, shiny black semicircles or crescents encircling the interior of the rim.

The first of these samples consists of 59 sherds from a depth of 0–20 cm below the surface in Square M6. Six of these sherds are illustrated in Figure 9.48, and the full list is as follows:

Camacho Reddish Brown
 Jars with slightly flaring rims: 2 rims
  (Figure 9.48a, b)

Jar with thin plain rim: 1 rim (Figure 9.48c)
 Open bowl rim, painted black and white
  over red wash: 1 (Figure 9.48e)
 Body sherds: 44 (mostly fire-blackened)

Camacho Black (Standard Variety)
 Body sherds: 3

Pingüino Buff
 Open bowl with large black crescents paint-
  ed on interior: 2 rims (Figure 9.48f)
 Body sherds from bowl: 1
 Jar neck, painted "graphite" black: 1 (Figure
  9.48d)
 Jar body sherd, traces of black and gray
  paint: 1
 Body sherds: 3

The second sample from 0–20 cm below the surface comes from Square N6 and consists of 37 sherds. Six of these sherds are pictured in Figure 9.49, and the total list is as follows:

Camacho Reddish Brown
 Neckless jar with everted rim: 1 rim (Figure
  9.49f)

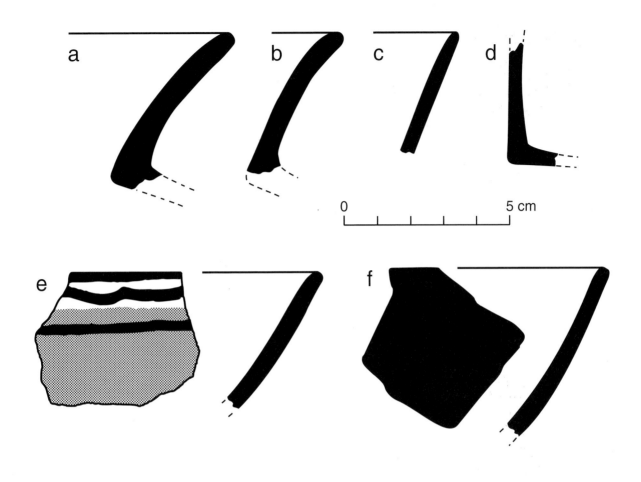

Figure 9.48. Sherds from 0–20 cm below the surface in Square M6, Terrace 11, Quebrada 6. *(a, b)*: Camacho Reddish Brown, slightly flaring rims from jars; *(c)*: Camacho Reddish Brown, plain rim from jar. *(d)*: Pingüino Buff, vertical jar neck, painted "graphite" black on the exterior; *(e)*: Camacho Reddish Brown, open bowl rim, given a dark red wash (10 R 3/4) on the interior and painted in black and white over that; the red is shown as a medium screen; *(f)*: Pingüino Buff, open bowl rim, painted shiny black on the interior, probably in the form of large crescents (see Figure 9.49a).

Jar with slightly flaring rim: 1 rim (Figure 9.49e)
Open bowl, burnished: 1 rim (Figure 9.49d)
Carinated bowl: 1 rim (Figure 9.49c)
Strap handle fragment: 1
Body sherds: 30

Pingüino Buff
Open bowl with large black crescents painted on the interior: 1 rim (Figure 9.49a)
Jar body sherd, traces of black and gray motif over cream wash: 1 (Figure 9.49b)

Summary of Terrace 11

Terrace 11 of Quebrada 6 seems to have been used mainly as a place to dump midden debris from one or more of the nearby tapia compounds. This dumping seems to have begun during the main period of occupation seen in Structures D and 9 and continued virtually until the end of the Late Intermediate era. The coal black color that attracted our attention to Terrace 11 seems to have resulted from the action of salt fog on richly organic dark brown midden. The quantity of fish bone in the midden can be seen as supporting the argument that rancid fish oil added to the dark color.

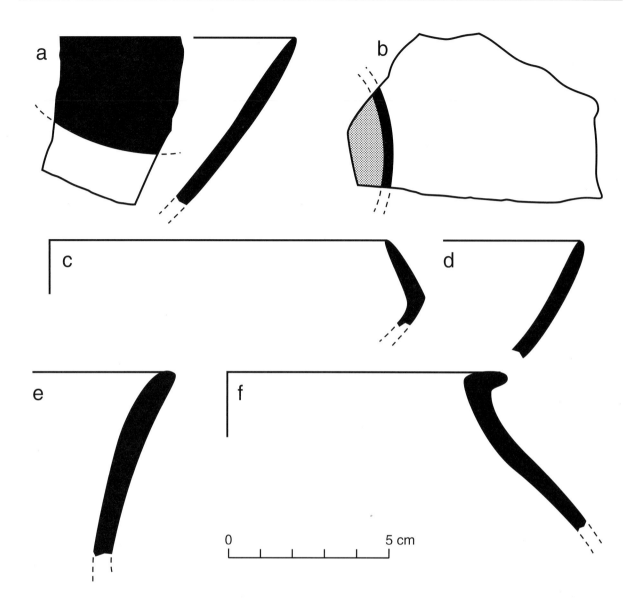

Figure 9.49. Sherds from 0–20 cm below the surface in Square N6, Terrace 11, Quebrada 6. *(a)*: Pingüino Buff, open bowl with an area of black paint on the interior; this sherd is also painted black on the top of the rim; *(b)*: Pingüino Buff, jar body sherd with burnished cream wash, over which a circular motif has been painted in gray (shown as light screen) and black; *(c)*: Camacho Reddish Brown, carinated bowl, fire-blackened on the exterior. *(d)*: Camacho Reddish Brown, open bowl, burnished inside and out and fire-blackened; *(e)*: Camacho Reddish Brown, slightly flaring rim from jar; *(f)*: Camacho Reddish Brown, neckless jar with everted rim.

QUEBRADA 6, TERRACE 12

My attention was drawn to Terrace 12 of Quebrada 6 while we were working on Terrace 11. As I looked down on Terrace 12, I could see the kind of depression we had come to associate with a looted burial cist.

As soon as we had completed our excavation of Terrace 11, I laid out a grid of 1 × 1 m squares

on Terrace 12. Once again, I began in the middle of the alphabet so that we could expand in any direction. We eventually wound up excavating eight squares: J6–J9 and K6–K9 (Figure 9.50).

Terrace 12 is very different from Terrace 11. Rather than having been used as a place to dump midden debris, Terrace 12 had been the venue for a burial cist, a storage cist, and an ash-filled earth oven. These constructions were set not in an ashy

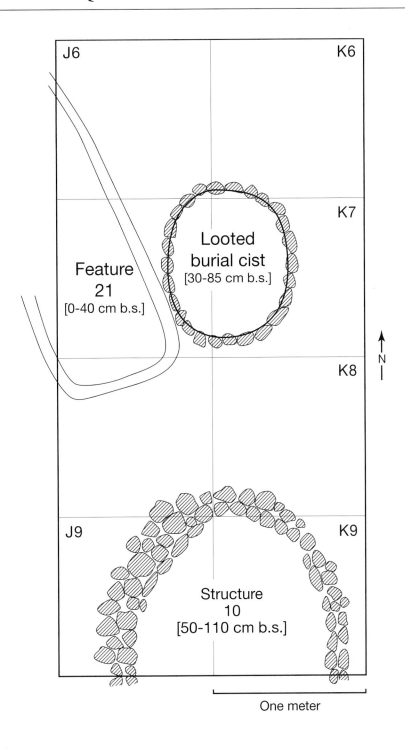

Figure 9.50. Quebrada 6, Terrace 12: plan of structures and features encountered in Squares J6–K9.

midden matrix, but in a 40- to 60-cm-thick layer of beach gravel brought in for that purpose.

Figure 9.51, a north–south cross section through our eight-square excavation block, shows the stratigraphic history of Terrace 12. The lowest layer is sterile hardpan that had formed above bedrock. Over this hardpan, someone had created a burial cist and a storage cist from readily available scree stones set in clay; these structures were held in place by the thick layer of beach

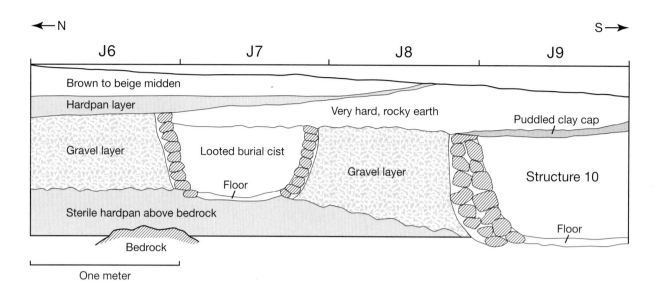

Figure 9.51. Quebrada 6, Terrace 12: east profile of Squares J6–J9.

gravel mentioned above. At a later date, someone had excavated down into the gravel layer and created a clay-lined subterranean earth oven.

There followed a hiatus during which a layer of very hard, rocky earth slid down over Terrace 12. A layer of sterile hardpan formed above this. Finally, a quantity of brown to beige midden from Terrace 11 eroded down over the rest of Terrace 12.

Now let us look at the constructions shown in Figure 9.50. The burial cist (roughly 70 × 100 cm and oval) had been emptied by looters, and was not given a structure number. The earth oven, designated Feature 21, extends outside our excavation block and could not be fully measured; its width is about 85–90 cm. Feature 21 contained ash, burnt bone, and fragments of maize.

The most nearly intact of the three structures is the storage cist, designated Structure 10 (Figure 9.52). In addition to its stone masonry wall, this cist had a clay floor and was sealed by a puddled clay cap (Figure 9.51). It, too, extends outside our excavation block and could not be fully measured; its internal diameter is approximately 1.25 m. The clay cap was still intact, allowing us to conclude that Structure 10 had not been looted. It might have been used to store something perishable, but there is no evidence it had ever been used for burials. When opened, it contained only pieces of decomposing nets or net bags, cordage, and marine shell.

Sherds from Terrace 12

Because so much of the matrix in Terrace 12 is sterile beach gravel, we recovered sherds only from the uppermost 20 cm—mostly from the brown to beige midden that had eroded down from a higher terrace. This pottery sample, seven sherds of which are illustrated in Figure 9.53, contains elements that appear in Late Horizon deposits elsewhere at Cerro Azul. Included in the latter are annular bases from bowls. The full inventory is as follows:

Camacho Reddish Brown
    Cooking pots with restricted orifice, bolstered rim, burnished exterior, fire-blackened: 3 rims (Figure 9.53a–c)
    Hatun maccma body sherd with raised (modeled) area in form of keyhole: 1 (Figure 9.53e)
    Body sherds: 3

Camacho Black (Standard Variety)
    Jar with flaring rim: 1

Pingüino Buff
    Ring bases from bowls; white wash; burnished on interior and exterior: 2 (Figure 9.53f, g)
    Slender vessel spout with bridge, slipped black: 1 (Figure 9.53d)
    Body sherds: 2

Figure 9.52. Structure 10, partially excavated. This stone-lined cist was found in Terrace 12, Quebrada 6. The north arrow is marked both in centimeters (R) and inches (L).

Comment on Quebrada 6: Our excavations on Terraces 11 and 12 of Quebrada 6 reinforce my suspicion that we had only scratched the surface of Cerro Camacho. The diversity of terrace use there was such that even had we dug two or three times as many localities, I believe that there would have been surprises with every new excavation. Some terraces were pure midden, virtually without intrusive features. Other terraces were created out of beach gravel and rocks for the express purpose of holding storage cists, burial cists, or earth ovens. I also began to suspect that while some burials had cists created just for them, other burials might have been placed in former storage cists that had outlived their previous usefulness.

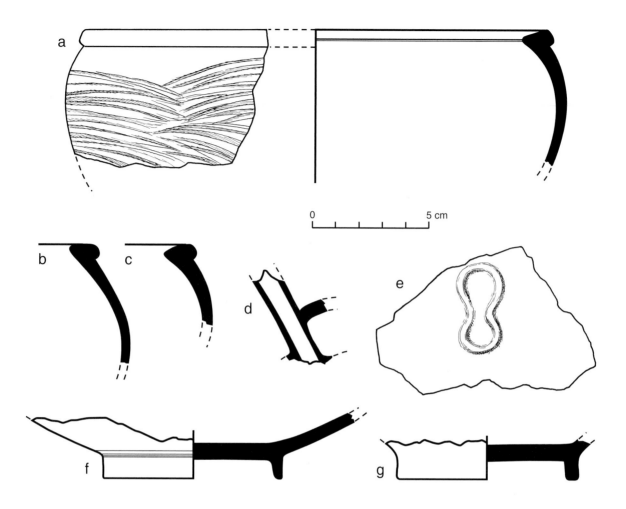

0   5 cm

Figure 9.53. Sherds from 0–20 cm below the surface on Terrace 12, Quebrada 6. *(a–c)*: Camacho Reddish Brown, cooking pots with restricted orifice, bolstered rim, brushed exterior, and fire blackening. (The "brushing," indicated on *a*, is very coarse—that is, whisk broom size rather than hairbrush size.) *(d)*: Pingüino Buff, fragment of bridge spout, from a vessel slipped glossy black on the exterior; *(e)*: Camacho Reddish Brown, body sherd of large jar or *hatun maccma* with a raised, modeled "keyhole" on the exterior; *(f, g)*: Pingüino Buff, ring bases from bowls, given a white wash and burnished on the interior and exterior.

CHAPTER 10

Interregional Comparisons and Cultural Inferences

Chapters 3–9 have presented the Late Intermediate pottery of Cerro Azul, its varied archaeological contexts, and the way the differences in context affected the mix of pottery types. One of my points of emphasis has been that the different activities in residential rooms, storage rooms, kitchens, breweries, middens, and burials strongly influence the size and typological makeup of sherd collections.

In this chapter, I turn to three additional topics. First, I consider those neighboring regions that share stylistic similarities with Cerro Azul's pottery. Second, I infer what those similarities might mean in sociocultural terms. Finally, I end the chapter by passing along some lessons learned at Cerro Azul, especially the value of distinguishing primary, secondary, and tertiary contexts and obtaining room-by-room inventories.

INTERREGIONAL COMPARISONS

Before my Cerro Azul project got underway, many of the Andean scholars to whom I spoke expected Cañete's strongest ceramic ties to have been with the well-known pilgrimage site of Pachacamac, which lies in the Lurín Valley to the north (Uhle 1903; Strong and Corbett 1943). What I discovered, however, is that Cerro Azul's Late Intermediate pottery was more similar to that from the valleys to the south, especially Chincha and Ica. These connections to valleys south of Cerro Azul had, in fact, been noted for more than 100 years, since the earlier work of

Max Uhle, Alfred L. Kroeber, and William Duncan Strong, among others (Uhle 1924; Kroeber and Strong 1924a, 1924b; Kroeber 1937; Lumbreras 2001). Those scholars referred to the Late Intermediate artifacts and pottery at Cerro Azul as the "Late Cañete culture" and compared them to the "Late Chincha culture" from the valley of the same name. Cañete and Chincha seem to have shared a particularly strong tradition before the arrival of the Inka.

As a result of discoveries made during his 1925 season (described earlier in this volume), Kroeber was struck by the similarities between whole vessels of the "Late Cañete culture" and those of "Late Chincha culture" (Kroeber 1937:244). He saw the pottery of these two cultures as "no more than local variants of the same type . . . the cultural relation is not one of complete identity but of a strong and pervading similarity."

In drawing comparisons between Cerro Azul and Chincha, Kroeber relied on the two types I have called Camacho Black and Pingüino Buff (Chapter 3). Both wares have counterparts in Chincha. To be sure, Kroeber and Strong did not assign specific names to those counterparts; they simply called the former "black ware" and described the latter as "combining red, white, and black on the same vessel" (Kroeber and Strong 1924a:16–18).

Uhle's work in the Chincha Valley between 1899 and 1901 produced numerous funerary vessels, some of which can be compared to the pottery

313

of Cerro Azul. Many vessels from Chincha are similar in shape and surface treatment to those found in burial cists at Cerro Azul and even to a few of the elite vessels in Structure D (Figure 10.1). Chincha graves usually included vessels for eating (*mikuna*) and drinking (*upiana*), the kinds of activities in which elite individuals would engage during their afterlife.

Uhle's burials, however, produced very few utilitarian vessels such as plain cooking pots and storage jars. In contrast, Sandweiss's excavations at Lo Demás in Chincha (Sandweiss 1992) yielded thousands of sherds from utilitarian vessels, particularly from cooking and storage pots, since he was excavating a midden comparable to Features 6 and 20 at Cerro Azul.

In addition to similarities in shape and surface treatment, Cerro Azul's Late Intermediate pottery shares motifs and style with painted Late Intermediate pottery from the Chincha Valley (Figure 10.2). Furthermore, Late Intermediate figurines from the Chincha Valley (Kroeber and Strong 1924a:Pl. 14; Sandweiss 1992:Figs. 33, 37) are similar to those found at Cerro Azul (Marcus 1987a:Figs. 21, 22). More than 100 years ago, Uhle noted that these figurines occurred only in graves that dated to his Late Chincha period; his Late Horizon graves contained no ceramic figurines. Uhle's statement is repeated by Kroeber and Strong, who say, "It is thus clear that the white figurines of Chincha are characteristic of the Late Chincha I graves, are practically lacking from Late Chincha II graves, and wholly absent from Inca ones" (Kroeber and Strong 1924a:29).

In front of the important ruins of La Centinela in the Chincha Valley, Uhle found pre-Inka graves whose pottery was later described as follows: "[T]he prevailing colors are red, white, and black in combination on the same vessel" (Kroeber and Strong 1924a:16). Kroeber and Strong (1924a) attributed the globular jar sherds I illustrate in Figure 10.2a, b to "bevel lip bowls," noting that they have "a characteristic heavy lip with beveled edge." In both sherds (Figure 10.2a, b) "the pattern is disposed in a zone just below the beveled lip, or below the neck, extending downward to or nearly to the latitude of greatest diameter of the vessel" (Kroeber and Strong 1924a:16–17).

Earlier, Uhle had astutely noted that the designs seen on these sherds were reminiscent of textile patterns; indeed, some textiles of the period also show conventionalized flocks of birds or schools of fish like those on the ceramics. Kroeber and Strong (1924a:18) also suggest that "several of the continuous patterns might well have been copied directly from a fabric onto the bowl." In addition to the painting of motifs such as schools of fish, the pottery of both valleys shows similarities in the creation of zones, panels, and registers (Figure 10.2).

Some jars from the Ica Valley are also similar to those from Cerro Azul (for example, Menzel 1976:Pl. 47, no. 14; Pl. 50, no. 30). Uhle—after

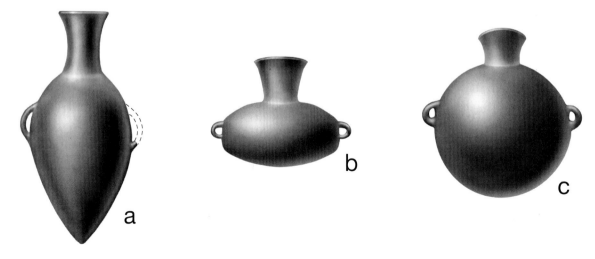

Figure 10.1. Blackware vessels of the Late Chincha I period that resemble Camacho Black pottery from Cerro Azul. *(a)*: amphora; *(b)*: drum-shaped jar; *(c)*: globular jar (redrawn from Kroeber and Strong 1924a:Figs. 7, 8).

Figure 10.2. Painted vessels from the Late Chincha I period that resemble Pingüino Buff specimens from Cerro Azul. *(a, b)*:sherds from globular jars with everted rims, painted black/white/red with the "school of fish" motif (redrawn from Kroeber and Strong 1924a: Fig. 6); *(c)*: jar with funnel neck and geometric motifs; *(d)*: jar with human face modeled on neck (*c* and *d* are redrawn from Kroeber and Strong 1924a:Pl. 12).

remarking on attributes shared by vessels from Chincha and Ica—noted that Chincha's ceramics were more similar to Ica's than to materials from Pachacamac. This assessment is particularly noteworthy because Uhle had excavated extensively at Pachacamac, and if the Chincha ceramics had been more similar to Pachacamac's, he certainly would have remarked on it.

I have to agree with Uhle, Kroeber, and Strong in recognizing a multi-valley ceramic sphere that includes the lower valleys of Cañete, Chincha, Pisco, and Ica. However, although these valleys share many ceramic shapes and motifs, additional excavations at Late Intermediate sites in each valley will surely isolate numerous local elements as well. We should also remember that all these valleys would have had interaction with sites in the *chaupi yunga* and interior zones of their respective drainages, as well as less direct relations with sites north of Cerro Azul.

UTILITARIAN POTTERY

Any Andeanist attempting to find comparisons for a complete ceramic assemblage, such as the one from Cerro Azul, quickly runs into a problem: a dearth of illustrated utilitarian pottery from neighboring regions. For many valleys, the entire sequence is based on whole vessels from graves, which generally do not include mundane cooking and storage wares. Exceptions to this situation are provided by Lo Demás in the Chincha Valley (Sandweiss 1992), which was essentially a domestic midden, and some of the stratigraphic cuts excavated at Pachacamac (Strong and Corbett 1943).

The most common Late Intermediate pottery type at Cerro Azul is Camacho Reddish Brown, a cooking and storage ware that includes the kinds of vessels every household would use. Many Camacho Reddish Brown cooking vessels show evidence of having been exposed to fire, their original surface color obscured by soot or fire-blackening. At Lo Demás in Chincha, the frequency of fire-blackened sherds is also very high; indeed, from 52% to 65% of all sherds in each stratigraphic complex display exterior soot (Sandweiss 1992:Table 5). "In most cases, the sherds are so heavily sooted or charred that they must certainly have been exposed to fire" (Sandweiss 1992:43).

One of the most common shapes at Cerro Azul is a cooking pot with a slightly restricted orifice and two handles, a shape broadly similar to some from the Chincha and Ica valleys. The two handles could be loops or straps, set either vertically or horizontally. Where and how the handles were set presumably depended on how the vessel was to be lifted, and whether the lifting was done with one's fingers or with a rope harness.

Also common at Cerro Azul is a jar with a cambered rim, a ceramic lip that hangs down over the rim like a shingle on a roof (Figures 3.2, 3.3, in Chapter 3). A series of alternative rim forms at Cerro Azul includes plain rims, rolled rims, beveled rims, and everted rims; some of these rim forms are also seen on vessels from the Chincha and Ica valleys (Kroeber and Strong 1924a, 1924b; Menzel 1966, 1976; Sandweiss 1992; Uhle 1924).

OTHER INTERREGIONAL SIMILARITIES

Perhaps the most elaborate plastic decoration on jars and amphorae at Cerro Azul is a modeled human face. On Camacho Black, such faces usually seem to represent dead people with puffy "coffee-bean" eyes. Similar faces on necks occur on Late Intermediate vessels in Late Chincha graves (see Kroeber and Strong 1924a:Pl. 12). On Pingüino Buff jars and amphorae, the faces are generally of living, open-eyed individuals with red facial paint. Pingüino Buff was also considered an appropriate medium for geometric and naturalistic painted motifs, counterparts for which can be found in the valleys of Chincha and Ica.

Typical Pingüino Buff vessels are pale brown and well made, but we also recovered a coarser variety we called the "atypical orange variety" of Pingüino Buff (Chapter 3). Stoltman (Appendix A in Chapter 3) suggests that this atypical orange variety may have been nonlocal. In this regard, it is interesting that from the quebrada east of Sector IV at Lo Demás in the Chincha Valley, Sandweiss (1992:43) discovered sherds "made of pure orange paste with medium-fine temper, [which] have an exterior red slip and black pendent triangles on the interior of the rim." It would be interesting to see whether these orange sherds from Chincha are related to the atypical orange variety of Pingüino Buff at Cerro Azul.

Another ware finding counterparts in valleys to the south is the highly burnished ("graphite") variety of Camacho Black. This highly burnished variety was most often used for burial offerings and effigy vessels, many of them miniatures. Very similar vessels occurred in Chincha graves (Figure 10.1).

SOCIOCULTURAL INFERENCES

To learn that Late Intermediate Cañete shares pottery attributes with Chincha to the south requires us only to look at illustrations of ceramics. To understand *why* it does so demands a higher level of sociocultural inference.

Why were Cerro Azul's ties with Pachacamac not stronger? That great religious center in the Lurín Valley is known to have had an important oracle that attracted pilgrims to the *Señorío de Ychma* (Rostworowski 1977, 1992); surely it would have had a significant influence on Cañete. Indeed, it may have had such an influence during the Middle Horizon and the early part of the Late Intermediate, the period to which the site of Cerro del Oro belongs. The deepest levels in Terrace 9 of Quebrada 5a had pottery with white "Life Savers" painted over a purple slip. Pachacamac is described as having some pottery with white rings and some with a purple slip that may be vaguely similar (e.g., Strong and Corbett 1943:62–65).

What could have happened to shift Cerro Azul's attention to the south? There are clues in the ethnohistory of the region. A 1558 document called the *Relación de Chincha* says that the valleys of Cañete, Chincha, and Ica each had its own independent ruler at the time of the Inka conquest (Castro and Ortega Morejón [1558] 1934). Most scholars have taken this to mean that the Late Intermediate period was a time in which the Andean coast was dotted with multiple autonomous polities, *curacazgos*, and *señoríos* whose lords established multiple alliances of different kinds, some for military or economic reasons. In speaking of the chronicler Cabello Balboa, Menzel (1959:125) says, "It can, perhaps, be inferred from Cabello Balboa's statements about common policy toward the Inka invaders that there was some sort of political connection between the valleys of Mala, Cañete, and Chincha, but the connection need have been no more than a temporary military alliance."

Most importantly, Chincha was by this time not only the seat of a wealthy and prestigious ruler, but also a religious center with its own Oracle of Chinchaycamac; this oracle was said to be none other than the son of the great Pacha-

camac oracle (Rostworowski 1992:52). This situation presented the people of Cañete with an important nearby pilgrimage center, much closer than the one at Pachacamac. Thus we should not be surprised if the pottery of Late Cañete and Late Chincha began to reflect a closer relationship between the two kingdoms.

Despite the relationship seen in their shared ceramic attributes, this group of south coast valleys differed in their response to the Inka conquest. Cabello Balboa (1945) indicates that Chincha and Cañete did not submit peacefully to the Inka conquest, but that Ica, Nazca, and Acarí did.

We have already described the violent Inka conquest of Huarco in Chapter 1. What happened in Chincha was different. A critical feature of the Inka transformation of the Chincha capital was their co-option of the oracle, which was probably associated with La Centinela's tallest pyramid complex. The Inka reoriented access to the shrine through their newly built imperial compound. As was their practice in newly incorporated territories, the Inka also built a Temple to the Sun (their imperial religion) in Chincha (Cieza de León [1553] 1959:346). Token respect was paid to the official Sun Cult by the occupants of La Centinela, but the major object of their worship was the shrine of their local oracle.

According to Pedro Pizarro ([1571] 1917:32), the lord of Chincha was such a powerful and close ally of the Inka ruler that he was still riding in his litter on the day the Inka empire fell to the Spaniards. Another account says that the lord of Chincha was one of several coastal lords who came to Pachacamac to meet Hernando Pizarro (de Estete [1534] 1968]). An *aviso*, another sixteenth-century document [1570], tells us that Chincha had three specialized groups: one devoted to agriculture, a second to fishing, and a third to long-distance trading with the coast of Ecuador and the southern highlands. Rostworowski (1970) has indicated that the principal commodity acquired in Ecuador was *Spondylus* shell, while in the southern highlands it was metal ore.

In contrast to Cerro Azul, the architectural and ceramic evidence in La Centinela's elite areas indicates a complex form of parallel rule, or co-rulership, involving the Lord of Chincha and the

Inka ruler. At La Centinela, Inka influence was profound and not limited to the highest levels of leadership. The most notable features at La Centinela were a palace for the local lord and an adjacent palace for the Inka (Morris, in press; Wallace 1998). The representatives of the Inka had access to a space through one doorway they had built for the local leader, and the local leader had reciprocal access through another doorway into a space in the Inka palace. The adjoining palaces with their paired spaces allowed the allied leaders, both as hosts and guests, to interact in surroundings appropriate to their ranks. After laboring to figure out this intricate architectural puzzle at La Centinela, Craig Morris (in press) came across a sixteenth-century statement that refers to the treatment meted out to local leaders who had been cooperative:

> to them [the Inka] bestowed favors and gave gifts, both gold cups and clothing from Cuzco, and in honor of their obedience he ordered that in each of those provinces a house be built for the said lord beside that which he had built for himself . . . [Fernando de Santillán [1563] 1927:14–15].

At La Centinela in the Chincha Valley, Morris documented dual plazas and paired palaces. In making a detailed study of one of the local compounds from earlier Chincha times (one that had been slightly modified by the Inka), Morris discovered that the modest architectural changes had had a profound impact on the organization and use of the compound. Major differences in ceramics confirmed the new dual character of the compound, with one side having much more Inka material than the other side. Before the Inka arrived, La Centinela, according to Morris, was already a very hierarchical and tightly structured polity, and in recognition of that hierarchy the Inka ended up co-ruling that polity for a while.

Needless to say, the Inka takeover of Chincha left a very different set of archaeological traces than did their massacre of the local elite in Huarco. La Centinela is rich in Cuzco-style pottery, gifts from the Inka and local imitations thereof. At Cerro Azul, on the other hand, we recovered only one imitation of an Inka *aryballos* in a Late Horizon midden, Feature 4 (Figure 5.15). Indeed, when Morris examined our pottery collections from Cerro Azul, he remarked, "You have virtually no Inka at all."

THE SOURCES OF LATE INTERMEDIATE CERAMIC VARIATION

In the course of preparing myself for the Cerro Azul project, I read a number of books and articles on the pottery of the central and southern Peruvian coasts. One of the things that struck me about this literature was the frequent assumption that all (or at least most) variation in vessel shape and decoration was related to chronological change. As Moseley (in press) has recently pointed out, synchronic variation has been underemphasized in Andean pottery studies. I would therefore like to end this volume with a discussion of the sources of variation in Late Intermediate ceramics.

At the highest and most general level there is regional variation, for which there are usually sociocultural reasons. I have already established that Cerro Azul exhibited elements of a regional style shared by the valleys of Cañete and Chincha, and I offered one possible reason for the shared style: Chincha's role as an influential pilgrimage center with a highly respected oracle.

At a somewhat lower level, there is functional variation. The Late Intermediate pottery of Cerro Azul consists of four recognizable pottery types, some of which come in more than one variety. The mix of types, varieties, vessel shapes, and decorative attributes very much depends on context. Sherd samples from kitchen areas tend to have high frequencies of Camacho Reddish Brown. Samples from elite residential rooms have a much higher frequency of Pingüino Buff and Trambollo Burnished Brown, and are more likely to contain unusual vessel shapes, unusual decorative attributes, and possible foreign wares. Breweries have significant concentrations of *hatun maccma*, chicha storage vessels too large to be portable. Burial cists (and some elite residential areas) have much higher frequencies of highly burnished variety of Camacho Black, including miniature or effigy vessels with a shiny, graphite-like surface color.

This variation makes it clear that limited excavations, confined to areas with only one or two functions, would not produce a well-rounded picture of the whole pottery assemblage. Kroeber and Strong saw graphite-black amphorae as typical of Late Chincha because they studied grave lots. Such lots contained none of the fire-blackened reddish brown cooking wares recovered by Sandweiss at Lo Demás in the same valley, and by the same token, the middens he dug had little in the way of graphite-black miniatures.

To be sure, some middens—as a result of having received basketloads of trash from many different proveniences—can have a more representative sample of ceramics than specific rooms or even buildings. However, we have already seen that a midden from an elite residential compound (Feature 6, Structure D) and a midden from a storage facility staffed by commoners (Feature 20, Structure 9) can have different mixes of types, varieties, shapes, and decoration—differences that, decades ago, might have been attributed to chronological variation.

Even a single room, as I learned repeatedly, could change its function over time. Perhaps the most dramatic example was the Room 1/Room 3 complex in Structure D. Originally designed to be an elite residential apartment, it had been so badly damaged by an earthquake that it was converted to fish storage. The ceramic samples from its original floor and its later fill are noticeably different.

This brings us, finally, to the differences between primary, secondary, and tertiary context, already mentioned in Chapter 3. Sherds from pots left in situ and crushed by overburden are, on average, twice the size of sherds moved only once. Sherds moved only once are, on average, twice the size of those that had been moved over and over, eventually winding up on one of the terraces of Cerro Camacho.

One of the lessons of Cerro Azul is that Andeanists cannot produce a reliable ceramic chronology simply by comparing grave lots, or by putting a few 2 × 2 m pits into a large archaeological site. To produce a real chronology, we have to be able to distinguish chronological variation from synchronic variation. That means diversifying our excavation units until we are sure we have an understanding of the differences among utilitarian cooking and storage wares, commoner serving vessels, elite serving vessels, and funerary vessels. All of these forms and wares will change over time, but not necessarily at the same rate; utilitarian pottery may change more slowly, elite serving vessels more rapidly, and so on.

If the above plan sounds like a lot of work, it is only because periods like the Late Intermediate are so complex, reflecting cultures with different social strata, different occupational specializations, and multiple functional contexts. Neither the purposes to which they put pottery, nor the way they treated it after it broke, were designed to make things easy for the archaeologist.

Bibliography

Acosta, José de
  [1550] 1940   *Historia natural y moral de las indias.*
                Fondo de Cultura Económica, México.
Angulo, Domingo
  1921   Don Andrés Hurtado de Mendoza y la
                fundación de la villa de Cañete. *Revista
                Histórica* VII:21–89. Lima.
Archivo General de Indias (AGI), Sevilla, Spain
                Escribanía de Cámara 498–B—año 1575.

                Audiencia de Lima–Legajo 1630—año
                1562—Términos de la villa de Cañete.

                Justicia 45, folio 1928.

Aviso
  1570   Aviso de el modo que havia en el govier-
                no de los indios en tiempo del inga y
                como se repartian las tierras y tributos.
                Tomo XXII, *Miscelánea de Ayala*, folios
                261–273v. Biblioteca del Palacio Real de
                Madrid (see *Apéndice I* in Rostworowski
                1970).
Barth, Fredrik
  1959   *Political Leadership among Swat Pathans.*
                Athlone Press, University of London,
                London.
Betanzos, Juan de
  [1551] 1968   *Suma y narración de los incas.*
                Biblioteca de Autores Españoles.
                Ediciones Atlas, Madrid.
Biblioteca Nacional de Madrid
  1571   Manuscript No. 3042, año 1571.
Bronk Ramsey, C.
  1995   Radiocarbon Calibration and Analysis of
                Stratigraphy: The OxCal Program. *Ra-
                diocarbon* 37 (2):425–430.
  2001   Development of the Radiocarbon
                Calibration Program OxCal. *Radiocarbon*
                43 (2A):355–363.
Brüning, Hans Heinrich
  2004   *Mochica Wörterbuch/Diccionario Mochica.*
                Edición e introducción a cargo de José
                Antonio Salas García. Universidad de San
                Martín de Porres, Lima.

Cabello Balboa, Miguel
  1945   *Miscelánea antártica. Obras*, Vol. 1, pp. 91–
                443. Editorial Ecuatoriana, Quito,
                Ecuador.
Castro, fray Cristóbal, and Diego Ortega Morejón
  [1558] 1934   Relación y declaración del modo
                que este valle de Chincha y sus comarca-
                nos se gobernaron antes que hobiese in-
                gas y después que los hobo hasta que los
                cristianos entraron en esta tierra. *Colección
                de libros y documentos referentes a la historia
                del Perú*, Tomo 10, segunda serie, edited
                by Horacio H. Urteaga, pp. 134–149.
                Lima.
  [1558] 1974   Relación y declaración del modo
                que este valle de Chincha y sus comarca-
                nos se gobernaron antes que hobiese
                ingas y después que los hobo hasta que
                los cristianos entraron en esta tierra. *His-
                toria y Cultura* 8:91–104. Museo Nacional
                de Historia, Lima, Perú.
Cieza de León, Pedro
  [1553] 1943   *Del señorío de los incas.* Ediciones Ar-
                gentinas "Solar," Buenos Aires.
  [1553] 1959   *The Incas.* Translated by Harriet de
                Onis. University of Oklahoma Press, Nor-
                man.
Cobo, fray Bernabé
  [1653] 1956   *Historia del nuevo mundo.* In *Obras
                completas del P. Bernabé Cobo.* Edición de
                Francisco Mateos. Biblioteca de Autores
                Españoles, Tomos 91–92. Ediciones Atlas,
                Madrid.
Conrad, Geoffrey W.
  1974   Burial Platforms and Related Structures
                on the North Coast of Peru: Some Social
                and Political Implications. Ph.D. disserta-
                tion, Department of Anthropology,
                Harvard University, Cambridge, MA.
  1982   The Burial Platforms of Chan Chan:
                Some Social and Political Implications. In
                Chan Chan: Andean Desert City, edited by
                Michael E. Moseley and Kent C. Day, pp.

87–117. University of New Mexico Press, Albuquerque.

Day, Kent C.
1973   Architecture of Ciudadela Rivero, Chan Chan, Peru. Ph.D. dissertation, Department of Anthropology, Harvard University, Cambridge, MA.

de Estete, Miguel
[1534] 1985   Relación del viaje que hizo el señor capitán Hernando Pizarro por mandado del señor Gobernador, su hermano, desde el pueblo de Caxamalca a Parcama y de allí a Jauja. In *Verdadera relación de la conquista del Perú y provincia del Cuzco llamada la nueva castilla*, by Francisco de Xerez. Crónicas de América 14, Historia 16. Concepción Bravo, Madrid.

Gillin, John
1947   *Moche: A Peruvian Coastal Community*. Institute of Social Anthropology, Publication No. 3. Smithsonian Institution, Washington, DC.

Harth-Terré, Emilio
1923   La fortaleza de Chuquimancu. *Revista de Arqueología* I (1):44–49. Organo del Museo Victor Larco Herrera, Lima.
1933   Incahuasi. Ruinas inkaicas del valle de Lunahuaná. *Revista del Museo Nacional* II (2):101–125. Lima, Perú.

Hyslop, John
1985   *Inkawasi, the New Cuzco, Cañete, Lunahuaná, Perú*. British Archaeological Reports, International Series 234. Oxford.

Johnson, George R.
1930   *Peru from the Air*. American Geographical Society, Special Publication No. 12. New York.

Kolata, Alan L.
1982   Chronology and Settlement Growth at Chan Chan. In *Chan Chan: Andean Desert City*, edited by Michael E. Moseley and Kent C. Day, pp. 67–85. University of New Mexico Press, Albuquerque.

Kroeber, Alfred L.
1937   *Archaeological Explorations in Peru*, Part IV: *Cañete Valley*. Field Museum of Natural History, Anthropology Memoirs, Vol. II, No. 4, pp. 220–273. Chicago.

Kroeber, Alfred L., and William Duncan Strong
1924a   The Uhle Collections from Chincha. *University of California Publications in American Archaeology and Ethnology*, Vol. 21, No. 1, pp. 1–54. Berkeley.

1924b   The Uhle Pottery Collections from Ica. With Three Appendices by Max Uhle. *University of California Publications in American Archaeology and Ethnology*, Vol. 21, No. 3, pp. 95–133. Berkeley.

Larrabure y Unánue, Eugenio
1874   *Cañete. Apuntes geográficos, históricos, estadísticos y arqueológicos*. Imprenta del Estado, Lima.
[1893] 1935   *Historia y arqueología—valle de Cañete*. Manuscritos y Publicaciones, Tomo II. Imprenta Americana, Lima, Perú.

Le Maitre, R. W., editor
2002   *Igneous Rocks: A Classification and Glossary of Terms*. Cambridge University Press, Cambridge.

Lizárraga, Reginaldo de
[1605] 1946   *Descripción de las Indias*. Los Pequeños Grandes Libros de América. Editorial Loayza, Lima.

Lumbreras, Luis G.
2001   Uhle y los asentamientos de Chincha en el siglo XVI. *Revista del Museo Nacional* 49:13–87. Lima.

Marcus, Joyce
1987a   *Late Intermediate Occupation at Cerro Azul, Perú: A Preliminary Report*. University of Michigan Museum of Anthropology Technical Report 20. Ann Arbor, MI.
1987b   Prehistoric Fishermen in the Kingdom of Huarco. *American Scientist* 75:393–401.
2008   A World Tour of Breweries. In *Andean Civilization: A Tribute to Michael E. Moseley*, edited by Joyce Marcus and Patrick Ryan Williams. Cotsen Institute of Archaeology at UCLA, Los Angeles.

Marcus, Joyce, Ramiro Matos Mendieta, and María Rostworowski de Diez Canseco
1985   Arquitectura inca de Cerro Azul, valle de Cañete. *Revista del Museo Nacional* XLVII:125–138. Lima.

Marcus, Joyce, Jeffrey D. Sommer, and Christopher P. Glew
1999   Fish and Mammals in the Economy of an Ancient Peruvian Kingdom. *Proceedings of the National Academy of Sciences* 96:6564–6570.

McCormac, F. G., P. J. Reimer, A. G. Hogg, T. F. G. Higham, M. G. L. Baillie, J. Palmer, and M. Stuiver
2002   Calibration of the Radiocarbon Time Scale for the Southern Hemisphere: AD 1850–950. *Radiocarbon* 44 (3):641–651.

Menzel, Dorothy
　1959　The Inca Occupation of the South Coast of Peru. *Southwestern Journal of Anthropology* 15 (2):125–142.
　1966　The Pottery of Chincha. *Ñawpa Pacha* 4:77–144. Institute of Andean Studies, Berkeley.
　1976　*Pottery Style and Society in Ancient Peru: Art as a Mirror of History in the Ica Valley, 1350–1570*. University of California Press, Berkeley.

Middendorf, Ernst W.
　[1894] 1973　El valle de Chincha. In *Perú: Observaciones y estudios del país y sus habitantes durante una permanencia de 25 años*, Tomo II:101–108. Publicaciones de la Universidad Nacional Mayor de San Marcos, Lima, Perú.

Moore, Jerry D.
　1989　Pre-Hispanic Beer in Coastal Peru: Technology and Social Context of Prehistoric Production. *American Anthropologist* 91:682–695.

Morris, Craig
　1979　Maize Beer in the Economics, Politics and Religion of the Inca Empire. In *Fermented Food Beverages in Nutrition*, edited by Clifford F. Gastineau, William J. Darby, and Thomas B. Turner, pp. 21–34. Academic Press, New York.
　1982　The Infrastructure of Inka Control in the Peruvian Central Highlands. In *The Inca and Aztec States, 1400–1800: Anthropology and History*, edited by George A. Collier, Renato I. Rosaldo, and John D. Wirth, pp. 153–171. Academic Press, New York.
　2004　Enclosures of Power: The Multiple Spaces of Inka Administrative Palaces. In *Ancient Palaces of the New World: Form, Function, and Meaning*, edited by Susan Toby Evans and Joanne Pillsbury, pp. 299–323. Dumbarton Oaks, Washington, DC.
　In press　Links in the Chain of Inka Cities: Communication, Alliance, and the Cultural Production of Status, Value and Power. In *The Ancient City*, edited by Joyce Marcus and Jeremy A. Sabloff. SAR Press, Santa Fe.

Morris, Craig, and Donald E. Thompson
　1985　*Huánuco Pampa: An Inca City and its Hinterland*. Thames and Hudson, London.

Moseley, Michael E.
　In press　Stylistic Variation and Seriation. In *Contending Visions of Tiwanaku*, edited by Alexei Vranich. Cotsen Institute of Archaeology, University of California, Los Angeles.

Moseley, Michael E., Donna J. Nash, Patrick Ryan Williams, Susan D. deFrance, Ana Miranda, and Mario Ruales
　2005　Burning Down the Brewery: Establishing and Evacuating an Ancient Imperial Colony at Cerro Baúl, Perú. *Proceedings of the National Academy of Sciences* 102 (48):17264–17271.

Munsell Color Company
　1954　*Munsell Soil Color Charts*. Munsell Color Company, Baltimore, MD.

Murra, John V.
　1960　Rite and Crop in the Inca State. In *Culture in History*, edited by Stanley Diamond, pp. 393–407. Columbia University Press, New York.
　1980　*The Economic Organization of the Inca State*. JAI Press, Greenwich, CT.

Museo Naval Madrid
　Manuscrito No. 468.

ONERN (Oficina Nacional de Evaluación de Recursos Naturales)
　1970　*Inventario, evaluación y uso racional de la costa: cuenca del Río Cañete* (Junio). Vol. 1. Lima.

Pizarro, Pedro
　[1571] 1917　*Descubrimiento y conquista de los reynos del Perú*. Biblioteca de Autores Españoles, Tomo 168. Madrid.

Ravines, Rogger
　1978　Almacenamiento y alimentación. In *Tecnología andina*, edited by Rogger Ravines, pp. 179–188. Instituto de Estudios Peruanos, Lima.

Rostworowski de Diez Canseco, María
　1970　Mercaderes del valle de Chincha en la época prehispánica: un documento y unos comentarios. *Revista Española de Antropología Americana* 5:135–178. Madrid.
　1977　*Etnía y sociedad: costa peruana prehispánica*. Historia Andina 4. Instituto de Estudios Peruanos, Lima.
　1978–80　Guarco y Lunaguaná—dos señoríos prehispánicos de la costa sur central del Perú. *Revista del Museo Nacional* 44: 153–214. Lima.

1992   *Pachacamac y el señor de los milagros: una trayectoria milenaria.* Instituto de Estudios Peruanos, Lima.

Rowe, John H.
  1946   Inca Culture at the Time of the Spanish Conquest. In *Handbook of South American Indians*, edited by Julian H. Steward. *Bureau of American Ethnology* 143, Vol. 2, pp. 183–330. Smithsonian Institution, Washington, DC.

Sandweiss, Daniel H.
  1992   The Archaeology of Chincha Fishermen: Specialization and Status in Inka Peru. *Bulletin of the Carnegie Museum of Natural History*, No. 29. Pittsburgh.

Santillán, Fernando de
  [1563] 1927   Relación del origen, descendencia, política y gobierno de los Incas. *Colección de libros y documentos referentes a la historia del Perú*, edited by Horacio H. Urteaga, Vol. 9, 2nd series. Sanmartí, Lima.

Santo Tomás, fray Domingo de
  [1560] 1951a   *Lexicon.* Edición facsimilar. Instituto de Historia, Universidad Nacional Mayor de San Marcos, Lima.
  [1560] 1951b   *Gramática o arte de la lengua general de los indios de los reynos del Perú.* Edición facsimilar. Instituto de Historia, Universidad Nacional Mayor de San Marcos, Lima.

Shelley, David
  1993   *Igneous and Metamorphic Rocks under the Microscope.* Chapman & Hall, London.

Stoltman, James B.
  1989   A Quantitative Approach to the Petrographic Analysis of Ceramic Thin Sections. *American Antiquity* 54 (1):147–160.

Strong, William Duncan, and John M. Corbett
  1943   A Ceramic Sequence at Pachacamac. In *Archaeological Studies in Peru, 1941–1942*, by William Duncan Strong, Gordon R. Willey, and John M. Corbett, pp. 26–122. Columbia Studies in Archeology and Ethnology, Vol. I, No. 2. Columbia University Press, New York.

Stuiver, Minze, and Paul D. Quay
  1980   Changes in Atmospheric Carbon-14 Attributed to a Variable Sun. *Science* 207 (4426):11–19.

Stumer, Louis M.
  1971   Informe preliminar sobre el recorrido del valle de Cañete. *Arqueología y Sociedad* 5:25–35. Universidad Nacional Mayor de San Marcos, Lima.

Uhle, Max
  1903   *Pachacamac. Report of the William Pepper Peruvian Expedition of 1896.* Department of Archaeology of the University of Pennsylvania, Philadelphia.
  1924   Explorations at Chincha. *University of California Publications in American Archaeology and Ethnology*, Vol. 21, No. 2, pp. 57–94. Berkeley.

Villar Córdova, Pedro Eduardo
  1935   *Las culturas pre-hispánicas del departamento de Lima.* 1st edition. Lima.
  1982   *Arqueología del departamento de Lima.* 2nd edition. Ediciones Atusparia, Lima.

Wallace, Dwight T.
  1963   Early Horizon Ceramics in the Cañete Valley of Peru. *Ñawpa Pacha* 1:35–39. Institute of Andean Studies, Berkeley, CA.
  1998   The Inca Compound at La Centinela, Chincha. *Andean Past* 5:9–33.

Williams, Carlos, and Manuel Merino
  1974   *Inventario, catastro, y delimitación del patrimonio arqueológico del valle de Cañete*, Tomos I, II. Centro de Investigación y Restauración de Bienes Monumentales, Instituto Nacional de Cultura, Lima.

Wilson, Brian, and Michael Love
  1962   "Surfin' Safari." Capitol Records, Los Angeles.

Index

Note: Page numbers in italics indicate a color photo; an *f* following a page number indicates a figure.

Tambo de Locos, 6
Tambo de Palo, 6
tambos, 6
tectonic movement. *See* earthquake
    damage
temper. *See also* latite temper
    amount of, 64–65
    petrographic analyses of, 65, 65f,
      66f
    source of, 27–28
temple, 11
Temple of the Sun, 6, 317
Terrace 9 (Quebrada 5a), 284–295
    deep sounding into, 285f
    first uses of, 295
    looting of, 284
    Zone A of, 285–286
    Zone B of, 286, 290–292
    Zone C of, 286–290
Terrace 11 (Quebrada 6), 295–307
    black color of, 295, 298f, 307
    excavation of, 297f, 298f
    function of, 307
    midden contents of, 298–299,
      299f
    pottery from, 299–307
    Square M6 of, 300, 306
    Square M7 of, 302
    Square M8 of, 300–301
    Square N6 of, 300, 306–307
    Square N8 of, 302–303
    squares of, 295–296
Terrace 12 (Quebrada 6), 308–312
    hardpan and, 309–310
    plan/features of, 309f
    sherds from, 310–312
    squares of, 308, 310f
    as storage/burial cist, 308–309
Terrace 16 (Quebrada 5), 264–272
    disuse of, 271–272
    function of, 270
    implications of, 271–272
    mussel shells in, 265–266
    sea-lion roasting in, 271–272
    strata profile of, 265f
    testing of, 264–265, 264f
    Zone A1 of, 266
    Zone A2 of, 266, 270f
    Zone B of, 266
    Zone C of, 266
    Zone D1/D2 of, 265
    Zone E of, 265
    Zone F of, 265
    Zone G of, 265, 266

terraces
    agricultural, 259
    black color of, 295
    from dumps to cemeteries, 284–285
    formation of, 260, 263f
    history/function of, 259, 311
tertiary contexts, sherd counts from,
    62, 259, 319
textile fragments, 169, 174
textiles, 260
thin-section analyses, 27, 63, 67
tinajón, 96, 97f, 112, 208, 222, 224,
    226f
    with bolstered rim, 117f
    maize cob lug from, 245f, 246
    rim of, 108f, 211f, 243, 244f, 251,
      290
toenail trimmings, 96
tombs. *See* burial cist; elite tombs
totora, 140
trachytes, 64
traders, 2
Trambollo Burnished Brown, 27, 60–
    62, 93, 105f, 205
    with cambered rims, 155, 156f
    with funnel neck, 116, 118f
    as hemispherical bowls, 28, 60, 61f,
      102, 105f, 116, 134, 136f, 150,
      155, 156f, 161, 208, 211, 211f,
      212, 242, 269, 269f, 271, 271f
    as incurved-rim bowl, 203
    for individual meals, 157
    miniature size of, 199, 203, 204f
    paste of, 60, 65f, 66f
    as pot stand/pot rest, 151f
    punctate lug from, 94f
    with restricted orifice, 290, 291f
    rims of, 266, 267f
    surface treatment of, 60
    temper/grain size of, 28
    thin sections of, 70, 71f
    as "turtle tail" vessel, 165
    with "worm" motif, 293f
trapezoidal niches, 4
triangular lug, 242, 243f
tunaukuna (handstones), 186, 189
turtle effigy vessels, 45, 56f, 160f
"turtle tail" vessel, 160f, 165, 165f

Uhle, Max, 313, 315
Ungará. *See* Fortress of Ungará
urpu, 187, 195

Vilcahuasi, 6, 11

wall. *See* defensive walls; fortification
    wall; fortresses; muralla
wall buttresses, 210–212
weaving, 82, 83, 141, 174. *See also*
    textile fragments
weaving implements, 141, 169, 174
weaving shuttle, 169, 183
West Complex
    Room 5 (Structure 9) of, 233–241,
      233f
    Room 6 (Structure 9) of, 233f, 234,
      241–244
    Room 7 (Structure 9) of, 244–
      246
    Room 13 (Structure 9) of, 220,
      221f, 246
    of Structure 9, 233–246
willow (*Salix*), 134
willow branches, 134, 183
wood, 286. *See also huarango*;
    huarango post
    radiocarbon dating of, 147, 288
    reused, 147, 183
wool, 141. *See also* camelid wool
"worm" motif, 293f

Yauyos, 7
yunga, 1, 10, 316

Zone A (Terrace 9), 285–286
    radiocarbon dating of, 286
    sherds from, 293
Zone A1 (Terrace 16), 266, 270–271
Zone A2 (Terrace 16), 266
    hearth trench in, 170f, 265
    sherds found in, 270–271
Zone B (Terrace 9), 286, 290–292
Zone B (Terrace 16), 266, 270
Zone C (Terrace 9), 286–290
    deep sounding of, 286
    lower, 286
    middle, 286–287
    radiocarbon dates for, 288, 290
    upper, 288
Zone C (Terrace 16), 266, 270
Zone D (Terrace 16), 265
    D1/D2 of, 265
    sherds found in, 268–270
Zone E (Terrace 16), 265, 267–268
Zone F (Terrace 16), 265
    drilled body sherds and, 267, 267f
    sherds found in, 266–267
Zone G (Terrace 16), 265, 266
zoomorphic motif, 45